TEACHING
SCIENCE in
Elementary&
Middle School

This book is dedicated to all those elementary and middle school science teachers who love their work—and those who will!

TEACHING SCIENCE in Elementary & Middle School

A Cognitive and Cultural Approach

Cory A. Buxton **&** Eugene F. Provenzo, Jr.

University of Miami, Coral Gables

SAGE Publications

Los Angeles · London · New Delhi · Singapore

For information:

 SAGE Publications, Inc.
2455 Teller Road
Thousand Oaks, California 91320
E-mail: order@sagepub.com

SAGE Publications Ltd.
1 Oliver's Yard
55 City Road
London EC1Y 1SP
United Kingdom

SAGE Publications India Pvt Ltd
B 1/I 1 Mohan Cooperative
   Industrial Area
Mathura Road, New Delhi
India 110 044

SAGE Publications Asia-Pacific
   Pte Ltd
33 Pekin Street #02-01
Far East Square
Singapore 048763

Printed in the United States of America

Library of Congress Cataloging-in-Publication Data

Buxton, Cory A.
Teaching science in elementary and middle school : a cognitive and cultural approach / Cory A. Buxton, Eugene F. Provenzo, Jr.
    p. cm.
Includes bibliographical references and index.
ISBN-13: 978-1-4129-2497-9 (pbk.)
    1. Science—Study and teaching (Elementary) 2. Science—Study and teaching (Middle school) I. Provenzo, Eugene F. II. Title.

LB1585.B88 2007
372.3′5—dc22

2006032001

This book is printed on acid-free paper.

07   08   09   10   11   10   9   8   7   6   5   4   3   2   1

Acquisitions Editor:	Diane McDaniel
Editorial Assistant:	Ashley Plummer
Associate Editor:	Elise Smith
Production Editor:	Catherine M. Chilton
Copy Editor:	Diana Breti
Typesetter:	C&M Digitals (P) Ltd.
Proofreader:	Ellen Brink
Indexer:	Wendy Allex
Cover Designer:	Michelle Kenny
Marketing Manager:	Nichole Angress

Brief Table of Contents

Preface   xx

Part I   Creating the Context for Science Education   1

CHAPTER 1   The Nature of Science   5

CHAPTER 2   Science Education in Social Context   37

CHAPTER 3   Toward a Philosophy of
Hands-On Inquiry-Based Science Education   69

CHAPTER 4   Diverse Learners in the Science Classroom   87

CHAPTER 5   Observing as a Scientist
and as a Science Teacher   121

Part II   Teaching and Learning the Science Disciplines   143

CHAPTER 6   Understanding and
Teaching Earth and Space Sciences   149

CHAPTER 7   Understanding and Teaching Biology   203

CHAPTER 8   Understanding and Teaching Chemistry   259

CHAPTER 9   Understanding and Teaching Physics   299

Part III   Making the Transition From
Preservice Teacher to Inservice Teacher   341

CHAPTER 10   Teacher Professional Development:
Growing as a Teacher of Science   343

Appendix   The National Science
Education Standards for Science Content   363

Glossary   365

Index   373

About the Authors   395

Detailed Table of Contents

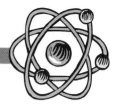

Preface   xx

Part I Creating the
Context for Science Education   1

CHAPTER 1   **The Nature of Science**   5

What Is Science?   6

Theory Into Practice 1.1: *Nature of Science Cards*   11

What Science Is Not   13

How Science Is Done   16

Theory Into Practice 1.2: *Hidden Shapes*   19

Patterns That Connect   20

Qualities of Scientific Inquiry   23

    Replicability   23
    Control of Variables   24
    Systematicity   24
    Communication   24
    Creativity   25
    Informed Skepticism   26

Combining the Qualities of Scientific
Inquiry to Address Scientific Questions   27

Theory Into Practice 1.3: *The Hypothesis Box*   29

Paradigms and Paradigm Shifts in the Nature of Science   31

Summary   34

Student Study Site   34

Reflections on Science   34

Internet Connections: Nature of Science Resources   35

References   35

CHAPTER 2   Science Education in Social Context   37

The Historical Role of Science Education in Our Society   38

Theory Into Practice 2.1: *What Would Life Be Like
Without Certain Inventions?*   48

Science Education Within Broader Educational Reforms   49

Sputnik and Education   49

Theory Into Practice 2.2: *Education Reform and You*   52

The Contemporary Role of Science Education in Our Society
and the Current Wave of Science Education Reform   52

Theory Into Practice 2.3: *Definitions of Scientific Literacy*   56

Learning to Speak the Language of Science   58

Theory Into Practice 2.4: *Metaphors in Science*   60

Ethics in Science and the Concept of Human Progress   61

Theory Into Practice 2.5: *Ethics and the Humane
Treatment of Experimental Animals*   63

Summary   64

Student Study Site   64

Reflections on Science   65

Internet Connections: Science Museums on the Internet   65

References   66

CHAPTER 3   Toward a Philosophy of
Hands-On Inquiry-Based Science Education   69

Piagetian Constructivism and
Learning Through Rediscovery   70

Theory Into Practice 3.1: *Helping Students Make
Meaning of Experience*   74

Designing Experiments and
Learning Through Project-Based Science   75

Theory Into Practice 3.2: *Learning by Design*   79

Sociocultural Theory and Learning
Through Legitimate Peripheral Participation   80

Theory Into Practice 3.3: *Learning Theories Textbook Review*   83

Summary   84

Student Study Site   84

Reflections on Science   84

Internet Connections: Design-Based Learning   85

References   85

CHAPTER 4 **Diverse Learners in the Science Classroom**   87

History of Diverse Learners in the Science Classroom   88

Theory Into Practice 4.1: *Draw a Scientist*   98

Current Science Education Reforms
and Their Impact on Diverse Learners   99

     Science for All Americans: Setting the Agenda   99

     *National Science Education Standards:
Reform Into Practice*   100

Theory Into Practice 4.2: *Mapping the Increasing Diversity
in American Classrooms*   102

Strategies for Working With
Diverse Learners in the Science Classroom   102

     *Strategies for Working With
Girls in the Science Classroom*   102

Theory Into Practice 4.3: *Two-Column Girls
and Scientists Activity*   104

     *Strategies for Working With Students
From Diverse Racial, Ethnic, and
Cultural Backgrounds in the Science Classroom*   104

     *Strategies for Working With
Children From Low-Socioeconomic
Backgrounds in the Science Classroom*   107

     *Strategies for Working With Students
With Disabilities in the Science Classroom*   108

Theory Into Practice 4.4: *Modifying Lab Activities*   110

     *Strategies for Working With English
Language Learners in the Science Classroom*   110

Theory Into Practice 4.5: *Sheltered Second-Language Activity*   112

Gifted and Talented Students in the Science Classroom   112

Theory Into Practice 4.6: *Debating the "Fairness" of Gifted Education*   115

Summary   116

Student Study Site   116

Reflections on Science   117

Internet Connections: Science for Diverse Learners   117

References   118

CHAPTER 5   **Observing as a Scientist and as a Science Teacher**   121

Scientific Observation   122

Theory Into Practice 5.1: *Observation Experiment: Watching a Traffic Pattern*   123

Observation in the Classroom   124

From Observation to Assessment of Science Learning   126

Field Experiences, Peer Teaching, and Other Opportunities to Practice the Craft of Science Teaching   128

Observational Forms   129

Theory Into Practice 5.2: *Science Lesson Observation Form*   130

Theory Into Practice 5.3: *Observing in a Science Museum or Other Non-School Setting*   132

Theory Into Practice 5.4: *Interviewing a Teacher After Observing a Science Lesson*   134

Beyond Observation: Other Science Process Skills   136

Creating a Science Educator's Portfolio   137

Portfolio Content and Structure   138

Theory Into Practice 5.5: *Looking at Electronic Portfolios*   140

Summary   141

Student Study Site   141

Reflections on Science — 141

Internet Connections: Scientific Observation — 142

Part II Teaching and
Learning the Science Disciplines — **143**

CHAPTER 6 **Understanding and
Teaching Earth and Space Sciences** — 149

The Place of Earth and Space Science in Science Education — 150

Measuring and Estimating in Earth and Space Science — 152

Estimating Large Numbers of Objects — 152

Experiment 1: *Estimating the Number of
Books in Your School Library* — 153

Determining Direction Using a Compass — 152

Experiment 2: *Orienteering* — 154

Measuring Deep Time: How Old Is the Earth? — 155

Experiment 3: *Geologic Time on a Football Field* — 156

The Cosmos: The Sun, Planets,
Solar System, Stars, and Beyond — 155

Scale of the Solar System — 155

Experiment 4: *Solar System Model* — 158

The Expanding Universe — 155

Experiment 5: *Expanding Universe Model* — 159

Star Power — 157

Experiment 6: *Hot Enough to Fry an Egg* — 162

Astronomy: Observing the
Heavens From Earth in the Past and Present — 161

Phases of the Moon — 161

Experiment 7: *Modeling Phases of the Moon* — 163

Changes in the Seasons — 161

Experiment 8: *The Changing Seasons* — 165

Exploring Shadows — 167

Experiment 9: *Changing Lengths of Shadows*   168

Restless Earth: Earth's Composition, Layers,
Movements, and Impacts in Surface Features   167

     Convection Currents: Heat Within the Earth   167

Experiment 10: *Convection Currents*   169

     Plate Tectonics   170

Experiment 11: *Mountain Building With Towels*   170

     Earthquake Simulation   171

Experiment 12: *Earthquake-Resistant Structures*   172

Rocks and Minerals: Formation, Identification,
and Human Use of Common Rocks and Minerals   173

     Growing Crystals   173

Experiment 13: *Crystals in Your Kitchen*   174

     Mineral Identification Strategies   175

Experiment 14: *Identifying Minerals*   176

     What's in Soil?   175

Experiment 15: *Determining Soil Type*   178

Earth Cycles: Many Processes on Earth Operate in Cycles   175

     Water Cycle   175

Experiment 16: *Building an Aquifer Model*   180

     Rock Cycle   177

Experiment 17: *Edible Rock Cycle*   181

     Atmospheric Cycle   182

Experiment 18: *Cloud in a Bottle*   183

Weather and Climate: Weather Patterns,
Climate Zones, and Climatic Change Over Time   182

     Tracking Rainfall   184

Experiment 19: *Tracking Rainfall*   186

     Measuring Wind   185

Experiment 20: *Making an Anemometer*   187

     Rainforest Terrarium   185

Experiment 21: *Rainforest Terrarium*   190

Atmosphere: Atmospheric Movement, Layers,
Pressure and Cloud Formation, Smog and Pollution   189

    Why Are Clouds White?   189

Experiment 22: *Why Are Clouds White?*   192

    Why Is the Sky Blue?   191

Experiment 23: *Why Is the Sky Blue?*   193

    Making Smog   191

Experiment 24: *Smog in a Can*   194

Water and Oceans: Fresh Water/Salt Water
Distribution, Interactions, and Contamination   195

    How Salty Is the Ocean?   195

Experiment 25: *How Salty Is Too Salty?*   197

    Probing the Ocean Floor   196

Experiment 26: *Mapping the Ocean Floor*   198

    Oil Spill Clean-Up Activity   196

Experiment 27: *Oil Spill Clean-Up*   199

Student Study Site   201

Reflections on Science   201

Internet Connections: Earth and Space Science   202

CHAPTER 7   **Understanding and Teaching Biology**   203

The Place of Biology in Science Education   204

Measurement in Biology   205

    Measuring Peak Flow Rate of Breathing   205

Experiment 28: *Measuring Peak Flow Rate*   206

    Estimating Lengths of Very Small Objects   205

Experiment 29: *Estimating Lengths of Very Small Objects*   207

    Measuring Population Change   208

Experiment 30: *Measuring Population Change*   208

Classification   209

    Classifying Using All of Your Senses   209

Experiment 31: *Observation in the Bag* — 212

Classification Systems — 209

Experiment 32: *Developing a System of Classification* — 213

The Linnaean System of Classification — 209

Experiment 33: *Classifying Different Animals* — 214

Plants — 211

Seed Germination — 215

Experiment 34: *Seed Germination* — 216

Plant Cells — 215

Experiment 35: *Making a Plant Cell Model* — 217

Variables in Plant Growth — 219

Experiment 36: *The Effect of Acid Rain on Plant Growth* — 219

Animals — 221

Dissecting Owl Pellets — 221

Experiment 37: *Owl Pellet Dissection* — 222

Animal Cells — 221

Experiment 38: *Making an Animal Cell Model* — 223

Bird Census and Journal on Animal Behavior — 221

Experiment 39: *Conducting a Bird Census* — 225

Neither Plant nor Animal:
Protista, Monera, Viruses, Bacteria, Fungi — 224

Microscope Studies of Pond Water — 226

Experiment 40: *Exploring Pond Water* — 227

The Action of Yeast in Dough — 226

Experiment 41: *The Power of Yeast* — 228

Looking for Helpful Bacteria in Our Food — 226

Experiment 42: *Making Yogurt* — 229

Ladder of Life: The Building Blocks of Organisms — 226

Cell Packing — 226

Experiment 43: *Cell Packing* — 231

Photosynthesis-Transpiration Interactions — 232

Experiment 44: *Photosynthesis and Transpiration*   233

Cells as Natural Forms   232

Experiment 45: *Minimal Surfaces in Natural and Biological Forms*   235

Code of Life: All Life Is Based on the Same Genetic Code   232

Modeling the DNA Double Helix   234

Experiment 46: *Making a Model of the DNA Double Helix*   236

DNA "Fingerprints" for Solving Mysteries   237

Experiment 47: *Black Marker "Fingerprints"*   238

Genetic Defects   237

Experiment 48: *Hearing Loss Simulation*   240

Evolution: Natural Selection and Evidence for Species Evolution   237

Bird Beak Models   239

Experiment 49: *Bird Beak Models*   241

Stereoscopic Vision   242

Experiment 50: *Experimenting With Stereoscopic Vision*   244

Evolutionary Adaptations to Fill Ecological Niches   242

Experiment 51: *Design-an-Organism*   245

Biomes and Ecosystems: Interactions Between Plants, Animals, and the Non-Living World   243

What Is a Biome?   243

Tracing Food Webs   246

Experiment 52: *Tracing Food Webs*   247

Measuring the Greenhouse Effect   246

Experiment 53: *Greenhouse Effect Model*   248

Unintended Consequences   246

Experiment 54: *Unintended Consequences*   250

The Human Body and Human Health   249

Tracking Food Choices   249

Experiment 55: *You Are What You Eat*   251

    Creating a Model of the Human Arm   253

Experiment 56: *Modeling the Human Arm*   252

    Spreading Infectious Illnesses   255

Experiment 57: *Spreading Infectious Disease*   254

Student Study Site   256

Reflections on Science   256

Internet Connections: Biology   256

References   257

CHAPTER 8   **Understanding and Teaching Chemistry**   259

The Place of Chemistry in Science Education   260

Measurement in Chemistry   262

    Estimating Volume   262

Experiment 58: *Estimating Volume*   263

    Measuring Temperature Using a Thermometer   264

Experiment 59: *Making a Thermometer*   265

    Counting Particles: Understanding Parts per Thousand   264

Experiment 60: *Serial Dilution of Colored Liquid*   267

Atoms, Elements, and Molecules   266

    Building Simple Molecules   268

Experiment 61: *Marshmallow Molecule Models*   270

    Physical Properties of Molecules   268

Experiment 62: *Evaporating Molecules*   271

    Elements You Eat   268

Experiment 63: *Elements You Eat*   272

Matter   268

    The States of Matter and the Organization of Matter: Physical and Chemical Changes   268

    Hot Air Rises   273

Experiment 64: *Hot Air Rises*   274

Densities of Liquids 273

 Experiment 65: *Densities of Liquids* 275

Making Salt Crystals 276

 Experiment 66: *Making Salt Crystals* 277

Bonding 276

 Experiment 67: *Floating a Needle on Water* ... 278

Separating Mixtures 276

Experiment 68: *Separating Mixtures* 279

Making Water "Wetter" With Soap 280

Experiment 69: *Comparing Soaps* 281

Temperature 280

Evaporation: Effects on Temperature 280

Experiment 70: *Evaporation of Alcohol and Water* .. 282

Hot and Cold Water Interactions 283

 Experiment 71: *Hot and Cold Water Mixtures* ... 284

Making Ice Cream 283

Experiment 72: *Making Ice Cream* 285

Pressure 283

Burning Candles: A Temperature/
Pressure Relationship 286

 Experiment 73: *Burning Candles* 286

Creating a Vacuum 286

Experiment 74: *Creating a Simple Vacuum* 288

How Air Pressure Changes With Depth 289

Experiment 75: *Cartesian Diver* 290

Fuels 289

Measuring the Energy in Batteries 289

Experiment 76: *Building a Voltaic Pile* 292

Harnessing Solar Energy 291

Experiment 77: *Making a Solar Water Heater* 293

Energy in Fossil Fuels 294

Experiment 78: *Peanut Power*   295

Student Study Site   296

Reflections on Science   296

Internet Connections: Chemistry   296

References   297

CHAPTER 9   **Understanding and Teaching Physics**   299

The Place of Physics in Science Education   300

Measurement in Physics   304

Standards for Measuring Length   305

Using a Balance to Measure Mass   308

Using a Stopwatch to Measure Time   308

Experiment 79: *Using Standard and Nonstandard Units of Length*   307

Experiment 80: *Determining Relative and Absolute Weights Using a Pan Balance*   309

Experiment 81: *Using a Stopwatch to Measure Time*   311

Force: Gravity, Velocity, Acceleration, Newton's Laws   310

Inertia   312

Experiment 82: *Flipping a Card off Your Finger While Leaving a Quarter in Place*   312

Centrifugal Force   313

Experiment 83: *Swinging a Bucket of Water in a Circle Without Getting Wet*   314

Air Flow: Creating Lift   313

Experiment 84: *Demonstrating "Lift" with a Ping-Pong Ball and Straw*   316

Forms of Energy   315

Trading Potential and Kinetic Energy With Superballs   317

Experiment 85: *Bouncing Superballs*   318

Modeling Nuclear Decay and Half-Life   317

Experiment 86: *Modeling Nuclear Half-Life*   319

Static Electricity   317

Experiment 87: *Creating an Electroscope
to Detect Static Electricity*   320

Simple Machines   321

   Pulleys   321

Experiment 88: *Experimenting With Pulleys*   322

   Ramps   321

Experiment 89: *Experimenting With Ramps*   323

   Levers   324

Experiment 90: *Experimenting With Levers*   325

Sound   324

   Sound Conduction   326

Experiment 91: *Demonstrating the Conduction of Sound*   327

   Harmonics   326

Experiment 92: *Experimenting With Harmonic Sound*   328

   Resonance   326

Experiment 93: *Experimenting With Resonance*   329

Light and Color   326

   Persistence of Vision   330

Experiment 94: *Making a Thaumatrope*   331

   Color Blending   330

Experiment 95: *Color Blending*   332

   Bending Light   330

Experiment 96: *Bending Light*   333

Electricity and Magnetism   330

   Magnetic Fields   334

Experiment 97: *Observing Magnetic Fields*   335

   Electrical Circuits   334

Experiment 98: *Making a Simple Circuit*   336

   Electromagnets   334

Experiment 99: *Making an Electromagnet*   337

Student Study Site   339

Reflections on Science   339

Experiment 100: *Design Your Own Experiment*   338

Internet Connections: Physics   339

References   340

Part III Making the Transition From Preservice
Teacher to Inservice Teacher   341

CHAPTER 10   Teacher Professional Development:
Growing as a Teacher of Science   341

History of Teacher Professional Development   343

The Current State of Teacher Professional Development   345

Theory Into Practice 10.1: *Recertification
Requirements Across States*   347

Action Research: From Research "On" to Research "With"   347

Japanese Lesson Study   349

Theory Into Practice 10.2: *The TIMMS Video Project*   351

Video Study Groups   351

Parental Involvement and Parental Engagement   352

Theory Into Practice 10.3: *Parent Interview*   354

Professional Organizations: NSTA   355

Advanced Study   357

National Board Certification   357

Theory Into Practice 10.4: *Interviewing an NBCT
in Your School District*   358

Applying for Grants   359

Theory Into Practice 10.5: *If I Had $500 . . .*   361

Student Study Site   362

Reflections on Science   362

References   362

Appendix   The National Science
Education Standards for Science Content   363

Glossary   365

Index   373

About the Authors   395

Preface

This book provides an introduction to basic science concepts and methods of science instruction for preservice and inservice elementary and middle school teachers of science. It is also a book about learning to think like a scientist, and one that we hope will enable the reader to better understand the role of science in our day-to-day lives and in the history of Western culture.

The book is a unique collaboration: Its lead author, Cory A. Buxton, is a science educator with a background and interest in social and cultural issues—particularly as they relate to science and science education. Its co-author, Eugene F. Provenzo, Jr., is a theorist in education and cultural studies with a strong interest in the history of science and technology. This collaboration has led to a book with several unique features, a text that neither author could have written alone.

Most current textbooks on teaching science follow a fairly generic model, common to teacher education methods courses, that tends to emphasize pedagogical practice over disciplinary knowledge. Reflecting our personal interests and backgrounds, we have tried to create a text that integrates the teaching of both core science concepts and scientific methods within a unified model of teaching and learning. We emphasize the connections between content and methods, not by sprinkling hands-on science inquiry activities throughout chapters focusing on aspects of pedagogy, but instead by presenting the book in two distinct parts. Part I highlights historical, methodological, and pedagogical issues concerning the teaching of science to children. Part II is organized around teaching the core concepts in each of the major science disciplines.

We feel that *Teaching Science in Elementary and Middle School: A Cognitive and Cultural Approach* distinguishes itself in four key ways:

1 The systematic introduction of key experiments for teaching core standards-based science concepts within a methods instruction model. Our experience indicates that as a beginning, or even a moderately experienced, teacher, you likely have concerns about your ability to teach science effectively. This is based on the fact that if you are a typical elementary or middle school teacher, you have had limited academic training in science and the courses that you have taken were introductory lectures that rarely allowed you to engage in actual **scientific inquiry**. In an attempt to overcome these concerns, our approach builds on an understanding of the crucial interactions between hands-on manipulation of original materials, the development of scientific language necessary in the formation of scientific reasoning, and the connection between content knowledge and effective inquiry-based pedagogy. To this end, a large portion of this text focuses on 100 core experiments that clearly demonstrate key standards-based science concepts that are an essential part of most science instruction at the elementary and middle school levels.

2 An introduction to the historical, social, cultural, and linguistic construction of science in American culture; in particular, how it functions as a human undertaking and endeavor. We feel that the social and historical context of science is underemphasized in most science materials for educators. We believe, however, that you, as a teacher, must have at least a basic understanding of these ideas in order to teach science in a way that will be meaningful and engaging for your students. Drawing on examples from the history of science is, in our opinion, among the clearest and most engaging ways to explain features of the scientific worldview. As a result, we infuse historical examples and historical experiments throughout the text.

3 Emphasis on the idea that science is connected to the world around us. In this context, we use Gregory Bateson's model from *Mind and Nature*, which emphasizes the need for students to understand the interrelatedness and connectedness between things, what he calls "the pattern that connects." Thus, we emphasize the integration of scientific knowledge with the other academic disciplines, including language arts, social studies, mathematics, and visual arts. Such a model suggests to us possibilities for using your local community to contextualize and "make real" the various aspects of science and scientific thinking that you will introduce to your students.

4 Emphasis on the development of the basic principles underlying scientific methods of thought and inquiry. Just as content without sound pedagogy is ineffective, teaching science concepts without a strong grounding in scientific methods and principles will not impart **scientific literacy** to you or your students. While most science methods texts discuss science process skills and scientific methods in depth, they tend to do so in ways that are disconnected from the presentation of the standards-based science content knowledge to which these methods must be applied in classroom science teaching. This text infuses the teaching of scientific methods and process skills into

Image P.1.   Artistic Depiction of Sir Isaac Newton

the teaching of the core science concepts. We believe that this kind of
connectivity is absolutely necessary to foster scientific literacy, both for
yourself as a teacher and for your students.

Above all, we wish the reader to come away from this text with an
enhanced appreciation for the power and elegance of a scientific understanding of the natural world. For us, the image of Isaac Newton above (Image P.1)
idealizes this vision—the scientist not as technical master of facts and procedures, but as wonderer and explorer of the forces underlying the natural world.

Pedagogical Features of the Text

Several special pedagogical features are included in *Teaching Science in
Elementary and Middle School: A Cognitive and Cultural Approach* to provide preservice and inservice teachers with opportunities to engage individ-
ually and collectively in reflection about teaching and learning science.

Theory Into Practice

The chapters in Part I and Part III of the text include activity boxes referred to as Theory Into Practice. These activities can generally be done either during class or as out-of-class work and focus on practical examples to clarify and reinforce the theoretical ideas being introduced.

Reflections on Science

End-of-the-chapter synthesis questions allow the reader to reflect upon and extend the main ideas and concepts in each chapter. These questions generally ask the reader to make connections between science and his or her personal life and experiences.

Internet Connections

Each chapter concludes with a list of exemplary Internet sites that can extend the learning on topics presented in the chapter. In some chapters, these sites are thematic (e.g., Science Museums on the Internet in Chapter 2) while in other chapters, they are more varied.

Historical Connections

Throughout the text, historical examples and connections are provided that trace the development of our scientific understandings from their historical roots. This does more than just provide "flavor" and interesting anecdotes. Many basic scientific ideas can best be understood by considering how they were first discovered.

Experiments

As mentioned earlier, Part II of the text is largely composed of 100 core experiments that demonstrate 100 fundamental scientific principles. These experiments, both historical and modern, allow the student to learn key science concepts in a memorable and lasting way. The experiments are clustered into groups of three to provide sufficiently detailed exploration of key topic areas. The experiments are designed to use only simple, readily available materials and most can be done in under 30 minutes.

Standards

Each of the experiments in Part II includes a list of the relevant content standards from the National Science Education Standards. These standards are then listed in full in the Appendix.

Icons

Within the text you will find icons representing the four major science disciplines that are designed to help orient the reader to the various activities in the book. These images should help you mentally categorize the activities you are doing with the appropriate science discipline. When all four of the images appear together, this indicates that the activity is not specifically related to one of the core science disciplines (for example, the Theory Into Practice boxes in Chapters 1-5 and Chapter 10).

 Chemistry   Physics

 Earth and Space Science   Biology

When taken together, these pedagogical features should enhance the utility and effectiveness of the text.

Organization of the Text

This book is divided into three sections: Part I consists of five chapters on the theme of "creating the context for science education." We begin with Chapter 1 on the nature of science, what distinguishes science from non-science, the qualities of scientific inquiry, the asking of testable questions, and the connections that exist both across the scientific disciplines and between the scientific disciplines and other academic disciplines. Numerous historical and contemporary examples provide a taste of how the history of science and social foundations of education infuse this methods text. Chapter 2 moves on from a discussion of science to the consideration of science education, its social and cultural context, and an exploration of both historical and contemporary science education. This chapter highlights the importance of the language of science as a component of scientific literacy and the question of how to make science and science education relevant to today's students (and teachers). Chapter 3 lays out the theoretical and conceptual basis for "hands-on," "inquiry-based," and "standards-based" science teaching by tracing the history and philosophy of teaching science from the eighteenth century to the present, with an emphasis on the social and psychological theories that have been used to support these pedagogical approaches. Chapter 4 introduces the topic of diverse learners in the science classroom and includes ways to meet various learning styles, a consideration of gender and science, and meanings of multicultural science. It also addresses working with **English Language Learners** and students from disadvantaged socioeconomic backgrounds and accommodating the needs of students with exceptionalities—both students with disabilities and gifted students. We conclude Part I with Chapter 5, focusing on the importance of observation to both scientists and teachers. We discuss the importance of classroom **observations** as a learning tool for teachers, the role of science process skills beyond observation for learning to engage in scientific problem solving, the critical role of **assessment** and how it is connected to observation, and the process of preparing a science teaching **portfolio**. Our goal throughout Part I is to engage the reader in the reasons science teaching should be an important part of the elementary and middle school classroom.

Part II includes four chapters that deal, in turn, with the four major science disciplines: **Earth and space science, biology, chemistry**, and **physics**. Each of these four chapters opens with a brief discussion of the defining aspects of the discipline and a bit about its history. Each chapter then moves on to highlight the key topic areas within the discipline and to present three core inquiry-based experiments that can be used to teach key standards-based concepts associated with that topic. One of the unique features of these chapters is that they include numerous historical and contemporary experiments. The historical experiments serve the dual purpose of teaching the development of scientific understanding while presenting elegant and simple ways to teach key science concepts. We begin with Earth and space science in Chapter 6, followed by biology in Chapter 7, chemistry in Chapter 8, and finally, physics in Chapter 9. Throughout these chapters, we highlight both the similarities and the differences across the disciplines. It is our experience that preservice teachers who have the opportunity to work through many of these key experiments leave the course feeling well-prepared to begin their professional journeys as teachers of science.

A concluding chapter draws this book to its end (Chapter 10) and focuses on the topic of "Teacher Professional Development: Growing as a Teacher of Science." This chapter includes discussions and activities on teacher certification and recertification; ongoing professional development activities in science for inservice teachers, such as Japanese lesson planning, video study groups, and action research; the importance of joining professional organizations and attending professional conferences; the value of graduate school and National Board Certification; and an introduction to writing small grant applications in support of inquiry-based science learning.

The Appendix provides a list of the National Science Education Standards content standards.

🦋 Supplemental Materials

In addition to the text, ancillary materials further support and enhance the learning goals of *Teaching Science in Elementary and Middle School: A Cognitive and Cultural Approach*:

Instructor's Resource CD

This CD offers the instructor a variety of resources to supplement the book material, including PowerPoint® lecture slides, Teaching Guide for the Science Standards-Based Lesson Plan Project, Theory into Practice resources, Reflections on Science assignments, Web resources, and more. The CD also includes video clips of select experiments and a Teaching Guide to help instructors integrate the videos into the classroom. Also included is a Test Bank, which consists of 20–30 multiple-choice questions with answers and page references, 10-15 true/false questions, as well as 10–15 short answer and 5–10 essay questions for each chapter. An electronic Test Bank is also available so that instructors can create, deliver, and customize tests and study guides using Brownstone's Diploma test bank software.

Student Resource CD

This CD is bound into the back of the text and offers students video resources to supplement the book material. Video clips are included to illustrate select experiments from the text as well as other key science concepts. A learning guide accompanies the video clips to assist student learning.

Web-Based Student Study Site

http://www.sagepub.com/buxtonstudy

This Web-based student study site provides a variety of additional resources to enhance students' understanding of the book content and take their learning one step further. The site includes comprehensive study materials such as chapter objectives, flash cards, practice tests, and more. Also included are special features, such as Resources for Experiments, the Links to Standards from U.S. States and associated activities, Learning from Journal Articles, Theory into Practice resources, Reflections on Science exercises, a Science Standards-Based Lesson Plan Project, and PRAXIS resources.

🦋 Acknowledgments

We would like to acknowledge the many people who have helped to create this book. First and foremost are our wives, Jean-Marie and Asterie. Jean-Marie shot several of the photographs in the book and provided constant support, keeping the kids in line during late afternoons of writing. Asterie provided her usual critical insights and editorial support. Her coffee rocks! Cory's three children, Jonah, Remy, and Lindy, constantly reminded us that "why" questions must be at the heart of good science teaching. They also put in cameo appearances in several of the photographs. Thanks to Donner Valle for creating many of the line drawings throughout the text. Special thanks go to Jeanne Schumm, our department chair when we wrote the bulk of this book, as well as to our other colleagues at the University of Miami School of Education. Fred the cat was a constant companion but not such a good critic.

Diane McDaniel, our editor at SAGE Publications, was patient and insightful. Her input throughout the planning and writing of this book made it a much better product. Our sincere thanks also go to Erica Carroll at SAGE for her help and advice with all the details that go into finishing a project of this kind, and to Elise Smith, Production Editor Catherine Chilton, and Copy Editor Diana Breti.

This book was much improved by the suggestions of its reviewers. We would specifically like to thank John Trowbridge (Southeastern Louisiana University), Claudia Balach (Duquesne University), Willis Walter (Florida A&M University), Benjamin Ngwudike (Jackson State University), Linda Easley Roach (Northwestern State University of Louisiana), and Jiyoon Yoon (University of Minnesota, Duluth). The careful and detailed feedback provided by Professors Trowbridge and Easley Roach was especially appreciated.

This book was great fun to write, and we hope that this comes across to you, the reader.

Cory Buxton
Gene Provenzo
Miami, FL, 2006

Part I
Creating the Context for Science Education

 Becoming a Teacher of Science in the Age of Standards-Based Instruction

Historically, science instruction has often been overlooked in elementary school classrooms, losing out to the "core" subjects of language arts and mathematics. When science has been taught at all, it has generally been presented as a collection of vocabulary and facts, read from a textbook, then memorized for a test. This approach to science teaching was never adequate and today is completely unsatisfactory. Thus, one of our aims in the first part of *Teaching Science in Elementary and Middle School: A Cognitive and Cultural Approach* is to explore how science, when presented as a process of inquiry-based problem solving, can be used to engage students in authentic explorations that promote reasoning and problem-solving abilities. This kind of instruction will support learning not just in science, but across the content areas. In the same way that learning to decode text without developing reading comprehension or learning mathematical algorithms without understanding mathematical principles are not satisfactory student outcomes, memorizing scientific vocabulary without understanding what science is or how it is practiced will not prepare students for the scientific and technological world in which they will live.

Becoming an effective elementary or middle school teacher of science is a complex and multifaceted task. First you need to develop the necessary science content knowledge and skills. Yet, as an elementary or middle school teacher, your job requires you to be a generalist rather than a specialist. Thus, it is unrealistic to expect you to develop a deep science content knowledge similar to that which might be expected of a high school science teacher. It would be natural, then, for you to ask questions such as "What science is the most important for me to learn?" or "How will I determine what science to teach my students?" This is where standards come into play. The national and state standards have been developed to provide exactly that type of guidance. If you are learning the science concepts that go along with the relevant science standards for the grade level you are teaching, then you can be confident that you are learning the science that you most need to know.

Still, there is more to being an effective teacher of science than having a firm grasp of the relevant science content. You may have experienced this if you have ever had a science instructor who clearly had a mastery of the content that he or she was trying to teach but did not seem to have the ability to make that content comprehensible to you as a student. Thus, in addition to being knowledgeable about science, to be an effective science teacher you must also master appropriate forms of pedagogy. This is the primary goal for the first part of this text, to help you reflect on how best to teach science to your students. We refer to this process as "creating the context for science education." The five

chapters that compose Part I of this text each address a different aspect of teaching science well. When you combine them with the science concepts you will learn in Part II of the book, you will be well on your way to becoming an effective teacher of science.

Chapter 1 considers the nature of science and the qualities of scientific inquiry. We start here to help create a shared understanding of what science is and what it is not, an understanding we will draw upon throughout the rest of the text. We also introduce numerous historical examples to help clarify our ideas, another theme you will see throughout the text. In Chapter 2, we move from a discussion of science to a consideration of science education—both its history and its contemporary practice. While this topic may not seem to be directly relevant to developing your skills as an effective science teacher, ideas such as the importance of the language of science and how to make science relevant to today's students are topics that effective science teachers often consider.

In Chapter 3, we discuss both the theoretical and the conceptual ideas behind why it is important to use "hands-on," "inquiry-based," and "standards-based" approaches to science teaching. We again highlight the history and philosophy of teaching science from the eighteenth century to the present, to provide evidence that supports these pedagogical approaches. Chapter 4 explores the topic of diverse learners in the science classroom. You may have a wonderful grasp of science concepts, but if you are not also well-trained in how to accommodate your students' various learning styles, how to help culturally and linguistically diverse students in your classroom, and how to address the special needs of students with exceptionalities or students from disadvantaged socioeconomic backgrounds, you are unlikely to be an effective science teacher.

Finally, we conclude Part I with a chapter on the importance of observation to both scientists and teachers. Science is not just about concepts; it is also about process, and skillful scientific observation plays a central role in that process. We discuss topics such as the importance of classroom observations as a learning tool for teachers and the critical role of assessment and how it is connected to observation. Our goal throughout Part I is to show the reader why science teaching should be an important part of what takes place in the elementary and middle school classroom. Learning to be an effective science teacher comes with practice, experience, and a willingness to experiment with new approaches. These are the skills that we will be highlighting throughout this text. If you don't currently view the teaching and learning of science as something that is both fun and engaging, we hope that you will come to see it that way by the time you are done with *Teaching Science in Elementary and Middle School: A Cognitive and Cultural Approach*.

The Nature of Science

Consider the following statements about science and the scientific process:

Science can purify religion from error and superstition. Religion can purify science from idolatry and false absolutes.

—**Pope John Paul II**[1]

If I have seen further than others, it is by standing upon the shoulders of giants. [I made discoveries] by always thinking unto them. I keep the subject constantly before me and wait till the first dawnings open little by little into the full light.

—**Sir Isaac Newton**

"The scientific method," Thomas Henry Huxley once wrote, "is nothing but the normal working of the human mind." That is to say, when the mind is working; that is to say further, when it is engaged in correcting its mistakes. Taking this point of view, we may conclude that science is not physics, biology, or chemistry—is not even a "subject"—but a moral imperative drawn from a larger narrative whose purpose is to give perspective, balance, and humility to learning.

—**Neil Postman**

Science is the tool of the Western mind and with it more doors can be opened than with bare hands. It is part and parcel of our knowledge and obscures our insight only when it holds that the understanding given by it is the only kind there is.

—**Carl Jung**

5

🐝 What Is Science?

The quotes above paint varied pictures of what science is: a collected body of facts and knowledge for explaining the natural world; a systematic and orderly way of thinking and problem solving; a counterpoint to other ways of knowing, such as religion or historical thinking; or a cultural frame of reference that guides much of modern Western philosophy and thought. What, then, is science?

The *Oxford English Dictionary* (1998) defines science as "those branches of study that relate to the phenomena of the material universe and their laws." Dictionary definitions, however, do not give us a conceptual understanding of the culturally and historically rich enterprise that is science. Science is much more than definitions: science is an integral part of our daily lives. In modern society, it surrounds us in everything we do. This has not always been the case for human beings, nor is it equally the case for all people around the world. Science as we know it, in its most limited models and manifestations, has existed for only several thousand years—a tiny fraction of the history of humankind.

Modern science is an even more recent newcomer, originating in the late Renaissance and Early Modern period (roughly 1550–1700). Beginning with the work of the Italian scientist Galileo (1564–1642; see Image 1.2), and continuing with the discoveries of the Englishmen Sir Francis Bacon (1561–1626; see Image 1.1) and Sir Isaac Newton (1642–1727; see Image 1.3), a new way of looking at the world emerged. It was an approach based upon systematic observations and **measurements** that were then codified into a series of rules and principles. These principles gradually came to be divided into distinct disciplines such as physics, chemistry, biology, and Earth and space science. Each discipline has grown and evolved in its own way, developing its own rules, codes, and methods and even subdividing into discrete subdisciplines (e.g., molecular biology and organismal biology), yet always remaining part of a larger identifiable whole that is science.

Prior to the rise of modern Western science (i.e., before about 1550), much that we now think of as science was considered to be magic. The science fiction writer Arthur C. Clarke (1985) has commented that "any sufficiently advanced technology is indistinguishable from magic" (p. iv). In Mark Twain's novel *A Connecticut Yankee in King Arthur's Court*, a man born in the late nineteenth century is transported back to the Middle Ages. Even with a limited scientific knowledge, he appears to his medieval hosts to be a magician or wizard.

As a new elementary or middle school teacher, you probably do not have an extensive background in the natural sciences. If you are typical of most college students, you've studied general science and biology, and

SOURCE: Wikimedia Commons (http://commons.wikimedia.org/wiki/Image:Francis_Bacon.jpg).

Image 1.1. Sir Francis Bacon (1561–1626)

SOURCE: Wikipedia (http://en.wikipedia.org/wiki/Image:Galileo.jpg).

Image 1.2. Galileo (1564–1642)

SOURCE: Painting by Godfrey Kneller, 1689 (Wikipedia, http://en.wikipedia.org/wiki/Image:GodfreyKneller-IsaacNewton-1689.jpg).

Image 1.3. Isaac Newton (1642–1727)

perhaps chemistry and physics, in high school. You have probably fulfilled a general science requirement of two to three unrelated science courses as part of your college or university's general studies program. Science is probably not something you spend a lot of time thinking about and is something you largely take for granted.

Why should science, and more to the point of this book, learning to teach science well, be of interest to you? The answer lies, at least in part, in the degree to which science shapes the world in which we live. Think for a moment about the extent to which your life differs from life just 100 years ago. To begin with, 100 years ago your life expectancy would have been much shorter, probably only about 50 years (possibly far less, depending on the type of work you did). There is a high likelihood that if you had brothers or sisters, one or more of them would have died of natural causes before they reached adulthood. Diseases and illnesses that we take for granted as being manageable or curable today were fatal just 100 years ago. Polio, for example, killed and debilitated millions until the mid-1950s when Jonas Salk (1914–1995) developed the first effective vaccine. Tuberculosis could only be controlled with the advent of antibiotics in the 1940s (and even today, in parts of the developing world where basic antibiotics can be difficult to come by, tuberculosis still kills two to three million people annually). One hundred years ago, appendicitis would most likely have proven fatal.

It is possible to argue that the fact that you are alive at your age is most likely a direct result of scientific discoveries made in the past 100 years.

Today's highly efficient systems of transportation are another example of how science has changed our world. Have you traveled on a vacation in the last year or two? Are you attending college or university away from home? Do you routinely travel hundreds of miles or more to visit family or friends? Modern transportation—such as airplanes and automobiles, both relatively recent marvels of science and technology—makes this possible (see Images 1.4, 1.5).

Look at how communication has been revolutionized in just the past decade. Ten years ago, cellular telephones were a novelty item, large and clunky devices of limited range and utility carried by "techno-geeks" and the occasional electrician and telephone repairer. Today, cell phones are a ubiquitous accessory, carried by nearly every adolescent and adult in the developed world (see Image 1.6). You are probably well aware of the technology that you use—especially the latest gadgets that you do not yet possess but hope to own soon. You are probably much less aware of the science that underlies this technology.

Of course, the wonders of science and its "advances" also cause complications, ethical dilemmas, and sometimes tragedy. Until you owned a car, you likely did not have to worry about paying for gas or insurance. Cell phones will soon be required to contain a global positioning system (GPS) locator, which will allow others to follow your every move. If you are worrying about finding a lost child who is carrying a cell phone, this might be a good thing. But what if you are, for example, a celebrity who is being tracked by a stalker, or simply a citizen whom the government wants to keep an eye on? "Big Brother," in George Orwell's nightmare dystopia *1984,* immediately comes to mind.

Image 1.4. Steam-Powered Train

Think how different life was 100 years ago when steam-powered trains were the main means of transportation.

SOURCE: Photograph by John T. Daniels courtesy of the Library of Congress.

Image 1.5. The Wright Brothers' Aeroplane

The first powered flight was made on December 17, 1903. Think how the world has changed as a result of the scientific discovery of flight.

SOURCE: Photograph by Jean-Marie Buxton.

Image 1.6. Cell Phone

Think how access to cell phone technology has changed the life of children as well as adults.

Since the atom bomb was dropped on Hiroshima on August 8, 1945, we have lived under the threat of nuclear annihilation. Every terrorist bombing that takes place around the world is made possible through science, as was the horrific destruction of the World Trade Center buildings on September 11, 2001. As a result of the power that comes from access to scientific and technological knowledge, human beings are now able to destroy the world in which we live (see Image 1.7). As General Omar Bradley (1893–1981) once claimed, "The world has achieved brilliance without conscience. Ours is a world of nuclear giants and ethical infants." Still, this surely does not mean that humankind would be better off without science and technology, only that it is imperative that we be thoughtful about how we use this extraordinarily powerful knowledge.

Image 1.7. Nuclear Test, Las Vegas, Nevada, November 1, 1951

Troops of the Battalion Combat Team, U.S. Army 11th Airborne Division, watch a plume of radioactive smoke rise after a D-Day blast at Yucca Flats, as the much prepared exercise "Desert Rock" reaches its peak.

Taking all of this into account, it is imperative that we, as citizens and teachers, have a clear understanding of the role of science in our lives. Equally important is the ability to communicate this understanding to the students whom we teach. One of the things we would like to emphasize in this textbook is that teaching science is not just about teaching a body of facts, skills, and processes but must also be about teaching the next generation to think about and reflect on the impact that science has on our lives, our work, and our society.

Theory Into Practice 1.1

Nature of Science Cards

As we continue to consider what science is, it may be valuable to pause and reflect upon your own beliefs about science. The following statements represent a variety of perspectives on scientific inquiry and the values and processes that underlie it. Alternatively, your instructor may have created a set of cards containing these or other statements about science. The procedures for the activity are as follows:

1. Select four science statements with which you agree:
   - "Only science can tell us what is really true about the world."
   - "Science is fundamentally responsible for most of our modern woes."
   - "Science is a powerful tool for understanding the natural world."
   - "Science and religion are fundamentally at odds."
   - "Scientific progress has made possible some of the best things in life and some of the worst."
   - "Scientists should have much greater influence in government."
   - "Scientific knowledge is of much greater value than any other type of knowledge."
   - "Science is always changing and therefore is not very reliable."
   - "The scientific methods should be followed in all fields of study."
   - "Science is one of several valuable ways of knowing."
   - "Science and technology always operate in somebody's interest and serve someone or some groups of people."
   - "Science begins with observations, which lead to generalizations."
   - "Science and technology are two sides of the same coin."
   - "Unless an idea is testable it is of little or no use."
   - "Good science cannot be done without good theories."
   - "Observation is central to all of science."
   - "There is no one scientific method."
   - "Theories serve to give direction to observations, that is, they tell a person where to look."
   - "Facts do not speak for themselves; they must be interpreted by theory."
   - "The destruction of nature is often done in the name of scientific progress."

- "The predominance of men in the sciences has led to bias in the choice and definition of the problems scientists have addressed."
- "A scientist should not allow preconceived theoretical ideas to influence observation and experimentation."
- "Money spent on projects such as NASA space flights would be better spent on health care for the needy."
- "If theory without observation is empty, then observation without theory is blind."
- "Scientific knowledge is always objective and self-correcting."
- "Scientific facts are manufactured through social negotiations."
- "Formal and informal networking among scientists is crucial for the success of scientific research."
- "Before beginning an experiment, a scientist should have an expectation of what will happen."
- "Seeing is believing."
- "Women and minorities are underrepresented in science because they have not been treated in the same encouraging ways as have white men."

2. Find a partner (who has also selected four statements) and discuss your statements and why you selected them (i.e., Why do you agree with these statements?).

3. Together, select the four statements that both of you can best agree upon (discard the remaining four statements—note that you may have duplicates).

4. With your partner, find another pair of students who have also completed Step 3 and, as a group of four, discuss the eight science statements you have selected.

5. Together, select the four statements that the four of you can best agree upon (discard the remaining four statements).

6. Collectively, write a paragraph titled "What we believe about science." Be sure to include the four statements that you agreed upon. Share this paragraph with the rest of your class, looking for similarities and differences between the various groups' paragraphs.

What Science Is Not

We have already stated that science is only one possible way of knowing or understanding the world. Science is a rule-bound system guided by specific procedures and checks. Science does not, for example, generally move forward by faith. A scientist may have faith in her ideas, may believe in what she is doing, or may have a hunch about how to proceed, but when doing science, faith alone is not sufficient. The procedures, methods, and reasoning of a scientist must be transparent so that they can be subjected to peer review and possible replication. This is not necessarily the case for other ways of knowing. A priest, for example, can base his or her knowledge on faith—faith that cannot and need not be proven through replication or peer review.

The current cultural debates about whether "intelligent design" should be taught in the science classroom as an alternative to evolutionary theory is a case in point. While many aspects of evolutionary theory can be tested, peer-reviewed, and refined over time, intelligent design must be accepted or rejected primarily on faith, and thus cannot be considered a **scientific theory**. This is not to say that science is a "better" way of knowing than faith-based knowledge, only that there are clear qualities of scientific knowledge that must be maintained. It is a misrepresentation of science to claim as scientific ideas that do not adhere to these qualities.

Science is also not about magic. Magic proposes that there are supernatural forces at work in the world and that phenomena can take place or things can be transformed through processes that defy natural explanation. While some science and technology may seem, at first, to be like magic, in the end it must withstand the scrutiny and the explanatory power of natural laws.

Science and magic are often confused and have, at times, even overlapped. In chemistry, for example, many of the physical transformations that early alchemists tried to perform became the foundation for chemical discoveries. Many early scientific discoveries were made by people who were trying to practice what would today be considered magic, rather than science.

An example is the German alchemist Hennig Brandt (unknown–1692) and his discovery of the **element** phosphorus. Brandt wanted to see whether he could create gold from other, less valuable elements found in nature. He reasoned that because urine from animals—including humans—was gold colored, it would be possible to extract the precious element from it. After collecting large amounts of urine in tubs, he let the urine set until it became a dry paste. Although the dried urine did not contain any gold, it did have an unusual property: It glowed in the dark! The dry paste was the element phosphorus.

It was soon discovered that phosphorus had other properties as well. When exposed to the air, white phosphorus would spontaneously burst into flame. The accidental discovery of phosphorous by an alchemist eventually led to other scientific and practical discoveries, including the invention of the safety match in 1855 by the Swedish inventor John Lundstrom (1815–1888).

Again, we wish to emphasize that although science is a powerful and useful way of knowing, it is not necessarily the best or the only way to understand the world. Historical, theological, aesthetic, intuitive, and other ways of knowing frequently help people to make sense of the world around them. When it comes to explaining causal relationships involving natural phenomena, however, it is generally agreed that scientific methods are the most reliable way of knowing.

We often underestimate how science has profoundly shaped our society and culture. We frequently take its results for granted, rather like the fish in the aquarium who does not think about the water in which it swims. Take, for example, the use of hay to feed farm animals. If you are like most people, you probably think that farmers have always had hay. But, in fact, the idea of cutting tall grass and drying and storing it so that domesticated animals could feed on it during the winter developed in the Middle Ages. As the physicist Freeman Dyson (1988) explains,

> Nobody knows who invented hay, the idea of cutting grass in the autumn and storing it in large enough quantities to keep horses and cows alive through the winter. All we know is that the technology of hay was unknown to the Roman Empire but was known to every village of medieval Europe. Like many other crucially important technologies, hay emerged anonymously during the so-called Dark Ages. (p. 135)

So, you might say to yourself, why is the discovery of hay so important? Have you thought that its discovery might have political and social ramifications? That it may have reshaped modern European history and the rise of countries such as Germany, France, and England?

> According to the Hay Theory of History, the invention of hay was the decisive event which moved the center of gravity of urban civilization from the Mediterranean basin to Northern and Western Europe. The Roman Empire did not need hay because in a Mediterranean climate the grass grows well enough in winter for animals to graze. North of the Alps, great cities dependent on horses and oxen for motive power could not exist without hay. So it was hay that allowed populations to grow and civilizations to flourish among the forests of Northern Europe. Hay moved the greatness of Rome to Paris and London, and later to Berlin and Moscow and New York. (Dyson, 1988, p. 136)

The discovery of hay as a source of feed for domesticated animals such as horses and cows represents a natural discovery that profoundly reshaped history. A seemingly simple mechanical discovery that changed European history was the stirrup. First introduced into Europe from Asia during the twelfth century, the stirrup made it possible for knights to ride armored horses without falling off (see Image 1.8). As a result, a new type of warfare was introduced into European culture, in which highly skilled military troops were trained with sophisticated weapons (lances, armor, etc.). The warriors who fought using this new technology required extensive training and a great deal of money to stay active in the field. Social systems involving a noble class, special privileges, and taxation evolved, which redefined the social and political direction of European culture. Without the stirrup, there would not have been knighthood as we know it, and the **evolution** of the social systems of countries such as England, France, and Germany would probably have taken profoundly different directions (White, 1962).

SOURCE: Etching by Albrecht Dürer, 1513.

Image 1.8. Knight, Death, and Devil

How Science Is Done

We have discussed what science is and what it is not. Now let us turn to the question of how science is done. Scientific inquiry is a process of trying to explain observations made of the natural world around us. There are certain rules involved in this process, including the generation of theory (explanatory hypotheses or predictions), the collection of data through observation and/or measurement, and the analysis and interpretation of those data in an attempt to answer an initial question (other common qualities of scientific inquiry are discussed in more detail under "Qualities of Scientific Inquiry," below). Still, the widely held belief that there is one overarching and invariant "Scientific Method" is largely a misconception (or at the very least, a vast oversimplification). As was mentioned earlier, science sometimes advances in part through taking leaps of faith, and sometimes discovery is even the result of pure accident. The vulcanization of rubber, for example, is an essential technology we make use of whenever we drive a car, take off or land in an airplane, or go on a bike ride. Like the discovery of phosphorus by Brandt hundreds of years earlier, the discovery of vulcanized rubber by Charles Goodyear (1800–1860; see Image 1.9) in 1839 was largely an accident.

SOURCE: Engraving by W. G. Jackman courtesy of the Library of Congress.

Image 1.9. Charles Goodyear (1800–1860)

Goodyear was trying to find a way to take raw rubber from a rubber tree and turn it into a shock-absorbing covering for the metal wheels that were common on wagons and other wheeled vehicles of the day. Unfortunately, the raw rubber in its unprocessed state was not sufficiently durable to make a good tire. Goodyear set about experimenting by mixing the rubber with various chemicals but repeatedly met with failure until he accidentally discovered the solution when he dropped a piece of raw rubber onto a hot stovetop. He "discovered" that by subjecting the rubber to a high **temperature,** he achieved the increased durability he was looking for through a process he came to describe as "vulcanization." What does this anecdote say to us about the process of scientific inquiry? It suggests that scientific discovery is not always (in fact, is rarely) a straightforward, linear process. Scientific inquiry is full of false starts and dead ends. It also can involve luck. However, scientific discoveries, even when made "accidentally," are almost always part of a process of systematic inquiry in which a scientist or group of scientists literally kept their eyes open for new results. As the great French scientist Louis Pasteur put it, "in the field of observation, chance favors only the prepared mind."

Even dreams have sometimes played a role in new scientific discoveries, as can be seen in the case of the benzene ring. Benzene is an industrial solvent used in the production of many plastics; it was discovered in 1825 by the British chemist Michael Faraday, who isolated it from oil **gas**. The formula of benzene (C6H6), however, was a mystery for some time after its discovery. Molecular structures were long believed to be linear in nature, a "fact" that could not explain many properties of benzene, nor account for all of its bonds (carbon usually forms four single bonds and hydrogen one).

In one of the most famous instances of dream-discovery, the German chemist Till Kekulé (1829–1896) deduced the ring structure of benzene while sleeping. He described this experience to a meeting of scientists as follows:

> I turned my chair toward the fire place and sank into a doze. Again the atoms were flitting before my eyes. Smaller groups now kept modestly in the background. My mind's eye, sharpened by repeated visions of a similar sort, now distinguished larger structures of varying forms. Long rows frequently rose together, all in movement, winding and turning like serpents; and see! what was that? One of the serpents seized its own tail and the form whirled mockingly before my eyes. I came awake like a flash of lightning. This time also I spent the remainder of the night working out the consequences of the hypothesis. (Von Baeyer, 1989)

Still, as Nobel Prize-winning physicist Richard Feynman (1918–1988) has noted, the scientific community has developed certain ingrained cultural norms that serve to at least partially obscure these "messy" and nonlinear aspects of the scientific process of discovery. In his 1966 Nobel lecture, Feynman claimed,

> We have a habit in writing articles published in scientific journals to make the work as finished as possible, to cover up all the tracks, to not worry about the blind alleys or describe how you had the wrong idea at first, and so on. So there isn't any place to publish, in a dignified manner, what you actually did in order to get on with the work.

Different scientific disciplines also have different norms for conducting inquiry and different limitations on what kinds of experimentation are possible. Some branches of science, such as geology and **astronomy**, are not conducive to controlled experiments. One cannot, for example, change the

SOURCE: Courtesy of NASA.

Image 1.10. Annie Jump Cannon (1863–1941)

way a star or a planet behaves to study the result; one can only observe what happens under various conditions that already exist in nature. The early twentieth-century American astronomer Annie Jump Cannon (1863–1941; see Image 1.10) spent 30 years at the Harvard College Observatory **classifying** more than 500,000 stars and creating a catalog of stars that is still used in attempts to understand stellar evolution. Throughout all this work, Cannon never once carried out a true experiment or followed the "scientific method" as it is taught in most science classes.

Still, there are a number of procedural and conceptual activities that are frequently practiced during a scientific investigation: asking questions; hypothesizing; designing experiments; making predictions; using apparatus; observing; measuring; evaluating **accuracy**, prediction, and error; recording and interpreting data; consulting data records; evaluating evidence; verifying evidence; reacting to contradictory or anomalous data; coordinating theory and evidence; performing statistical calculations; and formulating and revising models and theories. While no scientist practices all of these activities during any single experiment, every scientist routinely engages in a variety of these practices. For the purpose of doing science with elementary and middle grade students, we have simplified and condensed these practices into more general qualities of scientific inquiry that we present in the next two sections of the chapter.

Theory Into Practice 1.2

Hidden Shapes

The following activity is meant to demonstrate how scientific practice often includes a combination of observation and inference.

1. Cut two sets of shapes out of colored paper—one set of regular geometric shapes (circle, square, triangle, and rectangle) and one set of irregular shapes that resemble regular shapes but have missing or additional pieces (see Image 1.11 below for examples).

2. Glue these figures in sets onto pieces of plain white paper.

3. Take two manila office folders and cut or punch numerous small holes in one side and then tape closed two of the three open sides of the folder.

4. Slide the paper with the colored shapes into the folder so that small pieces of the shapes are revealed through the holes.

5. Give each folder to a group of three to five students and ask them to draw a picture of what is on the paper inside the folder using only the information they can observe through the holes (i.e., they cannot remove the paper from the folder).

6. It is likely that based on what they can see, both groups will draw regular geometric shapes because humans naturally seek pattern and order (whether it is there or not).

7. When both groups are done, tell them they can remove the sheet from the folder and compare what they have drawn with what is actually there.

The group with the irregular shapes is likely to feel "tricked."

This activity can be used to discuss how scientists often must try to explain phenomena based on only partial information or observation as well as how nature often, but not always, seems to adhere to regular patterns (a topic discussed further in the following section).

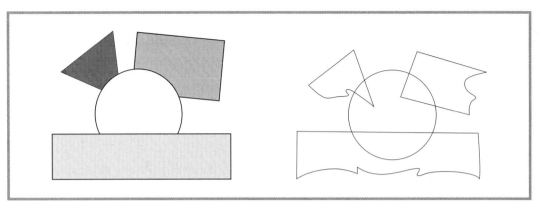

Image 1.11. Regular and Irregular Hidden Shapes

Patterns That Connect

Our philosophy is that science needs to be understood not just in isolation, but also in its connection to other things. Thus, an invention like the automobile needs to be understood not only in terms of how it functions mechanically, but how it is connected to other things in the world. Think for a moment about how our cities have developed as a result of the invention of the automobile just a little more than 100 years ago. How would they be designed differently if the car had never been invented? What would have been emphasized or omitted? To begin with, our cities would not have superhighways passing through them, gas stations on nearly every major corner, or stoplights. Houses and businesses would need to be designed to be within walking distance of each other, instead of driving distance. On a larger scale, the invention of the automobile has necessitated the importation of oil from foreign countries, involving not only new technologies of exploration, refining, and transportation, but also political negotiations and alliances that probably would not otherwise exist. The invention of the automobile has also led to the increased emission of pollutants into the atmosphere, contributing to the **greenhouse effect** and the warming of the Earth's atmosphere.

As we can see in the example above, understanding the relationship between science and the larger world is an extremely complicated process. The British anthropologist and social theorist Gregory Bateson (1904–1980) provides some insight into how we might think about these relationships. In his book *Mind and Nature,* Bateson (1980) argues that our educational system provides almost no training for the crucial issues we must confront in our lives—what he refers to as "the pattern which connects." He asks, for example, why our schools so rarely address questions related to social thinking and relationships between seemingly disparate ideas? According to Bateson, if you "break the pattern which connects the items of learning . . . you necessarily destroy all quality." Bateson asks what the crab and lobster, the rose and primrose, mean to one another. What do these four life forms mean to the amoeba? To man? (p. 8). In other words, "What is the pattern which connects all the living creatures?" (p. 9).

This is why we consider it so important for students, and particularly for those who wish to teach, to have an adequate understanding of science. Science provides us with powerful tools for considering how things are connected and related to one another, for understanding the world around us and our place in it as human beings. Conversely, having a weak understanding of science places one at a serious disadvantage when it comes to understanding these relationships.

Think for a moment about the shape of a chambered nautilus seashell (see Image 1.12). How is it connected to the spiral shape of a galaxy (see Image 1.13)? Are the two related? Did you know that chambered nautiluses and spiral galaxies both conform to the mathematical and architectural ratio known as the Golden Mean? Did you know that the Golden Mean Proportion exists throughout nature? It appears in organic and inorganic **matter**, in the structure of the human body, in the growth patterns of plants and animals, and even in viruses and **DNA**. Did you know that mathematically the pattern of a chambered nautilus or a spiral galaxy is actually a Fibonaccian sequence? The Fibonaccian sequence is a number sequence dis-

Image 1.12. The Rigid Open Chambers Within a Chambered Nautilus (*Nautilus pompilius*)

covered by the medieval mathematician Leonardo Fibonacci (1175–1250), in which the first two numbers in a sequence or series equals the third number in the same sequence (1, 1, 2, 3, 5, 8, 13, 21, 34 . . .).

Look, for example, at the rectangle in Image 1.14. It is a Golden Section or Phi (the ratio of 1:1.6180339 . . .) and is derived from a Fibonaccian sequence.

Notice the pattern of squares that make up the rectangle in Image 1.14. What do you observe? Notice also that by drawing an arc across each square between its most distant ends, we create a spiral that is identical in shape to the spiral found in a chambered nautilus or spiral galaxy. Is this simply an incredible coincidence, or is it a "pattern that connects" of the

SOURCE: Courtesy of NASA.

Image 1.13. The Spiral Galaxy NGC 4414

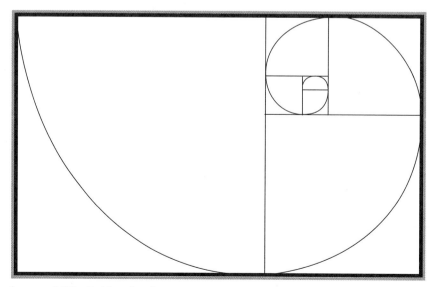

Image 1.14. Golden Section

type that Bateson is talking about? What about the shape of a sunflower or the branching of a tree? Did you know that these form Fibonaccian sequences too? Is it possible that there is some sort of "sacred geometry" at work here? Some sort of scientific law or principle?

Qualities of Scientific Inquiry

As we have seen, much of science is about discovering the patterns that exist in the natural world around us. But how do we make these discoveries? Scientific inquiry generally holds to certain qualities that improve the likelihood of such discoveries.

Replicability

If the same procedures are conducted under the same conditions, then the same results should be achieved. Thus, in billiards, if the cue ball strikes one of the bumpers at an angle of incidence of 45 degrees, then a person with some knowledge of **force** and motion would likely hypothesize that the ball will move off as a result of this collision at an angle of reflection also equal to 45 degrees (see Image 1.15). Whatever the result of the first trial, an interested observer would want to repeat the experiment several times to check the consistency of results. Suppose on the third trial the cue ball strikes the bumper but does not go off at the same angle after the collision. What might have happened? This brings us to a second quality of scientific inquiry: **control of variables.**

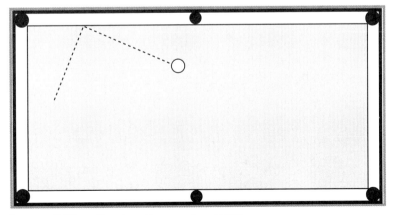

Image 1.15. Billiard Ball Bouncing Off Bumper

Control of Variables

A variable is any factor that could change, intentionally or unintentionally, during the course of scientific inquiry. In the above example of the pool table, the observer's hypothesis—that the cue ball will move off at an angle equal to the angle at which the ball hit the bumper—is only likely to be correct if certain other variables are held constant. Thus, the hypothesis assumes that the table is level, that the surface of the table is smooth and clean, that the bumper is straight, and that the ball is hit evenly with the cue stick without applying significant "spin." A scientist conducting an experiment needs to identify all possible variables that could change, control the ones that she can, and take into account those that she cannot control.

Systematicity

The process of discovery by "messing around with things" is an important part of the creative process found in science as well as in art, literature, and other creative fields. It is an approach that is also consistent with constructivist models of learning based on the theoretical ideas of psychologists such as Jean Piaget (1896–1980) and Lev Vygotsky (1896–1934), scientists whose work has significantly influenced the field of education and whose ideas will be discussed in detail in Chapter 3. While such "messing around" may seem to be haphazard, when it comes to science, this process must be tempered by a certain degree of **systematicity**, or following a previously determined, systematic plan. An example can be found in the work of the well-known American inventor Thomas Edison (1847–1931).

Edison did not simply have brilliant ideas; he worked systematically on problems, trying every possible combination and permutation until he came up with a solution to the thing he was trying to invent. Thus, his invention of the light bulb was a systematic inquiry in which he tried numerous burning filaments inside a **vacuum** chamber. He experimented with a vast range of different materials. One day, he went rummaging around in his wife's sewing basket and pulled out a thin strip of bamboo. He carbonized (burned) it and placed it inside the vacuum flask. The carbon filament of bamboo provided a bright and long-lasting glow, setting Edison on the path that led to the invention of an affordable, commercially available light bulb. This seemingly simple invention, one that revolutionized the way modern humans live and work, would not have come about were it not for Edison's systematic approach to scientific inquiry.

Communication

Scientific discovery also relies on a continual process of **communication** within the scientific community so that its members can build upon the work of others. Today, such communication is greatly facilitated by technologies such as e-mail, videoconferencing, and air travel. Even hundreds of years ago, however, communication of ideas played a central role in science. In the early nineteenth century, for example, Michael Faraday (1791–1867) had a clear understanding of the electrical experiments that had been conducted previously by people such as Benjamin Franklin (1706–1790), Alessandro Volta (1745–1827), and Antoine Lavoisier (1743–1794). Because they had published their work in detail, Faraday was able to build on their ideas to develop his understanding of electromagnetic properties and to build the first functioning electrical motor.

In our own era, scientific communication has played a critical role in many significant discoveries. The identification and isolation of the AIDS virus in the early 1980s was a direct result of thousands of scientists around the world researching a new and confusing disease, then communicating with each other about what they were finding and eventually identifying its culprit virus. In fact, credit for the final identification of the AIDS virus has been given to two separate scientific labs, one in France (L'Institut Pasteur) and one in the United States (U.S. National Cancer Institute), for their simultaneous work on the disease.

Creativity

Another important quality of scientific inquiry is **creativity**. An example is the ability to bring things that seem dissimilar or unrelated together in new ways. Scientific inventions frequently result from the integration and refinement of different prior discoveries.

One specific example is the invention of the motion picture. The scientific precursor to motion pictures dates back to 1826 and the work of British scientist John Ayrton Paris (1785–1856). Paris was interested in the physiology of the eye. He invented a device called the thaumatrope ("wonder turner" in Greek) to demonstrate the phenomenon of persistence of vision (see Experiment 94 in Chapter 9).

The thaumatrope then gave rise to the phantascope, a spinning wheel on a handle containing equally spaced vertical slits on one side and a set of sequential pictures (such as a horse galloping) on the other side (see Image 1.16). When this device is put in front of a mirror and spun, the viewer perceives a single, moving picture.

SOURCE: "Phantascope" (1881).

Image 1.16. A Phantascope

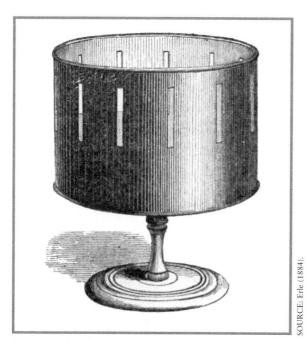

SOURCE: Erle (1884).

Image 1.17. A Zoetrope

From the phantascope was developed the zoetrope, which was an upright version of a phantascope consisting of a revolving drum with slits in the side through which a sequential picture could be viewed (see Image 1.17).

The zoetrope was then modified so that a light was projected through it and a lens focused the image—essentially, a primitive projector. Modern movies became possible when movement was recorded at high speed on strips of acetate film and then run through a projection device, replicating the principles of the primitive zoetrope projector.

While some scientific discoveries create something completely new, like motion pictures, other discoveries evolve from a scientist's desire to improve upon an old idea. Perhaps you have played with a "superball"—a rubber ball that bounces higher than other balls. The superball was invented by the chemist Norman Stingley in the early 1960s. He had been experimenting with compressing synthetic rubber at over 3,500 pounds per square inch and came up with a formula that was both resilient and capable of bouncing very high (three times higher than a normal rubber ball). He eventually took his invention to Wham-O, who manufactured the Frisbee and the Hula Hoop; they saw the superball's terrific potential as a toy. Since the introduction of the superball, over 20 million have been manufactured (see Experiment 85 in Chapter 9 for an experiment using superballs).

Informed Skepticism

While scientists should always be open to new ideas and new theories that purport to better explain natural phenomena, their enthusiasm must also be tempered by a sense of skepticism. Within the scientific community, acceptance of new theories is often a lengthy process. It is a process in which the proponents of the new theory attempt to provide evidence that their theory is better at explaining and/or **predicting** observations than other competing theories, as well as explain how their theory fits in and connects with other existing theories. This process of verification and refutation can often take years and can be highly contentious. In fact, the German physicist Max Plank (1858–1947) argued that "a new scientific truth does not triumph by convincing its opponents and making them see the light, but rather because its opponents eventually die, and a new generation grows up that is familiar with it" (Kuhn, 1970, p. 17).

When taken together, these qualities of scientific inquiry—(1) **replicability**, (2) control of variables, (3) systematicity, (4) communication, (5) creativity, and (6) **informed skepticism**—create a productive framework for addressing questions about the physical and natural world, a topic we take up in the next section.

🐝 Combining the Qualities of Scientific Inquiry to Address Scientific Questions

We can see how the six qualities of scientific inquiry that we have discussed can be combined in an authentic context by considering a pair of case studies—one historical and the other more current. Let's begin with the example of the work of the pioneer epidemiologist John Snow (1813–1858). Snow, who was an unassuming London physician, became concerned about the many severe cholera epidemics that threatened London during the 1840s. As a physician, he was interested in the cause and transmission of the disease. In 1849, he published a short article, "On the Mode of Communication of Cholera," suggesting that cholera was a contagious disease caused by a poison that reproduced in the human body and was transmitted by water contaminated with this poison. His view was at odds with the commonly held theory that the disease was transmitted by the inhalation of disease-ridden vapors. His work was largely discounted until the next epidemic in 1854, at which point he set out to prove his theory. He began by systematically collecting data and tracing the location of the outbreak by mapping the home address of each person who died from the disease. When he looked at the map after collecting the data, it was very clear that there was a central geographical point around which the deaths had occurred.

Snow discovered that at the center of the neighborhood where the most deaths occurred was a water well that nearly all of the victims had used. He deduced that the well water was infected and responsible for transmitting the cholera. To test this hypothesis, Snow convinced the city officials to remove the handle from the pump to the well (the Broad Street well) to prevent people from using it. The epidemic quickly came under control. His hypothesis seemed to be confirmed. But Snow still needed to consider whether any other variables had affected the situation besides the removal of the pump handle.

Earlier in this chapter, we discussed Gregory Bateson's idea that science is ultimately about discovering the patterns that connect. Snow saw the pattern between the death of the people living around the Broad Street well and his earlier idea that cholera might be a water-borne disease. Snow's work represents science functioning at its best—working to discover the patterns that connect.

It is interesting to note that Snow did not actually identify the infectious agent that was causing the cholera (a bacillus bacteria). In fact, the discovery of the causal agent was not made until more than 50 years later, in 1905. Thus, in the case of Snow, it was possible to isolate the source of the disease, control it, and even set up public health procedures that would save people's lives without fully understanding the exact nature of the problem.

A second, more recent example of how scientific practices work in addressing scientific questions is cold fusion. In 1989, two chemists working at the University of Utah, Martin Fleischmann and Stanley Pons, claimed to have developed an apparatus for producing "cold fusion" in their lab. They said it effectively harnessed the power of the sun without the dangers or the multi-billion dollar price tag of experiments with "hot fusion." Their announcement of this achievement was met at once by both excitement and informed skepticism within the scientific community. Fleischmann and Pons communicated their findings and their apparatus design to scientists at other institutions. In order to verify Fleischmann and Pons's findings, others attempted to replicate their work. While several labs at first seemed to be getting positive results from their experiments, other labs were failing to find the requisite amounts of either heat or nuclear byproduct **molecules** that would prove that nuclear fusion was actually taking place. It gradually became clear that many of the supposedly positive results could be explained away by experimental errors. The results of Fleischmann and Pons's experiment were called into question. Eventually, the scientific community came to the conclusion that the two scientists had been in error. Cold fusion remains an elusive and theoretically questionable possibility.

The case of cold fusion and many other cases of controversial science are not quite as clear-cut as they may seem on the surface. As historians of science Harry Collins and Trevor Pinch (1993) point out, using replicability to ascertain the existence of a phenomenon may be problematic when the phenomenon's existence is in doubt. If you are trying to detect something that you are not sure is there, does a negative result mean that, in fact, it is not there? Or, does it simply mean that you didn't use the "right" procedure or did not have a sensitive enough instrument? Thus, in the case of cold fusion, believers in the positive results obtained by Fleischmann and Pons could explain away the negative results of other groups as due to faulty procedures or slight differences in the conditions under which the experiment was conducted (remember the earlier example of the slightly angled pool table bumper). True replicability means that everything is held exactly the same. This can be much more problematic than it first appears. In the case of the Fleischmann and Pons experiment, the University of Utah where the research was conducted is perched high in the Rocky Mountains. Potential replicators of the study at MIT, for example, were working at sea level. What if altitude made a critical difference in the results? Those who failed to find evidence of cold fusion, however, could just as easily argue that they found nothing because there was nothing to find and that it was Fleischmann and Pons who had been in error in their measurements.

How, then, is the issue of controversial science to be resolved when replicability of results is inconclusive? Collins and Pinch (1993) argue that in such cases, communication and credibility win the day. The "expert" community of scientists within a given discipline generally comes to a consensus based on theoretical predictions, until such time as those theories may be more conclusively overturned through experimentation. In the case of cold fusion, the high-energy physics community had long held that cold fusion was theoretically impossible (or at least, highly unlikely). Fleischmann and Pons, who were chemists rather than physicists (an additional strike against them in terms of credibility), thus needed to meet a higher standard of experimental irrefutability than they were able to achieve in order to overturn the theoretical consensus. The point of this story is that while science is a rule-bound system, it is also a human enterprise governed by social conventions as well as by experimental ones.

Theory Into Practice 1.3

The Hypothesis Box

This activity is meant to model the so-called "black box" effect that experimental scientists must sometimes contend with. Sometimes it is possible to control the starting conditions of an experiment and then, after some period of time, observe the outcome of the experiment without observing what took place between the starting point and the end point—what takes place in between is thus a "black box" that cannot be penetrated, and what takes place "inside" must be inferred.

1. Construct the box as per Image 1.18 using six funnels, coffee filters, rubber tubing (must be able to fit over the outflow of the funnels), and a large cardboard box.

2. Prepare the box in advance of its use by placing coffee filters in three of the four interior funnels and placing four or five drops of food coloring in the center of each of the coffee filters (a different color in each filter) and corking (or otherwise sealing) the outflow from the fourth of the interior funnels.

3. Tell the class that you are going to pour something into the top funnel of the hypothesis box several times and that after carefully observing the procedure, they will have to draw a diagram of what they believe is happening inside the box.

4. Be sure the hose from the top funnel is pointing into one of the four internal funnels. Ask for a student volunteer to hold a beaker under

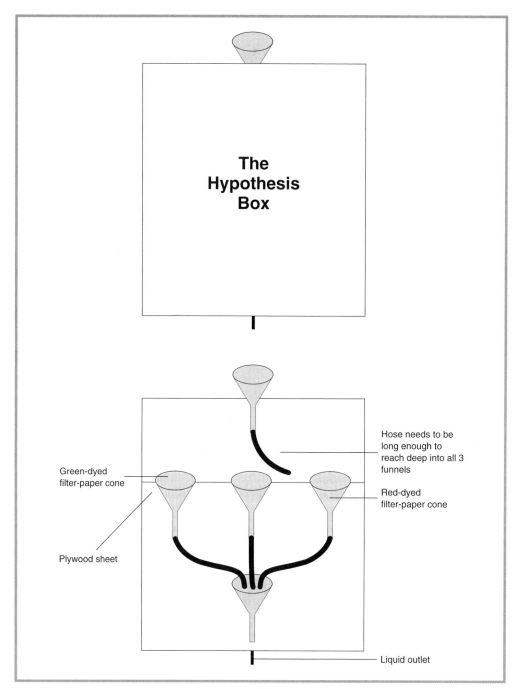

Image 1.18. Hypothesis Box: Internal and External Views

the bottom outflow tube, and pour several ounces of water into the top funnel—water of the first color should come out the bottom.

5. While the students are distracted observing the beaker of colored water, quietly turn the top funnel to the second position so that the tube is pointing toward the second color funnel.

6. Tell the class you are going to pour liquid in the top a second time and that they should observe closely. Have a second volunteer hold a second beaker under the outflow, and students should be quite surprised to see water of a different color come out.

7. While the students are distracted observing the second beaker of colored water, again quietly turn the top funnel to the third position. This should be the corked funnel, but could also be the third color. Repeat Step 6, but if it is the corked beaker, you should act surprised this time.

8. Repeat the above steps for the fourth position (either the third color or the stopped funnel).

9. Ask students to draw a diagram of what they believe the inside of the box looks like. Compare their diagrams, and finally, discuss how the box is like the way science sometimes works.

10. After the discussion, you can either show students the inside of the box right away or make the point that in science, the scientist doesn't always get the chance to "look into the box" right away and must sometimes move on with only partial information. Waiting at least until the next class period to show the class the inside of the box will make the activity more memorable for students and further emphasize the concept.

Paradigms and Paradigm Shifts in the Nature of Science

Thus far, we have provided evidence that science has a common core of ideals that can be used to evaluate the quality of a given scientific inquiry, but that scientific practice also varies from discipline to discipline, with quality sometimes being determined by negotiated consensus within a given scientific community. A number of socio-historical studies have contributed to this developing understanding of the nature of science, the two most famous of which are discussed below.

Sociologist Robert Merton (1910–2003) proposed four norms that he felt ought to drive scientific progress: (1) **universalism**, the idea that scientific results should be analyzed objectively and be verifiable or repeatable, without regard to the scientist's personal or social attributes; (2) **communism**, the idea that science is a communal activity in that scientists share their work with their community for the common good; (3) **disinterestedness**, the idea that scientists should have no emotional or financial attachments to their work; and (4) **organized skepticism**, the idea that scientists should wait until "all the facts are in" before a judgment is made about a particular theory (Merton, 1973, p. 267). Despite being focused on an idealized account of science rather than on scientists' actual practice, Merton's norms became widely accepted as a description of how science was done and are still often referenced today.

Merton's somewhat idealistic view of science was later challenged by sociologist Michael Mulkay. Mulkay argued that perpetuating Merton's vision of science, despite its inaccuracies, helped scientists in three ways: (1) raising scientists' social status; (2) increasing scientists' political power; and (3) enhancing the status of scientific knowledge (Mulkay, 1979). Mulkay proposed that while Merton's norms are, in fact, important guiding principles for scientific inquiry, there also exists a set of four "counter-norms" that can work against Merton's norms when scientists (as human beings) take actions to advance their professional careers.

Finally, no discussion of the nature of science would be complete without considering the work of the historian of science Thomas Kuhn (1922–1996). In his now famous book, *The Structure of Scientific Revolutions* (1970), Kuhn explored actual cases from the history of science, making a number of claims that flew in the face of the conventional understandings of science practice. Kuhn's main thesis was that science does not build upon itself in a linear fashion, but rather that it builds gradually for a time through routine science practice and then takes revolutionary leaps in unexpected directions during episodes of **paradigm shifts**. Thus, all scientific understanding must be viewed as specific to a given historical period and paradigm, rather than considered "finished" achievements that will remain unchanged. Kuhn also pointed out that agreement, or consensus, within the scientific community is the key to validating new knowledge claims, and that the criteria used in reaching this consensus are based on shared values as well as reasoned judgment.

According to Kuhn (1970), during the early stages of any field of science, researchers interpret their observations in many different ways (p. 17). After the initial stage of a field's development, however, these differences largely disappear as the field agrees upon a certain paradigm as the "correct" way to make sense of these observations. Kuhn also claimed that "to be accepted as a paradigm, a theory must seem better than its competitors, but it need not, and in fact never does, explain all the facts with which it can be confronted" (p. 17). At a future point, a new paradigm might be introduced that fundamentally changes the way the field explains and interprets these observations. Thus, scientific discovery often involves thinking about things in totally new ways. While it is important to look for patterns in science, it is also important to look for anomalies or things that do not agree with our assumptions.

Thus, the advancement of science is often based on breaking out of existing paradigms or models—in other words, thinking in new ways about things that are familiar. Some examples might help you understand the process a bit more clearly. There is a famous puzzle from the nineteenth century known as the "Columbus Egg Problem." Christopher Columbus is reported to have asked Queen Isabella of Spain how an egg could most easily be made to stand upright. The answer involves the use of a radical paradigm—by hard-boiling that egg and then lightly breaking its bottom, just enough so that the egg stays put. You may think that this is cheating, but no one said that the egg couldn't be boiled or that the bottom of the egg couldn't be broken. (You may want to challenge your students with this puzzle some day, but be prepared to clean up some broken eggs!)

Another example of breaking out of traditional ways of thinking (paradigms) is the classic puzzle of "thinking out of the box." The puzzle asks the viewer to connect nine points in the form of a square using just four straight lines that cannot cross each other (see Image 1.19). See how long it takes you to do it (and remember to "think outside the box!").

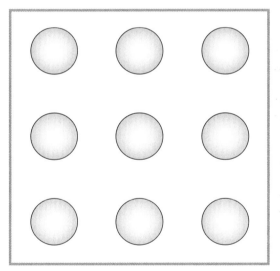

Image 1.19. Thinking Outside the Box

The observant reader will have noticed that in our discussion of the historical development of scientific inquiry, we have relied on examples from the work of scientists who are overwhelmingly white males of European descent. Does this mean that women and people of color have not made significant contributions to the development of science? As will be discussed in Chapter 4, there are several reasons why members of certain groups, women and people of color among them, have historically been underrepresented, both in terms of their actual participation in science and in terms of the credit they have been given for what they have legitimately accomplished. The most famous example of this is the case of Rosalind Franklin (1920–1958) and the discovery of the DNA double helix (a story that is taken up in more detail in Chapter 4). Even in the case of astronomer Annie Jump Cannon discussed earlier in this chapter, despite the recognition she receives now for her work in stellar classification, during her lifetime she was not able to hold a regular university faculty position and spent her entire career as a "research assistant" instead of as a professor.

Summary

In this chapter, we have discussed seven themes related to the nature of science. We took up the relatively short history of modern Western science and the enormous impact it has had on how humans live and work. We considered other ways of knowing about the physical and natural world and discussed the limitations of the scientific worldview. We then explored the fallacy of the "scientific method" as an invariant procedure for doing science, explaining instead how science is done through a mix of procedures and hunches, both following protocols and taking leaps of faith. This was followed by a discussion of the work of the social theorist Gregory Bateson and his belief that the fundamental role of education is to learn to make connections between seemingly unrelated things, an aspect of education that is often overlooked in today's schooling. We discussed six aspects of the practice of science, *replicability, control of variables, systematicity, communication, creativity,* and *informed skepticism.* We then provided two examples of how the qualities of scientific inquiry come together in practice: the work of the epidemiologist John Snow and more recent experiments by Fleischmann and Pons involving cold fusion. Finally, we highlighted the work of the historian of science, Thomas Kuhn, who revolutionized the way we understand how scientific disciplines are organized and how major conceptual changes (paradigm shifts) take place within those fields.

Student Study Site

The Companion Web site for *Teaching Science in Elementary and Middle School* http://www.sagepub.com/buxtonstudy

Visit the Web-based student study site to enhance your understanding of the chapter content and to discover additional resources that will take your learning one step further. You can enhance your understanding of the chapters by using the study materials, which include chapter objectives, flashcards, activities, practice tests, and more. You'll also find special features, such as Resources for Experiments, the Links to Standards from U.S. States and associated activities, Learning From Journal Articles, Theory Into Practice resources, Reflections on Science exercises, a Science Standards-Based Lesson Plan Project, and PRAXIS resources.

Reflections on Science

1. The nature of science means different things to different people. What does it mean to you? Write a short description of your understanding of what science is. Give it to someone (not in your class) to read and see whether it makes sense to him or her. Try to explain anything that he or she finds confusing.

2. Can you think of any times when you have used the process of scientific inquiry (outside of a school setting)? Describe the situation and how and why you used scientific inquiry.

3. Numerous historical examples of scientific discovery were presented in this chapter. Which one did you find most interesting and why? What does this example say about scientific inquiry?

4. What do you believe to be the greatest benefit to our society resulting from a scientific discovery? Why do you feel this way?

5. What do you believe to be the greatest problem faced by our society resulting from a scientific discovery? Why do you feel this way?

Internet Connections: Nature of Science Resources

AAAS Project 2061 on the Nature of Science
http://www.project2061.org/tools/sfaaol/chap1.htm

National Science Teachers Association (NSTA) Position Statement on the Nature of Science
http://www.nsta.org/positionstatement&psid=22

Nature of Science Lessons from Indiana University
http://www.indiana.edu/~ensiweb/natsc.fs.html

Lessons for Teaching the Nature of Science from University of California, Berkeley
http://evolution.berkeley.edu/evosite/nature/index.shtml

Comparison of Different Ways of Knowing from Arkansas Science Teachers Association
http://users.aristotle.net/~asta/science.htm

Evolution, Inquiry, and the Nature of Science
http://books.nap.edu/html/evolution98/evol6.html

Quackwatch Notes on the Nature of Science
http://www.quackwatch.org/01Quackery RelatedTopics/science.html

Note

1.   Except where otherwise indicated, quotations were obtained from the following Internet sites: http://www.lhup.edu/~dsimanek/sciquote.htm, http://www.wisdom quotes.com/cat_science.html, http://www .quotationspage.com/subjects/science/

References

Bateson, G. (1980). *Mind and nature: A necessary unity*. London: Fontana.

Clarke, A. C. (1985). *Profiles of the future*. New York: Warner Books.

Collins, H., & Pinch, T. (1993). *The Golem: What everyone should know about science.* Cambridge, UK: Cambridge University Press.

Dyson, F. (1988). *Infinite in all directions.* New York: Harper & Row.

Erle, T. W. (1884). *Science in the nursery; or children's toys and what they will teach.* New York: E. P. Dutton.

Eves, H. (1988). *Return to mathematical circles.* Boston: Prindle, Wever and Schmidt.

Kuhn, T. (1970). *The structure of scientific revolutions.* Chicago: University of Chicago Press.

Merton R. K. (1973). The normative structure of science. In R. K. Merton (Ed.), *The sociology of science: Theoretical and empirical investigations* (pp. 267–278).

Chicago: University of Chicago Press. (Reprinted from Science and technology in a democratic order. *Journal of Legal and Political Sociology, 1,* 115–126 [1942]).

Mulkay, M. (1979). *Science and the sociology of knowledge.* London: George Allen & Unwin.

Oxford English Dictionary. (1998). New York: Oxford University Press.

Phantascope. (1881, November 26). *Scientific American, 45,* 338.

Von Baeyer, H. (1989, January/February). A dream come true. *The Sciences,* 6–8.

White, L. T. (1962). *Medieval technology and social change.* Oxford: Clarendon Press.

Science Education in Social Context

Consider the following statements about science education and the scientific process:

E ducators may bring upon themselves unnecessary travail by taking a tactless and unjustifiable position about the relation between scientific and religious narratives. We see this, of course, in the conflict concerning creation science. Some educators representing, as they think, the conscience of science act much like those legislators who in 1925 prohibited by law the teaching of evolution in Tennessee. In that case, anti-evolutionists were fearful that a scientific idea would undermine religious belief. Today, pro-evolutionists are fearful that a religious idea will undermine scientific belief. The former had insufficient confidence in religion; the latter insufficient confidence in science. The point is that profound but contradictory ideas may exist side by side, if they are constructed from different materials and methods and have different purposes. Each tells us something important about where we stand in the universe, and it is foolish to insist that they must despise each other.

—**Neil Postman (1996)**

B asic research may seem very expensive. I am a well-paid scientist. My hourly wage is equal to that of a plumber, but sometimes my research remains barren of results for weeks, months, or years and my conscience begins to bother me for wasting the taxpayer's money. But in reviewing my life's work, I have to think that the expense was not wasted. Basic research, to which we owe everything, is relatively very cheap when compared with other outlays of modern society. The other day I made a rough calculation which led me to the conclusion that if one were to add up all the money ever spent by man on basic research, one would find it to be just about equal to the money spent by the Pentagon this past year.

—**Albert Szent-Györgyi (1970)**

Formerly, when religion was strong and science weak, men mistook magic for medicine; now, when science is strong and religion weak, men mistake medicine for magic.

—**Thomas Szasz, M.D.**

Science cannot resolve moral conflicts, but it can help to more accurately frame the debates about those conflicts.

—**Heinz Pagels (1989)**

The Historical Role of Science Education in Our Society

At the beginning of the previous chapter, we mentioned Mark Twain's novel *A Connecticut Yankee in King Arthur's Court*. It's the story of a man who is accidentally transported back through time to the Middle Ages (see Image 2.1). On his journey, he takes the knowledge of modern science with him. Imagine for a moment that you were, like Mark Twain's character, transported back 800 or 900 years. What do you know today that would set you apart from the medieval people whom you were visiting?

While you might know certain poems or stories or be aware of certain historical events, one of the things that would set you most apart would be your technical or scientific knowledge. Even if that knowledge is limited, it would be profoundly more sophisticated than that of the scientists of the period. You might seem to have supernatural powers. Perhaps, as in the case of the Mark Twain novel, you would be viewed as a magician or sorcerer. Something as simple as knowing that in order for surgery to be successful an antiseptic environment must be provided and instruments must be sterilized would place you at the forefront of medieval medicine. The knowledge that you would have would essentially reflect the scientific progress we have made in the past seven or eight centuries since the end of the Middle Ages (see Image 2.1).

SOURCE: Twain (1889).

Image 2.1. A Connecticut Yankee in King Arthur's Court

Science, in Western society, is typically associated with the improvement of the culture and also with issues of power. We take for granted that science is "progressive." Among historians, this notion is sometimes referred to as the "Whig" interpretation of history: that through the accumulation of greater and greater knowledge (in this case, scientific knowledge), we can achieve a greater perfection or enlightenment—that is, progress.

The idea of progress is an underlying principle of the French Enlightenment. In the decades prior to the French Revolution, the Enlightenment was a movement of philosophers who saw the perfectibility of humanity through the development of improved models of culture and science. From this perspective, scientific education of the general population and the creation of competent or effective scientists would bring with it the creation of an improved and better society. Several noted intellectuals of the Enlightenment contributed to the *Encyclopédie, ou Dictionnaire Raisonné des Sciences, des Arts, et des Métiers* (Encyclopedia, or a Systematic Dictionary of the Sciences, Arts, and Crafts), which was first published in 1751 (see Image 2.2). The intention of the *Encyclopédie* was to create a universal system of scientific knowledge—one that would reflect the advances of the Enlightenment. In the United States, this optimistic view of a steady march of progress, largely through science and technology, has been at the heart of our national identity

Image 2.2. Title Page of the First Volume of the French *Encyclopédie*

since the days of the American Revolution. Driven first by pre-industrial, then industrial, and now post-industrial economic innovations, America has always been seen as a scientific and technological innovator.

During the 1950s, a popular television program was hosted by Ronald Reagan, who eventually became the 40th president of the United States. The show was known as *The General Electric Theater*, and was sponsored by the

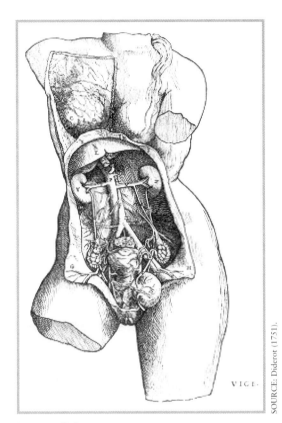

SOURCE: Diderot (1751).

Image 2.3. Illustration of Female Pelvic Anatomy

Vesalius's work represents the origins of modern medical illustration and the beginnings of modern scientific studies of anatomy.

General Electric Corporation, one of the country's main manufacturers of electrical components, appliances, and jet motors. As part of his commentary each week as the program host, Reagan would remind the TV audience that science was General Electric's "most important product." Implicit in this corporate message was the relationship between science and human progress and the notion that to maintain our progress, our society must also continue to advance scientifically (see Image 2.4). Continued scientific progress, in turn, requires satisfactory science education.

Science education for children dates back about 350 years to the late Renaissance and Early Modern periods. Jan Amos Comenius's *Orbis Sensualium Pictus* (1658) is commonly recognized as the first "modern" textbook for children. First published in Nuremburg, Comenius's work included extensive scientific illustrations and instruction (see Image 2.5). In it, Comenius included illustrated accounts of scientific concepts as well as Biblical stories of the second coming of Christ, indicating that science and religion have not always been viewed as mutually exclusive.

In the mid-eighteenth century, books such as *The Newtonian System of Philosophy Adapted to the Capacities of Young Gentlemen and Ladies by Tom Telescope* (1761) introduced young readers to the basics of Newtonian science (see Image 2.6). The "Tom Telescope" books are commonly attributed to the London children's book publisher John Newbery (1713–1767), who is most widely credited with the creation of the modern genre of children's literature. The main character in the book is a boy named Tom Telescope who uses examples from everyday life to introduce the basic scientific principles underlying the Newtonian system.

Through the late eighteenth and early nineteenth centuries, there continued to be a link between the presentation of scientific information and more traditional religious instruction. In works such as Sarah Trimmers's *An Easy Introduction to the Knowledge of Nature and Reading the Holy*

SOURCE: Courtesy of NASA.

Image 2.4. Space Station Freedom

Alan Chinchar's 1991 painting of the proposed space station "Freedom" in orbit around the
Earth with the Moon and Mars off in the distance. Implicit in pictures like this is the message of
technological and scientific progress.

Scriptures (1780), the argument was made that the sciences, and particularly
natural history, were a means of helping children to understand creation and
the creator.

It is not possible in this textbook to reconstruct all the science education
programs from the late eighteenth century onward. What is important to
note, however, is that science was increasingly incorporated into the education of children. By the beginning of the nineteenth century, science was considered to be critically important to the basic education of children in Great
Britain and France. In books such as Sir David Brewster's *Treatise on the
Kaleidoscope* (1819), Jeremiah Joyce's *Scientific Dialogues* (1829), and John
Ayrton Paris's *Philosophy in Sport* (1846), basic and newly discovered principles of science were introduced to young and old for the first time.

For example, while the kaleidoscope is largely disregarded today
as just another amusing toy, its significance for design conceptualization
(specifically, symmetrical pattern formation) during the early Victorian

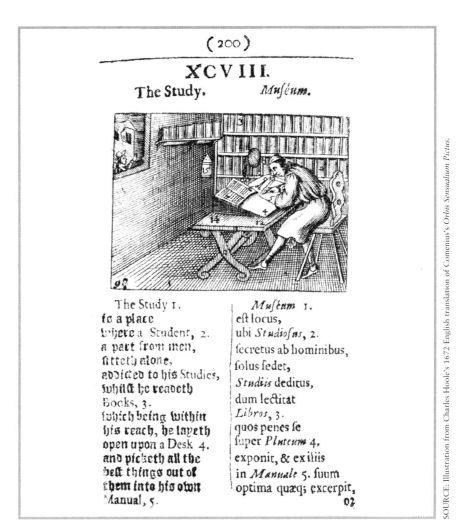

Image 2.5. A Lesson on Winds, Storms, Whirlwinds, and Earthquakes From *Orbis Sensualium Pictus*

First published in Nuremburg in 1658, Comenius's work included extensive scientific illustrations and instruction.

period cannot be overemphasized. The idea of repeating patterns in wallpaper and other decorative forms throughout the Victorian era was a direct result of Brewster's remarkable, yet simple invention (see Image 2.7).

Prominent Victorian scientists such as Michael Faraday, John Ayrton Paris, and Arthur Good also did much to lay the foundations of modern science education. For example, in *The Chemical History of a Candle* (1860/2000), his classic series of six Christmas lectures at the Royal Institution of Great

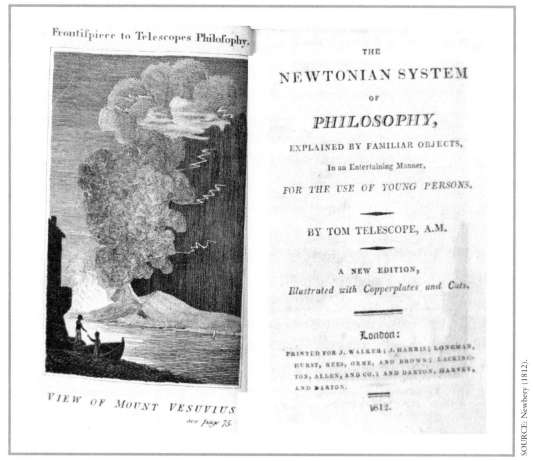

SOURCE: Newbery (1812).

Image 2.6. Title Page of *The Newtonian System of Philosophy*

The Newtonian System of Philosophy Adapted to the Capacities of Young Gentlemen and Ladies was first published in 1761 and was revised a number times, including this 1812 edition.

Britain, Faraday introduced English children to the fundamentals of chemistry. Arthur Good's three-volume collection of hands-on experiments for children, *La Science Amusante* (1893), represented the origins of hands-on "kitchen science" (see Image 2.8).

This approach to science education was later popularized on television. Beginning in the 1950s, Don Herbert brought hands-on science to American children through his program *Mr. Wizard*. In his series, Herbert drew on traditions of nineteenth-century "kitchen science" to introduce viewers to basic scientific principles. More recently, this tradition has been continued through the syndicated program *Bill Nye the Science Guy*.

SOURCE: Photo by Rodrigo Nuno Bragança da Cunha (Wikipedia, http://en.wikipedia.org/wiki/Image:Kaleidoscopic-pattern-00.jpg).

Image 2.7. A Pattern Made by a Kaleidoscope

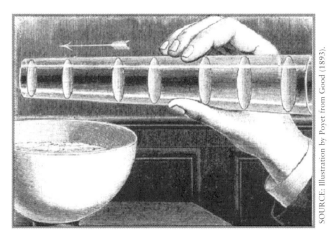

SOURCE: Illustration by Poyet from Good (1893).

Image 2.8. Reduction Tube

This experiment demonstrates through the use of a increasingly narrow glass tube how soap films always try to take up the least surface area possible. Good was part of an important late-nineteenth-century tradition of teaching hands-on science to children.

Other figures less directly associated with writing about science also contributed to the development of science education. The founder of the Kindergarten movement, Friedrich Froebel (1782–1852), who was trained as a crystallographer and naturalist, felt that science should be learned from nature and was an important part of the experience of young children. These ideas were continued in the work of other innovative educators. The great American educational philosopher John Dewey (1859–1952) incorporated many innovative, hands-on models of science education into his curriculum at the University of Chicago Laboratory School (see Image 2.9). Dewey's model involved the integration of all subject areas. As a result, students might conduct an experiment in which they

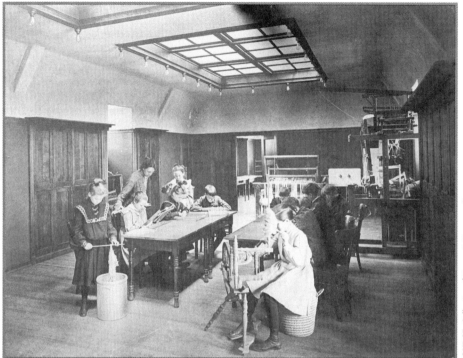

SOURCE: Collection of Eugene F. Provenzo, Jr.

Image 2.9. Sixth-Grade Students Dyeing, Spinning, and Weaving at the University of Chicago Laboratory School, c. 1905

not only learned about science, but also about history, mathematics, and literature.

At the Laboratory School, Dewey introduced science at the elementary level through shop work (mechanics) and cooking (chemistry and measurement). Handwork was, in Dewey's opinion, key to students obtaining the skills they needed to learn science. For him, the experimental nature of science required a high degree of manual skill and dexterity. As he explained,

> Science is largely of an experimental nature. It is a fact that may not have come to your attention that a large part of the best and most advanced scientific work involves a great deal of manual skill, the training of the hand and eye. It is impossible for one to be a first-class worker in science without this training in manipulation, and in handling apparatus and materials. (Dewey, 1907, p. 120)

Essentially, Dewey wanted children to learn science by doing science.

It is interesting to listen to Dewey 100 years after he began his experiment in education:

> Last year a good deal of work was done in electricity (and will be repeated this year), based on the telegraph and telephone—taking up the things that can easily be grasped. In mechanics they have studied locks and clocks with reference to the adaptation of the various parts of the machinery. All this work makes a most excellent basis for more formal physics later on. Cooking gives opportunity for getting a great many ideas of heat and water, and of their effects. The scientific work taken up in the school differs mainly from that of other schools in having the experimental part—physics and chemistry—emphasized, and is not confined simply to nature study—the study of plants and animals. Not that the latter is less valuable, but that we find it possible to introduce the physical aspects from the first. (Dewey, 1907, pp. 124–125)

To a large extent, Dewey's model of hands-on learning anticipated the theoretical insights of psychologists such as Jean Piaget (1896–1980) and Lev Vygotsky (1896–1934). In the case of science education, this means that children must be provided with simple hands-on experiments that they can integrate into the limited experience of their own lives. An example of this is the fairly complex idea of how the seasons relate to the movements of the planets and the tilt of the Earth. Students need to be shown that the tilt of Earth's axis affects the way the sun strikes the surface of the planet and that this, in turn, causes the change in seasons (see Experiment 8 in Chapter 6). This phenomenon is extremely difficult for most young children to interpret and understand without the use of a concrete physical model. Typically, this concept is most successfully introduced by using an **orrery**—a three-dimensional model that demonstrates the rotation of the planets around the sun and relative to each other (see Image 2.10). To make the concept even more concrete, one can take students out into a large open space and have them hold models or objects such as basketballs or beach balls, and then ask them to mimic the revolution and rotation of the planets around the sun.

This discussion of the value of concrete, hands-on science inquiry as an effective instructional strategy for young children might lead you to believe that Dewey's practices would have been widely adopted nationwide. This was generally not the case, however, and to a large degree science instruction at the elementary and middle school levels has been dominated by the memorization and repetition of fairly simple scripted information—the distance from the Earth to the moon, the various parts of a flower, the anatomical labeling of the human body, and so on. The more innovative approaches of people such as Dewey (1907) and Vygotsky (1987), in which students were involved in an active process of discovery and reflection, continue to be the exception rather than the rule.

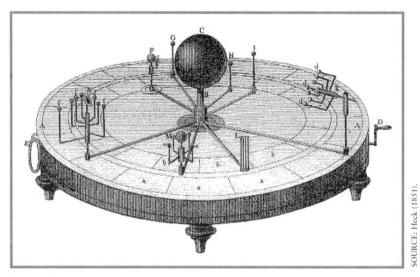

SOURCE: Heck (1851).

Image 2.10. Illustration of an Orrery

Theory Into Practice 2.1

What Would Life Be Like Without Certain Inventions?

We tend to take the science-based technology that surrounds us in our every-day lives for granted. In point of fact, our lives would be very different without certain inventions. Think for a moment about what your life would be like without electricity or cell phones.

Brainstorm a list of technologies and inventions that make your life significantly different from the lives of your great-great grandparents. Include at least five things. What do you gain from these inventions? What do you lose? Think for a moment about television or cell phones. What does our society gain and what does it lose with the incredible spread of inventions like these?

For one day, keep a log of all the inventions that you use (car, phone, washing machine, clock, toilet, etc.). Try to spend a day without using one of these inventions, such as a car, a cell phone, or a clock. How did this experience influence your daily life?

🐾 Science Education Within Broader Educational Reforms

Science education has always had a unique role within the broader expanse of educational reforms. This is due, at least in part, to the special role that science plays in our modern industrial and post-industrial societies. While the traditional "3 R's" of reading, writing, and arithmetic have always held the central focus of primary education, the importance of teaching the sciences has periodically been thrust to the forefront of the American educational debate. This was especially true during the aftermath of the Soviet launch of the **Sputnik** spacecraft in 1957.

Sputnik and Education

Sputnik 1, the world's first artificial satellite, was launched from the Soviet Baikonur Cosmodrome on October 4, 1957 (see Image 2.11). The satellite orbited the Earth every 96 minutes, broadcasting signals from two radio transmitters that could be picked up by amateur radio operators around the world. Thus, the launch of Sputnik literally heralded the start of the "space race," as the satellite remained in orbit, broadcasting for three months before falling back to Earth. While Sputnik marked an historic moment in space exploration, the event also marked an historic turning point in American education.

For the American public, this Soviet triumph symbolized a threat to American security and called into question American superiority in science and technology. In short, the United States was forced to ponder what it meant to be in second place scientifically, technologically, and perhaps militarily, in the midst of an era rife with ideological tension. As a result, educators, scientists, and mathematicians called for accelerated educational reforms. The public expressed support for the effort and, as a result, policy makers increased federal education funding.

Understanding the educational impact of the Sputnik launch requires placing this episode in its historical context. As the Cold War began to

SOURCE: Courtesy of NASA.

Image 2.11. Sputnik

unfold in the years following the end of World War II, the adversarial relationship between the Soviet Union and the United States touched nearly every aspect of public life in both countries. Public schools, as the institution responsible for shaping the thinking of the next generation, became one site for this ideological battle. The United States was committed to demonstrating to the rest of the world that the Soviet challenges to American-style democracy were both misguided and impotent. American schools, and the educational programs delivered therein, had a critical role to play in this mission. Thus, the movement toward educational programs that provided enhanced intellectual rigor and promoted economic and military dominance was already well underway before the launch of Sputnik (Rudolph, 2002).

The Soviet success in launching Sputnik made it clear to the American public that further changes to the educational system were in the national interest, particularly changes to curricula in mathematics and science. These changes were implemented at all levels, including the passage by Congress of the National Defense Education Act of 1958.

Research scientists and mathematicians from the country's most prestigious universities quickly became prominent voices in the discourse on educational reform. The scientists were empowered both by the successes they had in weapons development during World War II and by the goodwill that these successes engendered among the general public. Thus, when key scientists such as Admiral Hyman Rickover began to voice dissatisfaction with what they saw in the schools and then decided to turn their talents to educational reform, there were few objections. Scientists gained new and unprecedented influence in matters of public education policy.

These scientists had the support of the federal government to launch a sweeping reform of pre-collegiate science and mathematics education. At the heart of these policies was a focus on curriculum reform to emphasize content that the research scientists and mathematicians thought most important. The emphasis was on the "structure" of each discipline rather than on applications. Thus the structure of K–12 science education was brought into conformity with the science taught in the universities. Teaching the internal logic of each discipline as it was understood by university professors was the guiding objective. This was a radical shift away from the "life adjustment" curriculum that held sway in schools immediately following World War II. Built partly on Deweyan progressivism and partly on a psychological need to adjust from a wartime to a peacetime mentality, the life adjustment curriculum had focused on applications of knowledge in "real world" contexts. Thus science education, at least for the average student, focused on physical hygiene and general science rather than discipline-based areas such as physics, chemistry, and biology.

The Sputnik-era scientist-educators shared a common vision of education as the pursuit of excellence through high academic standards. This vision required banishing the life adjustment curriculum, replacing the emphasis on vocabulary and applied aspects of content with a focus on the structures and procedures of the science and mathematics disciplines. New curricula in science included work done by the Physical Science Study Committee (PSSC); the Biological Sciences Curriculum Study (BSCS); and the Earth Sciences Curriculum Project (ESCP), among others. New programs in mathematics included the University of Illinois Committee on School Mathematics (UICSM), the School Mathematics Study Group (SMSG), and the University of Maryland Mathematics Project (UMMP).

Just as social and political factors initiated and propelled the Sputnik-era reforms in mathematics and science education, new social and political realities, beginning in the mid-1960s, acted as oppositional forces to the philosophical underpinnings of these reforms. Specifically, the pursuit of excellence, rigorous academic standards, and the conceptual and methodological disciplinary focus in science and mathematics education were perceived as elitist. This model was also considered by some to be inattentive to the academic needs and the realities of an increasingly diverse student population. One alternative approach was the science-technology-society (STS) movement that grew through the 1970s and 1980s as an effort to foster science education that was humanistic, value-laden, and relevant to personal, societal, and environmental concerns (DeBoer, 1991). STS can be seen as teaching and learning science and technology in the context of human experience. It takes the position that lasting learning is most likely to occur when the learner feels connected to the topic of study and that STS connections naturally create such a learning environment.

While the Sputnik-era reforms were not carried forward as initially developed, their legacy can clearly be seen in recent science and mathematics education reforms more than 40 years after Sputnik. The National Council of Teachers of Mathematics (NCTM) *Principles and Standards for School Mathematics* (2000) and the *National Science Education Standards* (1996) developed by the National Research Council (NRC) built on the Sputnik-era legacy, both by including prominent research scientists and mathematicians in their development and by emphasizing disciplinary processes and high academic standards as key elements of the reform effort. This legacy is tempered, however, by an equal emphasis on attending to the learning needs of diverse students and promoting scientific and mathematical literacy for all. Additionally, the Sputnik-era focus on curriculum reform has now been broadened to include reforms in teaching, professional development, assessment, and policy factors because the reform of science and mathematics education is now viewed as a systemic and long-term project.

Theory Into Practice 2.2

Education Reform and You

Reform has been an underlying theme of American education throughout much of its history. Since the early 1980s and the publication of the *A Nation at Risk Report*, reform efforts have again dominated the schools. Much of the current reform effort has focused on standards. This has been true for science as well as for the other content areas such as mathematics, language arts, and social studies.

From your experience as a student in the K–12 educational system (and in light of your experiences now as a college or university student), how do you think these standards-based reform efforts have affected your education in science? Have these reforms influenced *what* you were taught? *How* you were taught? How you were assessed? Do you think these reforms have influenced the way science courses at your college or university are taught? If so, in what ways?

Exchange your ideas with a classmate, and consider areas of agreement or disagreement. Consider to what degree your points of view reflect the different schools you attended, different places where you grew up, different years you went to school, or any other variables you think are relevant.

The Contemporary Role of Science Education in Our Society and the Current Wave of Science Education Reform

There is considerable disagreement about what benefits can be expected from reforming science education in our schools. Four principal benefits have been proposed: *economic, aesthetic, environmental,* and *practical*.

Economic. The economic argument for including science education in the curriculum is that it will benefit not only individuals but the nation as a whole by producing highly skilled scientists and inventors. The belief is that we will have a greater competitive edge in the economic marketplace as a result of the new technologies and innovations they introduce into our economy (see Image 2.12).

Image 2.12. Wall Street

Wall Street symbolizes the economic power of the United States, a power that has shifted from industrial, to post-industrial, to information-based over the past century.

Aesthetic. The aesthetic argument is that science is something that is inherently interesting and beautiful. Learning about how atoms bond with each other to make complex molecules or the natural beauty found in the structure of organisms as simple as plankton or diatoms is inherently worthwhile (see Image 2.13). The argument follows that we are made richer as human beings by our understanding of science and the natural and physical order of the world.

Environmental. Related to the aesthetic argument for the study of science is the environmental argument. The environmental argument maintains that we need to be concerned about studying science because of our stewardship of the Earth. Natural systems are both fragile and closely interrelated (see Image 2.14). Understanding science can lead us to a greater respect for the world in which we live and greater understanding of how to preserve it for future generations.

Practical. The practical rationale for teaching science in the schools is that we need to know certain basic things to make our lives safer and to function more effectively. A basic understanding of germ theory, for example, teaches us to be careful about things that could spread infections (see

Image 2.15). Learning to wash our hands during cold and flu seasons is an example of applying scientific knowledge in a way that has practical outcomes. Likewise, understanding how the tides operate may be important for us if we are interested in sailing a boat or fishing in a coastal area.

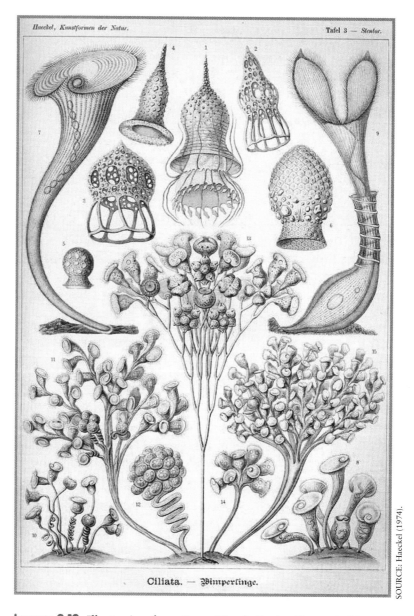

Image 2.13. Illustration from Ernst Haeckel's *Art Forms in Nature*

Image 2.14. Global Warming

Global warming is having a profound impact on the life and habitat of animals around the world—particularly those in the Antarctic.

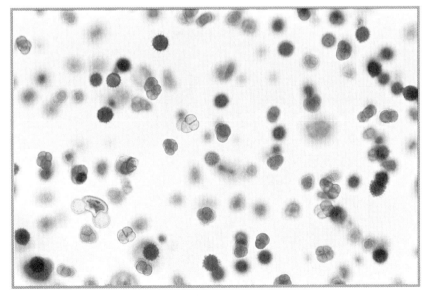

Image 2.15. Germ Theory

Basic understanding of germ theory prevents the spread of disease and promotes health among the general population.

Each of the four rationales for studying science represents an assumption that a certain level of scientific literacy is essential for every member of our society. Textual literacy is the ability to decode text-based information in its written or printed form in order to gain information from it. Numerical literacy (or numeracy) is the ability to interpret numerical information and use it in ways that are meaningful in our lives. Similarly, one interpretation of scientific literacy is the ability to take scientific information, decode it, and use it in meaningful ways in the world.

Theory Into Practice 2.3

Definitions of Scientific Literacy

According to the *National Science Education Standards* (NRC, 1996), "The goals for school science that underlie the National Science Education Standards are to educate students who are able to

- experience the richness and excitement of knowing about and understanding the natural world;
- use appropriate scientific processes and principles in making personal decisions;
- engage intelligently in public discourse and debate about matters of scientific and technological concern; and
- increase their economic productivity through the use of the knowledge, understanding, and skills of the scientifically literate person in their careers. (p. 27)

While this definition is the most commonly used by science educators, other definitions of scientific literacy have been proposed. For example, Bybee (1997) has described a continuum of scientific literacy with at least six identifiable points:

- Illiteracy—Inability to understand a question or locate the question in a given disciplinary domain
- Nominal literacy—Understanding the disciplinary basis of a question or topic, but displaying misunderstanding in response
- Functional literacy—Knowledge of scientific vocabulary within a specific context (i.e., defining a term on a test)

- Conceptual literacy—Understanding the way that disciplinary concepts relate to the whole discipline. Knowledge of both the parts and the whole of a discipline (i.e., the "big picture")
- Procedural literacy—Understanding the process of inquiry and the skills required to complete this process successfully. Linking concepts to the methods and procedures of inquiry used to develop new knowledge within a discipline
- Multi-dimensional literacy—Science as a cultural enterprise. Science as interconnected with society. Incorporates history and nature of science

According to the *National Science Education Standards*, the goals for scientific literacy listed in Theory Into Practice 2.3 above will be realized when students are able to gain competence in the content standards outlined in the standards document. The complete standards can be reviewed online at http://www.nap.edu/readingroom/books/nses/html/ (see also the Appendix).

While there has been academic debate about what it might take for the widest possible range of students to master the standards and whether the *National Science Education Standards* goes far enough in outlining what must be done to this end (e.g., Barton, 1998; Eisenhart, Finkel, & Marion, 1996; Lee & Fradd, 1998), the *National Science Education Standards* remains the key document underlying the current science education reform movement in most states (but see our discussion of the *California Content Standards for Science* below). How to develop a functional model of scientific literacy—one that drives the curriculum of the schools effectively—remains an open question. What do we need to do to make people truly scientifically literate? The view proposed in *National Science Education Standards* is that in order to make students scientifically literate, science must be based on hands-on discovery learning involving practical experiments, personal observations, and an opportunity to collaboratively construct meaning.

Other educators, supported by a vocal group of practicing scientists and mathematicians, have been arguing that science literacy is best learned through the transfer of a specific body of core science concepts from the teacher to the learner. In this model, it is the quantity of facts and information learned that will determine a student's degree of scientific literacy. This argument currently holds sway in the state of California, where the state science standards have been rewritten to reflect this fact-driven view of scientific literacy. The *California Content Standards for Science* can be seen online at http://www.cde.ca.gov/be/st/ss/scmain.asp.

Additionally, over the next few years, the No Child Left Behind Act (NCLB) is likely to change a number of aspects of science instruction. Signed into law in 2002, NCLB is a federal education reform law that is affecting virtually every aspect of K–12 education. The law already requires annual testing and reporting for all students in Grades 3–8 in mathematics and reading. In the 2007–2008 school year, such testing will be required in science as well, at least once in the elementary grades, again in the middle grades, and a third time in high school. Additionally, NCLB is affecting the preparation of science teachers by requiring that all core subjects (including science) must be taught by a "highly qualified" teacher; qualification will largely be determined by the ability to pass a content-area exam. How exactly NCLB requirements will change the actual practice of classroom science teaching remains to be seen, but it seems certain that the new testing requirements will lead to more attention being paid to science in the elementary and middle grades.

For the purposes of this text, we will take the position that while it is often useful to know specific facts about a given science topic, possession of facts is not equivalent to understanding. If the emphasis in science education is on teaching for factual knowledge rather than teaching for conceptual understanding, our students will ultimately know less science. Students often learn facts by rote memorization, a strategy that usually works only for a short time. Later, they forget most of what they memorized and misunderstand much of what they do remember. The long-term effect of this approach is little understanding of science. We argue that meaningful learning for most students occurs when scientific knowledge is integrated into the student's personal experience. Thus, experiential discovery learning through a series of guided experiments (provided in the second half of this book) is the approach we advocate as proponents of scientific literacy for *all* students. An essential part of this discovery occurs while talking about one's experiences and observations, a theme taken up in the next section.

Learning to Speak the Language of Science

Science, by definition, is a human construct. Implicit in any scientific construct is a set of human values and beliefs, and these values and beliefs are expressed through language. As we have considered above, many would define the goal of science education as teaching the basic concepts of the core disciplines: physics, chemistry, the life sciences, and the Earth sciences.

Yet one shortcoming of this approach is that it is an impoverished view to hold science to be just a body of concepts, laws, and theorems. Science is also a way of viewing the world, a series of habits of mind or processes of inquiry that guide how one interprets natural phenomena. Here, we discuss a second shortcoming of viewing science education as just the learning of scientific concepts. This approach implies a specific view of cognition grounded in a psychological model in which learning is fundamentally an individual and an internal mental process. This model assumes that learning goes on "between the ears" of each student, making the student the "receiver" of knowledge and the teacher the transmitter of the proper concepts. The Brazilian educator Paulo Freire has referred to this as a "banking model of education" (Freire, 1970, p. 72).

If, however, science is more than just concepts and is also values and processes, then science teaching must be about more than transmitting concepts to individual learners. It must also be about leading students to engage in tasks, to use the tools, to follow the processes, and to do things that allow them to develop scientific habits of mind. This means that a significant part of learning to reason and act scientifically has to do with discussing issues scientifically, that is, learning to use the language of science in conversation with others.

Models of learning other than the "banking model" or "learning as an individual mental process" can be found in the theories of social and developmental psychologists such as Lev Vygotsky (1978, 1987), Jerome Bruner (1986, 1990), and others (see Chapter 3 for a detailed discussion of these learning theories and how they apply to science education). From this social and developmental psychology perspective, science education is seen more in terms of what students should be able to do and how they need to communicate as part of doing these things. Learning becomes an act of participation and the acquisition of cultural tools and practices.

If we accept the view of learning proposed by the social and developmental psychologists, then teaching science becomes a question of modeling for students the way scientists go about their work. If scientists construct their conceptual understandings through dialogue and the exchange of ideas, with cultural value systems and disciplinary traditions exerting an influence on these ideas, then the teaching of science must model these practices as well. By doing so, teachers provide their students with a means by which to begin to adopt these practices.

Lemke (1990, 1995) has referred to the application of these sociological interpretations of learning to education as "social semiotics." By this he means that classroom learning is based on the combination of the details of what is said, what is written on the board, what is done at the lab table, and so on, and that all these details combine through socially shared action wherein the teacher and students jointly produce learning. Social semiotics thus becomes a powerful way to explore meaning-making practices through the things we learn to do as members of communities—in this case, the community of students and teachers of science.

Language is the most obvious marker of these meaning-making processes, with every community developing its own specialized language uses. Science practitioners, as members of one such community, have developed their own unique sets of specialized language. Just as this is true for words, it is also true for graphs, pictures, charts, and the other symbolic representations used as parts of the language of science. Thus, one of the goals of science education must be to empower students to use the various languages of science—not just the words, but also the pictures, graphs, and equations—in ways that allow them to communicate scientifically. Such an integration ought to be what we strive to instill in our students.

Theory Into Practice 2.4

Metaphors in Science

Metaphors are not simply literary devices for use in poetry and creative writing. Metaphors are active in much of our understanding and are perhaps even at the very basis of language. We use metaphors to describe our experience (*life is a journey*), the use of our senses (*his eyes were glued to the screen*), how learning is shared (*I got the idea across to her*), and so on.

Like other areas of language, science is rich with metaphors. For example, the following metaphors have been used, among others, to describe the scientific enterprise:

Science is a MACHINE

Science is a TEXT

Science is an ORGANISM

Science is a CIRCUIT

What are each of these metaphors saying about science and the work of scientists?

Come up with your own metaphor that describes how you see science. Write a paragraph that discusses your metaphor, what it means, and what it implies about science and scientists. Be explicit in your discussion of why science is like this thing/event/activity and the attributes it shares.

Share your metaphor paragraph with a classmate. Compare and contrast your two metaphors.

🐝 Ethics in Science and the Concept of Human Progress

In developing a model of science education, it is also necessary to define the ethical assumptions underlying our work. In our consideration of metaphors that describe Western scientific thought, one recurring metaphor is science as progress. Western culture is built on an essential faith in ongoing human progress. To a large extent, this faith or belief in progress has served Western society well.

Our faith in progress, however, is not without its perils. Often, through science, we employ new techniques that have unexpected and sometimes disastrous consequences. Thus, for example, our use of antibiotics to control disease has been one of the great medical breakthroughs of our time. It is also leading to the development of new super bacilli that are resistant to the antibiotics. In effect, an evolutionary process is taking place in which the bacilli are becoming resistant to our scientific ways of combating them. In this process, we are creating bacilli that are potentially even more dangerous that the ones we have subdued with antibiotics such as penicillin. Scientists must race to create new and improved antibiotics, and then the cycle begins again.

Thus, sometimes attempts to prevent one disease can lead to an equally or even more serious problem. This may be the case with AIDS, which has been hypothesized as having its origins in a viral infection that came from monkeys in Central Africa. There is a real possibility that during the 1960s, as the scientist Louis Sabin was experimenting with the development of an oral vaccine for the treatment of polio (one that has now come into common use and saved millions of lives), green monkeys, which he was experimenting with in Africa, may have transferred the AIDS virus to humans.

Similarly, we have seen the paradox posed by the development of nuclear power: We have created an enormously beneficial source of **energy** but now are faced with the problem of decaying nuclear power plants and large quantities of radioactive waste. Is the use of nuclear power worth the risk of the destruction caused when there is an accident such as the one that took place in Chernobyl in 1986 (see Image 2.16)? What is an acceptable risk when using certain technologies?

Ethical issues, such as those listed above, pose some of the most interesting and important questions scientists and the larger society must ask about their work. For example, is it justifiable for a scientist who is studying a disease such as AIDS to deliberately infect a rat? Is it justifiable to do so with a monkey? Can one legitimately inflict pain and even death on animals in the cause of scientific progress? One can argue that the potential harms of using the monkey for experimentation, including eventually killing it, are justified by the benefits gained by humankind. Is this viewpoint likely to be held by the monkey? Is it a viewpoint that can be justified if you are

Image 2.16. Radiation Hot Spots Resulting From the Chernobyl Nuclear Power Plant Accident

The nuclear power plant accident that occurred at Chernobyl in the former Soviet Union in April 1986 highlighted the potentially deadly long-term risks associated with nuclear power.

a Buddhist and believe that human beings do not have the right to harm other living things simply for their own benefit?

Thus, ethical differences over scientific issues often reflect profoundly different cultural values among different groups of people. What ethical considerations need to be taken into account as part of our attempt to add to our cumulative knowledge of science? These issues require a great deal of reflection, and our responsibility for addressing them should not be taken lightly.

Theory Into Practice 2.5

Ethics and the Humane Treatment of Experimental Animals

What are the limits that human beings should set for the ethical treatment of animals? When is it appropriate to use animals in experiments? It is highly likely that you believe that using experimental animals to test a new drug is justified in some cases. Thus, testing a new cancer drug by trying it out on a monkey may be justified, from your point of view. But, what about using experimental animals to test the toxicity of a new type of cosmetic? Is it justified, for example, to subject an experimental animal to a high degree of pain to find out whether a new mascara will cause eye irritation for its users? What do you think?

Where do we draw the line between ethical and unethical treatment of animals? How do we determine this? Who should make these decisions in the case of scientific experimentation?

Ask a classmate or friend where he or she stands on ethical issues such as these.

Summary

This chapter dealt with the social context in which science education takes place in the United States and how science education has evolved since the late Renaissance. We discussed the historical role that science education has played in Western society and looked at the beginnings of formal science education for children in Europe during the Enlightenment. In the United States, science education has long been connected with the ideas of progress, invention, and economic development. In the early decades of the twentieth century, the progressive educator John Dewey proposed a concrete, hands-on model of science teaching, but this model was rarely implemented until recently. We explored how science education reform fits with the broader education reforms of the second half of the twentieth century, particularly in response to the Soviet launch of the Sputnik satellite in 1957.

We then discussed the current wave of science education reform as part of the standards-based educational reform movement. We considered reasons for learning science, various meanings of scientific literacy, and our own beliefs about the most productive approach to teaching science to children. We highlighted the importance of language for both conceptualizing and communicating about scientific meaning-making. Students must learn to use spoken and written language as well as graphs and pictures to express their understanding of science. Finally, we turned to the question of ethical issues as part of the social context of science education. As science and technology continue to advance, new ethical dilemmas about their use, benefits, and risks continue to arise. Students need to explore these ethical issues as part of their science education.

Student Study Site

The Companion Web site for *Teaching Science in Elementary and Middle School* http://www.sagepub.com/buxtonstudy

Visit the Web-based student study site to enhance your understanding of the chapter content and to discover additional resources that will take your learning one step further. You can enhance your understanding of the chapters by using the study materials, which include chapter objectives, flashcards, activities, practice tests, and more. You'll also find special features, such as Resources for Experiments, the Links to Standards from U.S. States and associated activities, Learning From Journal Articles, Theory Into Practice resources, Reflections on Science exercises, a Science Standards-Based Lesson Plan Project, and PRAXIS resources.

Reflections on Science

1. How has the evolution of science education mirrored the evolution of our understanding of science?

2. How has the evolution of science education mirrored broader education reforms unrelated to science?

3. Why do you think there is such widespread agreement on the value of promoting scientific literacy but still such strong debate about how best to achieve this goal?

4. How is learning the "language of science" distinct from learning the language of mathematics or history or some other content area? Why is understanding this distinction important for you as a teacher of science?

5. How would you respond to a parent who criticized your decision to discuss age-appropriate ethically controversial science topics as part of your approach to teaching science?

Internet Connections: Science Museums on the Internet

Many important science museums have Web sites. Typically, these sites provide an introduction to the museum and its exhibits as well as information on current special exhibitions and programs. Some also include extensive educational materials that are of interest to elementary and middle school educators. Below is a list of some of the more useful museum sites available online. Try to find a museum convenient to you on the list, or go online and find out which science resources in your community have their own Web sites.

The Academy of Natural Sciences
   (Philadelphia, PA)
http://www.acnatsci.org/

Boston Museum of Science
http://www.mos.org/

The California Academy of Sciences
http://www.calacademy.org/

Carnegie Science Center (Pittsburgh, PA)
http://www.carnegiesciencecenter.org/

The Notebaert Nature Museum (Chicago, IL)
http://www.chias.org/

Explorit Science Center (Davis, California)
http://www.dcn.davis.ca.us/GO/EXPLORIT/

Fernbank Museum of Natural History
   (Atlanta, GA)
http://www.fernbank.edu/museum/

The Florida Museum of Natural History
http://www.flmnh.ufl.edu/

Fort Worth Museum of Science and History
http://www.fwmuseum.org/home/index.html

Institute and Museum of the History of
   Science (Florence, Italy)
http://galileo.imss.firenze.it/index.html

Manchester Museum
http://museum.man.ac.uk/

Miami Museum of Science
http://www.miamisci.org/

Canada Science and Technology Museum
http://www.sciencetech.technomuses.ca/

Natural History Museum of Los Angeles
    County
http://www.nhm.org/

EcoTarium (Worcester, MA)
http://www.ecotarium.org/

The New Mexico Museum of Natural History
    and Science
http://164.64.119.7/nmmnh/index.html

North Carolina Museum of Life and Science
http://www.ncmls.org/

Oregon Museum of Science and Industry
http://www.omsi.edu/

St. Louis Science Center
http://www.slsc.org/

Science Museum of Virginia
http://www.smv.org/

Science World (Vancouver, British Columbia,
    Canada)
http://www.scienceworld.bc.ca

SciTech Hands-On Museum (Aurora, IL)
http://scitech.mus.il.us/

The Smithsonian National Museum of
    Natural History (Washington, DC)
http://www.mnh.si.edu/

The Swedish Museum of Natural History
http://www.nrm.se/

University of Georgia Museum of Natural
    History
http://museum.nhm.uga.edu

References

Barton, A. C. (1998). Teaching science with homeless children: Pedagogy, representation, and identity. *Journal of Research in Science Teaching, 35*(4), 379–394.

Brewster, D. (1819). *Treatise on the kaleidoscope.* London: Archibald Constable & Co.

Bruner, J. (1986). *Actual minds, possible worlds.* Cambridge, MA: Harvard University Press.

Bruner, J. (1990). *Acts of meaning.* Cambridge, MA: Harvard University Press.

Bybee, R. (1997). *Achieving scientific literacy: From purposes to practices.* Portsmouth, NH: Heinemann.

DeBoer, G. E. (1991). *A history of ideas in science education: Implications for practice.* New York: Teachers College Press.

Dewey, J. (1907). *The school and society.* Chicago: University of Chicago Press.

Diderot, D. (Ed.). (1751). *Encyclopédie, ou dictionnaire raisonné des sciences, des arts et des métiers.* Paris: Le Breton.

Eisenhart, M., Finkel, E., & Marion, S. (1996). Creating the conditions for scientific literacy: A re-examination. *American Educational Research Journal, 33*(2), 261–295.

Faraday, M. (2000). *The chemical history of a candle.* New York: Dover Books. (Original work published 1860)

Freire, P. (1970). *Pedagogy of the oppressed.* New York: Continuum Press.

Good, A. (1893). *La science amusante* (Vols. 1–3). Paris: Le Librarie Larousse.

Haeckel, E. (1974). *Art forms in nature.* New York: Dover. (Original work published 1899)

Heck, J. G. (1851). *Iconographic encyclopedia of science, literature, and art, systematically arranged* (S. F. Baird, Trans. & Ed.). New York: Rudolph Garrigue.

Joyce, J. (1829). *Scientific dialogues: Intended for the instruction and entertainment of young people.* Philadelphia: John Grigg.

Lee, O., & Fradd, S. (1998). Science for all, including students from non-English-language backgrounds. *Educational Researcher, 27*(4), 12–21.

Lemke, J. L. (1990). *Talking science: Language, learning, and values.* Stamford, CT: Ablex.

Lemke, J. L. (1995). *Textual politics, discourse and social dynamics.* London: Taylor & Francis.

National Council of Teachers of Mathematics. (2000). *Principles and standards for school mathematics.* Arlington, VA: National Council of Teachers of Mathematics.

National Research Council. (1996). *National science education standards.* Washington, DC: National Academy Press.

Newbery, J. (1812). *The Newtonian system of philosophies adopted to the capacities of young gentlemen and ladies by Tom Telescope.* London: Ogilvy and Son. (Original work published 1761)

Pagels, H. (1989). *The dreams of reason.* New York: Simon & Schuster.

Paris, J. A. (1846). *Philosophy in sport made science in earnest: Being an attempt to illustrate the first principles of natural philosophy by the aid of the popular toys and sports of youth.* London: John Murray.

Postman, N. (1996). *The end of education: Redefining the value of school.* New York: Knopf.

Rudolph, J. L. (2002). *Scientists in the classroom: The cold war reconstruction of American science education.* New York: Palgrave.

Szent-Györgyi, A. (1970). *The crazy ape.* New York: Putnam.

Twain, M. (1889). *A Connecticut Yankee in King Arthur's court.* New York: Harper & Brothers.

Vygotsky, L. S. (1978). *Mind and society: The development of higher mental processes.* Cambridge, MA: Harvard University Press.

Vygotsky, L. (1987). *Thinking and speech.* New York: Plenum Press. (Original work published 1934)

Toward a Philosophy of Hands-On Inquiry-Based Science Education

3

Consider the following statements:

"Hands-on learning" has been a slogan, but there exists a lack of research to show how conceptual ("abstract") understandings arise from manipulating things in the physical world. Our own work … shows how hands-on learning affords new forms of observational and theoretical talk.

—Roth and Lawless (2002, p. 380)

Our inventions are wont to be pretty toys, which distract our attention from serious things. They are but improved means to an unimproved end.

—Henry David Thoreau

On the one hand, there are individual actions such as throwing, pushing, touching, rubbing. It is these individual actions that give rise most of the time to abstraction from objects.

—Jean Piaget

Optimist: "The glass is half full."
Pessimist: "The glass is half empty."
Engineer: "That glass is twice as large as it needs to be."

—Unknown

🐝 Piagetian Constructivism and Learning Through Rediscovery

Underlying this book is the belief, largely based on the work of the Swiss psychologist Jean Piaget (1896–1980), that learners construct knowledge and meaning for themselves by interacting with the world in which they live, an idea that is often referred to as **constructivism**. Learning takes place by actually doing real things. For Piaget, intellectual development was a combination of hereditary and environmental factors. Knowledge is invented and reinvented as children interact with the world around them. In his book *To Understand is to Invent* (1973), Piaget argued that "to understand is to discover, or reconstruct by rediscovery" (p. 20).

On a practical level, this means that for a child to learn and truly understand concepts about a topic such as electricity, he or she will probably have to reinvent and discover the concepts for himself or herself, much as early scientists did when they made their original discoveries. Thus, a learner interested in discovering how electricity works as a scientific principle should be guided toward re-creating many of the basic experiments of a scientist like Michael Faraday (1791–1867; see Image 3.1).

Faraday, whom we described as a pioneer of science education in the previous chapter, is most famous for having invented the electric motor and dynamo. Faraday's experimental device, which demonstrated the principle of an electric motor, did not look much like a modern motor (see Image 3.2). The upper end of the device was a stiff wire that hung from a pivot point; the lower part of the wire was suspended in a pool of mercury. Since mercury is a liquid, the wire was free to move. In the middle of the pool of mercury was a round magnet. When an electrical charge was run through the magnet, it flowed through the mercury and set the wire in motion.

This rather awkward device quickly evolved into something more practical. A coil of wire is wound around a piece of iron set on a pivot; it functions as an electromagnet when an electrical charge is run through it (see Experiment 99 in Chapter 9). If two magnets are set on either side of the coil with their poles facing opposite to one another and an alternating electrical current is run through the coil, the coil will begin to spin—that is, to **work** as a simple electric motor. A simple motor of this kind can then be used to power something as small as a toy electric car or something as large as a giant wind turbine (see Image 3.3).

Image 3.1. Portrait of Michael Faraday (1791–1867)

SOURCE: From the Project Gutenberg eBook *Great Britain and Her Queen*, by Anne E. Keeling (Wikimedia Commons, http://commons.wikimedia.org/wiki/Image:Michael_Faraday_--_Project_Gutenberg_eText_13103.jpg#file).

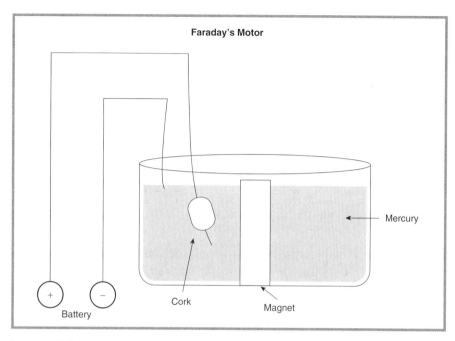

Image 3.2. Illustration of Faraday's Experimental Device Demonstrating the Principles of an Electric Motor

Did you understand how an electric motor works? Could you now explain it to someone else? Could you build one yourself? Probably not. Most learners cannot understand how a motor works by reading a description like the one above. Even when a diagram is added, few learners will gain a clear understanding of how the motor operates. For most students, the most effective way to construct deep understanding of this concept is to build a motor themselves. In doing so, they will actually invent and rediscover—much as Michael Faraday did—the way a motor works.

Learning through rediscovery has certain practical limits. Clearly, it does not seem reasonable to expect university science students to re-create all the findings of modern science. The scientific disciplines and subdisciplines have grown so complex and so specialized that learning through rediscovery does not seem feasible (although perhaps the teachers of university science courses should reflect upon the value of applying this approach in moderation). Still, we believe that this Piagetian rediscovery approach of "understanding through inventing" can be used effectively at the elementary and middle grade levels for a number of the basic principles of science. We feel that this is an enormously exciting idea—one that provides unusually interesting possibilities for teaching and learning. Our progress-oriented society tends to undervalue what can be learned from history. When it

SOURCE: Courtesy of NASA.

Image 3.3. Wind Turbines

Wind turbines are essentially an electric motor mechanism that is rapidly spun using the power of the wind to generate electricity.

comes to learning the fundamentals of science, however, we believe that history has much to teach us.

From this rediscovery perspective, toys and simple hands-on experiments become critical means by which learners can enter into the process of discovering science. In the 1840s, the French poet Charles Baudelaire (1821–1867) wrote an essay titled "A Philosophy of Toys," in which he argued that "the toy is the child's earliest initiation, or rather for him it is the first concrete example of art" (Baudelaire, 1986, p. 199). We believe, in a similar way, that toys are most children's first concrete experiences and encounters with scientific principles. Combined with simple hands-on experiments—many of which represent key discoveries in the history of science—we have the foundations for both a fundamental curriculum (laid out in Part II of this text) and a philosophy of science teaching and learning.

Think, for a moment, about a balancing toy like a skyhook. The toy is typically in the shape of an object such as a boat, with a long curved wire with a counterweight at its base. A pin or pivot point is set in the base of the boat near its center of gravity. When the pivot point is placed on an edge, such as a counter or table edge, the boat will maintain its balance while rocking back and forth. The toy demonstrates the fundamental concept of the center of gravity—the point at which the **weight** on all sides of an object is perfectly even and in balance.

Another toy, the Cartesian diver, demonstrates how compressing the air in a sealed chamber of water affects the buoyancy of an object suspended in it by raising the **pressure** on the air bubbles within the chamber. By playing with the toy, a child can begin to learn several of the fundamental properties of gases (see Experiment 75 in Chapter 8). Of course, this conceptual understanding does not necessarily take place unless the learner is supported in constructing an explanation of what he or she has observed. Thus, it is unlikely that playing with toys, in and of itself, will lead to meaningful learning of science concepts. In fact, a major criticism of much modern hands-on science instruction is that it devolves into simply "playing around" without sufficient time and attention given to developing a critical understanding of the underlying concepts being demonstrated. Students must be guided toward reflection on and discussion of the principles and concepts that were revealed by their actions and observations. This discussion should involve both student peers and more expert individuals, such as the teacher or older students.

While this eventual "expert" clarification of concepts is essential, we also believe it is critical that such clarification comes only after students have had sufficient time to play, explore, manipulate, and do as much re-creating of concepts as they can (see Image 3.4). In the push to cover as many topics as possible, many teachers feel tempted to take the shortcut of demonstrating how to do the activity and describing the underlying scientific principle in advance, to help "reduce student frustration" or to "limit off-task behavior." While such an approach may be tempting, especially for the new teacher who is often concerned with issues of classroom management, restricting students' opportunity to explore undermines the value of a hands-on inquiry-based approach to science learning. Lasting meaning is most likely to be constructed when the learner combines free exploration and critical analysis, allowing the child to integrate the significance of the experiment or the toy into his or her understanding of the world (Martin, 1992). This is what a good science educator must be most concerned with: bringing meaning to the learner's experience of the world (Vygotsky, 1978).

Psychologist David Ausubel believed that meaningful learning could be supported by an instructional model that helped connect new concepts to be learned to more inclusive concepts or ideas. He called these more inclusive ideas **advance organizers** and believed that teaching a new concept should always begin with the presentation of an advance organizer to aid the learner in conceptualizing how the new idea fits into a broader framework (Ausubel, 1978).

Building on Ausubel's notion of meaningful learning, Joseph Novak developed the instructional aid called the **concept map** to represent the meaningful relationships that exist between concepts (Novak & Gowan, 1984). A concept map consists of bubbles (called "nodes") that contain

Image 3.4. Young Children Observing the Natural World

descriptions of relevant concepts and arrows (called links or "propositions") that connect nodes and include labels describing the nature of the linkage between the concepts. Concept maps have become popular among science educators because they both provide a clear way to determine a learner's developing understanding of a complex topic and serve as a tool for discussion of those ideas.

Theory Into Practice 3.1

Helping Students Make Meaning of Experience

Teachers of science must develop the skill of guiding students to an understanding of science concepts without prematurely telling them what sense they should make out of their inquiry experiences. Much of this skill involves asking the right questions.

Try this. Pick one experiment from Part II of this book and do the activity with one student. Help the student understand the directions and then let her carry out the procedure. Observe what she does carefully. Make note of places where she gets stuck, but try to give the least amount of guidance as you can to get her unstuck.

After the student is done, interview the student and try to construct a concept map of the student's understanding of the key concept. First ask her what she did. The student should be able to describe the procedure fairly easily because she just completed it. Point out any places where the student seemed to be stuck and ask her what she was thinking at that point and how she decided to proceed.

Now, ask the student what she learned from doing the activity. Try to capture this understanding using nodes and links. Most students will not be able to give a complete description of the science concept that the activity demonstrates. Why do you think this is? What kinds of questions can you ask to help the student more clearly understand the concept? What kinds of questions proved helpful? What kinds of questions were not helpful for the student?

Share the concept map you made with the student and discuss it. Does the student feel that it matches his or her understanding of the concept? Modify the concept map together. What does this activity teach you about helping your students make meaning of science activities? How is this challenge increased when you are teaching an entire class of students?

Designing Experiments and Learning Through Project-Based Science

As we discussed in the previous chapter, since the Sputnik era there have been many changes in how we understand the teaching and learning of science. Simultaneously, there have been significant changes in our understanding of learning and learning environments. Our understanding of learning has shifted from a passive and individual project to an active process that is both individual and social in nature. This shift naturally implies that changes are needed in teaching—such as a shift in the teacher's role from being a manager of behaviors and knowledge distribution to being a manager of ideas, information, and interactions between learners.

For example, imagine a teacher planning a unit of instruction on birds for her second-grade class. Under an older "information processing" model of learning, this teacher would probably plan a series of lessons starting with basic information (What is the definition of a bird? What are its qualities?), then moving on to more specific information, often moving both downward in scale (What are the parts of a bird and their purposes?) and upward in scale (What is a bird's ecosystem like? Where do birds fall in a food chain?). Students might be asked to look at (and perhaps draw) pictures of birds, might watch an educational video on bird behaviors, and might label a diagram of bird parts or draw a food chain including a bird. The activities would be teacher-orchestrated and verified. Assessment might take the form of a short written test or a book report on one of a list of books preselected by the teacher. It is also quite possible that throughout the entire unit, students would never observe an actual bird in nature as part of the class activities. Only outside of school and on their own would students have the opportunity to integrate what they were learning in class with the birds they experienced in their everyday life.

Contrast the above experience with another second-grade teacher whose teaching philosophy is influenced by more modern views of learning. This teacher might begin the unit with a class discussion about students' prior experiences with birds (Where have they seen birds? What do birds like to do? How do they feel about birds? Has anyone ever had a bird for a pet?) and then construct a KWL chart (what you Know, what you Want to know, and what you Learned), filling out the first two columns and posting it prominently in the classroom. The teacher might then introduce the concept of a bird census (see Experiment 39 in Chapter 7), co-constructing with the class what sorts of data might be useful to collect as part of a bird census and then collaboratively designing a data collection form. Several times per week the students might go out on the school grounds and spend about 15 minutes observing birds and filling out their census forms. This data collection could go on for several weeks or, with less frequency, could be continued over a longer period of time.

In the classroom, the teacher would set up a center on birds with a variety of books including identification guides, possibly an audiotape of bird calls, and perhaps even some of the same activities that the first teacher had her class do (a labeling diagram or food chain). Each student would have several opportunities to spend time in the center looking at the resources and doing the activities. The class might do several inquiry activities such as exploring the relationships between characteristics of bird beaks and the kinds of foods that different birds eat (see Experiment 49 in Chapter 7). After several weeks, the class would revisit the KWL chart and discuss what they had learned (the third column) and revisit the questions in the second column to see which ones they could now answer and which ones still required additional knowledge. Assessment might take the form of a summary of and reflection on each student's bird census data or an illustrated poster highlighting a certain number of things that each student learned about birds.

The two examples above highlight ways in which changes in our understanding of children's learning should influence the ways we go about

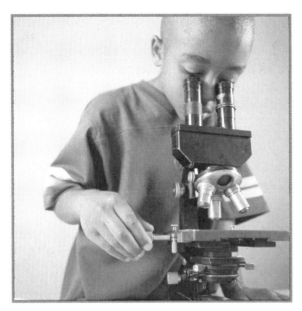

Image 3.5. A Boy Using a Microscope

teaching science. Additionally, as the practice of science itself continues to change and evolve, science educators must consider how these changes should be reflected in our science teaching. For example, new and more powerful technologies have led to an increase in the development and use of complex models in many science fields, often resulting in a corresponding decrease in the use of "classical" experimentation as it is generally conceptualized in science education (see Image 3.5). This is not to say that scientists no longer engage in experimentation, but rather that experiments are now more heavily contextualized in the process of designing, building, and revising models.

Thus, while we strongly believe in the value of teaching classical experimentation through the inquiry as rediscovery approach outlined above, we also feel that it is important for students to experience this perspective of science as building and testing models. How should we account for such shifts in the representation of science in our teaching? One approach has been the adoption of design-based or project-based immersion units (also sometimes referred to as "full inquiry" units, **Project-Based Science,** or PBS). Such units are usually several weeks long and provide students with one overarching problem or context for inquiry. Most of these full-inquiry projects have learning goals in areas including student communication about scientific ideas, students learning to evaluate the relative strengths of competing scientific explanations or arguments, and students developing scientific reasoning. The second of the two bird examples above has many of the features of a full-inquiry unit.

Design-based curriculum evolved out of an engineering model of teaching and learning and thus places a strong emphasis on applying science concepts to solve real-world problems. One example of such a curriculum is the Learning by Design project developed by researchers at Georgia Institute of Technology. The project has developed full-inquiry units for middle school students on topics such as "Vehicles in Motion," "Machines that Help," and "Managing Erosion." Each of the units has common design features including real-world constraints and criteria for success, interactive and iterative use of models through a series of refinements and improvements, and reflective and collaborative teamwork with an emphasis on learning how to constructively critique peers' work (and how to learn from others' critique of one's own work). More information on the Learning by Design project can be found at http://www-static.cc.gatech.edu/projects/lbd/.

Thus, our evolving understanding of both learning and science should be leading teachers of science to approach their task in new ways (Bruner, 1990). Just learning science facts and concepts is an insufficient goal for our students, but so, too, is just learning about science as a process of inquiry and experimentation. One of our overarching goals ought to be to help students learn to apply evidence and observation (inquiry) for the purpose of explanation and problem solving (design) while learning the concepts needed for the task (content knowledge). Such a model has been shown to be more successful when the learner is able to engage in a series of sequenced lessons on related themes, rather than being taught a stream of unrelated "stand-alone" science lessons. One common inquiry model that can support a design-based approach to science teaching is known as the "5Es" model. Developed by the Biological Sciences Curriculum Study group (BSCS) that was mentioned in Chapter 2, the 5Es model has the following components:

I. **Engagement:** The lesson begins with an attempt to capture the students' attention, get them thinking about the topic, and help them access prior knowledge.

II. **Exploration:** Next, students need to be given the time to plan, investigate, and collect data based on the topic of study. The focus here is on careful observation, measurement, model building, and so on.

III. **Explanation:** Third, students are asked to analyze and interpret their data. Simply collecting data and then being told by the teacher what it means is insufficient. Students' understanding is clarified through their own attempts to explain their findings.

IV. **Extension:** The focus in this section is to apply the concepts that have been learned to different contexts and especially to real-world situations. How is the concept similar and different in the new situation? These extensions can readily lead to additional explanations and repeated cycling through the 5E model.

V. **Evaluation:** How do you know whether each of your students gained an adequate understanding of the key concept(s)? What is your evidence for this?

Despite what we now know about cognition and learning, the individual and isolated lesson format remains the norm in American science classrooms. It is interesting to note that the standards-based reform movement may be unintentionally contributing to the continuation of this situation. Many states have piled on literally hundreds of standards and benchmarks, and districts have responded by creating rigid pacing guides to address all of them, resulting in many teachers teaching for "coverage" rather than teaching for depth of understanding. This march through the curriculum driven by a concern about not having time to cover all the required topics causes many teachers to rely on direct instruction and textbook-driven science as opposed to hands-on, inquiry-based instruction. In our presentation of core experiments in Part II of this book, we attempt a compromise by grouping our activities into "mini-strands" of three lessons each on various aspects of a given science topic. It is our hope that if teachers allow their students to engage in three related lessons on a topic, students will begin to develop a depth of understanding while teachers will still be able to move through the standards at a sufficient pace to address the pressures of the current "high-stakes" accountability systems.

Theory Into Practice 3.2

Learning by Design

Select one of the design-based science project Web sites listed at the end of the chapter. Read about the project and then consider the following questions:

1. What is the model of learning that is presented in this project?
2. What is the model of "doing science" that is presented in this project?
3. What science content or topics do students learn about in this project?
4. What reasons are given for why these topics and processes were selected?
5. What training do teachers involved in this project get?
6. Is this project consistent with a standards-based approach to science teaching? Why or why not?
7. As a student, do you think you would enjoy participating in this project? As a teacher? Why or why not?

🐜 Sociocultural Theory and Learning Through Legitimate Peripheral Participation

As we facilitate our students' engagement in science inquiry, we are simultaneously working in several interrelated domains: (1) the cognitive structures that students learn to adopt when reasoning scientifically (such as the learning through rediscovery approach); (2) the logic systems used when developing and evaluating scientific knowledge (such as the model-based design approach); and (3) the social and communicative processes that shape how scientific knowledge is represented. We have addressed the first two of these domains in the first two sections of this chapter, and we now turn to the third point.

When we engage our students in reasoning about science concepts, when we ask them to move beyond observations and evidence toward providing explanations, when we require them to build and revise models as part of this process, we are creating learning environments that are meant to foster collegial conversation and argumentation as part of the process of revision and acceptance of ideas (Rogoff, 1990).

From a sociocultural perspective, what individuals learn and know depends on the ways that they are allowed to participate in social practices (Cole, 1996). Relevant questions to ask are in what times and spaces, with what tools or representations, and with what goals or endpoints do social practices for learning take place? How have these practices been constructed over time? How do people, through their practices, make meaning in ways that reflect larger social structures? What are the implications of these questions for science?

Earlier we discussed that science is not a purely rational or objective pursuit of truth guided by the dictates of nature alone. Science is a human activity, influenced by biases and accidents, often guided by agendas of larger institutions and social movements like every other part of life. Learning science today is quite different from what it was even just a few decades ago, and each new generation of scientists must gradually remake our understanding of the world. Ultimately, it is through social and communicative processes that we shape how scientific knowledge is represented.

Anthropologists Jean Lave and Etienne Wenger proposed a model of learning they refer to as **situated cognition** theory, building on ideas of apprenticeship and community to explain learning through its situation in social relationships and social organization (Lave & Wenger, 1991). This theory of learning focuses on understanding "structuring resources" (such as artifacts, social organizations, linguistic forms, and identities) that move people from "newcomer" to "old-timer" status within a given community of practice. Think, for example, of a carpenter's apprentice. When beginning, the young apprentice is taught one basic task, such as how to select the right pieces of wood for a given project. While this is a simple task, it is an actual and necessary part of the larger task of building a piece of furniture.

Image 3.6. Students Using a Scale

Once this task is mastered, the apprentice is taught an additional task (e.g., how to attach the legs to a chair). In Lave and Wenger's terms, this is an example of "legitimate peripheral participation"—that is, a legitimate but not a central part of the process. Over time, as the apprentice learns and practices more and more tasks, he or she begins the gradual transition from apprentice to master, or from newcomer to old-timer. This transition requires, however, that the newcomers can and do engage in these practices. Thus, if the right social conditions don't exist, it is difficult to legitimately move newcomers to old-timer status.

Lave and Wenger (1991) criticize the structure of traditional schooling for failing to provide students with opportunities to engage in legitimate peripheral participation. The structure of schooling often functions to keep students in a perpetual newcomer state through disconnected teaching that does not build on itself in coherent ways. Just as students begin to master one task or topic, the focus often radically shifts to a completely different topic with no apparent connection to the first. Thus, in the context of the discussion earlier in the chapter, situated cognition theory also helps to explain the value of a full-inquiry or design-based approach to science teaching, as such approaches are more likely to promote legitimate peripheral participation. For example, students should learn to use the tools of science by doing projects that require the meaningful use of those tools as a legitimate part of problem solving (see Image 3.6).

In a related vein, another educational anthropologist, Jan Nespor, has studied the ways in which schools and academic programs are organized: how they use time and space, how individuals become categorized as "good" or "bad" members, and how tools and equipment are used to help promote and distinguish membership (Nespor, 1994). Thus, for Nespor, "learning" means becoming connected to a particular discipline, with all members of that discipline being connected across time and space through a shared network of understanding what it means to be a member—what he refers to as "actor-network theory." Learning is thus the process of becoming enculturated into a particular trajectory toward full membership. This is related to Lave and Wenger's (1991) notion of community, but Nespor sees community not as a geographically bounded entity, but rather as cutting across distant times and spaces.

Nespor (1994) analyzes how these practices create opportunities for students to learn and develop skills, social relationships, and identities within a given discipline. This framework can be applied to thinking about the teaching and learning of science in elementary and middle school classrooms. School is a powerful tool in the formation of identities and counteridentities; schools and teachers valorize certain ways of knowing and denigrate others. As a student, one cannot argue with this power. However, schools can use their power in ways that make change possible by striving to value multiple ways of learning and providing multiple points of entry into networks of "good student" membership.

How do the insights gained from learning frameworks such as those presented by Lave and Wenger (1991) and by Nespor (1994) help us conceptualize new ways of constructing schooling in general and science learning in particular? Can we utilize these insights to reconstruct definitions of the "educated person," of "knowledge," and of "learning" so that we do not continue to perpetuate the status quo of science education that is ineffective for many students? On a practical level, this sociocultural understanding of learning implies that more time must be devoted to topics of study, and connections must be made across topics. Students must be able to talk with each other about what they are learning and must be helped to make the connections between their formal school science experiences and their informal experiences with science topics outside school.

We must start by understanding that thinking and learning are active and communal processes conducted not just in and by the human brain, but by the whole body in communication with others, and making constant use of material tools and artifacts in the environment as well as systems of meaningful signs, such as language, diagrams, and mathematical symbols. Sociocultural perspectives on learning can help us to look at meaningful action and activity, at language in use, at all forms of verbal and nonverbal communication as integral parts of learning in community. When taken together with the other theories of learning discussed earlier in this chapter—Piagetian rediscovery and design-based learning—we have a rich, multidimensional picture of learning as well as some concrete ideas about the nature of learning activities and learning environments that can best make use of these theories to enhance the learning of science. In Part II of this text, we present core experiments that support this hands-on, inquiry-based philosophy of science learning while also attending to the realities of the current policy of standards-based instruction.

Theory Into Practice 3.3

Learning Theories Textbook Review

Borrow a copy of a "teacher's edition" of a science textbook that is used in a school district near you. The teacher's edition will have introductory material that explains the philosophy behind the book. Read this material and then consider the following questions:

1. Is there an explicit discussion of the learning theory or theories that influence how science is being taught in the book? If so, what theories are mentioned?

2. Is there any discussion (explicit or implicit) about Piagetian constructivism or learning through rediscovery? If so, what?

3. Is there any discussion (explicit or implicit) about design experiments or learning through project-based science? If so, what?

4. Is there any discussion (explicit or implicit) about sociocultural theory or learning through apprenticeship? If so, what?

5. Overall, does the approach to learning in this book take into account our current understandings about how students best learn science? Why do you think this is?

Summary

In this chapter we have laid out a philosophy that guides our thinking about how and why to teach a hands-on, inquiry-based approach to science. This philosophy is grounded in individual cognitive learning theories, historical and modern approaches to how science is practiced, and sociocultural theories about learning as a communal process. We began by focusing on the work of Jean Piaget and a model of learning through rediscovery (using experiments similar to those originally done during the discovery of the concepts being studied). We then considered new approaches to science learning that have emerged from research in cognitive psychology and from an engineering model of repeating cycles of designing and testing new tools—in this case, new learning tools. We discussed how learning can be seen as a sociocultural as well as a psychological construct. From this perspective, learning is about gradually gaining membership in a community of practice. This very different view of learning has implications for how we might go about teaching science in the classroom. When taken together, the ideas presented in this chapter should provide you with multiple lenses with which you can evaluate the quality of the science curriculum and instruction that you will encounter as a teacher.

Student Study Site

The Companion Web site for *Teaching Science in Elementary and Middle School* http://www.sagepub.com/buxtonstudy

Visit the Web-based student study site to enhance your understanding of the chapter content and to discover additional resources that will take your learning one step further. You can enhance your understanding of the chapters by using the study materials, which include chapter objectives, flashcards, activities, practice tests, and more. You'll also find special features, such as Resources for Experiments, the Links to Standards from U.S. States and associated activities, Learning From Journal Articles, Theory Into Practice resources, Reflections on Science exercises, a Science Standards-Based Lesson Plan Project, and PRAXIS resources.

Reflections on Science

1. Think back to the toys you played with when you were in early elementary school. Make a list of as many as you can remember. Now look at a list of science content standards for your state for the lower elementary grades. Do any of the toys seem to demonstrate concepts relevant to any of the standards? Describe.

2. What are models? Brainstorm a list of as many kinds of models as you can.

What is the purpose(s) of each of these models? How do scientific models fit within this broader framework of model types and purposes?

3. What does it mean to say that learning is a sociocultural process? Can you think of a time when you engaged in legitimate peripheral participation? Describe. What groups are you a member of? How do you know you are a member? Does membership in these groups cut across time and location? In what ways?

Internet Connections: Design-Based Learning

Discussions of Constructivism
http://www.stemnet.nf.ca/~elmurphy/emurphy/cle2b.html

http://www.leeds.ac.uk/educol/documents/00003562.htm

http://www.quasar.ualberta.ca/edit573/Links/constructivism.htm

The Center for Learning Technologies in Urban Schools (LETUS)
http://www.letus.org/

Science Controversies On-line: Partnerships in Education (SCOPE)
http://scope.educ.washington.edu/

Web-Based Inquiry Science Environment (WISE)
http://wise.berkeley.edu/

Modeling for Understanding in Science Education (MUSE)
http://www.wcer.wisc.edu/ncisla/muse/

Learning by Design
http://www-static.cc.gatech.edu/projects/lbd/home.html

References

Ausubel, D. (1978). In defense of advance organizers: A reply to the critics. *Review of Educational Research, 48,* 251–257.

Baudelaire, C. (1986). A philosophy of toys. In J. Mayne (Ed. & Trans.), *The painter of modern life and other essays* (pp. 189–212). Cambridge, MA: Da Capo Press.

Bruner, J. (1990). *Acts of meaning.* Cambridge, MA: Harvard University Press.

Cole, M. (1996). *Cultural psychology.* Cambridge, MA: Harvard University Press.

Lave, J., & Wenger, E. (1991). *Situated learning.* Cambridge, UK: Cambridge University Press.

Martin, J. R. (1992). *Schoolhome: Rethinking schools for changing families.* Cambridge, MA: Harvard University Press.

Nespor, J. (1994). *Knowledge in motion.* Philadelphia, PA: Falmer.

Novak, J., & Gowan, D. (1984). *Learning how to learn.* New York: Cambridge University Press.

Piaget, J. (1973). *To understand is to invent.* New York: Grossman.

Rogoff, B. (1990). *Apprenticeship in thinking.* New York: Oxford University Press.

Roth, W.-M., & Lawless, D. (2002). Science, culture, and the emergence of language. *Science Education, 86,* 368–384.

Vygotsky, L. (1978). *Mind in society.* Cambridge, MA: Harvard University Press.

Diverse Learners in the Science Classroom

Consider the following statements about science and diversity:

We are at a critical juncture where there is a rapidly growing need in the technology and science work force, and we cannot afford to waste anybody. Women's and girls' experience is needed to contribute to the development of these fields.

—**Linda Basch, Executive Director,**
National Council on Research for Women

While few solid figures exist, corporate officers uniformly agree that increased diversity in companies has a beneficial effect on the bottom line. The mixture of ideas from several different cultures, they feel, automatically makes scientific teams and entire laboratories more productive.

—**Peter Gwynne, American Association**
for the Advancement of Science

The great and invigorating influences in American life have been the unorthodox: the people who challenge an existing institution or way of life, or say and do things that make people think.

—**U.S. Supreme Court Justice William O. Douglas**

America is not like a blanket—one piece of unbroken cloth. America is more like a quilt—many patches, many pieces, many colors, many sizes, all woven together by a common thread.

—**Rev. Jesse Jackson**

🐝 History of Diverse Learners in the Science Classroom

Our perceptions of science and scientists come from a variety of different sources. They may start with personal experiences with science in school and then be further reinforced by the media; the larger culture; and by one's family, friends, and community. Thus, when science is portrayed, sometimes subtly and at other times blatantly, as the domain of smart, eccentric white men working in laboratories, we all respond to these portraits in different ways (see Image 4.1). Some will see this as an inaccurate stereotype, others as a statement about who can be successful in science, and still others as evidence of an inequity in need of redress. Many children and young adults are familiar with this stereotype and, as a result, have feelings of adequacy or inadequacy, reinforced by the media, pop culture, and their personal experiences in school science classes.

For much of the past decade, how science is presented and represented in modern Western society has been a topic of debate in the science education community. Broadly speaking, two camps have emerged. One argues that the culture of science, whatever its shortcomings or flaws, has developed in ways that are self-monitoring and self-correcting, and thus, issues such as underrepresentation of women or people of color will be corrected over time. Additionally, science, as it has been practiced, has been highly successful and has led to important discoveries that advance the human condition. Proposing changes, therefore, to how science is done or to how it is represented in science education runs the risk of disrupting scientific progress. Individuals in this "camp" argue that students, whatever their backgrounds, need to be taught to adopt this culture and its worldview if they wish to participate in scientific endeavors (e.g., Good, 1995; Loving, 1997).

In contrast, others have argued that science educators need to be responsive to traditions of bias and prejudice that have existed in the culture of science and recognize that science has largely been the domain of privileged white males. This tradition has both limited the potential contributions of those underrepresented groups and minimized the contributions that have been made. According to this argument, creating a model of science education that acknowledges and addresses these biases

Image 4.1. Stereotypical Scientist

Scientists are often stereotyped as wild eccentrics and almost always as white men.

SOURCE: Smithsonian Institution, National Museum of American History.

Image 4.2. The Geneticist Barbara McClintock's Microscope

will encourage the development of scientific learning for women, people of color, and other underrepresented groups. The model would include reforms to curriculum, instruction, and assessment that take into account issues such as learning styles, motivation, cultural and linguistic differences, and role models (e.g., Atwater, 1993; Brickhouse, 1994; Duschl, 1988; Stanley & Brickhouse, 1994).

For the purposes of our discussion in this book, we will consider diversity along five dimensions: gender, race/ethnicity, socioeconomic status (SES), learning exceptionalities, and linguistic difference. While other dimensions of diversity such as urbanicity (e.g., rural vs. urban), sexual orientation, and nationality might also be considered, we believe that the five dimensions we address are the ones that have played the most substantive roles in how opportunities to engage in science education have been allocated in this country.

We begin with a brief discussion of how each element of diversity has influenced the opportunity to learn and succeed in science and science education. We also provide examples of scientists from diverse backgrounds who have succeeded in making recognized contributions to science. We then map the role that the new wave of science education reform has played in promoting an awareness of issues of diversity in science education. Finally, we discuss concrete strategies that teachers can use to enhance the opportunities for diverse learners in the science classroom.

Gender in the Science Classroom. Historically, girls and women have faced inequality of representation and participation in the practice of the natural sciences. Pioneering women scientists like geneticist Barbara McClintock had to overcome significant barriers to their professional development to have their work recognized and accurately credited (see Image 4.2). While they have found increased opportunity in the sciences in recent years, women are still not represented in proportion to the national demographics (Rosser, 2000; Rossiter, 1997; Tonso, 1999). Also, the higher the status of the science field, subfield, or position in question, the greater the degree of inequality that persists in terms of the representation of women (Phillips, 1990; Traweek, 1989). Additionally, even women who are successful in the natural sciences report less job satisfaction and more stress in their personal lives than their male colleagues. For example, Seymour and Hewitt (1997) conducted a detailed study of the reasons women drop out of university science majors and how these reasons often differ from the reasons that males give.

Feminist critiques of science and science education have largely been ignored in the scientific community. It is probably an unfortunate reality that most practicing scientists have not given much thought to issues of equity in their work. One of the most common responses to this claim is that science is fundamentally meritocratic and self-correcting. Thus, while it is possible that women have been discriminated against in the past, such inequities are being resolved now that women have equal access to the required training opportunities. The increased enrollment of women in medical and veterinary schools, where women now make up the majority of students, is often cited as evidence of the self-correcting nature of the field. A number of studies point out, however, that the widespread perception of science as male or masculine continues to be one of the greatest barriers to adolescent girls' willingness to pursue advanced science education or to enter scientific fields (Howes, 1998; Oakes, 1990; Rosser, 1997; Tonso, 1999).

Table 4.1 provides a sampling of notable women scientists and their contributions to the field. Examples such as these can be used to complement the strategies for supporting girls in the science classroom that are discussed later in the chapter. It is worth noting that women's contributions to science date back to ancient Egypt, India, and Greece. However, for the vast majority of this history, women scientists faced additional barriers to opportunity and access while striving to contribute to the field.

Race/Ethnicity in the Science Classroom. Racial discrimination has played an important part in the history of American education. In the case of science education, facilities have often been inadequate and opportunities to attend elite universities where scientific training is the best have been few and far between for students of color. Important exceptions to this tendency have occurred in historic black colleges, which during the late nineteenth and early twentieth centuries provided some of the only scientific training available to African Americans in the United States. Institutions such as Howard University in Washington, DC, for example, established not only dental and medical schools but sophisticated bacteriology and chemistry research and teaching labs that provided advanced scientific training for its students (see Image 4.3).

Racial discrimination in science education has also come in the form of white role models being emphasized more than black persons who have contributed to the development of science. One of the important results of the civil rights movement and the black history and pride movement during the 1960s was the rediscovery of significant black individuals, including

Table 4.1. A Sampling of Notable Women Scientists

Scientist	Description
Hypatia (310–415)	Probably the first well-known woman scientist, Hypatia was primarily a mathematician. She also studied science, however, and was eventually murdered by a mob that objected to scientific study.
St. Hildegard of Bingen (1098–1179)	Like many scientists of her era, as was discussed in Chapter 1, St. Hildegard simultaneously studied the natural and supernatural worlds. She wrote extensively on the use of plants, animals, and metals in medicine.
Marie Curie (1867–1934)	Surely the most well-known woman scientist, Curie won the Nobel Prize twice for her pioneering work in both chemistry and physics, most notably for the study of radioactivity.
Florence Rena Sabin (1871–1953)	Sabin was the first woman to be elected to the National Academy of Sciences, over 80 years after it was founded by President Lincoln. Sabin was a medical researcher who primarily studied the disease tuberculosis.
Maria Goeppert Mayer (1906–1972)	The second woman to be awarded the Nobel Prize for physics in 1963 after a 60-year gap (Marie Curie was a recipient in 1903). Mayer's work was primarily on the shell theory of the structure of atoms.
Dorothy Crowfoot Hodgkin (1910–1994)	The second woman to receive the Nobel Prize in chemistry in 1964 (again, after Marie Curie, who was awarded the prize in chemistry in 1911). Hodgkin researched the structure of the antibiotic penicillin.
Edith Hinckley Quimby (1891–1982)	Quimby was the first to determine that radiation could be used in the treatment of cancer. The fact that Quimby became known as "America's Madame Curie" further highlights the huge role that Curie played as a trailblazer for women in science.
Jane Goodall (1934–)	Well-known for her studies of the behavior of chimpanzees in the wild, Goodall, as well as other women primatologists, is often cited by feminist scholars as an example of how women can bring alternative perspectives and modes of inquiry to science that men would be unlikely to adopt.

SOURCE: Courtesy of the Library of Congress Prints and Photographs Division, Washington, DC.

Image 4.3. Students in the Bacteriology Laboratory at Howard University in 1900

scientists, as potential role models. Highlighting the scientific contributions of people such as Benjamin Banneker, George Washington Carver, and Charles Drew is important not only for black students but for all students because it gives the scientific community a more diverse human face. More examples of the contributions of black scientists can be found in Table 4.2.

Despite the important contributions of black scientists described here, and the significant advances in educational equity since the 1960s, it must also be realized that many black students continue to attend schools with inadequate resources for the teaching of science. Good science instruction is expensive and takes a social and educational commitment to be fully realized. Racial discrimination in the education of Hispanic students in the United States has a shorter history and a lower profile than that of African American students. As the Hispanic population in the United States continues to grow, however, inequity of opportunity is now becoming evident in the science education of Hispanic students. The recognition of successful role models can again be one way to bring to light the importance and value of ensuring that all individuals be given the opportunity to study and pursue careers in science if they feel called to do so. Notable contributions of Hispanic scientists can be found in

Table 4.2. Notable African American Scientists

Scientist	Description
Benjamin Banneker (1731–1806)	Banneker became an accomplished mathematician and astronomer despite being almost completely self-taught. He is best known for his farmers' almanacs based on his astronomical calculations.
Rebecca Cole (1846–1922)	Cole was the second black woman to graduate from an American medical school in the aftermath of the Civil War (1867). She became well-known for advocating the importance of teaching hygiene and childcare to poor families.
Edward Alexander Bouchet (1852–1918)	Bouchet became the first African American Ph.D. recipient in physics in 1876. Because of his race, however, Bouchet was not able to get a university faculty position. He spent his career teaching high school at the Institute for Colored Youth in Philadelphia, where he inspired a generation of African American science students, some of whom did go on to hold the kinds of positions that Bouchet had been denied.
Daniel Hale Williams (1856–1931)	Williams was a medical doctor and surgeon who founded the Provident Hospital in Chicago in 1891. It was there that he performed the first successful open heart surgery in 1893.
George Washington Carver (1865–1943)	Probably the most well-known African American scientist, Carver was the director of agricultural research at the Tuskegee Institute in Alabama. He is remembered for his research on sustainable agricultural practices. He developed hundreds of applications for farm products such as the peanut, sweet potato, and soybean—most famously, peanut butter.
Charles Henry Turner (1867–1923)	Turner did important foundational research in entomology after receiving his Ph.D. from the University of Chicago in 1907. Among other discoveries, Turner was the first to prove that insects can hear.
Archibald Alexander (1888–1958)	Alexander was a distinguished civil engineer who designed two of the most famous bridges in Washington, DC.: the Tidal Basin Bridge across the Potomac River to the Jefferson Memorial and the Whitehurst Freeway.
Roger Arliner Young (1889–1964)	Young was the first African American woman to receive a Ph.D. in zoology. Rumor has it that she was accepted into graduate school because her first name was Roger. She went on to conduct research at the famous Woods Hole Marine Laboratory on Cape Cod, where she studied the role of osmosis in controlling the salt concentration in aquatic organisms.
Charles Richard Drew (1904–1950)	Drew was a medical researcher who studied blood plasma and transfusions. He discovered that blood could be preserved by separating the red blood cells from the plasma, which could then be frozen. This allowed for the creation of the first blood bank. Drew also organized the world's first blood drive.

Table 4.3. Notable Hispanic Scientists

Scientist	Description
Narciso Monturiol (1819–1885)	Monturiol was a physicist and inventor who was interested in underwater navigation. In 1859 he created and drove the first fully operable submarine.
Carlos Finlay (1847–1915)	Finlay was a medical doctor in Cuba who first proposed that yellow fever was transmitted by mosquito bites. He attempted to convince the Cuban government to begin a mosquito eradication and control program. It was not until 20 years later, however, that Finlay's theory was finally accepted and action was taken to control mosquito populations.
Severo Ochoa (1905–1993)	Ochoa was a biomedical researcher at New York University. His research helped us understand the role of ribonucleic acid (RNA) in carrying hereditary information during reproduction. He received the 1959 Nobel Prize in medicine for this discovery.
Luis Walter Alvarez (1911–1988)	Alvarez designed the ground-controlled radar system for aircraft landings and was awarded the Nobel Prize for physics in 1968. He also helped develop the meteorite theory of dinosaur extinction.
Baruj Benacerraf (1920–)	Benacerraf was awarded the Nobel Prize for medicine in 1980 for discovering the structures on the cell surface that control immunological reactions. This discovery has led to increased understanding of cell recognition, immune responses, and graft rejection in transplant patients.
Mario Molina (1943–)	Molina did the research showing that chlorofluorocarbons (CFCs) could destroy the ozone layer in the stratosphere, allowing more ultraviolet light to get through to Earth and potentially increasing the rate of skin cancer. This led to CFCs being banned in most countries. Molina received the 1995 Nobel Prize in chemistry for this work.
Ellen Ochoa (1958–)	Ochoa became the world's first Hispanic female astronaut in 1991. She is a mission specialist and flight engineer and has logged more than 900 hours in space on four flights.

Table 4.3. Equal education for all students—no matter what their race or background—remains a significant challenge for American educators.

Socioeconomic Status (SES) in the Science Classroom. While public schools are meant to be the great equalizer in addressing poverty in American society, the reality is that children in poor neighborhoods, whether urban, suburban, or rural, are less likely to have access to high-quality science education than students from more affluent backgrounds. As has been noted earlier, high-quality, hands-on, inquiry-based science instruction requires substantial material resources and well-prepared and qualified teachers, and it is substantially easier to do when class sizes are smaller. Schools that serve poor children frequently suffer in all of these areas, typically having limited and outdated science equipment, a higher percentage of uncertified teachers and higher rates of teacher turnover, and large class sizes. Additionally, schools that enroll large numbers of students from low-SES backgrounds are more likely to focus their instruction on "basic skills," such as basic literacy and numeracy, and are likely to devote less instructional time to science.

Because poverty and race/ethnicity tend to co-vary in the U.S., students of color are more likely to face the hurdle of under-resourced school science programs as well as the challenges they may face in school because of perceptions about their race. At the same time, white students from low-SES backgrounds are also likely to face many of these challenges to a high-quality science education.

Students With Exceptionalities in the Science Classroom. Disability affects everyone either directly or indirectly. It is estimated that there are between 38 and 52 million people with disabilities in the United States. Practically everyone will either experience disability directly or have a family member, loved one, or friend who has a mental or physical impairment.

People with disabilities are visible in society as never before, including in our public schools. Because of laws prohibiting discrimination—specifically Section 504 of the Rehabilitation Act and the Americans With Disabilities Act—people with disabilities are increasingly present in America's workplaces, stores, transportation systems, and public facilities. Prior to 1975 and the passage of the Individuals With Disabilities Education Act (IDEA—Public Law 94-142), many students with severe disabilities attended separate schools where they never interacted with their non-disabled peers. Students with even mild or moderate disabilities were usually taught in completely separate resource room settings and only occasionally interacted with their general education peers, perhaps during lunch or recess.

As a result of IDEA and the guaranteed right of all students to an education in the "least restrictive environment" that meets each individual student's needs, there has been an increased emphasis on inclusive education; students with disabilities are placed in general education settings to the greatest degree possible. Both teachers and non-disabled, general education students have increased exposure to students with disabilities.

While the placement of students with disabilities into general education classrooms has been shown to provide benefits to disabled and non-disabled students alike, teachers in these inclusive classrooms regularly face the difficult task of having to modify their curriculum, instruction, and assessment to meet the needs of students with a range of special needs. Without these modifications, students with disabilities often find themselves blocked from access to essential aspects of their education. Teachers have a legal as well as an ethical obligation to do their best to break down the barriers and assist these students to learn.

The teaching of science to students with disabilities involves some special challenges as well as some unique opportunities to provide meaningful and engaging education. A good teacher with the proper tools, preparation, and instructional methods can support and encourage each member of her class to participate directly in science learning experiences. Again, it should be noted that major contributions to science and technology have been made by individuals with a range of disabilities (see Table 4.4).

English Language Learners in the Science Classroom. Historically, students who spoke a language other than English as their home language (English language learners) were not provided with instruction in science until they demonstrated at least intermediate conversational fluency in English. The rationale for this decision was that it was more important for these students to put all their energy into learning English than it was for them to try to remain at grade level in the content areas of science, math, or social studies. The result of this approach was that English language learners either never received science instruction or by the time they did, they were already several years behind grade level (Rosebery, Warren, & Conant, 1992).

When science instruction did take place for these students, it was usually in a way that was grossly unequal to that of students in mainstream science classes. The "special" science instruction in English as a Second Language (ESL) classes was frequently inadequate for several reasons. First of all, science classes for linguistically diverse students were frequently taught by bilingual paraprofessionals rather than by certified science teachers. Second, in these settings, class work generally focused on learning science vocabulary, with a heavy dependence on worksheets, drill and practice methods, and an emphasis on lower-order thinking skills (Mason & Barba, 1992). At the other extreme, some English language learners, placed from the outset in mainstream science classes (the submersion or "sink or swim" model), were expected to learn science, often through a text and lecture format, at a level of English that was far beyond their comprehension. In either case, these students were not given an equal opportunity to learn science as compared to native English language speakers.

Another obstacle to content area success for linguistically diverse students is the inherent mismatch between the cultural backgrounds of these

Table 4.4. Notable Scientists and Inventors With Disabilities

Scientist	Description
Isaac Newton (1642–1727)	Newton, who articulated the theory of gravity and laws of motion that continue to govern our understanding of force and motion in the visible world, suffered both from epilepsy and from a speech impediment (stuttering).
Alexander Graham Bell (1847–1922)	Bell, who is most famous for inventing the telephone, suffered from a fairly severe learning disability that caused him to struggle in school and also inspired him to start a school for the deaf.
Thomas Alva Edison (1847–1931)	Famous for inventing the electric light and the record player, Edison suffered from partial deafness, learning disabilities (he didn't learn to read until he was 12), and, in later life, diabetes. It is said that Edison never developed good writing skills, yet his inventions literally changed the world.
Henry Ford (1863–1947)	Ford, one of the developers and the first to mass produce the automobile, suffered from dyslexia. As a youth, he struggled with reading and writing but had been drawn to tinkering with machinery, a path that eventually led him to engineering.
Albert Einstein (1879–1955)	Arguably the most well-known scientist of all time, Einstein is thought to have suffered from Asperger Syndrome, which is a from of autism, as well as dyslexia.
Stephen Hawking (1942–)	Probably the greatest living physicist, Hawking did much of the foundational work on black holes and has developed several theories about the nature and origins of our universe. Hawking has motor neuron disease (ALS) and is forced to use a wheelchair and voice synthesizer.

students and the mainstream culture of schools. Roland Tharp and his colleagues have explored how views of cultural difference are often used to explain student failure but are rarely accessed to support the content area instruction. They conclude that misunderstanding between the cultures of students and the culture of school is one of the major factors responsible for widespread school failure among students from culturally and linguistically diverse groups (D'Amato & Tharp, 1997).

Thus, the science classroom has often been overlooked as a place where academic success among English language learners can occur. We believe, however, that science learning can actually become one of the principle resources for simultaneously teaching linguistically diverse students English, providing them opportunities for academic success, and setting these students on a course that can lead to sought-after professional jobs.

By promoting strategies that aid in the development of academic (rather than just conversational) language skills, and by making explicit the kinds of content-specific learning strategies used by successful students, English language learners can develop and flourish in the science classroom. Failure of the teacher to attend to the language needs of these students, however, serves to continue the unfortunate historic trend of poor academic performance and high dropout rates later in school.

Theory Into Practice 4.1

Draw a Scientist

Perform the following visualization exercise with your students:

Close your eyes and picture a scientist. Summon up an image of what that scientist looks like and what that scientist is doing. When you have a clear visual image of your scientist, open your eyes and draw a picture of what your scientist looks like and what your scientist is doing.

As students finish, have them tape their pictures on the board. Next, ask everyone to take a look at all the pictures in the "scientist museum." Tell them to look for similarities and differences between the pictures.

While they are looking at the pictures, you may wish to slip on a lab coat and goggles and get a flask of colored water for effect.

Students are likely to note similarities (many) and differences (few) among their scientist pictures, as most will have drawn a stereotypical "geeky" scientist (usually white and male) with a lab coat, glasses, and crazy hair working in a lab with chemicals.

Why do you think that so many people of all ages, all education levels, both genders, and all races and ethnicities tend to draw the same stereotypical scientist?

Where do these stereotypes of scientists come from?

Are these stereotypes problematic? Why?

What can be done to combat these stereotypes?

♫ Current Science Education Reforms and Their Impact on Diverse Learners

In Chapter 2, we discussed the Sputnik-era reforms that led to increased attention to and funding for science education, which lasted into the late 1960s. Because the intention of the Cold War reforms was primarily to produce the next generation of competitive, highly trained scientists, females, students of color, students with disabilities, and English language learners failed to reap the benefits of these reforms proportionally with their more mainstream peers.

The 1990s saw a new wave of science education reforms brought about by a growing realization, based on international comparisons, that the U.S. was no longer at (or even near) the top when it came to science education. (See, for example, the U.S. TIMSS National Research Center Web site, http://ustimss.msu.edu/, for a detailed analysis of the results of the Third International Mathematics and Science Study.) A fundamental shift in science education reform has been the emphasis on scientific literacy for all students, as opposed to scientific mastery for a small, elite number of students. The push for broad scientific literacy has implications for the science education of diverse learners.

At the forefront of this latest reform effort has been the work of the American Association for the Advancement of Science (AAAS) through two books they have published: *Science for All Americans* (Rutherford & Ahlgren, 1990) and *Benchmarks for Science Literacy* (AAAS, 1993). In 1996, the *National Science Education Standards* (National Research Council [NRC], 1996) largely stemmed from the work of AAAS and the National Science Teachers Association. Still more recently, *Inquiry and the National Science Education Standards: A Guide for Teaching and Learning* (NRC, 2000) furthered the argument for hands-on, inquiry-based science for all students. In the following section, we briefly discuss the contributions of these reform documents.

Science for All Americans: Setting the Agenda

Science for All Americans (Rutherford & Ahlgren, 1990) was the first component of an AAAS endeavor named Project 2061, in reference to both the long-term, systemic perspective it takes toward the reform of science education in the United States and to the year of the return of Haley's Comet to Earth. *Science for All Americans* (SFAA) set an agenda for the reform movement and identified the basic scientific concepts that all citizens in today's technological world should be familiar with in order to be scientifically literate. While the stated goal of SFAA was to promote science for all, and current inequities experienced by female and minority students in science are condemned throughout, little space is devoted to concrete or specific suggestions for including traditionally underserved populations.

SFAA points out a number of educational practices, common in the typical science classroom, that are detrimental to the goals of science reform. Many of these practices are particularly harmful to culturally and linguistically diverse students. These include (a) an overemphasis on student competition with a focus on grades, rather than on student collaboration with a focus on learning (p. 193); (b) the role of imagination going unrewarded as compared to the role of memorizing and following directions (p. 191); (c) the tendency to keep science and mathematics restricted to the classroom, rather than expanding them into the larger community where children spend most of their time and do most of their learning (p. 193); and (d) the entrenched nature of the teaching schedule that does not allow time for collaboration and sharing of ideas (p. 201).

To make scientific literacy a reality for all, a serious and significant reform of the current education system will be required. SFAA concludes by recommending a series of "next steps" to achieve this goal. One of the book's concluding comments is that

> progress will have been made if, by 1992, educators and education policy makers have begun to develop a strong consensus on what it will take to restructure the school system so that all students—including especially those it has failed in the past—will emerge well educated in science, mathematics, and technology. (p. 213)

Clearly, this has not come to pass. In summary, while SFAA is short on concrete strategies to address the specific needs of diverse students in the science classroom, attention is paid to the importance of universal science literacy, inclusive of culturally diverse and traditionally underserved populations.

National Science Education Standards: Reform Into Practice

The current version of the *National Science Education Standards* (NRC, 1996) is meant to address and set standards for all aspects of science education. The document includes not only content standards, but also standards for teaching, professional development, assessment, science education programs, and science education systems. The importance of *all* in science education is given a central place in the *National Science Education Standards* (NSES). The first of the guiding principles said to drive the development of the NSES is "science is for all students" (p. 19):

> [The standards] emphatically reject any situation in science education where some people—for example, members of certain populations—are discouraged from pursuing science and excluded

from opportunities to learn science. Excellence in science education embodies the ideal that all students can achieve understanding of science if they are given the opportunity. (p. 20)

However, while support for the creation of a functional, inclusive science classroom is clearly present throughout the document, as is the case with SFAA, detailed discussion of the practical aspects of this guiding principle are scant. For example, Teaching Standard B, Substandard 4 states, "Teachers of science recognize and respond to student diversity and encourage all students to participate fully in science learning" (p. 36). The discussion of this substandard further states, "Students with limited English ability might be encouraged to use their own language as well as English and to use forms of presenting data such as pictures and graphs that require less language proficiency" (p. 37). Although these are two effective strategies that could be used by a science teacher working with English language learners, they are just the tip of the iceberg of the repertoire of strategies and techniques used routinely by language specialists.

Assessment Standard B, Substandard 3 addresses the issue of equal opportunity and equal access to quality instruction, stating, "Equal attention must be given to the assessment of opportunity to learn and to the assessment of student achievement" (p. 83). In other words, it is unfair to hold students who are receiving poor instruction to the same achievement standards as those students who are receiving high-quality instruction. Because many girls, students of color, students with disabilities, and English language learners have, in fact, been receiving inferior science instruction, this issue is highly relevant when considering diverse learners and science assessment, especially the high-stakes variety.

Standard D deals with issues of equality of resources, including updated texts, access to sufficient laboratory equipment, adequate time devoted to the study of science, and most importantly, well-trained professional teachers (pp. 218–220, 232–233). All of these resources, however, require substantial funding—funding that is often distributed to schools in a less than equitable fashion. Standard E deals with equitable access to the opportunities to achieve the content standards, and discusses issues of bias, exclusion, and tracking as ways that some students have traditionally been denied access to high-quality science education (pp. 221–222). In contrast to the economic equity issue, the task of ensuring that all students receive science education in an environment that is unbiased and inclusive seems more attainable; individual teachers have a significant amount of control over issues of inclusion in their classrooms. The standards summarize these issues as follows:

In particular, the commitment to science for all implies inclusion of those who have traditionally not received encouragement and opportunity to pursue science—women and girls, students of color, students with disabilities, and students with limited English proficiency. It implies attention to various styles of learning, adaptations to meet the needs of special students, and differing sources of motivation. (p. 221)

In summary, the NSES is a step forward in addressing the needs of diverse learners in the science classroom in that the standards point to many of the issues that have hindered the success of a wide range of students in science. However, increasing teachers' awareness of these issues is only a first step. Teachers must also learn to apply the specific skills that have been shown to increase successful science learning for girls, students of color, students with disabilities, and English language learners.

Theory Into Practice 4.2

Mapping the Increasing Diversity in American Classrooms

Using Web sites such as the Historical Census Browser (http://fisher.lib .virginia.edu/collections/stats/histcensus/) or the U.S. Census Bureau (http:// www.census.gov/), create a data table showing how the population of children attending school has changed over the last century. Look for data from 1900, 1950, and 2000.

Look for data on gender, race/ethnicity, disabilities, and home language.

Plot a graph showing your results and compare your graph your neighbor's.

If you have time, go back and look for data specific to your state. How does your state compare to the national figures?

Strategies for Working With Diverse Learners in the Science Classroom

Strategies for Working With Girls in the Science Classroom

As awareness of the need to more actively encourage girls in science has grown over the past few decades, support has come from several arenas.

Successful women scientists have begun to look at the educational and professional factors that allowed them to be successful and how these factors could be fostered in younger generations of girls and young women. Feminist science educators have worked to develop guiding principles for equitable science education grounded in feminist pedagogies. Teachers have reflected on the concrete, practical strategies they have found to be successful in encouraging success in science for the girls in their classes. Across this variety of settings and diversity of advocates, a fairly consistent set of recommendations and strategies has emerged for promoting women's and girls' success in science (as well as math and technology—two other areas where women and girls have historically faced challenges):

1. Assume that girls are interested in math, science, and technology, and make clear your expectations that they will succeed in these areas.

2. Have your class research and assemble a directory of "Women in Math, Science, and Technology in Our Community." This directory can then serve as a resource for setting up mentorship or internship opportunities. Have the students share the directory as part of a parents' night to educate parents about successful local women in math, science, and technology careers.

3. Promote and create mentorship and internship programs in the local community, to give girls and young women a realistic idea of potential careers in science.

4. Foster active and cooperative learning and group success over individual competition. At the same time, provide some opportunities for competition to teach students that competition is sometimes required but that collaboration is often the best way to achieve goals.

5. Integrate science, math, and technology with other disciplines, drawing connections to topics your students find engaging.

6. Arrange opportunities for younger girls to speak with older girls who are taking more advanced science and math courses, to share their experiences and insights.

7. Promote opportunities for girls and their parents to engage in science and technology together, such as a parent-daughter science and technology night at school. Encourage them to explore hands-on science activities or computer software together. Remember that girls need support and encouragement at home as well as in school to promote continued interest in math, science, and technology.

8. Present your students with current data on salaries for various careers in science, math, and technology as compared to salaries

for careers that have traditionally been "women's work," such as teaching, nursing, and administration.

9. Highlight a wide range of possible science careers, including those with community-building and people-helping components.

10. Review the science curriculum materials that are used in your school to ensure that they represent diversity issues in positive and proactive ways.

Theory Into Practice 4.3

Two-Column Girls and Scientists Activity

The following activity is meant to demonstrate how some of the characteristics associated with scientists are often constructed in opposition to the characteristics associated with girls, while other characteristics seem well-aligned.

1. Fold a piece of paper lengthwise, then unfold to make two columns.

2. Title the left-hand column "Girls" and brainstorm a list of all the qualities and characteristics that you associate with girls. Try to list at least a dozen.

3. Title the right-hand column "Scientists" and brainstorm a list of all the qualities and characteristics that you associate with scientists. Try to list at least a dozen.

4. Compare the two lists and, using a colored marker, connect terms that seem to be antonyms (opposites).

5. Compare the two lists and, using a colored marker, connect terms that seem to be synonyms.

6. Discuss the implications of the similarities and differences between your two lists.

Strategies for Working With Students From Diverse Racial, Ethnic, and Cultural Backgrounds in the Science Classroom

Much has been written in the past two decades about the role that multicultural education must play in our increasingly diverse schools and classrooms.

On the one hand, this literature has argued that all students, regardless of their racial, ethnic, and cultural backgrounds, must learn to be aware and tolerant of the differences between individuals and groups. On the other hand, some multicultural education literature has focused on ideas and strategies for more effectively teaching culturally diverse learners.

Within this second branch of multicultural education, which is focused on enhancing the education of non-mainstream students, the majority of the work has been content-general rather than content-specific. That is to say, it provides strategies that teachers might use in any situation to more effectively work with students from a particular cultural group or with non-mainstream students in general.

For example, McBay (1989) provided a list of recommendations for improving education for students of color: (1) early intervention in preschool and enhanced parental education; (2) restructured school systems to encourage success for all students; (3) curriculum that is sensitive to the ethnic and cultural identities of students; (4) making the best teachers available to the most needy students; (5) schools learning to also function as social service providers; (6) better communication between school services and other community services; (7) use of role models and support from the community; (8) earlier exposure to higher, more challenging levels of education; and (9) clarifying incentives for all students to participate in higher education.

Although strategies of this generic nature have been adopted, to a greater or lesser extent, in most schools with significant numbers of ethnically, racially, and culturally diverse students, it is our belief that content-specific strategies are at least as important, but are less often known to teachers. The multicultural education literature has few specific strategies for promoting science education for students from diverse races, ethnicities, and cultures. A study by Atwater (1993) is one often-cited example of this topic.

In the following section, we present six different perspectives based on the work of Banks (1995) that highlight how various generic principles of multicultural education can be explicitly applied to science teaching. Together, the following six perspectives on multicultural science teaching form a continuum from traditional science teaching, which does not consider multicultural issues, to a range of substantive changes. We believe that these changes are largely cumulative: A teacher who adopts one of the more substantive change models is also likely to adopt the less substantive changes as well. As someone preparing to be a teacher, you need to weigh these perspectives and consider which ones fit best with your personal philosophy about teaching science to diverse learners.

1. *No Significant Changes.* Students need to adapt to and learn Western science as it is. Science is a "culture of power," and to access this power structure, students must deal with science on its own terms. Modifying how we represent science in the classroom is doing a disservice to students because no one will make such modifications for them later in life if they wish to pursue careers in science.

2. *Additive Changes.* The most important issue is that diverse students fail to see themselves represented in positive ways within science. To address this problem, the teacher should look for opportunities to include contributions of minority and women scientists to Western science (e.g., posters in the classroom, special days celebrating the contributions of female scientists and scientists of color). Teaching of the actual science content is not modified in any way in this approach.

3. *Methods Changes.* The most important issue is that racially, ethnically, and culturally diverse learners are likely to have preferred learning styles that are somewhat different from their mainstream peers. To address this issue, instruction and assessment should be modified to better accommodate these learning styles, such as through greater use of cooperative learning, increased wait time, performance assessment, kinesthetic learning experiences, and so on. The teacher attempts to increase awareness of cultural differences between students and how this affects their preferred methods of learning. Again, teaching of the actual science content is not modified in any way in this approach.

4. *Substitution Changes.* The most important issue is that racially, ethnically, and culturally diverse students generally fail to see science as a worldview that comes from their cultural heritage, but rather as something that came from white European culture and has most benefited those of white European heritage. To address this incorrect notion that science has only Western European roots, the teacher looks to replace parts of the traditional curriculum with a study of the history of science, and especially how science evolved in other cultures, and how science is still used differently in other cultures today (see Teresi, 2002). For example, lessons and even whole curricula have been developed on topics such as Mayan and Incan agricultural practices (Incan farmers were doing controlled experiments on potato breeding long before the rise of science in Europe), Micronesian navigational practices (Micronesian sailors had mapped much of the Pacific Ocean while the Greeks were still constrained to the Mediterranean), and Egyptian architecture (the science behind the construction of the great pyramids fascinates people around the world to this day).

5. *Goal Changes.* The most important issue is that school culture and norms have evolved from a rationalist cultural model favored in Europe that leads to a focus on cognitive development of students without adequate attention to affective development. Students need to feel good about themselves as individuals, and about science as an area of study, if we expect them to be academic achievers and to conceive of themselves as potential scientists. Once a student has come to see science as a way of making sense of things that are important and valuable to him or her, then that student will feel good about science and be ready to succeed in learning academic science content. Thus, the teacher initially makes science content learning secondary to developing

lessons that allow students to see science as personally relevant to positive student interests. Topics such as fashion, music, sports, community service, safety, and cooking have all been used by teachers to promote affinity towards science with racially, ethnically, and culturally diverse students.

6. *Culture-Dependent Curriculum Changes.* The most radical end of the continuum advocates a fundamental overhaul of the science curriculum to align what is taught with the empowerment of the dominant ethnicity, race, and/or gender in the school or classroom. This ethnic, racial, cultural, or gender group determines the curriculum by focusing both on how science has been used successfully by members of this group (an extension of the substitution changes model discussed above) and on how science and technology have been used to disadvantage, marginalize, or control the group in question. This approach is generally only proposed in homogeneous school settings, such as single-gender schools or charter schools catering to a single racial or ethnic group. Thus, Afrocentric, Hispanocentric, and women's science curricula have all been developed under special circumstances, although the accuracy of some of the claims in these curricula has been challenged.

Strategies for Working With Children From Low-Socioeconomic Backgrounds in the Science Classroom

Children from low-SES backgrounds may also fall within one or more of the other diversity categories discussed in this chapter. For example, students of color are more likely to come from low-SES homes than are white children; thus, the teacher will want to consider strategies under the cultural and ethnic diversity section. Additionally, students from low-SES environments are over-represented in special education placement and diagnosis of **exceptionality**. Such placements seem to result, in part, from added health risks and developmental challenges that are associated with poverty, but also from misidentification because students from poor backgrounds may be less likely to exhibit the "good student" identities that convince teachers that a student is making adequate progress. Thus, teachers may also wish to consider whether some of the strategies for working with students with disabilities may prove helpful.

The following strategies may also prove helpful when working with students from low-SES backgrounds:

1. *Set high expectations but provide strong scaffolding.* Many teachers fail to realize that they hold substantially lower expectations for the academic success of students from low-SES backgrounds, expectations that their students readily pick up on. Students must first be convinced that they are expected to succeed before they are likely to believe it themselves.

2. *Learn about the students' out-of-school experiences and build on them.* Many teachers believe that students from poor backgrounds have only negative experiences in their communities. The stereotypes of drug- and

violence-infested inner cities paint a one-dimensional picture of the neighborhoods where poor students might live. While these students may indeed have witnessed or experienced frightening things that students in more affluent neighborhoods may not have, students from low-SES backgrounds have positive experiences in their neighborhoods as well. Teachers who take the time to learn about these positive experiences can then look for ways to connect these experiences to school topics in ways that help students to scaffold this learning.

3. *Provide experiences for students that they may not otherwise have.* While students from low-SES backgrounds are not devoid of meaningful experiences, it is also the case that these students are less likely to have had some of the experiences common among more affluent children that can help support science learning. Teachers can help narrow this "experience gap" through strategies such as supporting meaningful field trips, providing students with opportunities to use science tools and equipment, and inviting guest speakers to the classroom to share experiences that are unfamiliar to the students.

4. *Reciprocal Peer Tutoring and Cross-Age Tutoring.* Reciprocal peer tutoring is a strategy in which classmates of approximately the same age take turns teaching material to each other. Cross-age tutoring is an older student helping a younger student to learn something. Both of these strategies have been shown to promote confidence and competence in students from low-SES backgrounds, as long as the teacher has set clear expectations about the tutoring process.

5. *Parental/Family Engagement.* Parents and guardians from low-SES backgrounds often have numerous reasons why they feel uncomfortable becoming involved in their children's school. They may not have had good school experiences themselves, may not feel academically competent to help their children with their school work, may not speak English well, or may work multiple jobs and/or have multiple young children and simply not have the time to come to their children's school during regular hours. Despite these challenges, teachers who find ways to engage their students' parents in school activities report positive academic outcomes for their students as a result.

Strategies for Working With Students With Disabilities in the Science Classroom

Somewhat unlike the other areas of student diversity discussed in this chapter, the category of students with disabilities is extremely broad, covering a wide variety of disabilities, each with its own special needs. In this section, we will try to at least provide an overview of the kinds of student exceptionalities you might be asked to accommodate in your classroom and how you might begin that accommodation process.

Challenges in Gaining Knowledge

Many students with disabilities face challenges in gaining knowledge:

- A visual impairment requiring accommodation through materials in large print or Braille, on tape, or via computer;
- A hearing impairment requiring accommodation such as the use of an AM/FM system or an interpreter, additional printed materials, facing a student for lip reading, or increased use of an overhead projector or blackboard;
- A speech impairment requiring accommodations such as increased use of written or electronic communications where the ability to hear or speak is not required or the use of portable computer with speech output;
- A specific learning disability requiring accommodation such as increased visual, aural, and tactile demonstrations in class; extra time to complete assignments; and access to materials via a computer equipped with speech and/or large print output;
- A mobility impairment requiring accommodation such as in-class access to a computer with adaptive technology and a word processor, adaptive equipment for manipulating objects during a lab activity, or an adjusted table arrangement;
- A specific learning impairment (e.g., ADD or ADHD) requiring accommodations such as a specific seating location or attention to possible distracters in the classroom such as open windows that allow noise to filter in.

Challenges in Demonstrating Knowledge

Some students with disabilities face challenges in demonstrating their knowledge of a topic instead of, or in addition to, facing challenges in gaining that knowledge. The student might face challenges in writing, speaking, or working through a problem in a lab. Many of the same accommodations for assisting students in gaining knowledge that are discussed above can also help the student demonstrate mastery of a subject. Additional accommodations could include the following:

- A student with a visual impairment might need worksheets and tests in large print or Braille, on tape, or via computer, or access to adaptive technology that provides enlarged print, voice, and/or Braille as well as standard print output.
- A student with a specific learning disability may require extra time, alternative testing arrangements, or a particularly quiet space free of distractions.

- A student with a mobility impairment that leads to an inability to write may need in-class access to a computer with alternative native input (e.g., Morse code, speech, alternative keyboard) devices.

Students with a range of disabilities may require help from an itinerant special education teacher or paraprofessional to provide physical assistance in completing a test or assignment.

Theory Into Practice 4.4

Modifying Lab Activities

From Part II of this book, select three hands-on science experiments appropriate for the grade level you wish to teach.

Consider what accommodations you could make for each of the three activities to best meet the needs of students with the following disabilities:

A student with a visual impairment

A student with a mobility impairment who is in a wheelchair

A student who has ADHD

A student with a speech impairment

If you can, show your list of accommodations to a trained special educator to see what additional suggestions for accommodations he or she can provide.

Strategies for Working With English Language Learners in the Science Classroom

Inquiry-based science, because of its hands-on nature, is in many ways an ideal academic area in which English language learners can flourish. However, it can also be quite frustrating for these students as they try to figure out what to do, how to do it (often collaboratively with peers), and how to make sense of it. Remember that in a content-area class such as science, English language learners are being asked to learn the content and the language simultaneously—a cognitively demanding challenge! Meaning-rich learning opportunities can reduce the language load required for comprehension and promote student understanding. The combination of inquiry activities and non-linguistic means of expression (such as graphs and diagrams) can also help English language learners communicate their ideas.

The following strategies can be used to help English language learners simultaneously develop knowledge and skills in science and in English. Many of these strategies are valuable for all students and not just English language learners. Remember that all elementary and middle-grade students, even those whose first language is English, are still learning academic English as well as science content.

Multiple Representations. Ask students to express their ideas in multiple formats, such as drawings, graphs, and tables, as well as in written and oral communications. This will help students gain an understanding of the relationships among different modes of communication and the ideas they wish to express. Graphics production forces students to observe carefully, provides artifacts that foster discussion, and gives them something concrete and comprehensible to write about.

Key Science Terms in Multiple Languages. Science instruction is often associated with the use of many "scientific" terms. The acquisition of a massive science vocabulary should not be one of your instructional goals in teaching science. This applies to native English speakers as well as English language learners. Instead, you should guide students to comprehend and use a small number of key terms that are most important to the topic of study. It is worthwhile to create a multilingual basic vocabulary list in the languages prevalent in your class for the key science terms that you use repeatedly. Referring to these terms with the entire class will promote an understanding of science for your English language learners while promoting multiple language development in all your students. Keep this list posted on the wall and add to it throughout the year. Have native speakers of each language model correct pronunciation of the terms for the rest of the class.

Positional Terms and Phrases. In addition to key science terms, many English language learners, especially at the beginning levels of English acquisition, struggle to master positional terms, such as in/on, above/below, and inside/outside. These terms are critical in doing hands-on science because students are asked to make observations, take measurements, and draw pictures and graphs that all rely on correct use of positional terms. Participation in these activities can help English language learners to use these terms successfully, but only if the teacher is aware of students' language-learning needs and provides the kinds of input that helps students learn and use these terms.

Use of Tools and Objects. The value of hands-on science for making learning (and the corresponding language) concrete for English language learners has already been discussed. Use of tools and objects has the added advantage of giving English language learners legitimate ways to contribute to class or small-group activities even when their English language skills are still emerging. Once students understand what is to be done with a tool or object, they can carry out the task even if they cannot yet adequately express in English what they are doing. This legitimate participation further engrains the student into the workings of the class, helping build the relationships that are essential for developing opportunities for verbal communication.

Theory Into Practice 4.5

Sheltered Second-Language Activity

If you speak a second language (or can get the assistance of someone who does), teach a fairly simple hands-on inquiry-based lesson entirely in that language.

Be sure to use good ESOL teaching strategies such as modeling, gestures, repeated use of key vocabulary, simplified syntax, pictures, and so on.

Split the class into small groups. If there are some students in the class who speak the other language, so much the better—split them up between the groups.

Pose a question (in the second language) to be answered by manipulating the materials, then give each group some time to explore.

Let the students speak in English (or whatever language they prefer) while in their small groups to try to make sense of the task, but as you move around the class observing or answering questions, you should only use the second language. Likewise, when you bring the groups back together, have each group report what they did, but only in the second language—coach as needed.

Finally, switch back to English and debrief the experience. Many students are likely to express how frustrating and challenging it was to learn the content and language at the same time. Some may also point out, however, that with good teaching strategies, most of the students did manage to get at least the main ideas of the lesson even as they struggled with the language. Discuss how this experience was both similar to and different from the experiences of English language learners in their classrooms.

Gifted and Talented Students in the Science Classroom

All schools, no matter what other elements of student diversity might be present, have students who tend to think more quickly, more abstractly, and more divergently than their peers. Many of these students fall into the category of gifted and talented (a label that some argue should apply to as much as 15% of the student population, whether or not they have officially been placed in a program to receive special services). Whatever other supplemental services these students receive (often a pull-out program for a part of each day or several times a week), when they are in your classroom, it is your responsibility to adopt strategies to meet their learning needs. Science can be an ideal content area for pushing gifted students to explore and develop their full academic potential. Suggestions offered in this section will help you develop a science learning environment that will challenge and nurture gifted learners.

Attending to the needs of students who are gifted or talented in science while simultaneously teaching the other groups of students in a classroom is very difficult, especially in light of all the other special student learning needs we have outlined in this chapter. It would not be surprising if by this point you are ready to throw up your hands in dismay, wondering how you will ever learn to juggle so many needs for so many students at the same time. While this challenge is, indeed, daunting, you can take some comfort in knowing that many of the "special" strategies for learners with special needs that we have discussed in this chapter are actually, when used judiciously, teaching strategies that can benefit all your students.

For example, items on the following list of strategies and methods considered appropriate for gifted students are, we believe, equally valuable for all students when done in a thoughtful and reflective way:

1. Vary your use of group and individual activities to accommodate different abilities, skills, and learning rates.

2. Vary the level of cognitive demand of your activities, requiring students to develop both basic skills and higher-order thinking skills and strategies.

3. Allow students to negotiate self-selected topics for learning within established curriculum parameters.

4. Encourage students to question assumptions, including assumptions about their own learning and how they construct knowledge.

5. Demonstrate logical, critical, creative, lateral, and parallel forms of thinking.

6. Pay attention to both product and process, teaching students to visualize the desired outcome of a task, and then map the process backwards to determine how to accomplish the outcome.

7. Encourage students to help other students with their learning.

More specific strategies for teaching science to students who are gifted and talented include the following:

Independent Science Projects. Many gifted and talented students tend to finish their work rather quickly. In fact, teachers sometimes find that these students become behavior problems during this "free time." Have these students use this time to explore a special area of interest related to the science topic being studied. Many science texts, kits, and other curricular resources contain "extension" activities that teachers rarely have time to cover with the whole class. These extensions are frequently creative and engaging, and thus provide an excellent outlet for the gifted student's creative energy. They are sometimes referred to as "vertical enrichment" activities because they push the student to build more advanced knowledge rather than just do more of the same level work.

Academic Competitions. There are a growing number of academic science competitions for students of all ages: at the school level, such as a science fair; at the regional level, such as regional competitions of the Science Olympiad (http://www.soinc.org/); or even at national and international levels, such as Odyssey of the Mind (http://www.odysseyofthemind.com). Such experiences not only challenge students academically, they also provide an opportunity to develop skills in leadership and group dynamics.

Mentoring. Teachers frequently ask gifted students to work with struggling peers in the classroom as a peer tutor. There is a real cognitive and social value to be gained for the gifted student in attempting to teach his or her peers. It is true that one of the best ways to solidify one's own understanding of a topic is to attempt to teach it to another. However, such individual attention should be provided to the gifted student as well. Try to find a mentor who will work with the gifted student in an area of interest. Parents and other school volunteers are one source of potential mentors; school business partners and community organizations are another source. This outside expertise can provide your gifted students with opportunities to engage in areas of science learning that you may be unable to provide.

Learning Styles and Cognitive Demand. It is now well-accepted by most educators that all people possess "multiple intelligences" in varying degrees and that teachers should attempt to stimulate and develop in their students as many of these intelligences as they can (Gardner, 1993, 1999). This approach provides limitless possibilities for teaching science. Challenge your gifted students (and the rest of your class as well) to find ways to apply all of their intelligences to the learning of science. Push students to take the initiative to write a poem or a song, to build a model, or choreograph a dance that explores a science concept such as the change of the seasons or the structure of an **atom**. Likewise, considering Bloom's Taxonomy, or other models of cognitive demand, should help you determine whether you are requiring your students to engage in an appropriate mix of "lower order" cognitive demand (such as recall and basic comprehension) and "higher order" cognitive demand (such as analyzing and evaluating knowledge claims).

Learning Centers. Many teachers already use learning centers in their classrooms to allow students to work independently at their own speed on certain projects. Because gifted students frequently work faster than other students in their class, learning centers work well for these students as a place in the classroom to go and engage in something exciting (if they finish an assignment early).

Leveling Assignments. Leveling an assignment is the process of differentiating expectations of quality and scope of an assignment depending on your students' individual abilities. While teachers sometimes worry that setting different standards for different students does not treat their students fairly, in fact, using strategies that tailor the assignment to the needs of a given student is both more fair and more effective than expecting the same thing from every student. The one concern here is that using this approach puts the burden on the teacher to accurately diagnose students' abilities, and not, for example, "shortchange" what a given student knows.

Theory Into Practice 4.6

Debating the "Fairness" of Gifted Education

Gifted and talented programs sometimes come under criticism for funneling additional resources to students who already tend to be privileged in a number of ways. While almost no one would argue that a student with a visual or a mobility impairment should not receive special services to accommodate his or her disability, some have argued that providing special services to gifted and talented students is simply compounding advantages these students already have and that those resources should be used, instead, to provide additional services to academically struggling students.

Imagine that you are a teacher who has been asked to defend the value of your school's gifted program to a parent who does not believe that the program is fair.

Think about how you might respond to this parent and then write a one-page paper outlining your argument in support of gifted education programs.

Summary

In this chapter, we have discussed a wide range of diversity issues that are likely to influence the way you teach. While we have focused this discussion on teaching and learning science, issues of diversity obviously stretch across all content areas. We began by discussing the history of diverse learners in the science classroom, highlighting issues of gender; racial, ethnic, and cultural diversity; socioeconomic status (SES); students with exceptionalities; and English language learners and how each of these groups has historically been underrepresented both in science practice and in receiving high-quality science education. We then discussed the current wave of science education reforms and how they have impacted the education of diverse learners. While standards-based reforms make strong claims about the desirability of promoting science education for all students, they are generally short on substantive suggestions for how best to bring these changes about.

We attempted to address this shortcoming of the reform documents by providing a variety of specific strategies that can be used with diverse learners in the science classroom. Again, we focus on five categories of diversity: gender; racial, ethnic, and cultural diversity; SES; students with disabilities; and English language learners. We also highlighted the special needs of gifted and talented students in the science classroom. Working with gifted students in a general education setting differs from working with students with special needs: Teachers must push students to go beyond the standards rather than help students to meet the standards.

One thing we hope has become clear in this chapter is that the concept of a "mainstream student," one who can be taught effectively without attending to issues of diversity, is a myth. Every student you have in your classroom every year is different, and each will have his or her own "special needs." Some of the strategies we have discussed in this chapter will be effective for working with some students, and other strategies will be effective with others. Our best advice is to get to know each of your students as well as you can. Learning about and trying to draw pedagogical connections to their cultural and linguistic backgrounds, their likes and dislikes, their goals and aspirations is every bit as important as considering strategies based on the more obvious categories of gender, race, or diagnosed special needs. It is easy to label students as "at risk" or "problem students." It is much more challenging to learn to work with these students in ways that acknowledge and build on their strengths while helping them learn to compensate for or overcome their weaknesses. This is the true meaning of teaching diverse students.

Student Study Site

The Companion Web site for *Teaching Science in Elementary and Middle School* http://www.sagepub.com/buxtonstudy

Visit the Web-based student study site to enhance your understanding of the chapter content and to discover additional resources that will take your learning one step further. You can enhance your understanding of the chapters by using the study materials, which include chapter objectives, flashcards, activities, practice tests, and more. You'll also find special features, such as Resources for Experiments, the Links to Standards from U.S. States and associated activities, Learning From Journal Articles, Theory Into Practice resources, Reflections on Science exercises, a Science Standards-Based Lesson Plan Project, and PRAXIS resources.

Reflections on Science

1. Think back to when you were a student in elementary school. What memories do you have of students with special needs in your classes? If you don't have many memories, why do you think this is?

2. Have you ever taken a basic conversation course in a foreign language? What topics did you cover? Have you ever taken an academic subject course in a foreign language? What topics did you cover? What is the difference between these two cases? How does this relate to the situation of English language learners you might have in your classroom?

3. Does science benefit everyone evenly? Why or why not? Are there patterns or trends in who benefits most? Might this be related to why some students are more enthusiastic about learning science than others?

4. Are there ways in which the standards-based reform movement has improved the educational opportunities in science for students with special needs? For English language learners? For girls? For racially, ethnically, and culturally diverse students? For students from low-SES backgrounds? Are there ways in which the standards-based reform movement has damaged or hindered the educational opportunities in science for students with special needs? For English language learners? For girls? For racially, ethnically, and culturally diverse students? For students from low-SES backgrounds? Explain.

Internet Connections: Science for Diverse Learners

Notable Hispanic Americans
http://www.factmonster.com/spot/hhmbio7
   .html

Notable African Americans
http://www.infoplease.com/spot/bhmbios1.html

Notable Native Americans
http://www.infoplease.com/spot/aihmbioaz
   .html

Notable Asian Americans
http://www.infoplease.com/spot/asianambios
   .html

American Association of University Women
   (AAUW)
http://www.aauw.org/

National Association of Bilingual Education (NABE)
http://www.nabe.org/

Teachers of English to Speakers of Other Languages (TESOL)
http://www.tesol.org/s_tesol/index.asp

Council for Exceptional Children
http://www.cec.sped.org//AM/Template.cfm? Section=Home

References

American Association for the Advancement of Science. (1993). *Benchmarks for science literacy.* Washington, DC: AAAS.

Atwater, M. M. (1993). Multicultural science education: Assumptions and alternate views. *The Science Teacher, 60*(3), 32–38.

Banks, J. (1995). Multicultural education: Historical development, dimensions and practice. In J. Banks (Ed.), *Handbook of research on multicultural education* (pp. 3–24). New York: Macmillan.

Brickhouse, N. (1994). Bringing in the outsiders: Reshaping the sciences of the future. *Journal of Curriculum Studies, 26*(4), 401–416.

D'Amato, J. D., & Tharp, R. G. (1997). *Culturally compatible educational strategies: Implications for native Hawaiian vocational education programs.* Honolulu, HI: Center for Studies of Multicultural Higher Education.

Duschl, R. (1988). Abandoning the scientistic legacy of science education. *Science Education, 72,* 51–62.

Gardner, H. (1993). *Multiple intelligences: The theory in practice.* New York: Basic Books.

Gardner, H. (1999). *Intelligence reframed: Multiple intelligences for the 21st century.* New York: Basic Books.

Good, R. (1995). Comments on multicultural science education. *Science Education, 79*(3), 335–336.

Howes, E. (1998). Connecting girls and science: A feminist teacher research study of a high school prenatal testing unit. *Journal of Research in Science Teaching, 35*(8), 877–896.

Loving, C. (1997). From the summit of truth to its slippery slopes: Science education's journey through positivist-postmodernist territory. *American Educational Research Journal, 34*(3), 421–452.

Mason, C. L., & Barba, R. H. (1992). Equal opportunity science. *Science Teacher, 59*(5), 23–26.

McBay, S. M. (1989). Improving education for minorities. *Issues in Science and Technology, 5*(4), 41–47.

National Research Council. (1996). *National science education standards.* Washington, DC: National Academy Press.

National Research Council. (2000). *Inquiry and the national science education standards: A guide for teaching and learning.* Washington, DC: National Academy Press.

Oakes, J. (1990). Opportunities, achievement, and choice: Women and minority students in science and mathematics. In C. B. Cazden (Ed.), *Review of research in education* (Vol. 16, pp. 153–221).

Washington, DC: American Educational Research Association.

Phillips, P. (1990). *The scientific lady: A social history of women's scientific interests 1520–1918*. New York: St. Martins Press.

Rosebery, A. S., Warren, B., & Conant, F. R. (1992). *Appropriating scientific discourse: Findings from language minority classrooms*. Santa Cruz, CA and Washington, DC: National Center for Research on Cultural Diversity and Second Language Learning.

Rosser, S. V. (1997). *Re-engineering female-friendly science*. New York: Teachers College Press.

Rosser, S. V. (2000). *Women, science and society: The crucial union*. New York: Teachers College Press.

Rossiter, M. (1997). Which science? Which women? In S. G. Kohlstedt & H. Longino (Eds.), *Women, gender and science: New directions* (pp. 169–185). Chicago: University of Chicago Press.

Rutherford, F. J., & Ahlgren, A. (1990). *Science for all Americans*. New York: Oxford University Press.

Seymour, E., & Hewitt, N. M. (1997). *Talking about leaving: Why undergraduates leave the sciences*. Boulder, CO: Westview Press.

Stanley, W., & Brickhouse, N. (1994). Multiculturalism, universalism and science education. *Science Education, 78*(4), 387–398.

Teresi, D. (2002). *Lost discoveries: The ancient roots of modern science—from the Babylonians to the Maya*. New York: Simon & Schuster.

Tonso, K. (1999). Engineering gender—gender engineering: A cultural model of belonging. *Journal of Women and Minorities in Science and Engineering, 5*(4), 365–405.

Traweek, S. (1989). *Beamtimes and lifetimes: The world of high-energy physicists*. Cambridge, MA: Harvard University Press.

Observing as a Scientist and as a Science Teacher

Consider the following statements about observation:

You can observe a lot just by watching.

—**Yogi Berra**

Reason, Observation, and Experience—the Holy Trinity of Science.

—**Robert G. Ingersoll**

All of us are watchers—of television, of time clocks, of traffic on the freeway—but few are observers. Everyone is looking, not many are seeing.

—**Peter M. Leschak**

Nothing has such power to broaden the mind as the ability to investigate systematically and truly all that comes under thy observation in life.

—**Marcus Aurelius**

It is the theory that decides what can be observed.

—**Albert Einstein**

🐝 Scientific Observation

Systematic and controlled observation is fundamental to scientific inquiry. But what is involved in observation for a scientist? Why is it important? Why is teaching students how to observe a crucial part of their training to think and reflect like scientists? What is involved in measuring and accurately recording information in a scientific context?

As with science, systematic and controlled observation is also critically important to the study of education. Learning to be a good teacher requires that you observe and reflect on what takes place in your classroom. This involves many of the same skills possessed by good scientists, who observe and measure the world around them and then try to make sense of what they have seen.

SOURCE: Courtesy of the National Library of Medicine (Wikimedia Commons, http://commons.wikimedia.org/wiki/Image-Francesco_Redi.jpg).

Image 5.1. Italian Scientist Francesco Redi (1626–1698)

What are the characteristics of scientific observation? How does scientific observation differ from the causal observations we make in our daily lives? To begin with, scientific observation is usually focused on a guiding question. An example can be found in the question of spontaneous generation.

During the Ancient and Medieval periods, it was believed that animals such as frogs and flies could be spontaneously created from inanimate matter such as mud or spoiled food. It was causally observed that maggots (flies in their larval state), for example, would appear on a slab of meat left sitting in the sun in a market. People concluded that the maggots were being spontaneously generated from the meat. Was this what was actually happening? In 1668, the Italian scientist Francesco Redi (1626–1698) conducted a controlled observational experiment (see Image 5.1).

His logic involved the following steps:

He observed. Maggots seem to grow spontaneously on the side of decaying meat in a market.

He asked. What was causing the maggots to appear on the side of the meat?

He observed further. Redi carefully watched the meat as it lay in the market stalls of butchers. He observed that flies frequently landed on the meat.

He hypothesized. Redi hypothesized that the flies could cause the maggots, but he could not control the flies sufficiently to see how they might be connected to the generation of the maggots.

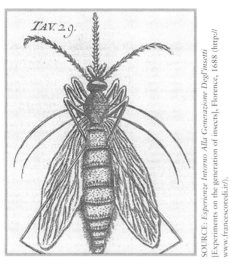

SOURCE: *Esperienze Intorno Alla Generazione Degl'insetti* [Experiments on the generation of insects], Florence, 1688 (http://www.francescoredi.it/).

Image 5.2. Illustration of a Fly

He controlled. Redi set up conditions in which he could control the degree of access the flies had to the meat by placing fresh meat in containers with different coverings.

He manipulated. Redi manipulated different variables by giving the flies access to the meat in some instances and denying them access in other cases.

He recorded. Redi recorded his observations in a systematic and precise way over a period of time (see Image 5.2).

He reflected and concluded. Redi reflected on what he had observed and recorded and came to the conclusion that the flies were laying eggs on the meat, which led to the appearance of the maggots.

Through his controlled observation of the flies and maggots, Redi created what is considered by many to be the first systematically controlled scientific experiments. Redi did not simply observe, he observed systematically, controlling in turn the different variables that might have affected what he was observing. It is also important to note that his observations were planned and guided by a prior theory he held: *Flies somehow generated the maggots found on the side of decaying meat.*

Theory Into Practice 5.1

Observation Experiment: Watching a Traffic Pattern

Have you even been waiting at a red light behind a line of other cars and wondered why, when the light turns green, you can't just all start moving forward at the same time? Theoretically, if all the drivers are paying attention and see the light turn green at the same instant, all the cars should be able to start to move simultaneously. But something else is going on here. Your assignment is to make careful and systematic observations to figure out what really happens.

Pick a fairly busy intersection at a time of day when traffic usually backs up.

After watching the traffic at the intersection for a few minutes, write down a hypothesis to explain why the cars at the light don't all start moving when the light turns green.

Develop a plan for systematically observing the cars in such a way that you will be able to test out your hypothesis.

Carry out your plan, making careful observations and recording your results.

Write a paragraph describing your findings and interpreting what they mean.

Observation in the Classroom

There are many introductory textbooks on doing observations in the classroom. In fact, you have probably already done observations as part of your fieldwork in other courses in your teacher education program. Observation in science classrooms is not necessarily different from other types of observation. You still need to be concerned about ethical issues (such as not compromising the privacy or rights of the people you are observing), getting yourself situated in an appropriate classroom or educational setting, keeping a record of your observations, and reflecting on the meaning of what you have observed.

In the context of observing the teaching of science, we will ask you to go back to the methods employed by scientists such as Francesco Redi to see whether you can follow many of the same steps. Let's suppose that you are asked by your instructor to observe patterns of behavior based on gender during hands-on science experiments. After watching a particular group of students in a classroom for several class sessions, you have noticed that most of the activity is being directed by the boys in the group. Let's imagine two boys and two girls grouped together to work on a project. The boys insist on running the experiments. When one of the girls gets involved in manipulating the experiment, the boys tell her she's doing it wrong and that she needs to "stop wrecking things." The girls are asked to keep notes and then write up the report that is due while the boys go off to use the class computer to search for pictures to include in the project.

Paralleling the steps that Redi took in his experiment with flies and maggots, you could take the following steps in conducting your own observational study:

You observe. Boys in this class seem to dominate the direction and manipulation of hands-on science activities.

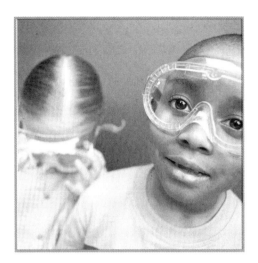

Image 5.3. Group work in the science classroom requires clearly defined norms of collaboration.

You ask. What classroom features are contributing to this uneven distribution of the opportunity to learn?

You observe further. The teacher has not posted a list of norms or expectations for collaborative group work, has not assigned students within groups to identifiable roles (e.g., materials manager, principal investigator, recorder, reporter), has assigned students to groups randomly by "counting off" rather than intentionally based on what she knows about the learners as individuals, and fails to move about the room to monitor student interactions.

You hypothesize. You hypothesize that by putting clear and explicit teacher expectations in place regarding collaborative group work, boys and girls will be more likely to engage more equitably in all aspects of the investigative process over time (see Image 5.3). However, because you are only observing the classroom you are not yet in a position to test your hypothesis.

You control. During later visits to the same classroom, you are allowed to conduct your own science lessons. You set up conditions to test your hypothesis by preparing several instructional strategies, such as intentionally assigning students to groups based on learner characteristics, explicitly stating expectations for group work, and assigning each student in a group to a specific role for that lesson.

You manipulate. During each of the science lessons you teach, you implement one of the selected instructional strategies to study the effect on group interactions.

You record. During each lesson you make careful and systematic observations of how the various groups in the class interact, focusing especially on who is manipulating the physical materials.

You reflect and conclude. You study and reflect on your observation notes from each of the class lessons and conclude that each of the instructional strategies appears to have had some positive impact on increasing the constructive engagement of the girls in the class, and that some strategies seem to be more effective for some students and other strategies for other students. You wonder what would be the effect of combining several strategies together. You decide that further observation and experimentation is needed. You plan to adjust your future classroom teaching based on what you have learned.

From Observation to Assessment of Science Learning

One of the jobs a teacher is expected to perform is to assess student learning. While assessment of science learning is not substantively different from assessment of the other content areas, the science teacher's focus on observation is well-suited to reflecting upon a range of assessment opportunities that arise in the classroom on a daily basis. When most people think about assessment in the context of science education, they tend to remember difficult exams on seemingly obscure science content that they were subjected to in their own schooling. While tests and exams are certainly a legitimate part of a well-rounded assessment plan, the current thinking on assessment in science education is clear: restricting assessment to the traditional model of homework, quizzes, and a final exam is insufficient. The research on learning that was discussed in Chapter 3 points to the need to better align assessment with the breadth and depth of our teaching goals.

The overarching goal of assessment is to help the teacher understand to what degree students have or have not gained mastery of the instructional goals and objectives. A secondary purpose of assessment is to help direct and focus future instruction by assessing students' prior knowledge. A third purpose of assessment is to provide instruction in its own right; that is, good assessment should teach the students something, rather than just measure what they already know.

Thus, one model of organizing assessment considers these three purposes and builds an assessment framework of **diagnostic assessment** (sometimes called pre-assessment), **formative assessment** (sometimes called ongoing assessment), and **summative assessment** (sometimes called cumulative or post-assessment).

Diagnostic assessment is done at the beginning of a new instructional unit or theme. It is meant to provide the teacher with information about what her students already know about the topic to be studied. Teachers who regularly engage in diagnostic assessment are routinely surprised, both by things that some students already know and by things that were assumed to be widely known, yet of which students are completely ignorant. Assessment strategies that are well-suited to diagnostic assessment include quizzes, interviews, concept maps, journal entries, and small-group discussions. While a whole-class discussion will give you some ideas about the prior knowledge of some of your students, the disadvantage of whole-class discussion is that unless you manage the discussion very strategically, there will be a number of students who do not contribute to the discussion. Thus, in reality you are only getting a diagnostic assessment of a subsection of the class, and this subsection might not be representative of the prior knowledge of the class as a whole.

Formative assessment should be ongoing throughout a unit of study. Formative assessment is critical for a proactive teacher who is committed to promoting the learning of all her students. In traditional assessment, primarily done at the end of the unit, a teacher may only find out that a given student has failed to understand the topic when that student fails the exam. At this point, it is too late to provide adequate help and support for that student because it is time to move on to the next topic. Formative assessment is meant to reduce this problem by allowing the teacher to identify students' confusion and misunderstandings with time enough to address them through continued instruction on the topic. Assessment strategies that are well-suited for formative assessment include homework (but only if the teacher checks for accuracy and not just for completeness), journal entries, exit slips (students must write down one thing they learned or one question they have on a slip of paper and hand it to the teacher as they exit the room), short class presentations, interview or small-group discussions, quizzes, lab reports, performance assessments (having the student demonstrate the use of some tool or technique), or running records (where the teacher circulates with a clipboard as the students are working and looks for evidence of a particular skill or idea).

Finally, summative assessment attempts to gain a more comprehensive picture of the degree to which each student has gained mastery of the key concepts addressed in a unit or theme. Although the traditional method of summative assessment is the final exam, teachers with a large assessment repertoire will often use other summative assessment strategies in place of, or in addition to, an exam. When you consider your learning goals for a unit of study, you are likely to conclude that in addition to learning goals about specific science content and concepts, you also have learning goals that have to do with processes of inquiry, with the use of tools and techniques, and with scientific habits or reasoning skills. While an exam may be appropriate for measuring mastery of the conceptual goals, it is much less suited to assessing the other goals. Assessment strategies that may prove useful include class presentations (with or without multimedia aids such as PowerPoint slideshows), research projects or papers, performance assessments (demonstration of how to use a tool or technique), a drama or play, a video or photo project, a concept map, a peer teaching lesson given to a younger group of students, a portfolio, a mock scientific conference, a debate, or a class-wide exhibit or museum display that could be shared with parents or other classes.

It is beyond the scope of this book to provide a thorough treatment of how to make use of all of the assessment strategies mentioned here. In fact, if your teacher preparation program is like most, you have had or will have an entire course devoted to the topic of assessment. For now, let it suffice to say that in addition to curriculum (what to teach) and instruction (how to teach), a thoughtful and reflective teacher will spend a great deal of time considering assessment (how well your students have learned, and by extension, how well you have taught them). A consideration of the ideas presented in this chapter will help you become a more astute assessor of your students' learning and of your own teaching.

Field Experiences, Peer Teaching, and Other Opportunities to Practice the Craft of Science Teaching

Going into classrooms and critically observing what is taking place is essential to begin to understand the social, cultural, and academic components of a teacher's life in the classroom. If you follow the kind of structured observational procedures that are outlined above, you will be conducting a type of basic controlled research (often referred to as "teacher action research") that includes many of the elements of good scientific data collection (see Chapter 10 for a more detailed discussion of action research).

Making the most of learning in the field requires not just scientific skills, however, but also diplomatic and human skills. You will need to situate yourself in a school or classroom setting. Entering into a classroom to do observations, you will need to use social skills that mark you as a professional. Politely introducing yourself, being discreet about the data you collect and analyze, being on time, and not interfering with the flow of normal classroom activity are just a few of the skills you will need to use.

If you are in a typical teacher education program, it is likely that your earliest experiences in fieldwork will be limited to basic observations in a traditional classroom. As you gain experience, you will move on to other types of field experiences such as one-on-one tutoring, small-group instruction, and finally, teaching in front of a full class. You may also find yourself working in less formal teaching settings, such as museums and summer camps.

Even if you are actively teaching, you can always be observing. One of the most important things that good teachers do is self-monitor their work. Often, this is done unconsciously and involves reflecting on the effectiveness of a lesson, how one is interacting with a particularly challenging student or group of students, whether or not learning materials are up to date and interesting, and many other features a teacher must manage. A journal of your teaching experience can be an invaluable data source in your effort to become a reflective and self-correcting practitioner.

To begin to develop these skills and habits, you may want to team up with another teacher education student and observe and critique each other's work. By engaging in a critique of each other's practice, you can go beyond yourself and learn much more about what you are actually doing in the classroom. An outside observer, for example, might see that you favor certain students over others during classroom discussion, or that you are not really clear when you explain certain materials. A careful and observant critic forces us to move beyond our biases and the ingrown habits we inevitably develop.

An essential part of a teaching field experience or practicum is the opportunity to reflect on the experience afterward. Teachers spend all day working with children, but unless they take the extra time to reflect on what they have done and why, it is possible that they will learn very little from the experience that will help them to become a better teacher. Practicum teaching experiences are intended to build on participants' prior learning, helping to reinforce and enhance the professional growth of beginning teachers. The general goals of such experiences should include the following:

1. They should help you reflect on your teaching experiences. In particular, they should improve your ability to consider how the practical aspects of teaching relate to larger theoretical issues. For instance, you might explore how the content and style of a particular lesson relates (or does not relate) to the "track" or socioeconomic status of the students you are teaching, or to your theoretical views on learning and teaching. This objective will be especially relevant if you are constructing a teaching portfolio because reflections that allow you to synthesize theory and practice are an essential component of a portfolio.

2. They should support you in exploring and developing your professional teacher identity.

3. They should promote professional and collegial communication among beginning and experienced teachers.

4. They should provide opportunities for discussing current or complicated educational issues, such as
   o Content area issues. What happens, for example, when you are expected to teach a topic with which you are unfamiliar?
   o Questions of professional responsibility and roles. For instance, how does a student teacher "respectfully disagree" with her or his mentor teacher?
   o Educational accountability. How do state accountability measures such as "high stakes" testing influence curriculum, instruction, and assessment?

5. They should help student teachers learn from students.

Observational Forms

Included here are some model observation forms that you may find helpful in conducting your field observations. They are specifically geared toward science education. Copy the forms to use in the field. We also recommend that you get a "field notebook" of some kind in which to keep your notes because individual sheets of paper can easily be lost.

Theory Into Practice 5.2

Science Lesson Observation Form

School (Use a Coded Name):	*Observer:*
Grade:	*Date:*
Science Subject or Area:	*Time In:* *Time Out:*

Directions: Observe a science class in which the students are participating in an experiment or hands-on activity.

Answer as many of the following questions as you can. Add your own questions as you see fit. Use the back of your observation form if you have a more extended observation or set of comments.

1. Note down as much as you can about what is taking place in the classroom.

2. Is anyone directing the lesson?

3. How do children interact with the instructor?

4. How do they interact with each other?

5. What are the goals of the lesson? Are they explicit?

6. What are the instructional strategies (lecture, supervised experiment, discussion, etc.) used during the lesson? Approximately how much time is devoted to each of these strategies?

7. Is creativity encouraged or discouraged? In what ways?

8. Do certain students stand out or fade away in the classroom? If yes, why?

9. What external factors seem to influence what occurs in the classroom?

10. Does the teacher demonstrate an adequate conceptual understanding of the subject content being taught in the lesson?

11. What overall teaching philosophy seems to underlie the instruction? For example, does the lesson seem to present science as a body of facts to be learned, a process of inquiry, a set of standards, or something else? Describe.

12. Are the students engaged in what they are doing? All students? Some more than others? Why might this be?

13. Do students have opportunities to take initiative in terms of their learning? How?

14. Do there appear to be students with special needs in the class? English language learners? Students with disabilities? What strategies or accommodations does the teacher use or provide to support the learning of these students?

15. Does the teacher have problems with discipline? What management strategies are used?

16. Is this a classroom in which you would have wanted to be a student when you were younger? Why or why not?

17. What type of language does the teacher model? Does it reflect scientific terminology and constructs? What analogies or models (if any) are used to explain complex concepts?

Summary Reflections: Review and reflect on your answers to the above questions and then summarize in the space below what you have learned from your classroom observation.

Theory Into Practice 5.3

Observing in a Science Museum
or Other Non-School Setting

School (Use a Coded Name):	Observer:
Grade:	Date:
Science Subject or Area:	Time In: Time Out:

Directions: Conduct this observation in a science museum, children's museum, or other informal education facility.

Answer as many of the following questions as you can. Add your own questions as you see fit. Use the back of your observation form if you have more extended observations or comments.

1. What is the museum's primary focus?

2. How do students interact with the content of the exhibits?

3. Is there a particular set of values, or point of view, that can clearly be seen in the exhibit (e.g., the need to create a world where natural resources are conserved)?

4. Is the language used to communicate scientific concepts accurate and clear? What age of student does it seem to be aimed at?

5. If a docent (museum guide) is leading a lesson, is she or he effective or ineffective? Why?

6. Is there cross-age (older and younger children learning together) or intergenerational (e.g., parents or grandparents and children learning together) interaction? If so, what does it look like?

7. Is there any evidence of racial, ethnic, cultural, and/or gender diversity expressed in any of the exhibits? If not, are there ways that more diversity could have been included?

8. If there are hands-on activities in the museum, are children reading or paying attention to the accompanying explanations, or are they simply running from one activity to the next?

9. How much learning do you think is actually taking place? What evidence do you have to support your perception?

10. Can you think of anything that would further enhance the learning experience in the museum? Could this realistically be added?

Summary Reflections: Review and reflect on your answers to the above questions and then summarize in the space below what you have learned from your museum observation.

Theory Into Practice 5.4

Interviewing a Teacher
After Observing a Science Lesson

School (Use a Coded Name):	*Observer:*
Grade:	*Date:*
Science Subject or Area:	*Time In:* *Time Out:*
Teacher Name (Use a Coded Name):	

Use the following interview questions to talk to a teacher after you have observed him or her teaching a science lesson. Ideally, the interview should take place as soon after the lesson as possible so that the details of the lesson are still fresh in your minds. Use the probe questions to get additional information if the answers to the initial questions are lacking in detail. You may decide to write down the teacher's responses in a notebook or else ask the teacher to allow you to record the conversation on a tape recorder. You can then listen to the tape and transcribe it at a convenient time.

1. Is this lesson a good example of the kind of work that you typically have your students do in science?

Probe:
      a. If yes, what makes it a good example?
      b. If no, why not? What would a better example look like?

2. What were the science ideas that you were trying to teach during the lesson?

Probe:
      a. What concepts were you trying to teach?
      b. What skills or abilities were you trying to teach?

3. What strategies did you use to try to promote your students' understanding of the science concepts in this lesson?

4. What strategies did you use to try to promote your students' use of inquiry in this lesson?

5. How well do you think your students understood the science concepts in this lesson?

Probe:
    a. How can you tell this?
    b. What learning difficulties, if any, did you notice with your students?

6. How well do you think your students engaged in the process of science inquiry in this lesson?

Probe:
    a. How can you tell this?
    b. What learning difficulties, if any, did you notice with your students?

7. Where do you think your students' understanding of science comes from?

Probe:
    a. Is it all from what you teach or does some of it come from other places? Where?

8. Do you think that your students will have a chance to use anything they learned in this lesson in their everyday lives? Why?

9. Was there a student who surprised you with his or her prior knowledge about the lesson or in how well he or she understood the lesson's main points?

Probe:
    a. If yes, what did the student do? Why did that surprise you?

Summary Reflections: Review and reflect on the teacher's answers to your interview questions. Write a detailed reflection on what you have learned from this teacher interview.

🐝 Beyond Observation: Other Science Process Skills

Science teachers often distinguish between science concepts and science processes. Science concepts are the ideas and discoveries that are the cumulative product of scientific investigation over time. Force, chemical elements, **photosynthesis**, and the rock cycle are all examples of science concepts. When people think about science, they most likely think about science concepts. Many of these fundamental science concepts are explored in Part II of this text. While science concepts account for most of the useful outcomes of science, these concepts cannot be explored and discovered except through the processes of science inquiry. Much of the discussion in Part I of this text has focused on how science gets done through inquiry processes. Thus, teachers of science must help their students understand that science is composed of these two parts—concepts and processes—and that the two are inextricably linked. The process of science inquiry leads to the discovery of new science concepts, and these new concepts lead, in turn, to new lines of science inquiry.

Thus far, this chapter has focused primarily on observation. Observation is one of the fundamental science process skills, but there are others that are equally important for conducting science inquiry.

Classifying. Classifying involves the grouping or ordering of objects or events into categories. These categories can be based on a range of properties or criteria. Classifying is fundamental to much of science because organization into categories makes it easier for scientists to see patterns and to explore similarities and differences. For example, living organisms are divided into a detailed classification system developed by the Swedish zoologist Carl Linnaeus (1707–1778). The Linnaean classification system of kingdom, phylum, class, order, family, genus, and species is still used to organize living things (see Experiment 33 in Chapter 7). While scientific classification can be very complex, even young children can begin to learn and practice the science process skill of classification.

Inferring. **Inferring** involves drawing a conclusion about something based on previously gathered information. For example, if a dish of water is left under a heat lamp and there is less water the next day, one can infer that water evaporated from the dish. There are other possible explanations for the decrease in water, but there is reason to believe, based on previously gathered information, that evaporation is the cause. Once students have learned to observe carefully, they can begin to draw inferences from their observations.

Predicting. Predicting involves stating an outcome for some future event based on past experience, observation, or other evidence. In science, predicting is often used synonymously with hypothesizing. While a prediction or hypothesis is much like a guess, the distinction that students must understand is that guesses can be random but predictions must be based on some evidence. For example, when rolling toy cars down a ramp covered by different textures, students might use their past experiences riding a bike or rollerblading to predict that the toy car will travel more quickly down a smooth piece of plastic than down a piece of artificial grass or a piece of sandpaper. Making predictions is an important science process skill that should be incorporated into most science experiments.

Measuring. Measuring involves the use of a variety of tools to quantify the dimensions of an object or event. Standard measurements appropriate for the elementary science classroom include length, weight, **volume**, temperature, time, speed, and **density**. Students need to learn to use the appropriate tools for each type of measurement, such as a ruler or tape measure for length, various types of scales and balances for weight, graduated cylinders and measuring cups for volume, thermometers for temperature, and so on. The other important aspect of measurement is that in the United States, both the metric and the imperial (British) systems of measurement are used, and students should become familiar with both. Additionally, estimating, or approximating a measurement without using a measurement tool, is a useful and related science process skill.

Communicating. Communicating what has been learned during an experiment is an essential science process skill. Communication can take many forms: words, tables, graphs, diagrams, models, concept maps, and many other types of symbolic representations. Communication about scientific findings generally emphasizes **precision**, clarity, and conciseness. Each of the science disciplines has its own technical vocabulary in which words have very specific meanings—meanings that sometimes differ from their everyday use. For example, the word "force" has a wide range of everyday meanings, but to a physicist, force has a very specific meaning: the product of the **mass** of an object multiplied by its acceleration. Elementary students can begin to learn this process skill of communicating scientifically.

In conclusion, there are a number of science process skills that students should begin to develop as part of an elementary-grade science program. When science is taught using a hands-on, inquiry-based approach, it is relatively easy to incorporate a range of these process skills. If science is taught primarily through a didactic lecture, text, and worksheet approach, however, students are likely to learn science concepts with little understanding of the processes that have led to the development of those concepts.

Creating a Science Educator's Portfolio

In recent years, teaching portfolios have come into widespread use in teacher education programs. Essentially, a portfolio is a compilation of your professional work. It can include lesson plans, personal reflections, observations, and even poetry or art. It is a tool for your professional development and potentially of value for your development as a teacher of science.

Portfolios are an example of "authentic assessment." The idea behind authentic assessment is to evaluate people by assessing things that actually take place in the real world. Thus, a teaching portfolio could include lesson plans that would actually be used in your teaching or observations of real classrooms and what takes place in them. Authentic assessment is often contrasted with traditional testing of students for right or wrong answers.

Perhaps you are already creating portfolio materials in other courses. You might be using an electronic portfolio system to create a record of your work or collecting artifacts in three-ring binders. A science teaching portfolio is much like any teaching portfolio; it will be a record of your development as a science teacher, one that can serve as an important professional development tool. A portfolio should represent you as a teacher—your teaching philosophy and style. Further, both the portfolio itself and the process of creating it should provide a stimulus for reflection on your teaching and on your developing identity as a teacher. A secondary purpose of the portfolio is as a document to be used in your search for a teaching position. It should serve this purpose well by providing potential employers with insight into your philosophy, experience, and skills as an educator.

Most teacher education programs require students to begin a portfolio during their coursework in teacher education and then to complete the portfolio during the semester in which they complete their student teaching or internship. Consequently, the portfolio represents a long-term work in progress. If you are planning to teach science, then you will naturally wish for your portfolio to have a science teaching focus. If, however, like most readers of this text, you are in an elementary generalist program and the teaching of science is just one facet of the teaching position you wish to have, then the teaching of science will play just one part in a more general portfolio.

Portfolio Content and Structure

There are many ways to structure and organize a portfolio. The model we present here is one that we have found to be particularly effective. Many states now have a list of key themes or practices in which all teachers are required to become proficient. For example, in the state of Colorado, these themes are Knowledge of Content and Learning, Communication, Assessment, Democratic Ideal, and Diversity. In the state of Florida there are twelve themes, including topics such as Critical Thinking, Continuous Improvement, Ethics, and Technology. While it may be a requirement in your state or program to include sections in your portfolio demonstrating competencies in all areas required by your state, we believe it is most useful to emphasize those themes that seem most central to your emerging professional philosophy as a teacher. Thus, if you plan to work primarily in inner city, multicultural settings with low-income children, issues related to diversity and social justice may be a particular focus in your portfolio.

What should a portfolio look like? We have included a model below that we think will serve most education students well. Use it as you see fit. Your program will very likely dictate at least some aspects of a format you should follow. Thus, the materials included below are meant to serve as ideas for how your portfolio can help you to be reflective about learning to teach.

Professional Statement and Portfolio Introduction

The first section of the portfolio serves as an introduction and guide for persons reading your portfolio. It should contain a relatively brief professional statement (one or two pages), a description of your teaching context (added once you are involved in student teaching), and a "reader's guide" to your portfolio.

Professional Statement. This statement should present your current (and evolving) philosophy of education. It may include a personal statement about why you have decided to become a teacher. It is essentially a reflective piece.

Teaching Context. This statement will help your reader get a clear picture of the various experiences you have had in your teacher education program and, more specifically, the classes and field settings in which you have worked. This section should provide a brief, nonjudgmental description of characteristics of the schools you have worked in, the length and nature of the experiences you have had, the cooperating teachers you have worked with, general descriptions of the students and classrooms you've worked in, and any other information you believe would help a reader understand the teaching/learning materials that follow.

Reader's Guide. This component provides an overview of the remaining sections, to guide the reader. It should be more than a table of contents; include, for example, a few sentences about each section that tie it to your professional statement or a concept map that shows the relationships between the various sections of the portfolio.

Professional Development Themes

Depending on your state or program requirements, there will be a number of sections exploring important themes about teaching and learning. Each of these theme sections should include the following types of information:

Theoretical Discussion. A statement elaborating your ideas about teaching and learning as it relates to the theme. This statement might be an expansion of a portion of your Professional Statement.

Practical Examples. These should include several examples of your experiences that highlight aspects of the professional development theme. For example, a section on Critical Thinking might include your description of the development of a series of hands-on activities showing students how to break paradigms or think outside the box.

Artifacts and Student Work. Provide samples of instructional materials (e.g., handouts, lesson plans) and student work associated with the teaching and learning activities you have described. Again, be sure to make explicit the connections between these artifacts and the professional development theme in question. That is, what do these artifacts say about you as a teacher in regard to the professional development theme? An example in science education for the theme of assessment would be your use of a scoring rubric that you actually used to evaluate the performance of students on a particular piece of work. You could include examples of student work with the completed evaluations. You could emphasize aspects of the evaluation, such as the range of scores by students, the rationale underlying student responses, and potential diagnoses for improved instruction. Remember that whenever you include student work you have an ethical obligation to protect student identities. Be sure to cross out any identifying information that might compromise the confidentiality of the student whose evaluation you are including in your portfolio.

Reflections. From a professional development perspective, your reflections on teaching and learning activities and associated materials are generally the most important part of the portfolio. This may not be the section that a reader is likely to focus on—the practical examples and artifacts are more visually interesting. However, in our experience, it is in writing these reflections and making explicit the connections between your theoretical ideas and your practical experience that you will learn the most.

Theory Into Practice 5.5

Looking at Electronic Portfolios

A quick search of the Internet will bring up literally thousands of examples of electronic teaching portfolios from students and teachers all over the country. Looking at other people's portfolios is a good way to reflect on the value of portfolios as well as to get some ideas about effective designs and layouts.

Use the Internet to locate three electronic teaching portfolios to review. Read through each of the three portfolios, and answer the following questions:

What do the portfolios tell you about what each teacher values the most?

What do the portfolios tell you about how each teacher thinks about instruction? About assessment?

What design features of each portfolio did you find to be particularly effective or ineffective in communicating the teacher's knowledge or beliefs?

Summary

This chapter explored the importance of observation (as well as other science process skills) in becoming an effective teacher of science. We began with a discussion of the qualities and the process of scientific observation, using Francesco Redi's famous observational experiment as an observational framework. We then explored how this same framework for scientific observation can be applied to making careful observations in the classroom. We discussed the importance of classroom field experiences as part of your professional development and emphasized the relationship between observation and reflection. We then provided a series of observation forms that can be used during classroom observations. These forms include a series of questions to help you get the most out of your observations. We discussed other science process skills that are complementary to scientific observation. Finally, we presented the purpose and structure of a teaching portfolio and included a model portfolio structure and a discussion of the value of electronic portfolios.

Student Study Site

The Companion Web site for *Teaching Science in Elementary and Middle School* http://www.sagepub.com/buxtonstudy

Visit the Web-based student study site to enhance your understanding of the chapter content and to discover additional resources that will take your learning one step farther. You can enhance your understanding of the chapters by using the study materials, which include chapter objectives, flashcards, activities, practice tests, and more. You'll also find special features, such as Resources for Experiments, the Links to Standards from U.S. States and associated activities, Learning From Journal Articles, Theory Into Practice resources, Reflections on Science exercises, a Science Standards-Based Lesson Plan Project, and PRAXIS resources.

Reflections on Science

1. Observation can involve more than just your sense of sight. Close your eyes and spend five minutes using your other senses to "observe." Write down everything you noticed with each of your other senses.

2. Children learn through observation from the time they are newborns (maybe even before that). Watch a baby for several minutes. What does he or she seem to be observing? Are there some things that seem to catch his or her attention more than other things? What does this imply about how babies learn?

3. Portfolios are just one way to document what you are learning about becoming a teacher. What are some other ways to evaluate what a teacher is learning? Do you think there is too much emphasis placed on teaching portfolios in your teacher preparation program? Why or why not?

Internet Connections: Scientific Observation

Characteristics of Scientific Observation
http://www.ccny.cuny.edu/bbpsy/modules/ char_of_sci_obs.htm

Scientific Observation for Kids
http://www.historyforkids.org/learn/science/ observation.htm

Additional Classroom Observation Tools
http://depts.washington.edu/cidrweb/Obs Tools.htm

Ideas for and Links to Electronic Portfolios
http://www.eduscapes.com/tap/topic82.htm

Part II
Teaching and Learning the Science Disciplines

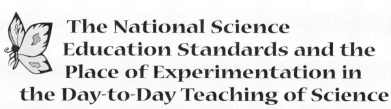

The National Science Education Standards and the Place of Experimentation in the Day-to-Day Teaching of Science

In Chapter 4 we briefly discussed the National Science Education Standards (NSES) and how they relate to questions of diversity in the science classroom. In this Introduction, we provide an overview of the standards as they relate to Part II of this text, "Teaching and Learning the Science Disciplines." Fundamental to the NSES is the idea that science education reforms must be systemic rather than piecemeal. By systemic, we mean that all components of the educational system must change together and synergistically if fundamental reforms are to be successful over the long term. If only one part of the system (e.g., content or assessment) is changed, that change is unlikely to be sustained in an effective way.

The six components of science education discussed in the NSES are science teaching, teacher professional development, assessment, science content, science education programs (at the school or school district level), and science education systems (at the state, national, and even international levels). Despite this call for systemic change in the National Standards, at the state, local, and classroom levels recent reform efforts have focused primarily on only one of these six components, science content. The science standards and benchmarks that have been adopted by most states and districts have centered on the overarching question of what science concepts should be taught to students and at what grade levels.

This focus on science content is perhaps only natural, as it is content rather than other aspects of the science education system that is being assessed by the high-stakes testing and accountability measures that are sweeping the nation. The other five components of the system play supporting roles in the development of high-quality science education programs. The reader will have noticed that Part I of this book dealt primarily with the other components of the system (science teaching, teacher professional development, assessment, science education programs, and science education systems). Part II turns to the question of science content for the elementary teacher.

One of the primary reasons we set out to write this book was to deal with science content as an integral part of learning to teach science. Many science methods texts have traditionally settled for providing an overview of the content standards outlined in the NSES, often with some examples of model lessons for addressing selected content standards. The rationale for this minimal treatment of content is that science content should be the purview of courses taken in the natural sciences, while methods courses should focus on how the teacher should make use of this content. While we agree that science content

courses taken in colleges of arts and sciences should indeed play a significant role in a teacher's development of science content knowledge, we are also aware that the organization, structure, and approach taken in most college and university science courses is very different from the assumptions that underlie the NSES. It is critical to understand that the NSES is driven by a focus on promoting science literacy for all K–12 students through an in-depth study of select topics, with a strong emphasis on science inquiry. In contrast, college science courses, especially the introductory survey courses that most pre-service elementary teachers take for general university requirements, survey a broad range of disciplinary topics and concepts, predominantly in a lecture format. This is meant to lay a foundation for science majors to build upon in subsequent classes—courses that non-science majors will likely not take. A separate lab section is often a requirement, but the approach taken in these labs is frequently one of cookbook-style verification exercises rather than one of critical scientific inquiry.

Thus, we set out to write a book that, in addition to considering the other components of a high-quality science teaching methods book, would provide elementary and middle-grade teachers with a more robust content framework from which they can develop their science teaching. While we agree that it is impossible to teach all the science content that an elementary or middle school teacher needs to know in one science teaching methods course, we have included 100 core experiments, both historical and contemporary, organized according to the four traditional branches of science (physics, chemistry, biology, and Earth and space science). Each of these experiments teaches a key science concept. When taken together, they provide at least a basic foundation for literacy in each of the principal science content areas. We are particularly interested in this approach because we feel that it also strongly correlates with the basic science experiments elementary and middle school teachers are likely to wish to teach in their classrooms.

The four chapters in Part II of this book each address one of the main science disciplines and provide core experiments and explanations of underlying concepts. The teacher (or student) who works his or her way through each of these experiments (and the other materials in these chapters) will have taken a major step toward achieving scientific literacy as described in the NSES.

While the NSES serves as an overarching model for what science education in the United States should look like, individual states each have their own standards. In order to explore the state standards to which you will be held accountable in your classroom, you will need to visit the Web sites for your state. Because these standards are frequently revised at the state level, we suggest that you find them online. A list of links to state department of education homepages is included below. Each of these sites has links to the state's specific academic standards for science. If your state is not included, you should easily be able to find the relevant links using an Internet search engine.

State Departments of Education

Alabama Department of Education
http://www.alsde.edu/html/home.asp

Arizona Department of Education
http://www.ade.az.gov/

California Department of Education
http://www.cde.ca.gov/

Colorado Department of Education
http://www.cde.state.co.us/

Florida Department of Education
http://www.fldoe.org/Default.asp?bhcp=1

Illinois State Board of Education
http://www.isbe.state.il.us/

Indiana Department of Education
http://www.doe.state.in.us/

Kentucky Department of Education
http://www.education.ky.gov/KDE/Default.htm

Massachusetts Department of Education
http://www.doe.mass.edu/

Michigan Department of Education
http://www.michigan.gov/mde

Mississippi Department of Education
http://www.mde.k12.ms.us/

New Jersey Department of Education
http://www.state.nj.us/education/

New York State Department of Education
http://www.nysed.gov/

North Carolina Department of Public Instruction
http://www.dpi.state.nc.us/

Ohio Department of Education
http://www.ode.state.oh.us/

Oklahoma State Department of Education
http://www.sde.state.ok.us/home/defaultns.html

Pennsylvania Department of Education
   Academic Standards
http://www.pde.state.pa.us/stateboard_ed/site/
   default.asp

Tennessee Department of Education
http://www.state.tn.us/education/

Texas Education Agency
http://www.tea.state.tx.us/

Virginia Department of Education
http://www.pen.k12.va.us/

Washington Office of Public Instruction
http://www.k12.wa.us/

Wisconsin Department of Public Instruction
http://www.dpi.state.wi.us/index.html

You will find that if you compare the standards from one state to another, most will be quite similar. The reason for this is that nearly all of the state standards are derived from the national science standards developed by groups such as the American Association for the Advancement of Science (AAAS; http://www.aaas.org/), the National Science Teachers Association (NSTA; http://www.nsta.org/), and the National Research Council (NRC; http://www.nationalacademies.org/nrc/). This is why it is possible to use a basic science text book in Georgia and use the same text book in California or Alaska. Despite this overall similarity, a trend in recent years in science education is to add materials specific to different geographic regions. Florida, for example, with its unique weather and geography, has materials addressing the Everglades, hurricanes, and the Gulf Stream—topics that are obviously not as relevant to students in Minnesota or Oregon. Thus, while the experiments in Part II of this text are relevant for students in any state,

as a teacher, you will also need to be aware of how the science content you teach is aligned with your own state standards.

A Note on the Importance of Safety When Doing Hands-On Inquiry-Based Science

Doing hands-on science is fun and engaging but can also be a safety risk for students. Teachers need to select safe science activities and make sure that proper safety procedures are followed in the classroom. Safety rules should be made clear to students, should be posted in the classroom, and should be included, as appropriate, in activity handouts. The following checklist is meant to help you consider some of the safety issues associated with doing hands-on inquiry-based science.

General Science Safety Checklist

All students should read and sign a lab safety contract at the start of the year. A copy should be sent home to the parent or guardian.

- All students should wear proper safety goggles when chemicals, glassware, or heat are used.
- Safety Rules should be posted in the classroom.
- All chemicals should be in clearly labeled containers and should be both stored and disposed of properly. Check

with your school district science support personnel if you are unsure of the safe way to dispose of any chemicals or other used science materials that could be hazardous.

- An emergency exit/escape plan should be posted.

- Live animals, whether class pets or experimental subjects, must be treated with care and respect.

- Potentially dangerous animals should not be brought into the classroom except under expert supervision.

- Teachers should always try an experiment ahead of time to identify possible dangers before allowing their students to do the experiment in class.

- Safety instructions should be discussed before beginning an experiment.

- Constant surveillance and supervision of students during experiments is essential.

- No one should be allowed to eat or drink in the classroom while science experiments are being done.

- Heat-safety items such as safety tongs and mittens should be used whenever materials are being heated.

- Teachers should set good safety examples when doing demonstrations and experiments by following all the safety guidelines that their students are expected to follow.

- Rough play or mischief should not be permitted in science classrooms or labs.

- Long hair and loose clothing should be pulled back when using heat or chemicals.

- Students should never conduct independent experiments that have not been approved by the teacher.

- Make certain all hot plates and burners are turned off when leaving the laboratory or classroom.

- The teacher should ensure that all lab equipment is in proper working order before allowing students to use it.

- Workspaces should be cleared of other materials before beginning a science experiment.

- Students should learn the proper way to check for odors or fumes using a wafting motion of the hand towards the nose rather than by sticking their nose close to the substance.

- Students should learn that many plants have poisonous parts and should be handled with care.

The following Web sites contain additional information on safety in the science classroom:

MSDS Online:
http://www.msdsonline.com

NSTA Lab Science:
http://www.nsta.org/positionstatement&psid=16

Flinn Scientific Safety Pages:
http://www.flinnsci.com

Environmental Protection Agency:
http://www.epa.gov

Centers for Disease Control:
http://www.cdc.gov

Understanding and Teaching Earth and Space Sciences

6

Consider the following statements about Earth and space sciences:

We learn geology the morning after the earthquake.

—**Ralph Waldo Emerson**

The primary role of the geologist is to recognize the existence of phenomena before trying to explain them.

—**B.M. Keilhau, 1828**

Finally we shall place the Sun himself at the center of the Universe. All this is suggested by the system of procession of events and the harmony of the whole Universe, if only we face the facts, as they say, "with eyes wide open."

—**Nicolas Copernicus**

Telescopes are in some ways like time machines. They reveal galaxies so far away that their light has taken billions of years to reach us. We in astronomy have an advantage in studying the universe, in that we can actually see the past.

—**Sir Martin Rees,
Astronomer Royal of Great Britain**

W ith every passing hour our solar system comes forty-three thousand miles closer to globular cluster 13 in the constellation Hercules, and still there are some misfits who continue to insist that there is no such thing as progress.

—**Ransom K. Ferm**

The Place of Earth and Space Science in Science Education

When the Apollo 11 astronauts landed on the moon in 1969, they were able to gain a new perspective on the Earth—the metaphor of a blue marble hanging in space. Humankind's limited forays beyond our biosphere have highlighted how we are suspended in a great void, a sphere hurtling through a mostly empty universe, a world both fragile and resilient.

The Earth and space sciences bring together aspects of each of the other science disciplines that will be discussed in this text. Like physics, the historical roots of the Earth sciences are grounded in attempts to understand the physical forms at work in our lives. The Earth sciences, however, did not generally have the prominence of the other sciences in the Renaissance and early modern period when physics, chemistry, and biology were flourishing. It was not until the eighteenth century that the beginnings of a modern field of geology began to develop with the work of men such as James Hutton (1726–1797) and Charles Lyell (1797–1875). During this time, the first attempts were made to explain the sources of materials such as fossils that were found in different geological formations.

The need to better understand the Earth came to be associated with the conquest and empire building of the great colonial powers. These European powers went to different regions of the world to gather natural resources such as diamonds in Africa, tin in Argentina, and silver and gold in Mexico. More recently, in the 20th century, the exploitation of oil and natural gas led to an increased interest in better understanding certain aspects of Earth science and the processes that led to the creation of these resources. While Earth science continues to play a central role in the quest for natural resources, Earth scientists today are also involved in a wide range of research to better understand the varied processes that shape the Earth.

In the first chapter of this book, we talked about the work of anthropologist Gregory Bateson. Bateson believed the ultimate goal of any researcher, whether astronomer or anthropologist, should be to observe and understand the pattern that connects. Implicit in understanding the idea of patterns in the Earth and space sciences is the realization that our planet Earth functions as a system. This means that nothing operates in a void, but instead, the existence of one condition or phenomenon in a geographic,

SOURCE: National Oceanic & Atmospheric Administration (http://www.nnvl.noaa.gov/hurseas2005/Katrina1545z-050828-1kg12.jpg).

Image 6.1. Hurricane Katrina

Hurricane Katrina, which decimated a large portion of the Gulf Coast region of the U.S. in August 2005, highlighted many aspects of the interconnectedness of Earth systems, including the atmosphere, hydrosphere, lithosphere, and biosphere.

oceanographic, or atmospheric system is shaped by other connected phenomena. Thus, taking the example of a hurricane, the forces that determine its strength and path are the results of a complex set of factors that come together to create a **weather** system (see Image 6.1).

Scientists who study the various systems on our dynamic planet have begun to learn how these systems work and how they interact. Some of the most important Earth systems that make up the whole are

Biosphere—all of Earth's living organisms

Atmosphere—Earth's relatively thin covering of gases

Lithosphere—Earth's surface and interior

Hydrosphere—Earth's circulating water systems

Energy system—the energy that powers all Earth's systems

As the human population of our planet continues to grow (there are currently more than six billion people living on Earth), humans are having a growing impact on each of these Earth systems. Our technologies and practices have the potential to dramatically change systems such as the Earth's **climate**, atmosphere, and the numbers and kinds of other living organisms. This ability to change the way our planet works presents both dangers and opportunities. In this chapter, we will examine the extraordinary planet on which we live and the sciences that involve earth, water, air, and the vast universe beyond our small and fragile planet.

Measuring and Estimating in Earth and Space Science

In the Earth and space sciences, objects need to be understood and considered on the local, the global, and sometimes even on the interplanetary scale. The ability to understand concepts of distance, time, and scale that range from the minute to the nearly infinite is essential to understanding many of the ideas in this discipline. Thus, measurement is a logical place to begin our experiments in the Earth and space sciences.

Estimating Large Numbers of Objects

Imagine that you were given the task of determining how many grains of sand were in a sandbox. How would you go about determining what that number might be? You certainly couldn't count every grain. A sand box five inches deep and four feet by four feet in area might very well have several billion grains of sand. If we want to find out the number of grains, we need a system of estimating. We would probably do this by determining the total volume of sand, to get a total number of cubic inches, and then we would have to figure out how many grains of sand are in one cubic inch. Even counting the grains in one cubic inch might be tedious, so we might measure out a quarter of a cubic inch and then do the math to estimate the total number of grains of sand.

Earth scientists frequently need to estimate large numbers of objects. Whether studying changes in plant coverage from satellite photographs, crystals in a mineral sample, or bone fragments in a fossil bed, accurate estimating is an important skill for a student of the Earth sciences. The following investigation will help you improve your skill at estimating large numbers of objects. (See Experiment 1.)

Determining Direction Using a Compass

The compass is arguably one of the most important inventions in human history. Prior to its introduction, people had to determine direction by the position of the Sun and stars. This was impossible to do during overcast weather and in parts of the world where the Sun is not visible for days on end. Such environmental conditions could make navigation quite challenging. The first compasses were used in China during the fourth century B.C. Compasses work because of the magnetic field caused by the rotation of the Earth, which can be detected using a metal needle free to pivot around a central point. While extremely simple in its operation, the compass's importance cannot be overemphasized. (See Experiment 2.)

Experiment 1: Estimating the Number of Books in Your School Library

In this activity, you will estimate the number of books in your school library.

Materials You Will Need for This Activity

- Access to your school library

What You Will Do

Image 6.2. Stack of Books

1. Look around the library and make an initial estimate of how many books you think there are. Write this number down. How can we improve the accuracy of our estimation? (Hint: One way is to break the estimate into pieces.)
2. Now focus on one bookshelf on just one bookcase. Estimate how many books are on that one shelf.
3. Count the books on that one shelf. How close was your estimate?
4. Estimate and then count the books on a second shelf of the same bookcase. Was your estimate more accurate the second time? Were there the same number of books on each shelf?
5. Now that you know about how many books are on each shelf, you need to estimate how many shelves are in the library.
6. Estimate how many shelves are on the typical bookcase in the library.
7. Next, count or estimate the total number of bookcases in the library.
8. Multiply the number of bookcases by the number of shelves per bookcase by the number of books per shelf to get your estimate of the total number of books in the library.
9. Ask the librarian whether he or she knows the actual number of books. How accurate was your estimate?

What you will learn: Estimating complex problems can be improved by breaking the estimate down into smaller pieces.

Core concept demonstrated: Estimation of large numbers of objects

Thinking like a scientist: When geologists or archaeologists are studying a fossil site, one of the first things they usually do is to mark out a grid of intersecting lines across the site. Why do you think they do this?

Correlation With National Science Standards: A.1; G.3

Experiment **2:**   Orienteering

In the following activity, you will use a compass to practice accurately finding directions.

**Materials You Will
Need for This Activity**

- A large open field
- A coin
- An orienteering compass (one with degrees as well as cardinal directions)

What You Will Do

Image 6.3. Compass Rose

1. Place a coin on the ground at your feet.
2. Set the compass to 60° and turn your body to face that bearing.
3. Walk forward 10 paces as straight as you can along this bearing and stop. It is important to keep your paces as regular in size as possible.
4. Add 120° to your current bearing. Your compass should now read 180° on the dial. Turn your body to face this new bearing and walk another 10 paces in the new direction. Stop.
5. Add an additional 120° to your last bearing so that the compass dial now reads 300°. Again, walk 10 paces along this new bearing.
6. You should have walked in a triangle and if you have been extremely accurate, your coin should be at your feet. Is it?
7. If you are not close to the coin, try again, focusing on keeping your paces as regular as possible and your line straight along the compass bearings.

What you will learn: Accurate measurement of distance and direction will allow you to navigate back to your starting point.

Core concept demonstrated: Determining direction with a compass

Thinking like a scientist: How can a compass help you find your way if you are hiking in the woods or sailing on a boat? Read about modern global positioning systems (GPS). How is GPS similar to a compass? How is it different?

Correlation With National Science Standards: A.1; E.2; F.5; G.1

Measuring Deep Time: How Old Is the Earth?

The history of the Earth (known as geologic time) is much longer than human history. Geological events take place over millions or even billions of years, whereas human history is much shorter. Humans have existed for between one and two million years. Modern human history dates back only three or four thousand years. Compare this to the history of the Earth, which was created between five and six billion years ago. Thus, the Earth has existed approximately four to five thousand times longer than humans have existed. If one compares Earth's history to modern human history (say, 5,000 years), the Earth has existed approximately one million times longer. This idea can be quite difficult for children (and even adults) to grasp. (See Experiment 3.)

The Cosmos: The Sun, Planets, Solar System, Stars, and Beyond

The planet Earth is a remarkably fragile spaceship making its way through the vast universe. Understanding the scale of solar and interstellar distances is essential to comprehending the place of the Earth in a remarkable and seemingly infinitely large universe. At the scale of our solar system, the radiant power of the Sun and its influence on all living things on Earth is equally remarkable.

Scale of the Solar System

As we saw in Experiment 3, one of the ways we can understand the size of extremely large things is by using a scale. For example, visualizing the distance from the Earth to the Sun—93,000,000 miles—is pretty difficult. But if you were to take the distance to the Sun and divide it by the circumference of the Earth (93,000,000/24,000 = 3,875), you could begin to imagine how far away the Sun is. Thus, to travel to the Sun would be the equivalent of going around the Earth nearly 4,000 times.

The distance from the Sun to Jupiter is 484,000,000 miles, equivalent to approximately 20,000 trips around the Earth. In Experiment 4, we establish a scale for measuring distances in the solar system that will help you grasp the relative distances of the planets from the Sun and from one another. (See Experiment 4.)

The Expanding Universe

Cosmology is the search for origins and answers to questions such as how the universe began. One such explanation is the Big Bang theory that has resulted from several important observations. In 1927, Edwin Hubble first observed that light from distant galaxies is "red shifted"; that is, it appears to be more red than it should be. Red shift occurs when the object you are observing is

Experiment **3:**   **Geologic Time on a Football Field**

In the following activity, you will explore the age of the Earth and significant events in Earth's history using a football field time line.

Materials You Will Need for This Activity

- Football field with the yard lines marked
- Paper and markers

Image 6.4. Football Field

What You Will Do

1. Go out to a football field.
2. Imagine that the goal line at one end of the field represents the time of the Earth's formation (about 4.6 billion years ago) and the other goal line represents the present time.
3. The teacher will assign each person, pair, or small group (depending on class size) one of the events in the Earth's history listed below.
4. Write the name of your assigned significant event in large letters on a piece of paper.
5. The teacher will tell each person where to position himself or herself on the field based on the age of his or her event, starting with the oldest events first. At this scale, each 10-yard increment represents 460 million years (each yard represents a 46 million-year period).
   - Earth's crust forms—own goal line
   - Oldest rocks found on Earth—own 17-yard line
   - First fossil evidence (blue-green algae)—own 21-yard line
   - First multi-celled organisms—visitor's 30-yard line
   - First jellyfish—visitor's 15-yard line
   - First fish—visitor's 11-yard line
   - First land plants—visitor's 10-yard line
   - First amphibians—visitor's 8-yard line
   - First reptiles—visitor's 7-yard line
   - First dinosaur—visitor's 5-yard line
   - First mammal—visitor's 4-yard line
   - First bird—visitor's 3-yard line
   - First flowering plant—visitor's 2-yard line

- Mesozoic mass extinction—visitor's 1-yard line
- First human ancestors—visitor's 1.5 inches from goal line
- First modern humans—visitor's 0.5 inches from goal line

What you will learn: When compared to the age of the Earth, life as we know it has existed for a very short time, and humans are extremely recent newcomers, barely visible on the overall scale.

Core concept demonstrated: Scale of geologic time

Thinking like a scientist: Where are the largest gaps between significant events that were marked on your timeline? What possible explanations for these gaps can you think of? Why does it become harder for scientists to study events in the Earth's history as they go further back in time?

Correlation With National Science Standards: A.2; D.5; G.3

moving away from you at a high speed. This is similar to the Doppler shift effect you hear whenever something like a fire truck or a race car moves past you quickly and you hear the pitch of the sound get lower. The red shift that Hubble observed indicated that the galaxies in all directions were moving farther and farther away from us. Second, Hubble determined that the farther away a galaxy is from us, the faster it is moving away. If the universe is expanding, then it must be the case that the galaxies of our universe were once closer together than they are now. By measuring how far apart galaxies are and how fast they are moving, one can calculate that it probably took about 15 billion years for the universe to grow to its present size. From these observations, one can theorize that the universe must have begun its expansion at a time when all the matter of the universe was together in one place: the awesome event that astronomers call the Big Bang. (See Experiment 5.)

Star Power

All stars produce both light and heat, but when we look into the night sky, not all stars look the same. Some stars appear brighter than others and some appear to be different colors. Some stars actually do produce more light than other stars, but one star may also appear brighter than another because it is closer to us here on Earth. Thus, a star that is closer may appear brighter than another star that actually produces more light and heat. Stars appear

(Text continues on page 161)

Experiment 4:   **Solar System Model**

In the following activity, you will create a model showing the relative distances between the planets.

Materials You Will Need for This Activity

- Pictures of the Sun and planets
- Roll of toilet paper
- Markers

What You Will Do

1. Place pictures of the Sun and planets at the front of the room where everyone can see them. List as many ways as possible to classify (group) the pictures.
2. In a hallway or open area, unroll a roll of toilet paper, and mark off the distances to the planets using a scale of one toilet paper square = 10,000,000 miles (see the chart below for distances).
3. Hold up the unrolled toilet paper and have someone hold each planet picture at the appropriate distance along the scale.

Object	No. of Toilet Paper Sheets From the Sun	No. of Toilet Paper Sheets From Previous Object
Sun	0.0	0.0
Mercury	3.6	3.6
Venus	6.7	3.1
Earth	9.3	2.6
Mars	14.1	4.8
Jupiter	48.4	34.3
Saturn	88.7	40.3
Uranus	178.7	90
Neptune	279.7	101.0
Pluto (avg. orbit)	366.1	86.4

What you will learn: The inner planets are relatively close to the Sun and relatively close to each other.

The outer planets are substantially more spread out, both from the Sun and from each other.

Core concept demonstrated: Relative distances between the planets of the solar system

Thinking like a scientist: Why is it so difficult for humans to travel between planets in our solar system? The closest star to us besides the Sun is Alpha Centauri, at a distance of 46 trillion miles. At the same scale used above, how many sheets of tissue would it take to represent the distance to Alpha Centauri?

Correlation With National Science Standards: D.2; D.6

Experiment 5: Expanding Universe Model

To watch a video clip related to this concept, go to the Student Resource CD bound into the back of your textbook.

In the following activity, you will study a model of the expanding universe.

Materials You Will Need for This Activity

- A balloon
- A pen
- A ruler
- A paper strip
- A paper clip

What You Will Do

1. Use the ruler to mark off the measurements on the paper strip.
2. Inflate a balloon just a little bit (1 breath) and then make 10 dots on the balloon, numbering them from 1 to 10.
3. Inflate the balloon part way (about 4 breaths). Fold the end of the balloon and paper clip it so no air escapes (don't tie it yet).
4. Using the paper strip, measure and record the distance between dot number one and each of the other numbered dots.
5. In the table below, record what happens to the 10 dots.
6. Now, blow up the balloon to about double the size it was before (this time you can tie the balloon). Again, use the paper strip to measure the distance from dot number one to all the other dots.
7. Calculate the difference for each dot between slightly inflated and half inflated and again between half inflated and fully inflated.

Image 6.5. Inflated and Deflated Balloons

Half Inflated

Dot	Initial Distance From Dot 1	Difference Between Slightly Inflated and Half Inflated
2		
3		
4		

(Continued)

(Continued)

5

6

7

8

9

10

Fully Inflated

Dot	Final Distance From Dot 1	Difference Between Half Inflated and Fully Inflated
2		
3		
4		
5		
6		
7		
8		
9		
10		

What you will learn: The more the balloon is inflated, the further the dots move apart and the more rapidly this happens.

Core concept demonstrated: The expanding universe

Thinking like a scientist: Do the dots get larger as the balloon expands? What happens to galaxies as the universe expands? If an object moving quickly away appears more red than normal (red shift), what do you think happens when an object is moving quickly toward you?

Correlation With National Science Standards: A.1; A.2; B.2; D.3; E.4; G.1; G.4

to be different colors because they are different temperatures. Hotter stars will usually appear white or blue and cooler stars will appear orange or red.

All stars, regardless of brightness or color, are giant balls of glowing gas. They shine because the gas inside them is so hot that a process of nuclear fusion takes place. Nuclear fusion occurs when two atoms fuse to form a different kind of atom. This fusion process gives off a lot of energy in the form of light and heat.

Energy from the Sun hits the Earth as heat and light. Of all this energy, about 19% is absorbed by the atmosphere and another 35% of the energy is reflected by clouds. Most of the remaining energy is in the form of visible and ultraviolet light. This energy is used by plants for photosynthesis and by animals for warmth. Humans also use this energy that has been stored for hundreds, thousands, or even millions of years when we burn wood and fossil **fuels** like coal and gas. (See Experiment 6.)

Astronomy: Observing the Heavens From Earth in the Past and Present

To a remarkable extent, the planets, the moon, and the stars that we observe in the night sky today appear nearly the same to us as they did to our distant ancestors. While the universe is constantly expanding and evolving, from our perspective, the march of the heavenly bodies through our sky is a consistent marker of the passing days, months, and years. In a certain sense, these vast celestial mechanisms function with the precision and consistency of the best-designed clockworks. It appears to be human nature to try to understand and predict the movement of these celestial objects, and nearly all cultures throughout history have explored the science of astronomy.

Phases of the Moon

For as long as humans have walked the Earth, we have gazed up into the heavens in wonder. One of the most fascinating aspects of the night sky is the constantly shifting appearance of the moon. As the moon goes through its lunar cycle, the light from the Sun reflects off it at different angles. The result is what we observe from Earth as the shifting phases of the moon: the new moon, crescent moon, quarter moon, full moon, and so on. In Experiment 7, you will create a model of these shifting phases.

Changes in the Seasons

Why do the seasons change? According to an ancient Greek myth, Persephone was the daughter of Demeter, the goddess of the harvest. Hades, who was the god of the Underworld, fell in love with Persephone and took her to his kingdom to be his wife. Demeter searched everywhere for her daughter but could not find her. Zeus, the king of the gods, finally

(Text continues on page 165)

Experiment 6:   **Hot Enough to Fry an Egg**

In the following activity, you will capture and focus the energy of the Sun and study star power.

**Materials You Will
Need for This Activity**

- 3 eggs
- 2 dark frying pans
- A piece of thick glass

Image 6.6. Fried Egg

What You Will Do

1. Take three eggs, two black frying pans, and one piece of thick glass outside on a hot, sunny day.
2. Crack one egg and put it directly on the sidewalk.
3. Crack the second egg and put it in one pan without a cover.
4. Crack the third egg and place it in the other pan and cover it with the piece of glass.
5. Observe the eggs carefully. Note which one fries the quickest.
6. Be sure you clean up the egg from the sidewalk afterwards. If you like, have an egg sandwich with the other eggs.

What you will learn: Solar energy heats the surface of the Earth. This energy can be concentrated by absorbing it with a dark surface, and it can be concentrated even more by focusing and trapping the heat with a glass covering.

Core concept demonstrated: Solar energy

Thinking like a scientist: Venus is very cloudy but also very hot. Why might this be? How would the solar energy on a planet with no atmosphere be different from the solar energy on a similar planet with an atmosphere?

Correlation With National Science Standards: A.1; B.3; D.4; F.5; G.1

Experiment 7:   **Modeling Phases of the Moon**

In the following activity, you will model the phases of the moon and explain why the moon appears to change its appearance when viewed from Earth.

Materials You Will Need for This Activity

- 8 small Styrofoam balls
- 1 medium Styrofoam ball
- 1 large Styrofoam ball
- Toothpicks
- Flat sheet of Styrofoam packing material or thick cardboard
- Flashlight
- Black marker

What You Will Do

1. Before making your model, you should keep a moon journal every night for at least a week (a month of observations is better). Each night, draw a picture of the moon. If you can't see the moon on a given night, the newspaper will probably have a drawing of the moon phase on the weather page.
2. To make your model, stick a toothpick in the large Styrofoam ball and stick the other end of the toothpick in the flat piece of Styrofoam or cardboard near one edge. This ball represents the Sun.
3. Do the same for the medium ball and place it in the center of the flat piece of Styrofoam. This ball represents the Earth.
4. Using the marker, color exactly half of each of the small balls black. These will represent the phases of the moon.
5. Draw a diagram on a piece of paper that shows the position of the moon, Sun, and Earth during each of the following phases of the moon. Be sure to label the diagram to indicate the names of each phase. You can look up the information in a book or on the Internet.
   - New
   - Waxing Crescent
   - First Quarter
   - Waxing Gibbous

(Continued)

(Continued)

- Full
- Waning Gibbous
- Third Quarter
- Waning Crescent

6. Create a 3-D model of your diagram by using toothpicks to attach the Styrofoam moon balls to the flat piece of Styrofoam in their proper positions relative to the Earth and Sun. Try to position the white and black sides of each moon in the proper orientation so it would been seen in the correct phase if you were standing on your Earth ball.
7. Darken the room and hold a flashlight next to your Sun to test your model. Move the balls as necessary to get the correct phase. Label each moon phase on the Styrofoam base.
8. Pick a phase of the moon and explain to a partner why we see that phase of the moon when we do.

What you will learn: We see the various moon phases from Earth as a result of the relative positions of the Sun, Earth, and Moon. The moon travels through a predictable series of phases approximately every 28 days.

Core concept demonstrated: Phases of the moon

Thinking like a scientist: What do you think it would be like to have several moons revolving around Earth? Would it change our calendar? Our poetry? Our tides?

What views do you think astronauts have of Earth and the moon as they orbit Earth?

Would the moon phases change if the moon revolved around Earth in the opposite direction? How?

Correlation With National Science Standards: A.1; B.2; D.3; G.1

told Demeter where Persephone was. Hades would not give her up completely but agreed that Persephone would live for half the year with Hades and for the other half with her mother. During the time that Persephone lived with Hades in the Underworld, Demeter was unhappy, and all the plants withered and died. But when Persephone returned each year, Demeter rejoiced and the plants grew again. This myth thus explained the reason for the changing seasons.

People are still interested in, and affected by, the consequences of these changes in season. In fact, the seasons have had a profound effect on human history: They establish the crop growing patterns in many regions, have led to historical migrations, and have even led to the development of hibernation among certain animal species. (See Experiment 8.)

 Experiment 8: **The Changing Seasons**

To watch a video clip related to this concept, go to the Student Resource CD bound into the back of your textbook.

In the following activity, you will create a model showing how the tilt of the Earth is responsible for the change in seasons.

Materials You Will Need for This Activity

- A sharp pencil or cooking skewer
- A medium Styrofoam ball
- A black marker
- A lamp

What you will do:

1. Push a pencil or skewer straight through the center of the Styrofoam ball. This represents the Earth's axis. Label the North and South Poles where the pencil pokes through.
2. Draw a circle around the middle of the ball, halfway between the poles, to represent the equator.
3. Darken the room and turn on the lamp.
4. Bring the ball a few feet from the lamp and tilt it slightly so the North Pole is about 23 degrees from straight up and down and pointing away from the lamp.

(Continued)

(Continued)

5. Describe the pattern of light and shadow on the ball on this day. What season do you think this is in the Northern Hemisphere? In the Southern Hemisphere?
6. Slowly move the ball counterclockwise around the lamp. Try to maintain the tilt—always pointing the North Pole out in the same direction in space (toward the same object in the room you are in).
7. Stop when you have gone a quarter of the way around the Sun. Describe the pattern of light and shadow on the ball on this day. What season do you think this is in the Northern Hemisphere? In the Southern Hemisphere?
8. Continue moving the ball counterclockwise. Stop when you have gone another quarter revolution. Describe what you observe as before.
9. Continue counterclockwise, stopping each quarter turn and describing the position and the season, until you get back to the starting point.

What you will learn: The Earth rotates on an axis that is tilted. In other words, our planet never stands upright—it is always leaning to the side. The direction of this lean never changes. As the Earth travels along its orbit, any particular place on the Earth sometimes leans toward the Sun and sometimes away from the Sun. This tilt determines the seasons by influencing the amount of direct sunlight that hits a given part of the Earth's surface.

Core concept demonstrated: Why the seasons change during the year

Thinking like a scientist: Many people believe that the seasons change because the Earth moves closer to and farther from the Sun during the year. Where do you think this belief comes from?

Would there be seasons on Mars? If so, how would the seasons on Mars be similar to or different from the seasons on Earth?

Correlation With National Science Standards: A.1; A.2; B.2; D.3; D.6; G.1

Exploring Shadows

The **sundial** is the oldest known device for measuring time and is probably the most ancient of all scientific instruments. A sundial works because the shadow of an object will move from one side of the object to the other as the Sun appears to travel across the sky during the day.

Sundials probably date back to the Sumerian civilization, about 3500 B.C. By 2500 B.C., both the ancient Babylonians and Egyptians were building obelisks to serve as timekeepers, dividing the day into two parts by indicating noon. Later, additional markers were added around the base of the monument to allow further time divisions.

In modern times, sundials have been replaced by clocks that are both more accurate and more convenient. It is, of course, still possible to estimate time using the Sun's shadow on a straight object. (See Experiment 9.)

Restless Earth: Earth's Composition, Layers, Movements, and Impacts in Surface Features

Looking down on the Earth from outer space, one might have the impression that the Earth is like a ball, round and smooth and unchanging. Nothing, in fact, could be further from the truth. In addition to the Earth's movement through space, which we have previously discussed, the internal and external features of the Earth are in constant and dynamic motion. This motion is the result of a number of interrelated systems shaped by tectonic forces, physics, chemistry, and even biology.

Convection Currents: Heat Within the Earth

The German geologist Alfred Wegener (1880–1930) was the first scientist to propose theories of continental drift and **plate tectonics**. He argued that a super-continent he called *Pangaea* had broken up about 200 million years ago, with the pieces drifting to their present positions. As evidence, he cited the fit of South America and Africa, fossil evidence, and similarity of rock structures across now-distant continents. Because he could not explain the mechanism for this continental drift, however, his ideas were widely discredited.

About 15 years after Wegener proposed his theory, the British geologist Arthur Holmes (1890–1965) proposed that the Earth's mantle undergoes thermal convection and that this could be the missing mechanism. This idea is based on the fact that as a liquid is heated, its density decreases and it rises to the surface until it is cooled and sinks again. This repeated heating and cooling results in a current, and this current might be enough to propel the great continents around the planet. While Holmes's idea received very little attention at the time, it turned out to be the correct mechanism to explain plate tectonics. (See Experiment 10.)

 Experiment **9:**   **Changing Lengths of Shadows**

In the following activity, you will explore how the lengths of shadows change during the day.

Materials You Will Need for This Activity

- Meter tapes
- Chalk
- Meter sticks
- Long pieces of paper (from a roll of paper) about 2 meters long

What You Will Do

1. Trace the length of the meter stick on the long piece of paper and record the length.
2. Take the paper and meter stick outside in the morning. Cast the shadow of the meter stick on the paper by placing one end of the meter stick on the ground, being sure to hold it as vertical as possible.
3. Trace the resulting shadow, measure it, and record the length and the time of day.
4. Repeat this procedure every 1 to 2 hours during the day. If possible, continue until the Sun goes down.
5. Compare the length of shadow cast at each time of day to the actual height of the meter stick.

What you will learn: When the Sun is lower in the sky, both in the morning and evening, shadows are extended and are longer than the height of the actual object. In the middle of the day when the sunlight is shining down closer to vertical, shadows are shorter than the length of the actual object.

Core concept demonstrated: How shadows are affected by the shifting angle at which sunlight strikes the Earth

Thinking like a scientist: Given what you have learned about the changing shadow length, how could you use this information to construct a basic sundial? Do you think the changing seasons would affect the lengths in your shadow experiment? Why or why not? If possible, repeat this activity three or four months after the first trial to answer this question: Would the changing seasons affect the way a sundial tells time? Why or why not?

Correlation With National Science Standards: A.1; A.2; B.2; D.3; D.6; G.1; G.4

Experiment 10: Convection Currents

To watch a video clip related to this concept, go to the Student Resource CD bound into the back of your textbook.

In the following activity, you will create a model to demonstrate how convection currents can move objects.

Materials You Will Need for This Activity

- 1 glass bread loaf pan or 8″ × 8″ square glass baking dish
- 2 ceramic coffee cups
- 2 cans Sterno
- Vegetable oil
- Ground spice such as cinnamon or nutmeg
- Spoon
- Matches
- Small pieces of balsa wood (optional)

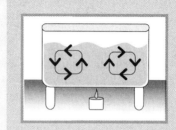

Image 6.7. Convection

What You Will Do

1. Pour a 1½ to 2-inch layer of the vegetable oil into the glass baking dish.
2. Mix in the spice. Stir thoroughly to distribute the spice. Carefully balance the dish on the coffee mugs, leaving space to place the Sterno cups in the center under the pan.
3. Observe the oil and spice mixture and describe what you see. Is there any movement of the liquid or the spices?
4. Light the Sterno cans and let the liquid heat up for a couple of minutes. Again, observe the oil and spice mixture and describe what you see. Is there any movement of the liquid or the spices now?
5. Look at the model several times during the experiment, both from above the dish and from the side of the dish. Draw a picture of what you observe.
6. If you have the balsa wood pieces, put them carefully in the center of the pan. Observe them for several minutes and describe what happens.

* Safety Notice—Both the lit Sterno cans and the hot oil are dangerous and can cause severe burns. Be sure that the experiment is placed on a solid and level surface and that students remain at a safe observing distance at all times.

What you will learn: The flow of the heating and cooling oil creates a convection current in which upward flow above the flame, due to heating, causes horizontal flow near the surface of the liquid. Cooling of the liquid near the ends of the container leads to an increase in the density of the liquid and produces sinking and a return horizontal flow toward the center of the container. This cycle of flow is known as a convection cell.

Core concept demonstrated: Convection currents

Thinking like a scientist: Is the pattern approximately symmetrical on the two sides of the heated area? Where do you observe upward flow? Where do you see downward flow? Where do you observe horizontal flow? How is this similar to or different from what goes on in plate tectonics?

Correlation With National Science Standards: A.1; A.2; B.2; D.1; D.4; D.5; G.1; G.4

Plate Tectonics

As discussed in the previous section, the English geologist Arthur Holmes discovered that convection currents explained how Alfred Wegener's theory of continental drift might be possible. But how and where exactly these convection currents might be operating was still unknown. The answer turned out to be hidden on the bottom of the oceans. American geologists Harry Hess and Robert Dietz studied ocean floor data collected by U.S. Navy submarines during World War II and concluded that the sea floors were gradually spreading apart and that new sea floor crust is continually being created along oceanic spreading ridges and then destroyed along the continental boundaries in deep trenches called subduction zones. This sea floor spreading served as the conveyor belt resulting from the convection currents below and, in turn, pushing the continents. As the continents were pushed in this way, they sometimes collided, resulting the creation of new mountain ranges. (See Experiment 11.)

Earthquake Simulation

In 1906, San Francisco was struck by an enormous earthquake that virtually destroyed the city. Arnold Gente, among others, left a remarkable photo record of the damage caused by the earthquake (see Image 6.8). Earthquakes are more common than many of us would like to believe. For example, a series of three massive quakes struck along fault lines near New Madrid, Missouri in 1811 and 1812. These quakes were so strong they could be felt as far north as Michigan and as far east as the Carolinas. More recently, a huge quake hit the city of Kobe, Japan in 1995, killing 5,000 people and causing billions of dollars in damage. As great as the damage was, it was mitigated by the fact that Japan, as a highly developed nation, is able to ensure that most structures are built to be somewhat earthquake resistant. Less-developed nations often struggle to ensure that buildings meet such safety codes. This sad reality could be clearly seen in the Asian tsunami of 2004 and the Pakistan earthquake of 2005, both of which caused horrific damage and loss of life. As more and more development occurs in earthquake-prone areas, structurally sound construction becomes critical. (See Experiment 12.)

SOURCE: Courtesy of the Library of Congress Prints and Photographs Division, Washington, DC.

Image 6.8. Houses Destroyed in the Aftermath of the 1906 San Francisco Earthquake

Experiment 11: Mountain Building With Towels

In the following activity, you will make a model to demonstrate how mountains are built up and erode as a result of plate tectonics.

Materials You Will Need for This Activity

- Three pairs of towels of three different colors/patterns

What You Will Do

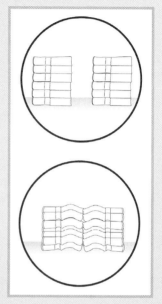

Image 6.9. Towels

1. Fold each towel into quarters, and make two identical stacks with three towels in each stack.
2. Place the two stacks of towels next to each other to serve as your model.
3. The towels represent different sedimentary rock layers. Where are the oldest rock layers in your model? (They are at the bottom of the stack, and the youngest will be at the top because newer sedimentary rocks are deposited over older rocks.)
4. The surface of the Earth in the model is represented by the top of the stack of towels. (The rest of the towels represent rock layers underground.)
5. Slowly begin to push the stacks of towels together. Describe what happens to the ground surface. How is this like what happens during the process of mountain building when two continental plates collide? (The rocks are pushed up as they crush together and the mountains gradually grow taller.)
6. Additionally, the process of erosion takes place as the younger rocks on top are gradually eroded away by water, wind, and ice. Simulate this erosion by slowly pulling back the top towels from both sides of the mountain and folding them under, while maintaining the tilt of the layers against the mountain flanks.
7. Model what will happen over time when the plates stop colliding and only erosion is now working on the mountains.

What you will learn: The continental plates move as a result of sea floor spreading. When two continental plates collide, the rock layers bend and fold and form mountains. The mountains will continue to grow as long as the plates are moving together. Erosion also takes place, and once the plates stop moving together, erosion will slowly decrease the height of the mountains as they are worn away bit by bit.

Core concept demonstrated: Mountain building as a result of plate tectonics

Thinking like a scientist: The two longest mountain ranges in the U.S. are the Rockies in the west and the Appalachians in the east. The Rockies are significantly taller. Give two possible explanations for this. How could you gather evidence to determine which of these explanations is correct?

Correlation With National Science Standards: A.2; B.5; D.1; D.4; D.5

Experiment **12:**   Earthquake-Resistant Structures

In the following activity, you will design model buildings to resist the effects of a simulated earthquake.

Materials You Will Need for This Activity

- 10 index cards
- 2 sheets of notebook paper
- 10 drinking straws
- 16 paper clips
- Metric ruler

- Tape measure
- Shoebox lid or Tupperware container
- Marbles to fill shoebox lid
- Tape

What You Will Do

1. The teacher will divide the class into three teams; each team will receive one of the structure challenges described below.
2. Construct a building at least 30 cm tall that passes the test for your team's challenge.
3. *Challenge #1:* Design a structure that will remain standing even when a heavy book is dropped onto the floor next to the structure.
4. *Test:* Put your building on a piece of paper on the floor. Trace the outline of the building on the paper. You may not fasten the building to the paper. Drop a heavy book onto the floor directly next to the structure from a height of 2 meters. Retrace the outline of the building on the paper and measure the distance that the foundation moved.
5. *Challenge #2:* Design a structure on a slanted surface so that it doesn't slide downhill even when an impact strikes the hillside. Build the structure on a slant so that one side of the bottom of the structure is about 8 cm higher than the other side.
6. *Test:* Trace the foundation of the building on a piece paper and place the paper on the hillside. Drop a small weight, like a box of crayons or a pack of index cards, from a height of about 30 cm above the uphill side of the structure. Retrace the outline of the building on the paper and measure the distance that the foundation moved.
7. *Challenge #3:* Build a structure on an unstable surface that will not fall down even when the surface moves beneath the building.
8. *Test:* Fill most of the shoebox lid or medium Tupperware container with a single layer of marbles so that the marbles can still roll. Set the building on the marbles. Slide the box back and forth a distance of 5 cm in each direction about once every 5 seconds. Increase the speed slowly until you are shaking

once per second. If the structure falls over, record the speed at which you were shaking when it toppled.

What you will learn: Basic design principles that can help reduce earthquake damage include construction with a wide base, a low center of gravity, and supports to reduce sliding.

Core concept demonstrated: Earthquake-resistant construction principles

Thinking like a scientist: Which features, if any, helped resist which challenges? Which features helped resist all challenges? What real-world limitations are there that can make it difficult to apply what is known about earthquake-resistant construction to all building projects in earthquake-prone areas?

Correlation With National Science Standards: A.1; A.2; B.4; B.5; D.1; E.2; E.3; F.5; G.1

Rocks and Minerals: Formation, Identification, and Human Use of Common Rocks and Minerals

The Earth is composed of a great variety of **rocks** and **minerals**. These rocks and minerals are created as a result of tectonic forces, volcanic activities, and other chemical processes and even the erosion of the older rocks and minerals. Understanding where rocks and minerals come from is essential to understanding how the Earth was formed as well as how it constantly renews itself. These processes, in turn, play an integral part in how life thrives and becomes abundant on the planet.

Growing Crystals

Have you ever seen a piece of rock candy or looked at table salt under a magnifying glass? Both the rock candy and the salt exhibit crystalline structures. How are these structures similar to or different from rock crystals that you have seen? Even though they are different in terms of their chemical composition, each of these crystals formed in approximately the same way. (See Experiment 13.)

Experiment 13: **Crystals in Your Kitchen**

In the following activity, you will compare the structures of several types of crystals.

Materials You Will Need for This Activity

- Magnifying glass
- Table salt
- Epsom salt
- Jar of honey
- Measuring cups and spoons
- Pencil

- String
- Sugar
- Paper clips
- A glass jar
- Hot plate, stove, or other heat source

What You Will Do

1. Use your magnifying glass to closely observe the table salt, the Epsom salt, and the rim of the honey jar.
2. Draw pictures of what you observe. In what ways are the crystals similar and different?
3. Dissolve 1 teaspoon of salt in 1 cup of water and heat the mixture over a low flame to evaporate the water.
4. Observe what is left using your magnifying glass and draw a picture of these crystals.
5. Pour 1 cup of boiling water into a dish and add 2 cups of sugar. Stir until the sugar is completely dissolved. Let the sugar water cool and then pour it into the glass jar.
6. Straighten out a paper clip so that it can lie across the mouth of the jar.
7. Tie a piece of string to the clip so that it can hang down into the jar and reach nearly to the bottom (but not touch the bottom).
8. Observe every day. After a few days, remove the string and examine the crystals under the magnifying glass.

* Safety Note—This experiment uses boiling water. Be sure that children maintain a safe distance from hot liquids and containers.

What you will learn: When liquids cool, they solidify. In some cases, under the right conditions, crystals will form. Crystals are made up of molecules that fit neatly together in an orderly way. All crystals of the same material formed under the same conditions should have the same structure and shape.

Core concept demonstrated: Development and appearance of crystal structures

Thinking like a scientist: How are the salt and sugar crystals that you grew in this activity similar to or different from the ones that you observed at the beginning of the activity? How are they similar to or different from mineral crystals you have seen before?

Correlation With National Science Standards: A.1; B.4; D.1

Mineral Identification Strategies

Geologists have developed a number of procedures by which to identify and differentiate the minerals in the Earth. A mineral is a naturally occurring, inorganic, crystalline solid that has a definite chemical composition. A rock is a combination of one or more minerals. Mineral identification can be important because some minerals (i.e., gold) are highly valuable and other minerals (i.e., pyrite, also known as fool's gold) are less so. Many minerals have properties that are desirable for manufacturing and building, and other minerals are sought simply because of their natural beauty. There are several simple tests that can be done to categorize and classify minerals. (See Experiment 14.)

What's in Soil?

We take the **soil** that we find beneath our feet pretty much for granted, but in fact soil is a complex mix of organic and inorganic materials that is essential for life on Earth. Soil typically includes small particles of rock, plant material in various states of decomposition, animal material both living and dead, and a variety of minerals. Soil is necessary for plant growth, which, in turn, is essential for all animal life. (See Experiment 15.)

Earth Cycles: Many Processes on Earth Operate in Cycles

What happens in the Earth's atmosphere, on the surface of the land, in the oceans, and deep underground is all part of a complex series of closely connected and interrelated phenomena. The Earth is a dynamic system in which there are many cycles. Three of the main cycles are the atmospheric cycle, the water cycle, and the rock cycle. These cycles provide evidence of two important facts about the Earth. First, the Earth is essentially a closed system with almost no net gain or loss in matter. That is, the matter on the Earth gets cycled through various systems, but there is very little new matter that comes into or leaves the system. Second, changes in one part of any of these systems can affect other parts of the system, and even other systems. Another way to think about this is that almost nothing occurs in isolation. Understanding the interrelationships between these cycles is fundamental to any understanding of Earth science.

Water Cycle

A rock formation that is porous and permeable enough to store water is called an **aquifer**. Water can be drawn from an aquifer through a well. Wells are holes drilled into and through the layers of rocks and down to a layer that contains stored water. Water that seeps into the ground, either from rainfall or another source, refills an aquifer. Thus, aquifers are renewable resources,

Experiment 14: Identifying Minerals

In the following activity, you will conduct several basic tests useful in mineral identification.

Materials You Will Need for This Activity

- Glass plate (for testing hardness)
- Streak plate (for testing streak)
- Iron nail (for testing for presence of carbonates)
- Vinegar (for testing for presence of carbonates)
- Magnet (for testing for presence of iron)
- 5 mineral samples (quartz, calcite, magnetite, pyrite, and galena)

What You Will Do

1. Observe the five mineral samples and describe each sample in as much detail as you can.
2. Construct a data table to record each of the test results for each of the samples.
3. Begin with the first mineral sample and conduct each of the tests on the sample. See below for the test procedures. When you have completed the tests, try to identify the mineral.
4. Follow the same procedures for each of the other mineral samples.
5. When you are done, compare your results with those of other students in your class.

Streak Test: Hold the ceramic tile flat on the desktop. Press a corner of the mineral firmly on the tile and try to draw a line using the mineral. Based on your observation, write "colored streak" or "no colored streak" in the streak column of your data table.

Hardness Test: Hold the glass plate flat on the desktop. Press a corner or edge of the mineral firmly on the glass and try to scratch the glass with the mineral. Write "does scratch" or "does not scratch" in your data table under the hardness column.

Fizz Test: Use the nail to scratch a small area on the mineral specimen. Put a drop of vinegar in this area. Watch closely to see whether the vinegar fizzes, so you know whether it reacts with the mineral. Write "fizz" or "no fizz" in your data table.

Luster Test: Look at the mineral sample closely. Does it look like it is made of metal? Is it shiny? Write "metallic" (if it looks like a metal) or "non-metallic" (if not).

Magnetism Test: Hold a magnet next to the mineral sample. Is the magnet attracted to the mineral? Write "magnetic" or "not magnetic" in the magnetic column of your data table.

* Safety Note—Mineral samples can have sharp points and edges, as do the glass and streak plates and the nail. It is important to set clear expectations and give clear instructions to students before beginning this activity.

What you will learn: Many common minerals can be identified through a series of simple tests.

- quartz—no streak, does scratch, no fizz, non-metallic, non-magnetic
- calcite—no streak, does not scratch, yes fizz, non-metallic, non-magnetic
- pyrite—yes streak, does scratch, no fizz, metallic, non-magnetic
- galena—yes streak, does not scratch, no fizz, metallic, non-magnetic
- magnetite—yes streak, does scratch, no fizz, metallic, magnetic

Core concept demonstrated: Physical and chemical characteristics of common minerals

Thinking like a scientist: Which mineral was the easiest to identify? What made this mineral easy to identify? Which two minerals were the most difficult to tell apart? What made them difficult to distinguish? If you were a field geologist, what tools would you want to take with you to help identify different minerals?

Correlation With National Science Standards: A.1; A.2; B.1; D.1; F.7

but if water is drawn out faster that it is replenished, eventually the aquifer will be depleted. Also, if the area near the aquifer becomes polluted, the water that seeps into the aquifer will become polluted, too. Aquifers have the ability to filter some pollutants out of the water, but groundwater can easily become polluted when people living above the aquifer are not careful about what goes into the ground. (See Experiment 16.)

Rock Cycle

The creation of geologic formations is a dynamic process in which different types of rock are formed and reformed. Molten rock, which is known as magma or lava, can cool to form igneous or crystalline rocks. These igneous rocks can then be transformed through additional heating and pressure into metamorphic rocks. Both igneous and metamorphic rocks can also be eroded, deposited in layers, and then compressed into sedimentary rocks. This cycle can occur over and over again with the same molecules passing from one form of rock to another. (See Experiment 17.)

Experiment **15:**   Determining Soil Type

In the following activity, you will use a classification system developed by soil scientists to identify several soil samples.

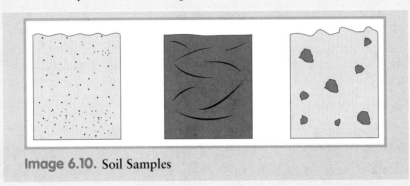

Image 6.10. Soil Samples

Materials You Will Need for This Activity

- Soil samples brought from class members' yards or neighborhoods
- Magnifying glass
- Tweezers
- Paper towels

What You Will Do

1. Spread the first soil sample out on a paper towel and observe it closely using the magnifying glass.
2. Take notes on what you observe. Consider observations such as the texture of the particles, presence of identifiable objects (leaf, twig, etc.), presence of any living organisms, and so on.
3. Using the flow chart in Image 6.11, follow the directions to determine the classification of your soil.
4. Repeat Steps 1 to 3 with a second soil sample.
5. Compare the soil type of your samples with the soil types of your classmates. Make a graph of the class results.

What you will learn: Soil is composed of several different types of particles (silt, clay, sand, and loam) and can be classified depending on the relative amounts of these constituents.

Core concept demonstrated: Components and classification of soils

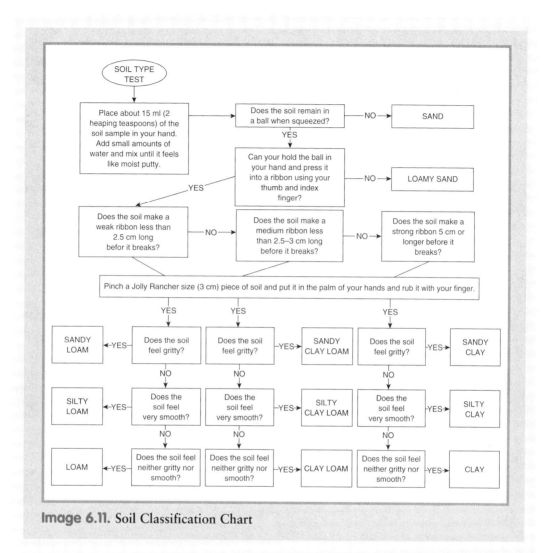

Image 6.11. Soil Classification Chart

Thinking like a scientist: Why might an engineer or an architect need to know about the types of soil present before planning a new construction project? Why might a gardener? Why do you think gardeners add peat moss or topsoil to their garden if it has a high clay content?

Correlation With National Science Standards: A.1; A.2; B.1; D.1; F.3; G.1

 Experiment **16:** **Building an Aquifer Model**

In the following activity, you will build a model of an aquifer and explore the effect of pollution on groundwater.

Materials You Will Need for This Activity

- Two-liter soda bottle
- Clay
- Gravel
- Topsoil
- Sand
- Pencil
- Piece of nylon cut from a stocking
- Twist tie
- Eye dropper

Image 6.12. Aquifer Model

What You Will Do

1. Cut the top half off a clear two-liter bottle and remove the label.
2. Layer clay, gravel, topsoil, and sand in the bottom half of the bottle. Observe the layers in the bottle. How do they appear similar and different?
3. Wrap the piece of nylon around the end of a pencil and secure it with the twist tie.
4. Make a simulated well by drilling a hole through the various layers with the pencil. Drill until you hit the clay layer.
5. Slowly, pour water in the area around the well and observe. Does the water filter through the layers like it would in a natural aquifer?
6. Untie the twist tie and slip the pencil out, leaving the nylon in the hole.
7. Use the eyedropper to extract water from the well. Describe what happens and observe the water.
8. Now, add a large amount of food coloring to the areas outside the well to simulate adding pollution to the aquifer.
9. Continue drawing water from the well using the eyedropper. What do you observe?

What you will learn: Water filters through the rock layers of an aquifer and can be pumped out of a well into the aquifer. If pollution is added anywhere it can seep into the aquifer, it is likely that the water will become contaminated.

Core concept demonstrated: How water is stored and filtered by aquifers

Thinking like a scientist: You caused your "pollution" with food coloring. What types of things in your home might actually contaminate drinking water if poured on the ground? In the model, only a few drops of food coloring were enough to "pollute" the well. How much of a pollutant do you think is necessary in the real world to pollute an aquifer or a well?

Correlation With National Science Standards: A.1; A.2; B.1; D.1; D.4; F.1; F.8; G.1

Experiment 17: **Edible Rock Cycle**

In the following activity, you will create a tasty model that demonstrates part of how the rock cycle occurs.

Materials You Will Need for This Activity

- Bowl
- Mixing spoon
- Wax paper
- Measuring cups and spoons
- $\frac{1}{3}$ cup evaporated milk (silt; erosion)
- 1 cup sugar (quartz crystals; uplift)
- 1 tablespoon margarine (organic sediments; time)

- 1 cup mini-marshmallows (limestone pieces; ocean)
- ¼ cup pecans or walnuts (sandstone pieces; weathering)
- ¾ cup chocolate chips (basalt pieces; heat)
- ½ teaspoon vanilla extract (crude oil; pressure)

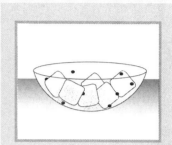

Image 6.13. Mixing Bowl

What You Will Do

1. Measure and add the silt, quartz crystals, and organic sediments to the bowl.
2. Mix them thoroughly with the spoon to simulate the effects of plate tectonics.
3. Place the bowl in the microwave for 45 seconds and then stir it to simulate increases in temperature and pressure. Repeat this step 3 times.
4. Break the sandstone pieces into smaller pieces to simulate weathering.
5. Measure and add the limestone, sandstone, basalt, and crude oil to the bowl.
6. Stir the sediments as they undergo metamorphosis, finally melting the limestone and basalt back into magma.
7. Use the spoon to scrape the magma back out onto the Earth's surface (wax paper).
8. Add another sheet of the Earth's surface (wax paper) over the top of the cooling igneous rocks.
9. Set aside overnight in a cool place or in the refrigerator. The next day, observe the newly formed igneous rocks.
10. Cut the rock into squares and enjoy!

What you will learn: Rocks many go through the rock cycle numerous times as they cool, are exposed to new temperatures and pressures, are eroded and deposited, are uplifted or subducted, are re-melted and reformed.

Core concept demonstrated: The rock cycle

(Continued)

(Continued)

Thinking like a scientist: Do all rocks necessarily go through all phases of the rock cycle? Why or why not? What might cause a rock to spend more or less time in a given phase of the cycle?

In our activity, the simulated rock went through the complete cycle in one day. How does this compare with actual rocks going through the cycle?

Correlation With National Science Standards: A.1; B.4; B.5; D.1; D.4; F.3

Atmospheric Cycle

Heat from the Sun warms the Earth. As air in the atmosphere is heated, it will rise, lowering the air pressure in the area. Colder air higher up in the atmosphere (higher up because it was once warm air) will fall, raising the air pressure in the area. Air then flows horizontally between high and low pressure areas, resulting in the atmospheric cycle. This movement between high and low pressure areas can be on a local scale, a global scale, or any scale in between. High-pressure areas are generally associated with clear skies and stable weather. Low-pressure areas are generally associated with unstable weather and also with cloudy skies, due to the increased evaporation of moisture in the upper atmosphere.

Clouds are nothing more than water vapor that condenses and gathers together into a visible form. Clouds are usually formed when moisture-filled air near the Earth's surface is raised higher into the atmosphere by the heat of the Sun. As the air is lifted, the pressure drops and the air is subsequently cooled. The combination of these two processes causes water vapor to condense. (See Experiment 18.)

Weather and Climate: Weather Patterns, Climate Zones, and Climatic Change Over Time

Weather and climate both result from the interactions of the various cycles that make up our dynamic Earth. Water, wind, temperature, topography, latitude, season—these and many other features influence the weather and climate that we experience. But what is the difference between weather and climate? Weather is the variety of atmospheric events that we observe on a daily basis.

 Experiment **18:** **Cloud in a Bottle**

In the following activity, you will create a model that simulates cloud formation in the atmosphere.

Materials You Will Need for This Activity

- A clear 2-liter plastic bottle with cap
- A measuring cup
- Cold and hot water
- Matches

Image 6.14. Cloud Bottle

What You Will Do

1. Pour $\frac{1}{3}$ cup of cold tap water into the clear bottle and place the cap on it.
2. Shake the bottle for 30 seconds and then set it on the table.
3. Squeeze the bottle and then release the pressure. Repeat this process several times.

   (Explanatory note—When you squeeze the bottle you increase the pressure and saturate the atmosphere inside the bottle. The increased pressure in the bottle also increases the air temperature. When the air is heated, more water moves into the air. When you release the pressure on the bottle, you decrease the air pressure inside. This lowers the air temperature and causes condensation in the bottle. You don't yet, however, have everything you need to make a cloud. There are not enough particles in the air to which water vapor molecules can attach themselves.)

4. Now, remove the cap from the bottle and light a match. Hold the match over the mouth of the bottle. Quickly squeeze the bottle to extinguish the match, then slowly release the pressure to draw smoke into the bottle.
5. Replace and tighten the cap.
6. Squeeze the bottle again and release. A cloud should now have formed above the water inside the bottle. Again, squeezing the bottle forced condensation inside the bottle. Now that smoke has been added to the bottle, the water has something to condense around. The condensed water forms the small cloud inside the bottle.
7. Finally, rinse the bottle thoroughly and pour $\frac{1}{3}$ cup of hot tap water into it. Shake the bottle for 30 seconds and place it on your table.
8. Squeeze the bottle and then release the pressure. Repeat this process several times. Then repeat the process of extinguishing a match over the mouth of the bottle and drawing the smoke inside. Squeeze and release the bottle again to create a cloud.

(Continued)

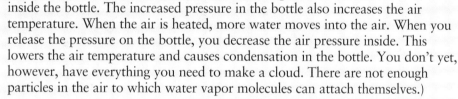 To watch a video clip related to this concept, go to the Student Resource CD bound into the back of your textbook.

(Continued)

What you will learn: The role that temperature plays in cloud formation. When the bottle is squeezed, the temperature of the air inside the bottle increases. When the air temperature is decreased, a cloud is created inside the bottle.

Core concept demonstrated: Cloud formation as a response to temperature and pressure change

Thinking like a scientist: When did a bigger cloud form in the bottle—with the cold water or with the hot water? Why might this take place? Why are some locations on Earth more susceptible to clouds than others? What can you tell about a city that only very rarely has cloud cover? About a city that is frequently shrouded in heavy clouds?

Correlation With National Science Standards: A.1; B.4; B.5; B.6; D.2; F.4; G.1

Climate is that larger pattern that helps us to understand the weather. Weather can change very rapidly, depending on whether it is hot or cold, wet or dry. The atmosphere reacts to a wide range of features that are changing hour to hour. Thus, the weather can change multiple times in a single day.

Meteorologists are scientists who study weather and climate. They record the weather every day, and this database of weather information helps us to understand the climate of an area. Climate is the average weather in a location over a prolonged period of time. For example, a location like Hawaii that gets large amounts of rain over many years would have a wet climate. A place like Alaska, where it stays cold for most of the year, would have a cold climate. Understanding the climate of an area is helpful for predicting the weather in that area.

So, when you look out the front door in the morning, you see weather. If you keep looking out the door every morning, and keep observing the weather each day, then you will begin to understand some things about the climate in your area.

Tracking Rainfall

Throughout history, people have been interested in forecasting the weather to guide agricultural practices like planting and harvesting, migrations, and even the timing of festivals. The ancient Babylonians, Chinese, and Greeks all developed systems for weather forecasting. However, these predictions were generally based on lore and personal observations with few systematic attempts at measurement using tools. It was not until the Renaissance that tools such as the thermometer and barometer were used systematically in weather observation.

Accurate record keeping and sharing of data across locations did not become common until the 1860s, which is generally considered to be the beginning of modern meteorology. Keeping accurate records over time is an extremely important part of weather prediction. Knowing the tracks of storms is important because weather patterns often repeat themselves. Thus, in an area like the southeastern United States, it is known that hurricanes appear consistently at certain times of the year and follow certain consistent tracks. This is also true for other types of weather in the north, like snow storms and blizzards.

Recording rainfall is one of the many types of data collection that are done as part of weather forecasting. (See Experiment 19.)

Measuring Wind

Hurricanes, which are called typhoons in the Pacific, are the most powerful storms in the Earth's atmosphere. They can have winds as high as 170 miles per hour and cause huge devastation not only because of the destructive winds, but also because of flooding from tidal surges and massive rainfall. In August, 2005, Hurricane Katrina destroyed much of the Gulf Coast region of the United States, flooding the city of New Orleans and causing tens of billions of dollars of damage. Even when it is not blowing with such destructive force, wind is an important aspect of both weather and climate. (See Experiment 20.)

Rainforest Terrarium

Rainforests are some of the most incredible ecosystems on Earth. They are forests full of tall, dense plant life that regularly receive high amounts of rainfall and are well-known for having an incredible range of biodiversity. While the vast majority of rainforests are in tropical and subtropical regions, smaller rainforests can be found in more temperate climate zones. Rainforests currently cover approximately 6% of the Earth's surface, but are thought to contain more than half of the world's plant and animal species. The climate of a rainforest is very hot and humid and is usually considered to have four distinct layers.

At the bottom is the forest floor, where it is usually very dark and, as a result, almost no plants grow there. Things on the forest floor tend to decompose very quickly; thus, the soil of the forest floor is rich in nutrients. Above the forest floor is the understory layer. There is still only a little sunshine that reaches down to this area, so many plants grow large leaves to reach the sunlight. Animals in the understory layer in tropical rainforests include jaguars, tree frogs, and leopards, as well as a large concentration of insects.

Above the understory is the canopy layer, which is the primary layer of the forest and forms a roof over the two layers below it. Trees in the canopy layer receive abundant sunlight, and most have smooth, oval leaves. Trees

(Text continues on page 188)

🌐 Experiment **19:** Tracking Rainfall

In the following activity, you will keep track of the rain that falls at your school over a one-week period.

Materials You Will Need for This Activity

- Glass or clear plastic container at least 10 inches high
- Marbles
- A permanent water-resistant marker
- A 12-inch plastic ruler

What You Will Do

1. Place marbles into the container and add about one inch of water. Draw a line on the bottle to indicate this water level. This will be your rain gauge. The marbles and water will steady the container and keep it from tipping over in the wind.
2. Put the rain gauge outside on a level surface, away from any overhanging trees or other things that could block rainfall. Leave the gauge outside all week.
3. Make a hypothesis about how much rain you think will fall over the next week.
4. Measure the rainfall every day at about the same time of day. Have one student hold the ruler against the side of the container, with the ruler's bottom end even with the base line. Have another student read the height of the water column.
5. Record readings and comments about the weather on an observation chart.

What you will learn: Rainfall may vary a great deal from day to day. If you keep accurate data over time, it becomes possible to see patterns and make predictions.

Core concept demonstrated: Systematic collection of weather data

Thinking like a scientist: Could you make accurate climate predictions about rainfall based on your one week of rain data? Why or why not? What could you do to improve your ability to make predictions? Could you use your rainfall data to predict other aspects of the weather, like temperature? Why or why not? What could you do if you wanted to predict other aspects of the weather as well?

Correlation With National Science Standards: A.1; A.2; D.3; E.2; F.5; G.1

Experiment **20:** Making an Anemometer

In the following activity, you will build a tool to measure wind speed and use it to make wind measurements.

Materials You Will Need for This Activity

- Plastic drinking straws
- Tape
- 4 small paper cups (the kind used in bathroom dispensers)
- A straight pin
- A pencil with an eraser
- A Marker
- A Beaufort wind scale

What You Will Do

1. Form a cross with two drinking straws and tape the straws together where they cross.
2. Tape one small paper cup to the end of each straw, making sure all the cups have their opening pointed the same way (right or left).
3. Push the straight pin through the center of the straws where they cross and then push the pin into the eraser on the end of the pencil.
4. Mark one cup with the marker to be a reference you can use to count as the cups spin around in the wind.
5. Go outside and measure the wind speed by counting the number of times the **anemometer** spins around in one minute.
6. Measure the wind speed in several different locations and record your results in a data table. (Your measurements will be in revolutions per minute, not miles per hour. Store-bought anemometers make this conversion for you.)
7. Compare the results you measure with your anemometer with the Beaufort wind scale (below). Look at the observable effects of the wind and then use the scale to estimate the wind speed in miles per hour.

What you will learn: Wind speed can be measured through direct measurement using an anemometer or through indirect measurement using the Beaufort wind scale and observed wind effects.

Core concept demonstrated: Measuring wind speed

Thinking like a scientist: Can you compare the measurements of the two systems? Why or why not? What would you have to do to compare them? How much did the wind speed change from place to place? If you wanted to keep accurate data over time, what would you need to do?

Correlation With National Science Standards: A.1; A.2; B.5; D.3; E.2; F.5; G.1

(Continued)

(Continued)

Scale	Description	Wind Speed (miles per hour)	Observable Effects
0	Calm	less than 1	Smoke will rise vertically.
1	Light Air	1–3	Rising smoke drifts; weather vane is inactive.
2	Light Breeze	4–7	Leaves rustle, can feel wind on your face, weather vane is inactive.
3	Gentle Breeze	8–12	Leaves and twigs move around. Lightweight flags extend.
4	Moderate Breeze	13–18	Moves thin branches, raises dust and paper.
5	Fresh Breeze	19–24	Trees sway.
6	Strong Breeze	25–31	Large tree branches move; umbrellas are difficult to keep under control.
7	Moderate Gale	32–38	Large trees begin to sway; noticeably difficult to walk.
8	Fresh Gale	39–46	Twigs and small branches are broken from trees; walking into the wind is very difficult.
9	Strong Gale	47–54	Slight damage occurs to buildings; shingles are blown off of roofs.
10	Whole Gale	55–63	Large trees are uprooted; building damage is considerable.
11	Storm	64–75	Extensive widespread damage.
12	Hurricane	above 75	Extreme destruction.

in the canopy layer are generally so close together that animals can easily move from tree to tree while remaining in the canopy. Many animals live in the canopy, including various snakes, birds, and tree frogs. Finally, trees that extend up above the canopy make up the emergent layer. These trees can be more than 200 feet tall with trunks that measure up to 16 feet around. There is plentiful sunlight in the emergent layer, and the trees tend to have broad leaves. Eagles, monkeys, bats, and butterflies are just some of the animal inhabitants of the emergent layer. (See Experiment 21.)

In addition to their incredible biodiversity, rainforests are interesting because they tend to create their own microclimates and localized weather.

🦋 Atmosphere: Atmospheric Movement, Layers, Pressure and Cloud Formation, Smog and Pollution

We live in a complex ocean of air that clings to the surface of our planet and forms our atmosphere. The atmosphere protects all the life on Earth by blocking out dangerous rays from the Sun. The atmosphere is composed of a **mixture** of gases that are thickest at the surface of the planet and gradually become thinner as they reach space and then disappear. The Earth's atmosphere is composed mainly of two gases: nitrogen (78%) and oxygen (21%). The remaining 1% is a mix of many other gases.

Oxygen is, perhaps, the most important gas in the atmosphere because it allows animals, including humans, to breathe. Some of the oxygen has gradually been converted into ozone, which is a special form of oxygen. The ozone in the atmosphere is primarily responsible for filtering out the Sun's harmful rays. A number of recent research studies have shown how humans have caused a hole to form in the ozone layer. This hole allows more dangerous radiation to reach the Earth's surface.

Another way in which humans are affecting the Earth's atmosphere is through a process often referred to as the greenhouse effect. Certain gases that we produce with our cars and industry, such as carbon dioxide, trap some of the heat that would normally be radiated away from the Earth. While there is some scientific and political debate about the environmental impact of this greenhouse effect, most atmospheric scientists now believe that the Earth's atmosphere is having trouble maintaining the balance that has generally existed for millennia. Still, the atmosphere that surrounds us is resilient in response to the various forces that act upon it. How the dynamics of this atmosphere affect the formation of clouds, the appearance of natural light, and even the creation of nuisances like smog is an important piece of the Earth sciences.

Why Are Clouds White?

You will learn in Chapter 9 that color is light energy and that when all (or most) of the colors of the visible spectrum (red, orange, yellow, green, blue, indigo, and violet) are present, the light appears white. If an object absorbs some of the wavelengths of the visible spectrum, the color of the object will be something other than white. If all of the wavelengths are absorbed, the object will appear black. Thus, if clouds appear white, they must be reflecting all of the wavelengths of the visible spectrum. But how does this occur? (See Experiment 22.)

 Experiment **21:**   **Rainforest Terrarium**

In the following activity, you will make a model rainforest in a bottle and observe how water cycles through this ecosystem.

Materials You Will Need for This Activity

- Heat lamp
- Small tropical houseplants
- Carrot seeds to simulate fern-like plants
- Bean seeds to simulate vines
- Potting soil
- Plastic 2-liter bottle (the kind with the extra plastic piece on the bottom)
- Ruler

Image 6.15. Rainforest Terrarium

What You Will Do

1. Rinse out a plastic 2-liter bottle and cut it in half about in the middle.
2. Pull the colored bottom piece away from the clear plastic.
3. Fill the colored plastic bottom piece with potting soil.
4. Arrange a few small tropical houseplants in the soil and drop carrot and bean seeds around the soil.
5. Add about ¼ cup of water to the soil.
6. Invert the clear plastic rounded part of the bottle and tightly seal it on the colored bottom.
7. The terrarium should remain closed from now on. Do not open it to water or observe.
8. Spread the terrariums for the class in various places so that they have different growing conditions. Place at least a few under a low heat lamp or plant light.
9. Observe your terrarium every day and take measurements of plant growth from the outside of the bottle.
10. Compare the growth in the various terrariums.

What you will learn: Plants will not suffocate in a closed container because they can use the same air over and over again. They do not need to be watered because water is also recycled in the terrarium. Plants take water from the soil and then release it through their leaves as water vapor. Normally this water vapor is transported away from the plant, but in a closed container, this vapor turns back into water droplets, drips back into the soil, and can be used all over again by the plants.

Core concept demonstrated: Model water cycle in a terrarium

Thinking like a scientist: What cycles or processes are occurring within the terrarium? How is the rainforest terrarium similar to and different from an actual rainforest? Why do you think we did not put any animals into the terrarium? What kinds of animals might survive? What kinds might not? Why? As the world's rainforests shrink due largely to human inhabitation and development of the land, how might the weather in the region be affected?

Correlation With National Science Standards: A.1; C.3; C.7; D.4; F.7; G.1

Why Is the Sky Blue?

Almost every child has asked his or her parents why the sky is blue. Like most things in nature, the answer to this question has to do with basic physical principles. While the sky is usually blue, it does, in fact, gradually change colors throughout the day. This has to do with the angle at which sunlight is filtered thought the atmosphere. (See Experiment 23.)

Making Smog

Have you ever seen a picture of Mexico City or Los Angeles or another big city where the air looks brown with pollution? This kind of air pollution is usually called "smog," from a combination of the words "smoke" and "fog." The term "smog" was first used in London in the late 1800s to describe the haze produced by the condensation of water vapor on soot particles from factories.

When the Sun heats two common kinds of air pollutants (hydrocarbons and nitrogen oxides), a chemical reaction takes place that produces smog (which is actually ground-level ozone). More than two-thirds of all the smog-producing pollutants come from the emissions of vehicles. Most of the rest of the pollutants come from smoke stacks and from chemical solvents. Either a lack of wind or a weather condition called a thermal inversion (where the warm air over a city, which would normally rise and escape, gets stopped by another air mass above it that prevents it from escaping) can cause smog to be trapped over an area. Smog has been shown to cause medical problems for people, such as irritation of the respiratory system and aggravation of asthma, emphysema, and other breathing problems. (See Experiment 24.)

Experiment 22: Why Are Clouds White?

In the following activity, you will determine why clouds generally appear white and how this occurs.

Materials You Will Need for This Activity

- Hard candy of various colors
- Hammer
- Magnifying glass
- Paper towels

What You Will Do

1. Observe several pieces of colored hard candy. What do you know about why they appear to be the color that they are?
2. Carefully crush several of the candies into a powder with the hammer (wrapping the candy in a paper towel before hitting it with the hammer will minimize flying candy pieces).
3. Observe the crushed candy pieces closely. Do they still appear to be their original color? Why or why not?
4. You may need to continue to crush the candy. At some point, the pieces will begin to lose their color and turn white. Why is this happening?
5. Use the magnifying glass to compare the sizes of candy pieces that maintain their color and pieces that now appear white. Try using the width of a human hair as a point of comparison. What do you observe?

What you will learn: Clouds reflect all visible wavelengths of the sunlight. Color scattering is usually due to particles whose size is smaller than the wavelength of the light. The water droplets in the clouds are generally many times larger than the wavelength of visible light, and there are many droplets and many surfaces to reflect the light, so the clouds scatter almost all the light and look white.

Core concept demonstrated: Why clouds appear white due to scattering of sunlight off water droplets

Thinking like a scientist: Clouds don't always appear white. For example, when the Sun is going down, the sky often appears red and this includes the clouds, which sometimes appear bright red. Why do you think this might occur? For a clue, think about this: What will happen if you shine a red flashlight on a white piece of paper? Why?

Correlation With National Science Standards: A.1; B.4; D.3

Experiment 23: Why Is the Sky Blue?

In the following activity, you will demonstrate why the sky is blue during the day and reddish near dawn and dusk.

Materials You Will Need for This Activity

- Clear glass container, about the size of a pitcher (clear plastic can be used, too, but glass works best)
- Flashlight
- Some milk or cream (whole milk or cream works best; if using skim milk, you'll need to add a bit more)

What You Will Do

1. Fill the container with water and add a few drops of the milk. Mix the milk in completely. Make sure the water is milky enough so that it's hard to see through the water.
2. Shine the flashlight into one side of the container.
3. Look at the water at a 90° angle from the light beam. Describe the color of the water.
4. To make a comparison, shine the flashlight away from the container for a moment and shine it back in, while looking at the milky water. Does the color of the water change at all?
5. Now look through the container directly at the incoming light.
6. Describe what you observe. Is there a difference in color compared to when you were looking from the side?

What you will learn: The light in the sky is scattered sunlight. The scattering is done by small particles. Even when the sky is "clear," there are still a great number of molecules and particles in it that can reflect the light, but these particles have a greater ability to reflect at the violet end of the spectrum. Thus, the color of the sky should really appear to be more "purplish," but our eyes are not very sensitive to violet. They are sensitive to the next most represented color, blue. There are decreasing amounts of green, yellow, and red, so overall, the sky usually appears blue.

Core concept demonstrated: Color scattering

Thinking like a scientist: Now that you understand why the sky appears blue during most of the day (the blue light is scattered because of collisions with molecules and particles in the atmosphere), can you explain why the sky often appears red in the evening shortly before sunset? Think about how much atmosphere the sunlight passes through and how this differs between midday and sunset. What would happen if all the blue light got scattered away before the light got to you?

Correlation With National Science Standards: A.1; A.2; B.3; B.4; D.3; G.1

Experiment 24: Smog in a Can

In the following activity, you will create a model of smog that will demonstrate what it looks like and how it behaves.

Materials You Will Need for This Activity

- Clean, dry wide-mouth canning or mayonnaise jar
- Heavy-duty aluminum foil (6″ × 6″ square)
- 2 or 3 ice cubes
- 6″ × 2″ strip of paper
- Matches
- Salt

What You Will Do

1. Fold the piece of paper in half lengthwise and twist it into a rope.
2. Make a lid for the jar out of the piece of aluminum foil. Put a slight depression in the foil lid where the ice cubes can rest without sliding off.
3. Put a little water in the jar, swish it around to wet the whole inside of the jar, and pour the remaining water out.
4. Light the twisted paper with a match, and drop both the paper and the match into the jar.
5. Quickly put the foil lid on the jar, making as tight a seal as you can, and put the ice cubes on top of the lid.
6. Sprinkle a little salt on the ice to help it melt.
7. Observe and describe what you see taking place in the jar. Draw a sketch.

What you will learn: Fog (a low lying cloud) is formed when warm, moist air is cooled. If smoke particles are present at the same time, then the smoke will mix with the fog, producing smog.

Core concept demonstrated: Creation and appearance of smog

Thinking like a scientist: How does vehicle use affect smog levels? Do you think that all vehicles contribute the same amount to smog production? Why or why not? Why are some cities, such as Mexico City, Los Angeles, and Denver, particularly prone to being blanketed in a layer of smog? Why was smog more common in London 150 years ago than it is today?

What do you think people with breathing problems should do on particularly smoggy days?

Correlation With National Science Standards: A.1; B.4; D.3; F.1; F.4; F.8

Water and Oceans: Fresh Water/Salt Water Distribution, Interactions, and Contamination

It has often been noted that when viewed from the far reaches of space, the Earth looks like a big blue marble. Any extraterrestrial visitor coming upon the Earth would identify it as our solar system's ocean planet. The oceans cover approximately 140,000,000 square miles, or 72% of the Earth's surface. While all of the oceans are, in fact, connected, geographers have traditionally identified five distinct oceans: the Antarctic, Arctic, Atlantic, Indian, and Pacific Oceans.

The Pacific Ocean is far and away the largest of the oceans, covering nearly 35% of the Earth, or nearly half of the ocean surface. The Pacific Ocean stretches from Asia in the west to North and South America in the east. The Atlantic Ocean is the second largest, covering nearly 21% of the Earth's surface. The Atlantic Ocean stretches from North and South America to Europe and Africa. The Indian Ocean is the third largest, covering 15% of the Earth's surface and stretching from Africa to Asia. The Antarctic Ocean (also known as the Southern Ocean) circles the globe, surrounding Antarctica. Finally, the Arctic Ocean covers the Earth's North Pole, and includes the great Arctic icecap and many icebergs.

The oceans play many important functions in the Earth's dynamic systems, such as influencing the planet's weather and temperature. For example, the ocean currents distribute the Sun's heat energy more evenly around the globe, heating the land and air during winter and cooling it during the summer. The chemical composition of the oceans, the tidal movements and currents, and the geology and life below the ocean surface are all core concepts in the Earth sciences.

How Salty Is the Ocean?

Water from rain runs through the soil and across the ground as it makes its way into streams and rivers. Water in rivers runs across the riverbed as it flows toward the sea. Throughout this process, the flowing water picks up small amounts of mineral salts from the rocks and soil of the ground. This very slightly salty water flows into the oceans and seas. Once in the ocean, this water only leaves by evaporating or by freezing into polar ice. In either case, the salt remains behind, dissolved in the ocean; it does not evaporate. Thus, the remaining seawater gets saltier and saltier. Over the history of the Earth, this process has led to the increasing concentration of salt in the oceans.

Salt, as a mineral, can literally be mined from the sea through evaporation of seawater, releasing fresh water into the atmosphere and leaving the salt crystals behind. Thus, rain is never salty even though most of the water that makes rain is evaporated out of the oceans. But just how salty is the ocean? The oceans are about three and a half percent salt (by weight). Salinity is generally reported in parts per thousand (ppt), which is equivalent to the number of pounds of salt per 1,000 pounds of water. The average ocean salinity is 35 ppt. (See Experiment 25.)

Probing the Ocean Floor

There is a famous parable about three men who are blind and who try to describe an elephant while each one holds a different part of the elephant's body. One man feels the elephant's trunk and says that an elephant is like a snake, one grasps its tail and claims an elephant is like a rope, and the third grabs its leg and says an elephant is like a tree. In fact, each has described a part of the animal but none has gotten a complete picture. This experience is very much like the process of sampling the sea floor with probes, like oceanographers did before the recent inventions of satellite imaging and global positioning system (GPS) technology. (See Experiment 26.)

Oil Spill Clean-Up Activity

In March, 1989, the oil tanker *Exxon Valdez* ran aground on a reef in Alaska's Prince William Sound, rupturing its hull and spilling nearly 11 million gallons of oil into the sea. This remains the largest oil spill ever to occur in U.S. waters and one of the largest anywhere in the world.

In addition to major oil spills like the *Exxon Valdez*, however, small oil spills in marine waters occur frequently, and their cumulative impact can also be quite large. These small spills generally receive little media attention and are rarely reported or cleaned up.

When oil spills in the ocean it floats on the surface (oil usually floats on fresh water as well). Oil usually spreads out quickly from the spill and forms a thin layer called an oil slick that gets thinner and thinner as it spreads farther and farther out.

Spilled oil can be extremely damaging to the environment and especially to the marine life that makes its home near where oil is spilled. There are many famous pictures from the aftermath of the *Exxon Valdez* spill of birds, otters, and other marine life dead or dying from being covered in oil.

Cleaning up an oil spill, however, is very difficult. The equipment used includes "booms," which are floating barriers that can be placed around a tanker that is leaking to collect the oil; "skimmers," which are boats that skim spilled oil off the water's surface; and "sorbents," which are like big sponges used to absorb oil. Chemical and biological agents can also be used to break down the oil into less hazardous chemical components. (See Experiment 27.)

Experiment 25: How Salty Is Too Salty?

In the following activity, you will compare the salt content of fresh, brackish, and ocean water.

Materials You Will Need for This Activity

- 3 glasses
- Water
- Salt
- Measuring spoon

What You Will Do

1. Fill three clean eight-ounce glasses with water from the sink.
2. Label the first glass "fresh," the second glass "brackish," and the third glass "ocean."
3. Add nothing to the first glass; add $\frac{1}{8}$ teaspoon of salt to the second glass; add one teaspoon of salt to the third glass.
4. Take a sip from each glass and describe the taste.
5. Do you taste any salt in the "fresh" water glass? Is the "brackish" water drinkable? Is the "ocean" water drinkable?

* Safety Note—Be careful not to swallow the salt water because ingesting too much salt can make you sick.

What you will learn: Freshwater salinity is usually less than 0.5 ppt. Water between 0.5 ppt and 17 ppt is called brackish and exists in the mixing zones where fresh river water meets with salty ocean water. The average ocean salinity is 35 ppt. This number varies between about 32 and 37 ppt. Rainfall, evaporation, river runoff, and ice formation cause these variations.

Core concept demonstrated: Salinity of fresh, brackish, and sea water

Thinking like a scientist: The Red Sea and the Persian Gulf have the saltiest seawater while the oceans in the polar regions are the least salty. Look at these regions on a globe—what might explain the greater and lesser salt concentrations? Why can't freshwater fish survive in sea water or ocean fish in fresh water? What must brackish water fish do when the tide moves in and out?

Correlation With National Science Standards: B.4; C.8; D.1; F.7

Experiment 26: Mapping the Ocean Floor

In the following activity, you will simulate how sonar has been used to map the surface of the sea floor.

Materials You Will Need for This Activity

- Graph paper
- Box of colored pencils
- A wooden dowel
- A completed shoebox (prepared in advance by teacher—this is done by spreading modeling clay or play dough across the bottom of the box to create whatever landforms are desired, such as mountains, plateaus, trenches, etc. To create the box lid, poke 3 rows of regularly spaced holes in the lid that are the correct size for the wooden dowel to fit through but small enough to prevent "spying")
- Ruler
- Modeling clay or play dough

What You Will Do

1. The shoebox has three rows of holes. Select one row to test first.
2. Insert the wooden dowel in the first hole of the row and measure the depth from the ocean surface (box lid) by marking it with your finger. Pull the dowel out and measure the distance from the end of the dowel to your finger. Record this data in a data table and on your graph paper.
3. Use the same procedure for each hole in the first row. Connect the dots on the graph to see the estimated topography of the sea floor underneath your first row of holes.
4. Using this one row of measurements, predict what the sea floor in the rest of the shoebox might look like.
5. Repeat the same testing procedure for the second row of holes, but use a different colored pencil on the graph. Compare your results from the first two rows. Are they the same? Does this change your prediction of what the rest of the sea floor in the box looks like?
6. Now, repeat the same testing procedure for the last row of holes, again using a different colored pencil on the graph.
7. When everything has been measured and graphed, open your shoebox and examine the bottom. Compare the results of your graph with the actual bottom of the shoebox.

What you will learn: Using a probing method that collects equally spaced data points will normally give a fairly good estimate of what is being probed. It is possible, however, that entire important features will be missed if they happen to fall between the probe points.

Core concept demonstrated: Strategies for getting information about difficult-to-observe locations such as the sea floor.

Thinking like a scientist: How accurate or inaccurate were your predictions about your sea floor? Were some groups' predictions more accurate than others? Why do your think this was? If you needed to increase the accuracy of your prediction, how might you change your data collection?

Correlation With National Science Standards: A.1; A.2; B.2; D.4; E.2; E.3; F.5; G.1; G.3

Experiment 27: **Oil Spill Clean-Up**

In the following activity, you will simulate the clean-up of an oil spill.

Materials You Will Need for This Activity

- Flat aluminum pan
- Cotton balls
- String
- Spoon
- Medicine dropper

- Piece of nylon stocking
- Piece of cardboard
- Straw (or dry grass)
- Drinking straws
- Plastic gloves

- Piece of sponge
- Cat litter
- Paper towels
- Plastic bags
- Salad oil

To watch a video clip related to this concept, go to the Student Resource CD bound into the back of your textbook.

What You Will Do

1. You will pretend that each group has been contracted to control or eliminate an oil spill that has just occurred in the ocean. You will have several materials to work with and can choose among them.
2. Fill the pans with water.
3. Lay out and discuss all the possible clean-up materials that can be used.
4. Predict which material(s) will be the most successful in cleaning up the oil spill. Each group should decide in advance what method they want to try first.

(Continued)

(Continued)

5. Pour a small amount (about 10 ml) of salad oil on the surface of the water. Together, the group members should attempt the cleanup using the method decided upon.
6. After about two minutes, assess the level of clean-up that has taken place in each group so far. At this point, groups can try other materials or other strategies or stick with the same strategy.
7. After another two minutes, check the results again.
8. As an extension, a simulation can be done of cleaning up the spill in "rough water." Repeat the clean-up process while one member of the group gently shakes the pan.

What you will learn: Oil spills are extremely difficult to clean up. A number of materials and techniques are used in attempts to clean up spills, but none are 100% effective. As the size of the actual spill increases and the location and/or conditions around the spill become more challenging, the effectiveness of the clean-up efforts are likely to decrease.

Core concept demonstrated: Oil spills and their consequences

Thinking like a scientist: Which materials and methods seemed to be the most effective at cleaning up the spill? Why do you think this method worked best?

Which materials and methods seemed to be the least effective at cleaning up the spill? Why do you think this method did not work well?

Can you think of any new methods that could be invented to make the clean-up more effective?

Correlation With National Science Standards: A.1; A.2; B.4; C.3; D.1; E.2; F.6; F.7; F.8; F.10; G.1

Student Study Site

The Companion Web site for *Teaching
Science in Elementary and Middle School*
http://www.sagepub.com/buxtonstudy

Visit the Web-based student study site to
enhance your understanding of the chapter
content and to discover additional
resources that will take your learning one
step further. You can enhance your
understanding of the chapters by using the
study materials, which include chapter
objectives, flashcards, activities, practice
tests, and more. You'll also find special
features, such as Resources for
Experiments, the Links to Standards from
U.S. States and associated activities,
Learning From Journal Articles, Theory
Into Practice resources, Reflections on
Science exercises, a Science Standards-Based
Lesson Plan Project, and PRAXIS resources.

Reflections on Science

1. In the introduction to this chapter, we
   discussed five major Earth systems that
   together make up the whole of our
   dynamic Earth system:
   - The biosphere—all of Earth's living
     organisms
   - The atmosphere—Earth's relatively
     thin covering of gases
   - The lithosphere—Earth's surface
     and interior
   - The hydrosphere—Earth's
     circulating water systems
   - The energy system—the energy that
     powers all Earth's systems

   What have you learned in this
   chapter about each of these systems
   and the role that each plays in the larger
   Earth system?

2. At the university level, astronomy is
   generally considered to be a part of
   physics. At the K–12 level, space science
   is generally taught with Earth science.
   Why do you think this might be?

3. Earth science tends to address topics
   that are more geographically localized
   than topics in the other science
   disciplines. For example, earthquakes,
   hurricanes, volcanoes, mountains, beach
   erosion, saltwater intrusion, and so on
   are topics that are directly observed and
   experienced by students in some parts
   of the country (and the world) but
   not in others. Is it important to teach
   these topics to students in all places,
   regardless of any direct experience they
   may have with these phenomena, or
   should Earth science education be
   taught in a more localized and targeted
   way? Explain your answer.

Internet Connections: Earth and Space Science

The following Web sites provide additional resources that may prove useful in teaching Earth and space science:

United States Geological Survey (USGS) Science Resources for Primary Grades (K–6)—a range of activities and information
http://education.usgs.gov/common/primary.htm

United States Geological Survey (USGS) Educational Resources for Secondary Grades—a range of more advanced activities and information useful for middle school and for teacher background knowledge
http://education.usgs.gov/common/secondary.htm

Geological Society of America (GSA) Resources for K–12 Earth Science Educators—activities, information, and resources
http://www.geosociety.org/educate/resources.htm

Mineral Information Institute Resources for Teachers—lesson plans and activities to teach about minerals and their uses
http://www.mii.org/teacherhelpers.html

NASA education and public outreach site for studies of the Earth's magnetic field
http://image.gsfc.nasa.gov/poetry/

Center for Educational Resources (CERES) Project—activities, information, and support for teaching astronomy in K–12 education
http://btc.montana.edu/ceres/

Franklin Institute's Space Science Hot List—many links to information on space science, organized by topic
http://sln.fi.edu/tfi/hotlists/space.html

Understanding and Teaching Biology

Consider the following statements about biology:

A thing is right when it tends to preserve the integrity, stability, and beauty of the biotic community. It is wrong when it tends otherwise.

—**Aldo Leopold**

I t is a monstrous abuse of the science of biology to teach it only in the laboratory—Life belongs in the fields, in the ponds, on the mountains, and by the seashore.

—**James G. Needham**

T he human mind evolved to believe in the gods. It did not evolve to believe in biology.

—**Edward O. Wilson**

W e travel together on a little spaceship, dependent on its vulnerable reserves of air and soil, committed for our safety to its security and peace, preserved from annihilation only by the care, work, and I will say, the love we give our fragile craft.

—**Adlai E. Stevenson**

🐝 The Place of Biology in Science Education

Biology is the study of life in all its myriad forms. Understanding the foundations of biological life in both plants and animals means addressing fundamental questions concerning the meaning of life and the act of creation. How is it possible that biological forms have come into being in what is essentially a harsh and inhospitable physical universe? The photograph of Earth taken from the moon by Apollo 11 in July 1969 caused human beings to see the world in a new way, as a tiny speck of teeming life in a vast and cold solar system, galaxy, and universe (see Image 7.1).

SOURCE: Courtesy of NASA.

Image 7.1. Photograph of the Earth Taken by Apollo 11 Astronauts From the Moon

The study of the biological sciences carries with it not only the need to understand issues about the nature of creation, but also questions concerning the appropriate use of life forms. Thus, the study of biology is a profoundly ethics-bound field. Should we experiment with the cloning of animals, for example? Should we use animals to test new drugs, or less important things like cosmetics? Should we manipulate plants to make better crops with which to feed people? Are we creating unforeseen dangers when we manipulate animals and plants for the advantage of human beings? What potential benefits to humankind might arise from embryonic stem cell research? At what cost?

The biological sciences bring to our attention the myriad complexity of living forms. Even the simplest of life forms are, in many ways, more complex than the most intricate inventions that humans have created. No one who studies animals or plants can help but wonder at both their complexity and their diversity. Biology suggests to us that life is diverse and coexistent, while at the same time competitive and often surprising.

Biology, perhaps more than any other branch of science, forces us to confront the finite nature of human endeavors and the extent to which we are passing and ephemeral moments in an ongoing parade of living organisms that have come and gone throughout the history of our planet. Gaining a basic understanding of core concepts in the biological sciences should help students better appreciate the beauty and diversity of life on Earth.

🐛 Measurement in Biology

As in other science disciplines, measurement is an important aspect of biological research. Not only does biological science require us to measure life forms, but also to determine issues of time related to the biological systems, such as how long it takes a plant to grow, how tall it grows, or, in the case of an animal, what its life span is or the number of heart beats it takes in a minute or for the duration of its life.

Measuring Peak Flow Rate of Breathing

We use many different means to monitor biological systems. In the case of human beings, medical devices provide an excellent example of the methods used to measure biological phenomena. Diabetics, for example, will use a glucometer, which samples the glucose or sugar level of their blood. This is done by taking a sample of blood and subjecting it to an electrical device that physically measures the glucose level in the blood sample. Another example is the measurement of heart rates that are done as part of an EKG. This is essentially a device that is able to measure the regularity of a heart beat of any animal and determine whether or not there are erratic patterns that could indicate a life-threatening condition.

One final example of a biological measuring device is a peak flow meter that is used by asthmatics to monitor the flow of their breathing. Peak flow is a measure of the ability to get air out of the lungs. It is measured as a rate, and the units of measure are liters per minute (LPM). (See Experiment 28.)

Estimating Lengths of Very Small Objects

During the Renaissance, a remarkable number of inventions were introduced that were responsible for the transformation of science. In the case of astronomy, the invention of the Galilean or optical telescope and the Newtonian reflecting telescope literally made visible planets and stellar systems that had previously been invisible to human stargazers. Along with the invention of astronomical devices came devices that allowed people to view things at a microscopic level. The most important of these was the microscope, which was initially a simple tube with a plate for the object at one end and at the other end a magnifying lens that would increase the size of an object by up to 10 times. The first truly modern microscope was developed by Anton van Leeuwenhoek (1632–1723), who experimented with developing very small but very powerful lenses with precise curvatures to give them very large magnifications—up to 270 times the size of the object. Leeuwenhoek's microscope was followed, in turn, by designs by Robert Hook, who significantly improved on Leeuwenhoek's creations. This constant improvement of microscopes is a process that has continued into our own era and includes the invention of computer-based electron microscopes. (See Experiment 29.)

To watch a video clip related to this concept, go to the Student Resource CD bound into the back of your textbook.

Experiment 28: Measuring Peak Flow Rate

In the following activity, you will compare the peak flow rates of the members of your class when they breathe.

Materials You Will Need for This Activity

- Peak flow meter (can be purchased at most pharmacies or drug stores for under $10)
- Alcohol wipe
- Graph paper

What You Will Do

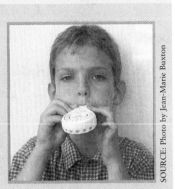

Image 7.2. Photograph of a Child Using a Peak Flow Meter

SOURCE: Photo by Jean-Marie Buxton

1. Have each student in the class measure the peak flow of air as he or she breathes. To do this, wipe the mouthpiece of the flow meter with the alcohol wipe to sterilize it, take a deep breath, and blow as hard and fast as you can into the meter.
2. Read the flow off the meter dial. Repeat two more times for a total of three trials.
3. Record your highest reading with your name in a table on the board in your class.
4. When everyone has recorded his or her peak flow of air, look for patterns in the data.
5. Brainstorm as many ways to graph the data as you can.
6. Make a bar graph of peak flow differentiated by gender. Is there a pattern?
7. Make a line graph of peak flow vs. height. Is there a pattern?

What you will learn: The peak flow of air varies by individual, but males, tall people, non-asthmatics, and those who are more physically active tend to have a higher peak flow rate.

Core concept demonstrated: Variation in a biological phenomenon across a population

Thinking like a scientist: Who uses peak flow meters and how is this activity related to the concept of environmental health? There have been a number of professional athletes with asthma. What do you think their peak flow rates would be?

Correlation With National Science Standards: A.1; C.4; F.1; F.8

Experiment 29: Estimating Lengths of Very Small Objects

In the following activity, you will learn how to estimate the lengths of very small objects.

Materials You Will Need for This Activity

- A magnifying glass
- A box of small straight pins
- A metric ruler
- A strand of your hair

Image 7.3. Magnifying Glass

What You Will Do

1. Place the ruler on a flat surface.
2. Line up pins side by side to determine how many pin widths make one centimeter and how many make one millimeter.
3. Place a strand of your hair on a white piece of paper.
4. Look at the hair under the magnifying glass.
5. Place a pin next to the hair and compare the widths of the two.
6. Using your knowledge of the width of the pin, estimate the width of the hair strand.

What you will learn: You can make accurate estimates of very small objects by comparing the object under magnification to a known standard.

Core concept demonstrated: Measuring very small objects

Thinking like a scientist: Could you use a similar procedure for even smaller objects, using a microscope? Describe what you would do.

Correlation With National Science Standards: A.1; C.1; F.10; G.4

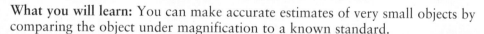

Measuring Population Change

In biological systems, it is extremely important to understand at what rate different species reproduce. With human beings, for example, this will determine population needs for schools, retirement homes, and pensions. Actuarial tables take into account the factors that influence the survival rate of various populations, making it possible for insurance companies to set costs that allow people to be insured without the insurance companies going out of business. (See Experiment 30.)

 Experiment **30:** **Measuring Population Change**

In the following activity, you will learn about population growth by exploring a classic model of rabbits reproducing.

Materials You Will Need for This Activity

• Paper and pencil

What You Will Do

1. Imagine that a newly born rabbit can reproduce when it is one month old. Suppose that the rabbit never dies and that it continues reproducing a new rabbit every month. This rabbit will then reproduce when it is one month old, two months old, and so on. Assuming that none of the rabbits die and that each rabbit reproduces every month, how many months will it take to have at least one million (1,000,000) rabbits?
2. Make a data table to help you keep track of the growing number of rabbits.

What you will learn: The number of rabbits doubles every month. This model of rabbit reproduction is based on an exponential numerical sequence. It is also based on what is known as a Fibonaccian sequence, in which the first two numbers in a sequence equal the third number in the same sequence and which is the basis for many other patterns found in nature. For example, as we discussed in Chapter 1, a chambered nautilus expands based on a Fibonaccian sequence, as does a spiral galaxy.

Core concept demonstrated: Exponential functions and population growth

Thinking like a scientist: Is this model of population growth likely to actually occur in the natural world? Why or why not? Do some animal or plant populations sometimes grow out of control? Why might this happen?

Correlation With National Science Standards: C.5; C.7; F.2

Classification

Understanding the complex forms of life found on Earth requires us to organize and classify them. In doing so, we see the relationship between different species, what seemingly different life forms have in common as well as what makes seemingly similar life forms different from one another. Biologists have estimated that there are somewhere between 10 and 40 million different species or organisms currently inhabiting the Earth. Of all these, only about 1.5 million have been classified scientifically.

The basis of biological classification is the species. A species is a group of interbreeding organisms that do not ordinarily breed with members of other groups. Thus, despite their wide variety of appearances, domesticated dogs all belong to the same species because they can interbreed. Two nearly identical looking black birds, however, may belong to different species and not interbreed.

Classifying Using All of Your Senses

We use many different means to observe and understand the world and then to classify what we observe. Our five senses provide different means to sense and decode what is around us. We see with our eyes, we hear with our ears, we taste with our tongue, we feel with our hands, and we smell with our nose. When used together, the five senses give us powerful observational tools. The senses provide an interface through which we understand the world around us and serve as the basis for how we classify things. (See Experiment 31.)

Classification Systems

The Swedish scientist Carlus Linnaeus (1707–1778) developed an important system of classifying things found in nature. In doing so, he made it possible to define the key differences between various plants and animals. It was Linnaeus who introduced the use of the term "species" to represent the most refined unit in the organization. Linnaeus also suggested that each organism should be classified using a distinct binomial name. In this classification system, the first term represents the organism's generic name (called the genus) while the second term represents the organism's species. The current classification systems used by modern biologists have been built directly upon the Linnaean system of classification (see Image 7.4). (See Experiment 32.)

The Linnaean System of Classification

The full system of classification for living things developed by Swedish scientist Carlus Linnaeus involves seven different categories (kingdom, phylum, class, order, family, genus, species, and variety). You can more easily remember this system and its order by using the following mnemonic or memory device: "King Phillip Came Over For Good Spaghetti and Vegetables."

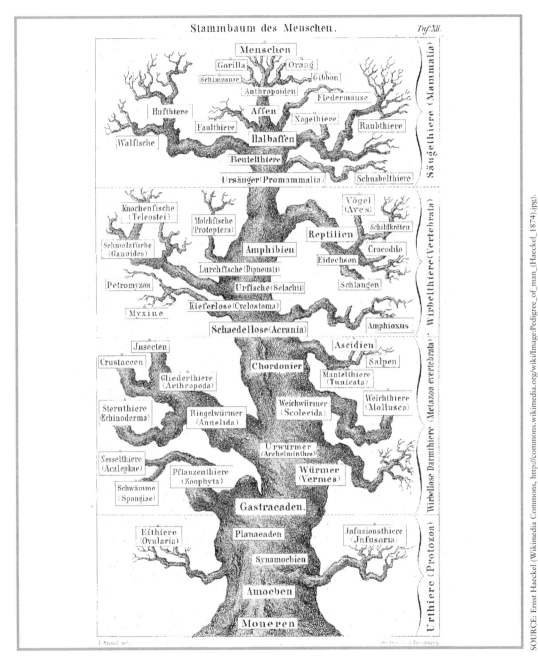

Image 7.4. Pedigree of Man, 1874

Classification systems are illustrated in this "Pedigree of Man," created by the German biologist Ernst Haeckel (1834–1919).

King = Kingdom
Phillip = Phylum
Came = Class
Over = Order
For = Family
Good = Genus
Spaghetti = Species
Vegetables = Variety

A Collie dog, for example, is of the kingdom Animalia, the phylum Cordata, the class Mammalia, the order Carnivora, the family Canidae (group with dog-like characteristics), the genus Canis (coyote, wolf, and dog), species Canis familiaris (domestic dog), and the variety Collie. (See Experiment 33.)

Plants

Plants are some of the most varied life forms on Earth and play many essential roles in supporting the planet's numerous ecosystems. Plants serve as producers and are at the bottom of many food chains, feeding the majority of animals. Plants are the only organisms that are able to convert light energy from the sun into food through the process of photosynthesis. Plants also play an important role in producing the oxygen that we, and all the other animals, breathe. Plants produce oxygen as a part of the process of photosynthesis. The oxygen that plants produce is then used by people and other animals when we breathe. In fact, all of the oxygen in our atmosphere originally comes from plants.

Another important ecological role that plants play is to provide a habitat for other organisms. A wide variety of animals of all shapes and sizes live in, on, and under plants. Plants provide shelter, safety, and food for these animals. Additionally, plants play a role in influencing the climate. For example, plants provide shade, which helps to moderate the temperature and serves as a buffer against wind and rain. In large enough numbers, such as in the rainforests, plants can modify entire weather patterns over large areas of the Earth. Plants also play an important role in creating and maintaining soil. The roots of trees and other plants help to hold the soil together, thus reducing erosion. One of the short-term consequences of deforestation is usually an increase in soil erosion because the soil no longer has the tree roots to help keep it in place. Plants help to create new soil as well. Soil is composed of broken-down rocks combined with the decomposed remains of plants. Without this plant matter, soil would be mostly sand and clay, lacking many of the nutrients that plants need to grow.

Many of us give little thought to plants, but it should be clear that plants play a significant role in our lives. Without plants, there could be no animal life on Earth.

Experiment **31:** Observation in the Bag

In the following activity, you will use all of your senses (except sight) to observe and classify objects hidden inside bags.

Materials You Will Need for This Activity

- Brown paper bags
- Small food samples such as raisins, chocolate chips, lemon, lime, grape, potato chip, apple, potato, orange, hard candy, cold cereal, etc.

What You Will Do

1. Number the bags from 1 to 5 and place a different food sample in each.
2. Make a data table listing the different senses in the columns and the bag numbers in the rows.
3. Use your sense of hearing to shake each bag, and write a description of the sound made.
4. Use your sense of touch to reach in each bag (without looking!), and describe the feel of each sample.
5. Use your sense of smell and sniff the contents of each bag, and describe the smell.
6. Close your eyes and taste a sample of each food; describe each taste.
7. Based on your data collection, draw a conclusion about what is in each bag.
8. Finally, look in the bag and check the accuracy of your conclusions.
9. How can you classify the items that were in the bags?

Image 7.5. Blindfolded Eating

What you will learn: The contents of the bags can be determined with reasonable accuracy using senses other than the sense of sight.

Core concept demonstrated: "Observation" in science often involves the use of more than just the sense of sight. Using multiple senses results in more robust observations and can aid in classification.

Thinking like a scientist: Which of the senses (besides sight) gave you the best clues to determine what the samples were? Why do you think that was? Which of the senses (besides sight) gave you the least information to determine what the samples were? Why do you think that was? Are there ways that you can classify the items based on your use of all your senses that you could not do based only on sight? Explain.

Correlation With National Science Standards: A.1; A.2; C.4; G.1

Experiment 32: Developing a System of Classification

In the following activity, you will experiment with creating systems of classification.

Materials You Will Need for This Activity

- Photographs of members of your immediate and extended family
- Chart paper
- Paper and pencil

What You Will Do

1. Look at the pictures of your family members. Consider how you can break them down into different classifications based on gender (male/female), age (young/old), responsibility, hair color, etc.
2. On the chart paper, draw boxes and place the pictures of family members showing how different individuals fall within different classifications. Rearrange the pictures several times to classify them in different ways.
3. Go outside on your school grounds and find an area with plants and animals.
4. List the living as well as nonliving things you find and classify them according to their various physical properties.
5. Try to list at least 20 different organisms sorted or classified into groups.
6. Look at each of your groups and see whether you can classify the group into subgroups.

What you will learn: All organisms have distinctly different characteristics that can be used for classification.

Core concept demonstrated: Humans divide the natural world into categories based on distinct properties or characteristics.

Thinking like a scientist: Think about how classification is an important part of not only our natural, but also our social lives. How do we classify nations? Think about features such as geographical setting, climate, politics, and religion. How do we classify people based on their race or ethnicity? How do we classify people based on their intelligence or ability?

Correlation With National Science Standards: A.2; C.1

Experiment **33:**   Classifying Different Animals

In the following activity, you will begin to classify different animals using the Linnaean categories.

Materials You Will Need for This Experiment

- Paper and pencil
- Animal pictures from books or magazines
- Internet access

What You Will Do

1. Try to classify as many of the taxonomic properties that you can for the following animals:
   - A Siamese cat
   - A goldfish
   - A grasshopper
2. Consult the Internet for help on classifying these animals. Use search terms such as "Linnaean classification" and "animal classification."
3. The Linnaean classification system is useful to scientists because it allows scientists from around the world to share a common understanding of which organism is being talked about. There are many other ways to classify animals, however. Look at the pictures of animals in the books or magazines and discuss how else they could be classified.

What you will learn: The Linnaean classification system helps to highlight the differences and similarities between various animals based on their natural characteristics.

Core concept demonstrated: How taxonomic classification systems break down the characteristics of living things

Thinking like a scientist: Think about the advantages and limitations of using various taxonomic systems. How can such systems potentially distort what things are like in the world? How can such systems help us understand what things have in common?

Correlation With National Science Standards: C.1; G.4

Image 7.6a. Cat

Image 7.6b. Goldfish

Image 7.6c.
Grasshopper

Seed Germination

Seeds are incredible biological devices. They contain the genetic information to grow an entire plant. In addition, they can lie dormant for long periods of time before the growth of a plant takes place. This is an important biological feature that makes possible much of life on Earth. A seed is grown, drops into the soil, and becomes active or germinates when the conditions of weather and moisture make it possible for the cycle of life to continue. (See Experiment 34.)

Plant Cells

Like all organisms, plants are composed of **cells**. Cells are the basic unit of life and the building blocks for all organisms, whether plants or animals. There are some differences, however, between plant cells and animal cells. Below is a brief overview of the parts of a plant cell and their functions. Every plant consists of millions of tiny plant cells. Every cell is made up of different parts that help it work. These cell parts are called *organelles*. All of the organelles in a cell work together to keep the cell alive. Each organelle in a plant cell has a unique set of functions. The analogy of a factory is sometimes used to describe the role of each organelle in the cell.

Cell wall—All plant cells have a rigid cell wall around them. The cell wall is like the brick wall of a factory; the cell wall helps to support the plant cell, just like the walls of a factory keep the building standing up.

Cell membrane—The cell membrane allows certain things to go in and out of the cell. It is like a screen door in a factory; it allows some things to go in and out, but not others.

Cytoplasm—The cytoplasm is the liquid in the cell in which all the other organelles float around. It is like the floor of a factory; it provides a surface that everything can stand on.

Ribosomes—The ribosomes make proteins. They put together the different pieces of proteins that the cell makes. Ribosomes are like the assembly line in the factory; they use certain materials to put together a product.

Endoplasmic reticulum (ER)—The ER is a transportation network that moves materials. The ER is like mail truck; it distributes materials around the cell.

Lysosome—The lysosome digests wastes in the cell. It is like the cleaning crew of a factory; it gets rid of materials in the cell that the cell does not need.

Nucleus—The nucleus controls what the cell does and contains its DNA. The nucleus is like the control room of the factory; it gives directions to all the other parts of the cell.

 **Experiment 34:** **Seed Germination**

In the following activity, you will explore and observe the **germination** of seeds.

Materials You Will Need for This Activity

- Paper towels
- Baby food jars
- Radish seeds
- Water
- Light source

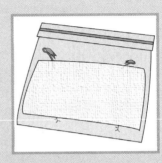

Image 7.7. Seed Germination

What You Will Do

1. Crumple a piece of paper towel, and place it in the bottom of your jar.
2. Add enough water so that the paper towel is wet and there is a layer of water on the bottom.
3. Place 5 radish seeds on the paper towel, keeping them out of the water.
4. Put your jar in the same place as the jars of your classmates.
5. Observe your jar each day for 10 days, and draw a picture of your seeds each day.

What you will learn: Seeds germinate and grow at different rates. The roots grow down regardless of how the seed is originally positioned.

Core concept demonstrated: Germination of seeds

Thinking like a scientist: Which grew first when your seeds sprouted, the root or the stem? What factors were present that may have helped your seeds germinate and grow? Is growth a physical or chemical process? Is energy gained or lost as the plant grows? What sources of energy did the seeds in this experiment use?

Correlation With National Science Standards: A.1; C.2

Chloroplast—The chloroplast helps the plant make its own food. It is also like a power supply; it provides the cell with the materials to make food. (See Experiment 35.)

Experiment **35:**   Making a Plant Cell Model

In the following activity, you will make a model of a plant cell.

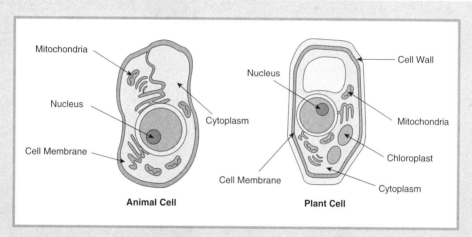

Image 7.8. Plant and Animal Cells

Materials You Will Need for This Activity

- Cytoplasm—yellow clay or play dough
- Endoplasmic reticulum—yarn or cooked spaghetti
- Ribosomes—cake sprinkles
- Vacuole—plastic-bubble packing material
- Lysosome—red clay or play dough

- Chloroplasts—green clay or play dough
- Cell wall—aluminum foil
- Cell membrane—plastic wrap
- Nucleus—blue clay or play dough
- Nuclear membrane—plastic wrap
- Chromosomes—pencil shavings
- Microscope
- Onion skin

(Continued)

(Continued)

What you will do:

1. Make the cell membrane by placing a large piece of plastic wrap on the table.
2. Make the cytoplasm by forming a ball of yellow clay or play dough, laying it on the plastic wrap, and pressing it into a "pancake" about 6 inches in diameter.
3. Using the materials listed above, find the supplies to represent each cell structure, and gently press each item into the cytoplasm, with the exception of the cell wall.
4. Wrap the cytoplasm pancake carefully around the cell parts and seal the edges together, forming a ball.
5. Wrap the cell membrane (plastic wrap) around the cytoplasm and then wrap the cell wall (aluminum foil) around the cell membrane.
6. Shape the cell into a rectangular form and then carefully cut the cell in half with a large knife to expose a cross section of the cell.
7. Now that you have made a model plant cell, you will look at a real cell. Take a small piece of onion skin and place it on a microscope slide.
8. Look at the onion skin under the microscope. Can you observe individual cells? Individual organelles? How do they appear similar to or different from your cell model?

What you will learn: Plant cells are composed of multiple components that are tightly packed into a cell structure.

Core concept demonstrated: Basic form and components of a plant cell

Thinking like a scientist: Why do you think a cell has so many component parts? Why do you think plant cells have cell walls and animal cells do not? What would happen if plant cells didn't have these cell walls? What would happen if animal cells did?

Correlation With National Science Standards: C.4; C.9

Variables in Plant Growth

Plants are extraordinary biological engines. They move and grow and process nutrients as animals do; however, the process by which they do this is different. Instead of processes such as eating, digestion, and muscular movement, plants employ the process of photosynthesis to grow. In the following experiment, we will explore variables that influence photosynthesis in plants. (See Experiment 36.)

 **Experiment 36:**   **The Effect of Acid Rain on Plant Growth**

In the following activity, you will simulate the effect of acid rain on the growth of radish plants.

Materials You Will Need for This Activity

- 3 Styrofoam cups
- Masking tape
- Marker
- Potting soil
- Radish seeds (note that if you already germinated radish seeds in Experiment 34 you can use these sprouts rather than sprouting new seeds)
- Ruler
- pH strips or pH soil test kit

Image 7.9. Acid Rain

What you will do:

1. Label three Styrofoam cups A, B, and C with masking tape and marker.
2. Fill each cup with potting soil.
3. With your finger, make a hole about three to five cm deep in the soil.
4. Place five radish seeds in each hole.
5. Cover the seeds with soil.

(Continued)

(Continued)

6. Water the seeds in cups A and B with 50 ml of water.
7. Water the seeds in cup C with 50 ml of vinegar.
8. Place the cups in a windowsill with sunlight.
9. Predict what you think will happen to the seeds in each cup.
10. Check your plants each day.
11. Using a ruler, measure their growth in centimeters every three days. Record this information in a data table.
12. Every other day, add 20 ml of water to cups A and B. Add 20 ml of vinegar to cup C.
13. After one week, continue to water only cup A every other day with 20 ml of water. Water pots B and C with 20 ml of vinegar.
14. Make new predictions about what you think will happen to the seeds in each cup.
15. Continue measuring and recording plant growth every three days.
16. After 21 days, take the last measurements of plant height and then measure the pH of the soil in each of the cups.
17. Using the data table you have made, construct a bar graph to display your results.

What you will learn: The lower pH caused by the vinegar will negatively impact plant growth. The more dramatic the pH change, the more pronounced the effect on plant growth.

Core concept demonstrated: Changing one chemical variable can affect plant growth rate

Thinking like a scientist: How did your results compare with the results of other groups? How can you explain any differences? How did your results compare with your predictions that you made at the beginning of the experiment? What changes could you make in this experiment, based on the information you now have, to extend your understanding of this topic? How could what you have discovered be used to make you a better gardener or farmer?

Correlation With National Science Standards: A.1; A.2; C.3

Animals

Many people think of the study of animals when they think of biology. Animals come in all shapes and sizes, from microscopic protozoa to mammoth whales, from the ancient jellyfish to the relatively modern *Homo sapiens*. The cellular and anatomical structure of animals, and how they differ from other forms of life such as plants, is one essential component of animal biology. At the ecological level, the ways animals interact with each other and with other elements of the environment is another primary component. For young scientists, the careful observation of animal behaviors provides insights into both the nature of animal life forms and the ways in which animals interact with their natural environment.

Dissecting Owl Pellets

Animal droppings or poop may be pretty gross stuff, but the elimination of fecal matter is an essential part of animal biology. All animals, whether they are reptiles, mammals, birds, fish, or insects, must eliminate biological waste. Nutrients are absorbed by the body, and the waste materials need to be expelled. Some creatures have developed unique ways to deal with this biological necessity. Owls, who eat small creatures whole, must expel sharp objects such as bones and hard-to-digest fur. Rather than expelling this material through fecal matter, owls regurgitate it as furry boney lumps called owl pellets. In the materials that are expelled, there is a great deal of interesting residue that provides information about the owl and its diet. Thus, owl pellets provide clues for biologists about what the owls have recently eaten. It is actually possible to take a pellet apart and reconstruct the skeleton of an owl's small prey, such as voles or field mice. (See Experiment 37.)

Animal Cells

Different life forms have different cellular structures. The basic structures of animal cells are different from those of plant cells. Animal cells don't have a cell wall. This makes them more flexible than plants with their rigid cells. Animal cells do not have chloroplasts because they are not involved in the process of photosynthesis. Instead, animal cells have Golgi bodies and vacuoles that help distribute nutrients that provide energy for cell functions. (See Experiment 38.)

Bird Census and Journal on Animal Behavior

Every 10 years the U.S. **Census** counts all of the people in the United States. In 2000, for example, it was determined that the population of the country was 282, 421, 906 (http://www.census.gov/). Census takers want to know more than just the number of people living here. They are interested, for example, in the number of men and women, children and adults, the types

(Text continues on page 224)

Experiment 37:   **Owl Pellet Dissection**

In the following activity, you will explore the contents of an owl pellet and attempt to reconstruct the skeleton and identify the last creature eaten by the owl.

Materials You Will Need for This Activity

- Owl pellet
- Paper plates
- Pair of tweezers
- Toothpicks
- Latex gloves
- Glue

Image 7.10. Owl

What You Will Do

* Safety Note—The owl pellets, which come from a biological supply house, have been sterilized to kill germs, but it is still recommended to wear latex gloves when handling the pellets.

1. Measure the pellet (length, width, and mass).
2. Carefully pull the pellet apart.
3. Separate the bones from the fur with the tweezers or toothpicks.
4. Set the bones on one plate and fur on another.
5. Organize and classify the bones into piles.
6. Count the number of each type of bone found in your owl pellet.
7. Record your bone count results on a bar graph.
8. Try to reconstruct the skeleton of the creature by laying out the bones on a flat surface.
9. Glue your skeleton to a piece of paper.

What you will learn: Owl pellets contain the skeletal remains of small prey that can be sorted and at least partially reconstructed.

Core concept demonstrated: Examination of reconstruction of an animal skeleton

Thinking like a scientist: What additional materials would help you to more accurately construct the skeleton of the owl's prey? How was your task similar to that of a paleontologist attempting to reconstruct a dinosaur skeleton? What makes the paleontologist's task even more difficult?

Correlation With National Science Standards: A.1; C.4

 **Experiment 38: Making an Animal Cell Model**

To watch a video clip related to this concept, go to the Student Resource CD bound into the back of your textbook.

In the following activity, you will make an edible model of an animal cell. Look at Image 7.8 for a picture of an animal cell compared to a plant cell.

Materials You Will Need for This Activity

- 1 package of Jell-O (light color)
- 1 package of Knox gelatin mixture (to make Jell-O stiffer)
- 1 paper plate
- 1 small plastic cup
- 1 plastic knife
- 1 plastic spoon
- Toothpicks
- 2 blue or green pieces of Fruit Roll-up (Golgi bodies)

- 2 red or yellow pieces of Fruit Roll-up (endoplasmic reticulum)
- 1 teaspoon of round cake sprinkles (ribosomes)
- 4 Hot Tamales (or similarly shaped candy) (mitochondria)
- 4 chocolate-covered raisins (vacuoles)
- 1 gum ball (nucleus)
- Microscope
- Microscope slide

What You Will Do

1. Mix the Jell-O gelatin according to the directions. Add some unflavored Knox gelatin to the Jell-O to make it stiffer.
2. Pour the Jell-O mixture into individual plastic cups until they are about two-thirds full. Put them in the refrigerator to set.
3. Remove the Jell-O from the plastic cup by turning it over and placing it on a paper plate.
4. Cut the Jell-O in half to form two cylinders.
5. Use a spoon to scoop out a hole in the bottom (larger) half of the Jell-O.
6. Place the gumball in the hole to represent the nucleus of the cell.
7. Continue in this way, using the spoon to make spaces to put the other cell parts into the cell as directed in the materials list above.
8. Parts can be put into both the top and bottom half of the Jell-O cell.
9. When all the parts are in place, carefully take the top part of the cell and place it back on the bottom half.
10. Now that you have made a model animal cell, you will look at a real cell. Use a clean toothpick to scrape the inside of your cheek.
11. Place the cheek cells on the microscope slide and look at them under the microscope. Can you observe individual cells? Individual organelles? How do they appear similar to or different from your cell model?

(Continued)

of jobs people have, where they live, and so on. This information is enormously important to better understand future trends in our country. For example, it allows sociologists to predict future demands on schools or the number of people who are going to be retiring.

Similarly, conducting censuses of animals is a very important source of information for biologists. An animal census can provide information about the stability or health of a population, as well as provide insight into the behaviors of particular species. (See Experiment 39.)

Neither Plant nor Animal: Protista, Monera, Viruses, Bacteria, Fungi

Plants and animals are not the only forms of life on Earth. Traditionally, living organisms have been divided into two main groups: the **monera**, including bacteria and blue-green algae (organisms whose cells lack a nucleus); and the **eucaryotes**, including protozoa, algae, plants, fungi, and animals (organisms whose cells contain a nucleus). This arrangement has been replaced by the more recent five-kingdom classification that divides the living organisms into five kingdoms: monera (the bacteria and blue-green algae), protista (the protozoa and some of the algae), fungi, plants, and animals. Currently, biologists are debating whether this classification system needs to be modified further. The protista, monera, viruses, bacteria, and fungi are easy to overlook when considering living organisms, yet all play important roles in the Earth's ecosystems.

Experiment **39:** Conducting a Bird Census

In the following activity, you will conduct a bird census by observing birds in your schoolyard and keeping track of their behavior over time.

Materials You Will Need for This Activity

- Bird guide (preferably specific to your state or region. Titles that are relevant to your geographic region can readily be found from online booksellers. Many of these books should also be available in your local library. In addition, your local Audubon Society may have information, including Web sites, for learning more about birds in your part of the country.)
- Binoculars (optional)
- Notebook and pencil

What You Will Do

1. Make a census table in your notebook with 3 columns: kind of bird, where the bird was, what the bird was doing.
2. Go outside in the schoolyard and look for birds.
3. For every bird you see, make an entry in your census journal, recording where the bird is, what the bird is doing, and, if you are able to, identifying the species or more general type of bird.
4. Make your observations for about 10 to 15 minutes.
5. Repeat your observations once a week for at least a month, but preferably for the entire school year.
6. Discuss in class how you can make graphs of the data in your table.

What you will learn: Within a given ecosystem, there is a wide variety of bird species with a wide variety of behaviors, both of which change over the course of the year.

Core concept demonstrated: Variation of species and behaviors in a given ecosystem

Thinking like a scientist: What kinds of birds were the most common in your schoolyard? Was this consistent over the year or did it change with the seasons? Were the bird behaviors consistent over the year or did they change? What might explain any changes you recorded over the year? How might a scientist make use of bird census data of this kind? How would conducting observations at the same time every day have affected your research?

Correlation With National Science Standards: A.2; C.3; C.7; G.1

Microscope Studies of Pond Water

One amazing thing about biology is the growing awareness of the variety of life that exists at all scales, even at the microscopic level. If you look at a pond, it usually appears to be just water with plants growing around the edges. On careful examination, however, you will typically find a complex ecosystem with a wide variety of plant and animal life. Small plants and animals are visible to the naked eye, but even more can be seen with the aid of a microscope. (See Experiment 40.)

The Action of Yeast in Dough

Organic material can be altered as a result of biological and biochemical processes. For example, the fermentation process that results in wine occurs when grapes are crushed and the sugars undergo a biochemical process. A similar process occurs in the making of bread. Bread "rises" because of the addition of yeast that acts as a leavener that produces a gas. Yeast feeds on the sugars in flour and gives off carbon dioxide in the process.

Yeast is a fungus. It is so small that just one gram contains over 20 billion yeast cells. These cells will produce carbon dioxide, as long as there is enough simple sugar present for the yeast to use as food.(See Experiment 41.)

Looking for Helpful Bacteria in Our Food

Have you ever cut yourself and put an ointment on the cut so it doesn't get infected? The reason you do this is to kill bacteria, which can easily enter an open wound and spread. Maybe you have also used an antibacterial soap to clean your hands. You probably think that bacteria are always harmful and will make you sick. This is true for some bacteria, but it is not always the case. Bacteria in food can be both good and bad. You don't want to eat a spoiled piece of food that has begun to rot and is growing bacteria. However, certain kinds of bacteria are necessary to make some of our favorite foods, including cheese, buttermilk, and yogurt. (See Experiment 42.)

🐾 Ladder of Life: The Building Blocks of Organisms

Cellular construction, photosynthetic processes, and the role of surface areas represent some of the basic structural principles underlying the development of various life forms. Understanding these principles provides us with a growing awareness of how different life forms respond developmentally to the range of forces that act upon them in the world.

Cell Packing

Biological forms consistently make use of the most efficient structures possible. This is almost certainly a matter of survival. In the case of cellular forms, cells generally arrange themselves in ways that allow the maximum

(Text continues on page 230)

Experiment **40:** Exploring Pond Water

In the following activity, you will take a sample of pond water and catalog the microscopic forms that can be seen.

Materials You Will Need for This Activity

- Pond water sample
- Petri dish or watch glass
- Magnifying glass
- Microscope
- Microscope slides and cover slip
- Field guide of pond organisms

What You Will Do

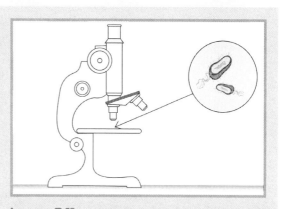

Image 7.11. Pond Water Under a Microscope

1. Collect a water sample from a nearby pond, stream, or canal and bring the sample back to the classroom.
2. Use the medicine dropper to place several drops of pond water into a small dish. Record anything you observe in your sample with the naked eye.
3. Next, observe the sample using a magnifying glass. Record anything you observe.
4. Get a microscope slide and a cover slip. Use the medicine dropper to put one or two drops of pond water on the middle of the slide, and put the cover slip on top of the pond water.
5. Look at the slide you made using the microscope. Make a sketch of what you observe under the microscope.

* Safety Note—Pond water may contain harmful bacteria or other substances. Never drink the water and try to keep it out of cuts or other injuries where it can cause infections.

What you will learn: There are a number of living organisms in pond water, some of which can be seen with the naked eye and some of which require magnification.

Core concept demonstrated: Protista are among the microscopic organisms found in pond water.

Thinking like a scientist: How can you tell whether the pond organisms you observed were animals, plants, or protista? What strategies can you use to differentiate the three? Which were the most common in your pond sample? Why might this be? Do you think this would hold true in samples from other ponds? Why or why not?

Correlation With National Science Standards: A.1; C.3; C.7

To watch a video clip related to this concept, go to the Student Resource CD bound into the back of your textbook.

 Experiment **41:** The Power of Yeast

In the following activity, you will look for evidence of the biochemical reaction that takes place when yeast feeds on sugar.

Materials You Will Need for This Activity

- 1 packet of active dry yeast
- 2 tablespoons sugar
- 1 cup very warm water (about 110° F)
- A large balloon
- An empty 16- or 20-ounce water bottle

Image 7.12. Bread Dough

What You Will Do

1. Stretch out the balloon by blowing it up several times.
2. Add the yeast and the sugar to the cup of warm water and stir.
3. When the yeast and sugar are dissolved, pour the mixture into the empty water bottle.
4. Attach the balloon over the mouth of the water bottle.
5. Observe the balloon every few minutes over the next 30 minutes.
6. Sketch what happens to the balloon.

What you will learn: Yeast feeds on sugar and produces the gas carbon dioxide. This is what happens in the balloon and it is also what happens when bread rises. The carbon dioxide gas gets trapped in many little balloon-like bubbles in the bread dough, and once it is baked, this gives the bread its texture.

Core concept demonstrated: Fungi such as yeast produce biochemical reactions.

Thinking like a scientist: What do you think would happen if you used twice as much yeast in this experiment? Half as much yeast? Twice as much sugar? Half as much sugar? Hotter water? Colder water? You might want to actually try some of these variations to compare them with your initial results.

Correlation With National Science Standards: A.1; A.2; C.1; C.2

 **Experiment 42: Making Yogurt**

In the following activity, you will use a bacterial culture to make yogurt.

Materials You Will Need for This Activity

- 1 gallon of 2% milk
- Box of instant nonfat dry milk
- Container of plain (no fruit added) yogurt (be sure the label indicates that the product contains a live culture)
- Kitchen thermometer
- Measuring cup
- Large saucepan
- Stove or hot plate
- Styrofoam cups or used yogurt cups
- Sugar (optional)
- Fruit preserves (optional)

Image 7.13. Yogurt Container

What You Will Do

1. Mix one gallon of 2% milk and 2 ¾ cups of nonfat dry milk in a large saucepan.
2. Sugar may be added to the milk before boiling, if desired. Try 1 cup the first time, and then adjust to taste in subsequent batches.
3. Heat the milk in the saucepan to boiling and then let the milk cool to 110°F. (Be careful not to let the milk boil over! Boiling the milk kills unwanted bacteria.)
4. Remove any "skin" that may have formed on the milk as it cooled.
5. Warm 1 cup of starter culture (plain yogurt bought at the store or dry starter culture can be purchased online) to 110°F in a warm water bath and then add the starter to the milk once the milk has also cooled to 110°F.
6. Mix well, but gently, so as not to stir in too much air.
7. Sanitize your yogurt containers (Styrofoam cups or used yogurt cups) by rinsing them in boiling water.
8. If fruit is to be added to the yogurt, first warm the fruit in a warm water bath so that its temperature is 110°F. Put the fruit in the bottom of the cups before adding the milk.
9. Pour the milk into the clean containers and cover them with a lid (plastic wrap can be used or the tops of used yogurt cups sterilized with boiling water).

(Continued)

Part 2   Teaching and Learning the Science Disciplines

(Continued)

10. The cups of yogurt must now be incubated, maintaining their temperature at 110°F until the milk coagulates with a firm custard-like consistency (this generally takes from 3 to 6 hrs). Do not stir the yogurt during this period.
11. There are several ways to control the temperature during incubation: Yogurt containers can be kept warm in an oven or a Styrofoam cooler box with a light bulb placed inside to generate heat; yogurt containers can be placed into pans of 110°F water in an oven or an electric frying pan that can be turned on to warm from time to time to maintain water temperature; electric heating pads or solar energy may also be used.
12. After a few hours at 110°F, check for coagulation by gently tilting the cups in which you have been making your yogurt.
13. Once the yogurt is firm, place it in the refrigerator. Eat when cold.

* Safety Note—Close adult supervision is required during the boiling process. As with all food preparation, all containers and materials should be thoroughly cleaned both before and after use.

What you will learn: Bacteria combined with milk during an incubation process results in the transformation of milk into yogurt.

Core concept demonstrated: Some bacteria are beneficial to humans and are part of what we eat.

Thinking like a scientist: Imagine that the batch of yogurt you made didn't turn out right—either it never coagulated or perhaps it tasted bad. What are some of the possible things that could have gone wrong? How could you test your ideas about what had gone wrong to see whether your explanation was correct or not? What would be the some of the hypotheses that you would generate?

Correlation With National Science Standards: A.1; A.2; C.4; E.4; G.1

Copyright © 2007 by Sage Publications, Inc. All rights reserved. Reprinted from *Teaching Science in Elementary and Middle School*, by Cory A. Buxton and Eugene A. Provenzo. Reproduction authorized only for the student who purchased the book to use in his or her teaching.

number of cells to be put into a minimal space. This makes it possible for the organism to be structurally stronger and to maximize the biological functions contained within it. The British scientist Darcy Wentworth Thompson (1860–1948) concluded in the 1930s that many biological forms, like cells, consistently have the same geometry and that this is primarily a result of efficient packing. In many cases, this results in hexagonal patterns that are highly efficient packing configurations. You can see this in the shape of a turtle shell, as well as in the shape of many plant cells. (See Experiment 43.)

 Experiment **43:**   **Cell Packing**

In the following activity, you will observe how materials are packed in ways that make them more efficient to stack.

Materials You Will Need for This Activity

- A 12-ounce can of Pringles© potato chips
- A 12-ounce bag of regular or loose potato chips
- A balance

Image 7.14. Chip Packing

What You Will Do

1. Empty the potato chips into two separate piles. You can open the bag of loose chips and simply dump it. Slide the Pringles© out of their can so that they remain stacked on top of one another.
2. Take the loose chips and drop them into the empty Pringles can. Be careful not to crush them. When the can is as full as possible without having crushed the chips, weigh the can on the balance. Record this weight.
3. Empty the can. Now slide the stack(s) of Pringles back into the can until it is full. Weigh the can. Record this weight and compare it with the weight of the loose chips.

What you will learn: How tightly objects can be packed together will depend on how they are shaped and how they are aligned.

Core concept demonstrated: Efficiency in design and packing

Thinking like a scientist: How can efficiency of the type demonstrated above be useful for people who must transport expensive goods great distances? If you were to design a space station, how might the characteristics of Pringles© inform the type of structure that you built and launched into space? Where can you see design principles of the type discussed here in nature and in fields such as architecture and engineering?

Correlation With National Science Standards: A.2; C.4; E.4; G.3

Photosynthesis-Transpiration Interactions

In addition to all the other functions a plant cell carries out (see Experiment 35), the chloroplasts in plant cells must produce the sugars that serve as food for the plant. This is done through the process of photosynthesis. The English chemist Joseph Priestly (1733–1804) discovered that when he captured air under an inverted jar and burned a candle in it, the candle burned out very quickly. He also discovered that placing a mouse in the jar with the candle would cause the candle to burn even faster. He then showed that when he placed a plant in the jar, the candle would burn longer. In 1778, Jan Ingenhousz repeated Priestly's experiments. He discovered that the candle kept burning because sun and light on the plant caused it to produce oxygen. (See Experiment 44.)

Cells as Natural Forms

The German biologist and philosopher Ernst Haeckel (1834–1919) is among the most famous scientists of the nineteenth century. Some of his most interesting work involved the study of radiolarians, a type of microscopic sea creature. He collected these organisms while he was working as a field biologist on the British ship HMS Challenger during the mid-1870s.

Haeckel drew extraordinarily detailed and beautiful drawings of different types of radiolarians, as well as many other sea creatures. A remarkable discovery was that as complex as these radiolarians appear to be, they take on shapes and forms that are highly predictable and that also correspond to the shapes taken by soap bubbles when suspended in differently shaped metal frames. This process is based on minimal surfaces; as part of an evolutionary process, the radiolarians take on the most structurally and energy efficient forms possible (Look back at Image 2.13 in Chapter 2 for a stunning image of Haeckel's radiolarians). The forces that shape radiolarians and soap bubbles can be seen at work in other contexts as well. For example, if you suspend vegetable oil in alcohol and water, it will take the form of a sphere, which is the most efficient and minimal form possible. (See Experiment 45.)

🐜 Code of Life: All Life Is Based on the Same Genetic Code

Biological systems have extraordinary means by which to communicate complex information and data. DNA represents a means by which biological systems can store and transfer this information using a genetic code. A genetic code is a set of rules that serve to map DNA sequences onto proteins in a cell. Almost all living things use the same genetic code. This code determines the characteristics and appearance of the organism as well as which characteristics will be modified or changed through the process of evolution.

Experiment 44: Photosynthesis and Transpiration

In the following activity, you will look for evidence that plant cells engage in photosynthesis and transpiration and the production of oxygen.

Materials You Will Need for This Activity

- 2 or more small pots
- A packet of pea seeds
- A bag of potting soil
- A spray bottle or mister
- A large cardboard box
- A glass bottle or jar

What You Will Do

1. Germinate the pea seeds by placing them on a damp paper towel in a tray and covering them with warm tap water. A root should spout in two to three days. After the roots appear, the seeds are ready to be planted in the pots.
2. Fill the pots with the potting soil mixture up to 2 ½ inches from the top.
3. Place the seeds carefully on top of mixture, and cover them with ¼ to ½ inch of soil.
4. Spray water over the top of the soil until the soil is well saturated.
5. Place half of the pots in a well-lit place and the other half of the pots in the closed cardboard box.
6. Spray all the plants lightly with water every two to three days, but otherwise be sure the plants in the box remain in the dark.
7. At the end of one week to 10 days, remove the pots from the closed box and compare them with the pots of seedlings that were grown in the light. What do you see?
8. Remove one seedling from each pot and compare the root structure of the seedlings grown in the dark with the seedlings grown in the light.
9. Leave the pots that were in the dark in the light for a few days, and compare the results.
10. Now place a glass bottle over one of the seedlings, and put it in the sunlight.
11. Notice after a couple of hours or a day condensation occurs on the inside of the bottle. This is the result of water vapor being given off by the plant when it exchanges oxygen for carbon dioxide in the transpiration process.

What you will learn: Comparing a plant left for a week in the dark with one exposed to sunlight allows you to see the key role of photosynthesis in plant cells. Covering a plant with a bottle allows you to see the condensation that is the result of transpiration and the production of oxygen.

(Continued)

(Continued)

Core concept demonstrated: Plant photosynthesis

Thinking like a scientist: Several of the largest mass extinctions of plants and animals in the history of the Earth seem to have been caused by asteroid or meteor impacts that filled the atmosphere with dust and debris for months or possibly even years. How does what you know about photosynthesis explain how such an event could cause this type of extinction? When the Indonesian volcano Krakatoa erupted in 1883, huge amounts of dust were expelled into the stratosphere. Weather was changed across the entire surface of the Earth. How do you think this eruption affected plant growth?

Correlation With National Science Standards: A.1; A.2; C.4; G.4

Modeling the DNA Double Helix

The DNA double helix holds the genetic code for all life on Earth, and as such, its discovery is seen as one of humankind's greatest scientific breakthroughs. The two names most closely associated with DNA are James Watson (1928–) and Francis Crick (1916–2004), who are widely credited with identifying its structure in the late 1950s. While Watson and Crick undoubtedly deserve credit, there exists a significant controversy around this key scientific discovery. Watson and Crick shared a 1962 Nobel Prize for this work with Maurice Wilkins, who had worked on DNA research independently of Watson and Crick. Wilkins worked in a lab at King's College, London with a chemist named Rosalind Franklin. Between 1951 and 1953, Franklin did most of the foundational work and came very close to solving the puzzle of DNA structure on her own. Tensions between Wilkins and Franklin, at least in part because Franklin was a successful woman in a field very much dominated by men at that time, led Wilkins to show critical parts of Franklin's work to Watson and Crick without Franklin's knowledge or permission. Watson and Crick were able to use this new information of Franklin's to quickly solve the puzzle of DNA's structure and publish their conclusions without giving credit to Franklin.

As a sad end to the story, Franklin developed cancer a few years later and died in 1958. The Nobel Prize guidelines prohibit posthumous awards; thus, Franklin was ineligible to even be considered when the prize was

(Text continues on page 237)

Experiment 45: Minimal Surfaces in Natural and Biological Forms

In the following activity, you will see how spheres are formed as vegetable oil takes on the most efficient form and shape possible.

Materials You Will Need for This Activity

- A flat-sided bottle
- Rubbing alcohol
- An eye dropper
- Vegetable oil
- Water

What You Will Do

1. Fill a flat-sided bottle (a round bottle will distort what you see) $\frac{2}{3}$ full with rubbing alcohol.
2. Using a eyedropper, place a few drops of vegetable oil on the surface of the alcohol.
3. Slowly add water to the bottle until the drops of oil float between the water and the alcohol.
4. No matter how many drops you add, the oil will always form into spheres.

What you will learn: Nature is essentially parsimonious and likes to save energy. Natural forms take on the simplest and most efficient shape possible. The shape that can hold the greatest volume within the least area is a sphere. This is why soap bubbles become round. What happens with the oil in this experiment is what happens when a soap bubble is formed. The surface area of the suspended soap bubble or oil causes it to take the shape of a sphere because this is the most economical way it can function—it saves energy and space. Similarly, whenever a drop of water falls through the sky as a raindrop, it will always form a sphere.

Core concept demonstrated: Minimal surfaces and volume

Thinking like a scientist: Why are raindrops not perfectly shaped spheres? What other factors influence their shape? What shape would a drop of water take inside a spaceship in outer space?

Correlation With National Science Standards: C.1; C.8; G.4

Experiment 46: Making a Model of the DNA Double Helix

In the following activity, you will create a model of the DNA double helix structure.

Materials You Will Need for This Activity

- Styrofoam balls (about 100)
- Double-end toothpicks (75)
- Wooden or metal ring stand to serve as a support
- Paint brushes for painting the Styrofoam balls
- Paints (6 colors)

What You Will Do

1. Decide what colors you want to use for the small molecules that make up a larger DNA molecule.
2. Paint all the balls and let them dry.
3. Start from the base of your stand, and connect the molecules to each other using toothpicks. The large DNA molecule must wrap around the stand's column.
4. Note that the bases of DNA are almost always found as base pairs. Adenine (A) pairs with Thymine (T) and Guanine (G) pairs with Cytosine (C). The prime features of the structure are two strands of DNA wrapped around each other, creating a right-handed helix.
5. Make a pair of C-G (Cytosine-Guanine) and then add a phosphate molecule to each end of the C-G pair. Attach this chain of 4 molecules to the backbone (stand).
6. Assemble the second row, which can be C-G again or A-T. Attach phosphates and then add to the stand as with the first row, but rotate a small amount clockwise relative to the first row.
7. Continue the ladder in this fashion until you run out of balls. Remember that each row must rotate a small amount clockwise relative to the prior row, to create the spiral.

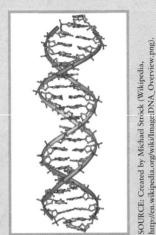

Image 7.15. Double Helix

SOURCE: Created by Michael Ströck (Wikipedia, http://en.wikipedia.org/wiki/Image:DNA_Overview.png).

What you will learn: A DNA molecule appears quite complex but, in fact, is made primarily of only two set pairs of molecules with a surrounding support structure.

Core concept demonstrated: Structure of DNA

Thinking like a scientist: Why do you think the DNA molecule has formed in the shape that it has? How can a repeating structure of only four basic molecules possess all the genetic code to grow a new organism as complicated as a human being? Think about minimal surfaces and some of the ideas developed in this book.

Correlation With National Science Standards: C.4; C.5; E.5; G.1; G.4

awarded to Watson, Crick, and Wilkins in 1962. Thus, despite her significant contributions, it seems unlikely that Rosalind Franklin will ever be anything but a footnote in the story of DNA's scientific discovery and description. (See Experiment 46.)

DNA "Fingerprints" for Solving Mysteries

Have you ever watched a detective show on TV in which the suspect was caught because of fingerprints he left behind? Fingerprints are unique to every individual, and fingerprint evidence has been used by police since the eighteenth century. Genetic information, in the form of DNA, is as unique to each of us as our fingerprints; we have a unique genetic code that identifies us. Thus, if a criminal leaves a hair at the scene of a crime, it can be used to identify that individual. When DNA is tested, a process called polymerase chain reaction (PCR) is used to amplify small well-defined strands of a DNA sample, which can then be compared to a known standard (such as for detecting genetic diseases) or to another sample (such as in the case of matching a suspect's DNA with that found at a crime scene). A similar process can be done using chromatography to see the "fingerprints" of colored DNA markers. (See Experiment 47.)

Genetic Defects

The chromosomes found within living cells represent extremely complex mechanisms for turning on and off different functions in cellular systems. The analogy can be made that chromosomes are like the keys that open the locks on a door and, in turn, allow certain cellular functions to take place. They can also be thought of as catalysts for setting these functions in motion. Genetic defects are generally a result of one or more abnormalities on one or more chromosomes. Many genetic defects can now be detected prenatally (before a baby is born), and other tests for genetic defects are routinely done with newborns while they are still in the hospital. One such test is a hearing test to check the baby for evidence of hearing loss or deafness. (See Experiment 48.)

Evolution: Natural Selection and Evidence for Species Evolution

Evolution can be defined as a change in the **gene** pool of a population over time. A gene is a hereditary unit that is passed on from generation to generation. The gene pool is the collection of all the genes in a given population. One of the most commonly cited examples of observed evolution is the case of the English moth. This moth comes in two colors, a light moth and a dark moth. In the mid-1800s, dark moths only accounted for about 2% of the English moth population. By 1900, however, approximately 95% of the English moths around the English city of Manchester were of the dark variety. In rural areas, however, light moths still made up the majority of the population.

To watch a video clip related to this concept, go to the Student Resource CD bound into the back of your textbook.

Experiment 47: Black Marker "Fingerprints"

In the following activity, you will use chromatography to identify a "mystery marker."

Materials You Will Need for This Activity

Image 7.16. Fingerprint

- 5 different brands of black markers
- Coffee filters
- Scissors
- Large bowl with about one inch of water in the bottom
- Ruler
- Tape

What You Will Do

1. Cut coffee filters into rectangular strips about one inch wide and six inches long.
2. Draw a horizontal line across each strip of coffee filter about one inch from the bottom, using a different black marker for each strip.
3. Label each strip, so you know which marker was used on it.
4. Place the ruler across the top of the bowl of water.
5. Tape the strips to the ruler so that the strips hang down with the water touching the bottom of the coffee filter, but not touching the ink.
6. The water should creep up the coffee filter strips and separate each ink line into a unique pattern.
7. Now have a person not in your group write a short note on a coffee filter using one of the markers, without telling anyone which marker was used. How can you solve the mystery to find out which marker was used to write the note?
8. Use the same procedure you used to test the five markers originally to find the "color fingerprint" of the mystery marker.
9. Compare the pattern from the mystery marker to the five standards you have created to see which one it matches. Check your answer with the person who wrote the note.

What you will learn: Even though the inks from different markers appear the same, they are actually made of many different dyes. Chromatography can be used to separate the dyes in the ink from different markers to make different patterns. A different type of separation technique is used in much the same way to identify DNA samples.

Core concept demonstrated: Separation techniques can be used to identify individual subjects.

Thinking like a scientist: What do you think would happen if you used colored markers instead of black markers? Would they separate into different components, or are the colors based on one dye? How else might chromatography be used in the study of proteins, in industrial chemistry, and so on?

Correlation With National Science Standards: A.1; A.2; C.5; C.8; F.10

The moths' color was determined by a single gene. Therefore, the increase in dark-colored moths represented a change in the gene pool, or evolution. The increase in number of dark moths was a result of natural selection. During England's industrial revolution, pollution from the factories darkened the bark of the trees that the moths frequently rest on. Against this dirty background, birds could more easily see the light-colored moths and ate more of them. As more of the light-colored moths were eaten, more dark moths survived to reproduce. The greater number of dark-colored offspring survived to continue this pattern. This is an example of natural selection.

It is important to understand that in evolution, individuals do not evolve. In the example of the English moths, no light-colored moths changed to a dark color to avoid being eaten. Instead, individuals that were dark color were selected because they were more likely to survive and reproduce, and over time the moth population evolved to include more dark moths.

Bird Beak Models

Have you ever gone to the zoo or watched a nature program and seen different types of birds? Have you noticed how different various birds' beaks are, depending on where they live and the types of food they eat? This is part of an evolutionary adaptation that has led to extraordinarily different types of bird beaks. A bird like a stork that primarily hunts small fish has a beak that allows it to spear its prey. By contrast, a parrot, which feeds largely on nuts that must be cracked, has a conical beak that is very strong (Never put your finger in a parrot's beak! Ouch!). (See Experiment 49.)

Experiment **48:** **Hearing Loss Simulation**

In the following activity, you will experience what life is like for people with a hearing loss.

**Materials You Will
Need for This Activity**

- Earplugs (with the greatest amount of noise blockage or attenuation you can find)
- Earmuffs, scarves, or wool hats

Image 7.17. Hearing Loss

What You Will Do

1. Divide the class into two groups: one that will simulate moderate hearing loss and one that will simulate minor hearing loss.
2. Group A (moderate hearing loss) will use earplugs to filter out most of the sound.
3. Group B (minor hearing loss) will use earmuffs, scarves, or wool hats to filter out some of the sound (but less than those wearing the ear plugs).
4. Students will spend the entire day with the simulated hearing loss.
5. All students will use a journal to record the following:
   - Which group they are in
   - How they were treated by other students and people they encountered
   - How they responded to the way others treated them
   - How they felt during the simulation
   - How the simulation changed or did not change their view of hearing loss

* Safety Note—The teacher should send a memo to other teachers in the school and to the students' homes prior to the day of the activity to advise them of the purpose of the activity. Instruct students to be careful not to do anything that might be dangerous because of their blocked hearing, such as crossing the street alone.

What you will learn: Hearing loss, which is often genetically based, affects many aspects of a person's life and requires the person to change and adapt many behaviors.

Core concept demonstrated: The effect of hearing loss on social behavior

Thinking like a scientist: In what ways did you have to adapt to your simulated hearing loss? What were the differences between the ways the group with moderate hearing loss and the group with minor hearing loss adapted? How might the adaptations in this activity be different from those that would be used in a simulation of vision loss?

Correlation With National Science Standards: A.2; C.4; C.5

Experiment **49**: Bird Beak Models

In the following activity, you will explore models of bird beaks and examine what type of beak is best suited for eating various types of food.

Materials You Will Need for This Activity

- Tweezers
- Nutcrackers
- Nut picks
- Slotted spoons
- Tongs
- Gummy worms

- Bird seed
- Goldfish crackers
- Apples
- Peanuts
- Bird guide books or other accurate pictures of birds

Image 7.18. Bird Beak

What You Will Do

1. Place in a tray the five representations of different types of bird foods and the five tools that represent different types of bird beaks.
2. Using the food and "beaks" in front of you, try to determine the foods that a bird with that type of beak would eat and why. Fill in the table below.

Tool/Bill	Type of Food	Best Fit? Why?
Tweezers		
Nut Picks		
Slotted Spoon		
Tongs		
Nutcracker		

3. Select six different bird pictures. Make predictions about the type of food each bird might eat based on the shape of its beak and what you learned from collecting food with the different model beaks.

What you will learn: Different species of birds have evolved over time to have different beak forms in order to compete effectively for specific kinds of foods.

(Continued)

(Continued)

Core concept demonstrated: Evolutionary adaptations

Thinking like a scientist: Did everyone agree with the matching between the types of foods and the model beaks? If there was any disagreement, how could you resolve it? Are all types of bird beaks equally common, or are some more common than others? Why might this be? How might geography play a role in bird beak adaptations?

Correlation With National Science Standards: A.1; A.2; C.4; C.8; G.1

Stereoscopic Vision

Almost all animals have two eyes. This is not an accident, but instead is an evolutionary adaptation. Animals that tend to be hunted as prey (e.g., deer, rabbits, many fish, and mice) usually have their eyes placed on the sides of their heads to allow for the greatest possible field of vision (see Image 7.19). Predators such as bears, foxes, lions, housecats, wolves, and humans have eyes that are located on the front of their heads facing forward and closely spaced to one another (see Image 7.20). This orientation of the eyes for predatory animals makes possible stereoscopic vision, which provides depth perception, which is a significant advantage for predators when hunting.

Stereoscopic vision results when the brain combines the images that are received from each eye into a single image. A slight offset of the two images allows the viewer to have greater depth perception. Depth perception is lost as you bring what is being observed very close to the viewer's eye. (See Experiment 50.)

Evolutionary Adaptations to Fill Ecological Niches

Have you ever thought about what a giraffe, an elephant, and a brachiosaurus dinosaur have in common? Each is (or was) a plant eater that evolved to eat plant material from tall growing plants. The brachiosaurus had a long neck that allowed it to reach its head high and feed from tall plants; the giraffe uses the same approach today. An elephant achieves the same goal by using its trunk to tear leaves off trees or to pick things up off the ground. Each of these three species evolved to fill an ecological niche, eating plant material out of the high trees, thus allowing them to successfully compete with the various other species living in the same environment. (See Experiment 51.)

Image 7.19. Sheep

This young sheep, a herbivore (plant eater) and a herd animal that is hunted by predators like wolves and mountain lions, has eyes that are set in the side of its head for increased field of vision.

Image 7.20. Bear

The close forward eye placement on this bear is typical of a predatory or hunting animal.

 # Biomes and Ecosystems: Interactions Between Plants, Animals, and the Non-Living World

What Is a Biome?

Biomes and **ecosystems** represent the settings in which plants, animals, and the non-living world interact. A **biome** is generally defined as a large area containing similar flora, fauna, and microorganisms. Examples of biomes include coniferous forests, deserts, tropical rainforests, and Arctic tundra. Each biome contains species that have adapted to survive in that biome's varying conditions. For example, elk and big horn sheep thrive in the high

(Text continues on page 246)

Experiment 50: Experimenting With Stereoscopic Vision

In the following activity, you will see how stereoscopic vision works.

Materials You Will Need for This Activity

- Two 3″ × 5″ cards
- Image 7.21
- A pencil or pen

What You Will Do

Image 7.21. Bird in Cage

SOURCE: Illustration by Poyet from Good (1893).

1. Draw the image of the bird and birdcage as illustrated in the upper right hand corner of Image 7.21. Your drawing should be divided in half and take up as much space as possible on the card.

2. Hold the card in front of your face like the man in Image 7.21. Make sure you hold the card you have not drawn on at a right angle to your drawing (on the dotted line marked B-A). Now, move your nose slowly toward the center of the picture. As you do so, you will see the bird move into the cage.

What you will learn: When your eyes get too close to an image, you lose your depth perception. Your brain can no longer distinguish the two different views of each image it is receiving from your eyes as it usually does. Instead, the two different images come together.

Core concept demonstrated: Binocular or stereoscopic vision as an evolutionary adaptation

Thinking like a scientist: What types of toys or visual devices can be created based on this phenomenon? Why is depth perception important? Why can't a person who is blind in one eye get a driver's license in some states?

Correlation With National Science Standards: C.4; C.6; C.8

 **Experiment 51:**   **Design-an-Organism**

In the following activity, you will design an organism that is well-suited for living in a specific environment.

Materials You Will Need for This Activity

- Paper and pencil
- Modeling clay

What You Will Do

1. Discuss the ecosystem around your school. What kinds of plants and animals live in this ecosystem? How have these plants and animals adapted so that they are well-suited to survive?
2. You will design a new organism (either plant or animal) to fit into a certain niche in this ecosystem. Think about the following questions:
   - How big is your organism?
   - What kind of food will it eat? How much food will it need to survive? How will it get this food?
   - What behaviors will your organism possess to aid its survival?
   - How will your organism reproduce? How often?
   - What niche will the organism fit into and what organisms already occupy that niche?
   - What will your organism look like? Make sure to consider both structure and function in your design.
3. Draw a picture of your organism and write a description of how each of its parts and behaviors helps it to survive in this ecosystem.
4. Finally, make a clay model of your organism, highlighting the features that allow it to survive and thrive in its environment.

What you will learn: A habitat is a place where an organism lives. A habitat contains the basic necessities for that organism, such as light, food, air, water, temperature, and sufficient space. A niche is the role and position of an organism within a particular habitat. Each organism in an established ecosystem tends to have a distinct niche. Thus, any newly introduced organism will likely have to engage in competition with an organism that is already occupying that niche.

Core concept demonstrated: Over time, species adapt to fill certain ecological niches in an environment.

Thinking like a scientist: Predict the impact of your new organism on the ecosystem. Will the other organisms currently filling the niche that your new organism is moving into be able to co-exist with the new organism? Why or why not? Is it common for a new organism to appear suddenly in an ecosystem it did not previously inhabit? What might cause this?

Correlation With National Science Standards: A.2; C.1; C.3; C.4; C.8

mountains while alligators and wading birds are well-suited to surviving in the marshlands.

Ecosystems are similar to biomes, only generally smaller in area. While some ecosystems can be quite large, such as the Amazon rainforest, ecosystems can also be as small as the stream running through your neighborhood. Ecosystems are often defined as the dynamic interactions between plants, animals, microorganisms, and their environment. Within an ecosystem, each organism has its own niche, or role, to play.

Tracing Food Webs

Think for a moment about a farmer in a pioneering region in the United States during the nineteenth century. Such a farmer might have some cows and pigs, a small vegetable garden, and might produce some larger crops such as corn or wheat. Every year the farmer might slaughter a certain number of animals to eat and might find a certain number of other animals, such as deer or wild turkey, he could hunt off the land. He would combine these animal food sources with the crops that he grew, plus other plants he foraged, such as wild nuts and berries. His cows and pigs would need to be fed corn or other grains, and the animal wastes might be composted, with the help of decomposers such as worms, and then used as fertilizer for the vegetable garden.

The ecosystem in which this farmer is the top-level consumer represents a complex web of consumers and producers. All living organisms are part of complex food webs in which some species are producers, others are consumers, and still others are decomposers. (See Experiment 52.)

Measuring the Greenhouse Effect

As you will recall from the previous chapter, the atmosphere is just one system within a complex collection of interconnected Earth systems. Earth's atmosphere extends to a distance of approximately 600 miles above the planet's surface. Life forms, however, cannot exist more than five or six miles above the Earth's surface. The conditions for life on Earth are profoundly shaped by atmospheric conditions, and changes in these conditions can affect a wide range of life forms. In recent years, the production of greenhouse gases though the burning of fossil fuels has led to changes in the Earth's atmosphere and, thus, changes in weather and global climate. (See Experiment 53.)

Unintended Consequences

In science, as in human life, doing something can often lead to unexpected consequences. For example, rabbits were introduced in Australia in 1895. However, they became a major pest because there were no predatory animals, such as foxes and coyotes, to keep the rabbit population under control. If people had realized the way in which rabbits would overrun the Australian countryside, they surely would not have introduced them.

 **Experiment 52:** **Tracing Food Webs**

In the following activity, you will role-play a food web as each member of the class takes on the role of one organism in an ecosystem.

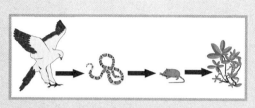

Image 7.22. A Food Chain

Materials You Will Need for This Activity

- Index cards with a holes punched in two corners and yarn tied through to hang around neck. Label the cards as follows:
  - 1 card labeled "sun"
  - 6 cards labeled "grass"
  - 5 cards labeled "grasshopper"
  - 2 cards labeled "chicken"
  - 2 cards labeled "frog"
  - 2 cards labeled "mouse"
  - 4 cards labeled "snake"
  - 2 cards labeled "hawk"

What You Will Do

1. Clear a space in the middle of the room and pass out the role cards, one per person.
2. The person representing the sun stands in the center of the room. Discuss the importance of the sun to all living things. What uses the sun to make food?
3. People representing the grass stand in a circle around the sun. The grass needs the sun to make food, so each person representing grass should place one hand on a shoulder of the sun. Discuss the importance of plants in the food chain.
4. Tell everyone else to find an organism that their organism eats. Have them stand behind the organism they eat, placing one hand on that person's shoulder.
5. There should be at least four people (counting one plant and the sun) in each food chain that makes up the food web.

What you will learn: There is a fundamental interdependence between consumers and producers, predators and prey. These organisms form intricate food webs that can be disrupted when there are too many or not enough of a given organism in an ecosystem.

Core concept demonstrated: Food webs

Thinking like a scientist: Did any of the organisms have a difficult time finding a place in the food web? Who is competing for food? Is it easier for an omnivore, an herbivore, or a carnivore to find food? What is the difference between a food web and a food chain?

Correlation With National Science Standards: C.3; C.7; F.2; F.7

Experiment **53:** **Greenhouse Effect Model**

In the following activity, you will create a model to study the effect of carbon dioxide on temperature changes as a result of trapped gases similar to those that create the greenhouse effect on the Earth's atmosphere.

Image 7.23. Greenhouse Model

Materials You Will Need for This Activity

- Two 2-liter plastic soda bottles (with their labels removed)
- Modeling clay
- Vinegar
- Baking soda
- Two thermometers
- Measuring spoons
- Sunlight

What You Will Do

1. Label one 2-liter bottle "With Carbon Dioxide" and label the other bottle "Without Carbon Dioxide."
2. Add two teaspoons of baking soda and then two teaspoons of vinegar to the bottle labeled "With Carbon Dioxide." This mixture will produce carbon dioxide gas.
3. Quickly cover the opening of the bottle with modeling clay to stop the carbon dioxide from leaking out.
4. Add two teaspoons of vinegar only to the bottle labeled "Without Carbon Dioxide" and cover the bottle opening with modeling clay.
5. Carefully make a small hole in the modeling clay covering the opening of each bottle and poke the thermometers through the holes.
6. Place both bottles in a sunny place.
7. Make a data table and record the temperature in each bottle every five minutes for a 30-minute period.
8. Make a line graph representing the temperature in each bottle over the 30-minute time period.

What you will learn: The heating effect you observed in this activity is known as the greenhouse effect because carbon dioxide in the Earth's atmosphere acts like the glass in a plant greenhouse. The carbon dioxide allows warm sunlight to enter the bottle but prevents the re-radiated heat from escaping the bottle. The greenhouse effect is a natural phenomenon that is actually very important to life on Earth. Without this effect at work, the average temperature on Earth would be approximately 30°C colder than it currently is. However, the enhanced greenhouse effect, also known as global warming, has the potential to create too much warming, which could result in a destructive global sea level rise, significant shifts in the planet's climate patterns, and other dire consequences for the inhabitants of Earth.

Core concept demonstrated: Greenhouse effect

Thinking like a scientist: There is currently both scientific and political debate about the enhanced greenhouse effect, how significant this effect might be in the future, and what the consequences might be. Why is it difficult to agree on concrete answers to these questions? What might allow for more definitive answers?

Correlation With National Science Standards: A.1; C.3; E.3; F.9; F.10; G.1

Unintended consequences can occur in other ways as well. Aspirin was introduced as a pain reliever in the late nineteenth century. It was eventually found that a small daily dose of aspirin also reduced the risk of heart disease. While this was beneficial, the introduction of other drugs have had unexpected tragic consequences. For example, in the 1960s, the drug thalidomide was used to help women deal with morning sickness during pregnancy. However, it was soon discovered that thalidomide caused birth defects, including missing limbs. (See Experiment 54.)

🐾 The Human Body and Human Health

In the sciences, we spend more money and time on research into the human body and its functioning than on any other topic. Human beings are complex organisms shaped by many different forces, including the mechanics of our bodies, the foods we eat, and the drugs we take to improve our health.

Tracking Food Choices

Different types of foods are good for us for different reasons. Too much or too little of a food can lead to a nutritional deficiency or other type of health problem. For example, too much sugar causes diabetics to have various

(Text continues on page 253)

Experiment 54: Unintended Consequences

In the following activity, you will explore the law of unintended consequences by analyzing social and geographical structures in a major city.

Materials You Will Need for This Activity

- Historical and modern maps of New York City
- Historical and modern photographs of New York City

Note—Alternatively, you could use maps and photos of the largest city in your state to make this activity more relevant for your students.

What You Will Do

1. Study the historical and modern maps and photos of New York City. New York City was founded in 1624 by Dutch fur traders and settlers. They chose the site because of the excellent harbor created by the Hudson River and the access the river gave them to the interior of the region.
2. Think about how establishing the city initially on the island of Manhattan influenced its early development. What happened as the city outgrew Manhattan? What technologies had to be implemented to cope with population growth?
3. Create a list of unexpected consequences resulting from the decision to establish a city at the mouth of the Hudson River.

What you will learn: Social systems, like natural systems, develop and evolve in unexpected ways.

Core concept demonstrated: Unintended consequences and their impact on environments

Thinking like a scientist: Why is the country's main theater district in New York and not in Iowa? Think about the other major cities in the U.S., such as Los Angeles, Chicago, or Houston. Why might they have developed where they did? What might be some of the unintended consequences of their development?

Correlation With National Science Standards: A.2; C.3; C.7; F.7; F.10; G.1

 Experiment **55:**   **You Are What You Eat**

In the following activity, you will track the food choices you make during a three-day period and consider how these choices function or do not function well for you.

Materials You Will Need for This Activity

- Food journal
- Food pyramid

What You Will Do

1. Keep a record of all the food you eat during meals and between meals over a three-day period.
2. For each day, list the foods you eat. When possible, try to write down an estimate of the amount of each food as well (e.g., 2 celery sticks, 4 Oreo cookies).
3. After three days, make a chart based on the categories found in the food pyramid at http://www.mypyramid.gov/pyramid/index.html.
4. Write the foods you ate each day in the proper category of the food pyramid and compare what you actually ate with what is recommended.

What you will learn: The six components of the food pyramid are grains, vegetables, fruits, milk, meat/beans, and physical activity, with vegetables and milk products recommended in higher amounts than the other food groups. Refined sugars (candy, cookies, etc.) are not part of the pyramid at all, meaning that they do not add to your daily nutrition in any substantial way.

Core concept demonstrated: The importance of proper nutrition

Thinking like a scientist: In what categories were you eating sufficient quantities of nutritious food? In what categories were you not eating enough? What social features in American society influence the food choices we make? How might these features be similar or different in other countries? Physical activity was added to the newly revised food pyramid. Why do you think this was done?

Correlation With National Science Standards: A.1; C.6; F.1; G.1

Experiment **56:**   **Modeling the Human Arm**

In the following activity, you will create a working model of the muscles that move the human arm.

Materials You Will Need for This Activity

- Tape
- Hole punch
- 2 empty toilet paper rolls
- 2 five-inch long balloons
- 1 pipe cleaner cut in half

What You Will Do

1. The two toilet paper roles represent the upper and lower arm. To connect the two arm parts, make two holes 180 degrees apart, $\frac{1}{2}$ inch from the end of each cardboard tube.
2. Thread a piece of the pipe cleaner through the holes on each side of the two tubes to connect them together, and bend the ends to form a joint. The pipe cleaner represents the ligaments that function to hold the muscles in place. The tubes represent the major bones in your arm.
3. Bend your model arm at the "elbow" to form an L shape.
4. Inflate one balloon slightly, and tape one end of the balloon to each arm part on the inside of the arm's L shape. This simulates the contracted biceps muscle.
5. Inflate the other balloon slightly and tape it to the arm parts on the outside of the L. This simulates the triceps muscle.
6. Move your model arm's lever up and down. What happens to the balloons?

What you will learn: Every moving bone in the human body has at least

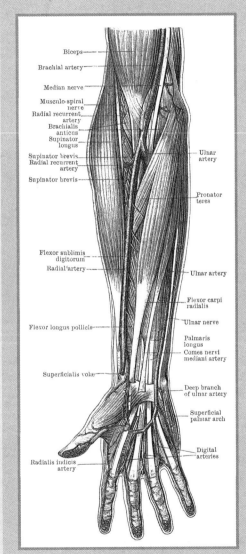

Image 7.24. A Nineteenth-Century Anatomical Drawing of the Human Arm

two muscles connected to it. These pairs of muscles work together to facilitate movement. When you bend your arm at the elbow, the top muscle (biceps) contracts and shortens. This causes your forearm bones to pull into a bent position. At the same time, the bottom muscle (triceps) stretches because it is relaxed. When you straighten your arm, the opposite occurs—the biceps relaxes and straightens, and the triceps contracts and shortens. The contraction of the triceps pulls down the bones of your forearm and your arm straightens out.

Core concept demonstrated: Basic physical mechanics of the human arm

Thinking like a scientist: Compare how your model arm moves with what you feel when you bend and straighten your own arm. Now, describe what you think happens in your legs when you walk or run. How does what you have learned influence how you would design prosthetic arms and legs for amputees?

Correlation With National Science Standards: A.1; A.2; C.4; C.8; G.1; G.4

blood circulation problems that can lead to blindness or the loss of limbs. Keeping a balanced diet is an extremely important part of people's health. (See Experiment 55.)

Creating a Model of the Human Arm

For as long as we have had consciousness, humans have been interested in the workings of our own bodies. The oldest recorded anatomical records can be found in Egyptian papyruses, dating to more than 3,000 years B.C. Diseases of the eyes, hemorrhoids, rectal prolapse, intestinal parasites, abdominal pain, fractures, and urological conditions are all mentioned in early Egyptian documents.

Medical research came later to Western culture, largely originating in ancient Greece. The Greek scholar Hippocrates (460–377 B.C.) is generally considered the father of Western medicine for proposing the concept that illnesses might have natural (rather than supernatural or spiritual) causes and cures. Hippocrates believed that the study of anatomy must be the foundation of medicine. In the East, the classic Hindu medical manuscript *Susruta Samhita* (A.D. 200) demonstrated an advanced understanding of surgery, describing more than 100 operations and the instruments that should be used. In the modern era, our understanding of human anatomy continues to grow as new technologies allow us to analyze and understand more and more information about the human body and disease.

One of the most interesting aspects of anatomy is its relationship to basic principles found in physics. In fact, the skeletal system of an animal

 Experiment **57:**   **Spreading Infectious Disease**

In the following activity, you will simulate how disease spreads as well as play the role of an epidemiologist trying to figure out who started the spread of the disease.

Materials You Will Need for This Activity

- Small (8-ounce) plastic cups
- pH strips or universal indicator
- Moderately strong acid or base such as dilute HCl or dilute sodium hydroxide (lye) (lemon juice or vinegar can also be used but are much more easily detected because of their odor)

What You Will Do

1. In advance, prepare one cup per student by filling halfway with water.
2. Add 10 drops of dilute HCl or NaOH (or 10 ml of lemon juice or vinegar) to one of the cups without allowing students to know this.
3. Tell the students that this activity simulates how germs (or many infectious diseases) spread. Warn students not to drink the liquid in their cups.
4. Give each student a cup of liquid and have students mingle in the center of the classroom.
5. Have each student share the liquid in his or her cup with another student by pouring the liquid back and forth several times between their cups and then putting half back in each cup.
6. Have students mingle some more and then repeat the sharing process with two other students (for a total of three).
7. The student needs to remember the three people with whom he or she shared and the order in which this took place.
8. Using the pH test strips or universal indicator, test each student's liquid to see whether the infection spread to him or her or not.
9. Now, ask students to think like an epidemiologist (or a detective) and see whether they can come up with a strategy for determining which student had the original contaminated cup ("patient zero").

* Safety Note—Be sure to warn the students not to drink their samples. While the amount of lye needed for the pH reaction is minuscule, at higher concentrations, lye is a very strong and dangerous chemical base.

What you will learn: Disease can spread rapidly through a population, potentially growing exponentially as every infected individual infects several others. Using reasoning and logic, it is sometimes possible to trace the spread of a disease backwards from those currently infected to the originally contaminated individual.

Core concept demonstrated: Spread of disease through a population

Thinking like a scientist: In this simulation, is it possible to figure out who the original patient zero was, or is the best that can be accomplished to figure out who the first two infected individuals were? Why is this so? Think back to Chapter 1, and the discussion of the Broad Street pump and the London cholera epidemic of the nineteenth century. How is solving the mystery in this activity similar to what Dr. John Snow did to solve the mystery in London? How is it different?

Correlation With National Science Standards: A.1; A.2; C.2; C.6; F.1; F.5; G.1

SOURCE: Courtesy of the Library of Congress.

Image 7.25. Demonstration at the Red Cross Emergency Ambulance Station in Washington, DC During the Influenza Pandemic of 1918

represents a complex system of levers and counterlevers. When connected together by muscles and cartilage, an animal's limbs provide the ability to perform an incredibly varied and complex range of activities. (See Experiment 56.)

Spreading Infectious Illnesses

An infectious disease like the flu represents a biological mechanism that has an extraordinary evolutionary capacity to spread itself across hosts. This can be seen in the case of the great flu epidemic of 1918 that killed more people worldwide than were killed during the fighting in World War I (see Image 7.25). In the two years that the pandemic took its course, a fifth of the world's population was infected. An estimated 675,000 people died from the disease. The 1918 flu was airborne and carried from person to person via germs that were carried on their hands, through sneezing, and so on. (See Experiment 57.)

Student Study Site

The Companion Web site for *Teaching Science in Elementary and Middle School* http://www.sagepub.com/buxtonstudy

Visit the Web-based student study site to enhance your understanding of the chapter content and to discover additional resources that will take your learning one step further. You can enhance your understanding of the chapters by using the study materials, which include chapter objectives, flashcards, activities, practice tests, and more. You'll also find special features, such as Resources for Experiments, the Links to Standards from U.S. States and associated activities, Learning From Journal Articles, Theory Into Practice resources, Reflections on Science exercises, a Science Standards-Based Lesson Plan Project, and PRAXIS resources.

Reflections on Science

1. Biology is sometimes divided into two categories: biology at the cellular or microscopic level (microbiology) and biology at the organismal and environmental level. Make a Venn diagram comparing and contrasting these two domains.

2. Most of the early study of biology focused on human anatomy and medicine, with the study of other life science topics generally coming substantially later. How could you explain this historical trend?

3. There are many exciting, yet ethically challenging, breakthroughs that could, in the next few years, potentially redefine how we understand and make use of certain aspects of biology. These topics include the human genome project, embryonic stem cell research, and cloning. How do you believe the decisions should be made to guide our understanding and application of these emerging topics in biology?

Internet Connections: Biology

The following Web sites provide information that may prove helpful for teaching biology:

The University of Arizona Biology Project— with information for teachers plus lesson plans
http://www.biology.arizona.edu/

Cells Alive—interactive Web site about all things cellular
http://www.cellsalive.com/

Dr. Saul's Biology in Motion—animated models on many biology topics
http://www.biologyinmotion.com/

Frank Potter's Science Gems: Life Science— links to numerous high-quality life science resources
http://www.sciencegems.com/life.html

Biosphere 2—a fascinating site on the
    Biosphere 2 project integrating many
    biology topics
http://www.bio2.com/

Net Frog—an online virtual frog dissection
http://curry.edschool.virginia.edu/go/frog/

Reference

Good, A. (1893). *La science amusante* (Vols. 1–3). Paris: Le Librarie Larousse.

Understanding and Teaching Chemistry

8

Consider the following statements about chemistry:

When we decode a cookbook, every one of us is a practicing chemist. Cooking is really the oldest, most basic application of physical and chemical forces to natural materials.

—**Arthur Grosser**

Chemists are, on the whole, like physicists, only "less so." They don't make quite the same wonderful mistakes, and much what they do is an art, related to cooking, instead of a true science. They have their moments, and their sources of legitimate pride. They don't split atoms, as the physicists do. They join them together, and a very praiseworthy activity that is.

—**Standen (1958)**

Referring to a glass of water: I mixed this myself. Two parts H, one part O. I don't trust anybody!

—**Comedian Steven Wright**

If it's green, it's biology. If it stinks, it's chemistry. If it has numbers, it's math. If it doesn't work, it's technology.

—**Unknown**

❦ The Place of Chemistry in Science Education

Chemistry is the study of matter and its interaction with energy. Because matter can take so many different forms, chemistry is generally divided into three different branches: physical chemistry, inorganic chemistry, and organic chemistry. Physical chemistry deals with the physical properties of chemical substances. It is different from inorganic chemistry, which is the study of the properties and reactions of inorganic **compounds** such as metals and plastics. The third branch of chemistry, organic chemistry, is the study of the structures, properties, and reactions of organic compounds (compounds that contain carbon and hydrogen).

Probably the earliest chemical experiments by humans involved food. As foods decay, they go through chemical changes. The chemical changes that take place can be highly desirable; for example, fermentation is necessary to make beer and wine. With the discovery of fire, humans could transform the chemical composition of foods by heating them. This chemical process changed the flavor of the food and also increased the length of time it could be preserved without spoiling. Chemical experimentation was also involved in the development of dyes used in weaving and cloth making in ancient cultures.

Chemistry has also played a central role in the development of weapons since ancient times. "Greek fire," for example, was developed in A.D. 673 by the Syrian engineer Callinicus. The weapon was first used by the Byzantine navy to set fire to enemy ships by emitting a highly combustible substance made from phosphorus through a bronze tube (see Image 8.1). Gunpowder was invented centuries earlier (in about 200 B.C.) in ancient China, although it was not introduced into Europe until the late Middle

SOURCE: From the Skylitzes manuscript in Madrid (Wikimedia Commons, http://commons.wikimedia .org/wiki/Image:Greekfire-dridskylitzes1.jpg).

Image 8.1. "Greek Fire" Used in a Naval Battle

SOURCE: *Etliche Tractaten, zum ander Mal in Truck ausgegangen. Vom Fodagra und seinem Speciebus* (Cohn, 1567). National Library of Medicine.

Image 8.2. Paracelsus

The Swiss alchemist Paracelsus (1493–1541) is the most famous alchemist from the Renaissance era.

Ages. The resulting widespread use of cannons and musketry changed the nature of warfare forever. More recently, potentially devastating chemical weapons and poisons have been developed that have led to the need for international treaties and agreements in attempts to limit the more destructive side of chemistry.

The roots of modern chemistry are generally traced back to the Middle Ages and the attempts of alchemists to change lead and other metals into gold (although, as we have already pointed out, humans had been experimenting with chemical changes long before this time). The alchemists were unsuccessful in their attempts at transmutation, but they did begin to learn about the creation of chemical compounds.

During the late Renaissance and Early Modern period, chemistry began to be codified and studied more systematically. For example, the Swiss alchemist Paracelsus (1493–1541), unlike most alchemists of his period, was interested in the use of chemical compounds to treat medical disorders (see Image 8.2). His pioneering work with elements such as zinc represents the beginning of modern pharmacology. As he explained, "Many have said of Alchemy, that it is for the making of gold and silver. For me such is not the aim, but to consider only what virtue and power may lie in medicines" (Holmyard, 1990).

Research in the field of chemistry expanded in the eighteenth and nineteenth centuries, when many of the ideas fundamental to modern chemistry were developed. The Englishman Joseph Priestly (1733–1804), for example, studied the behaviors of gases and discovered the element oxygen and the compounds carbon monoxide and nitrous oxide (as well as inventing the first "soda water," the precursor to modern soda pop). Antoine Lavoisier (1743–1794), who built on the experiments of Priestly and standardized many experimental procedures, is considered by many to be the father of modern chemistry. Lavoisier's success was due in no small part to his collaboration with his wife, Marie. Despite the fact that Lavoisier lived at a time when accomplishments were attributed to men, Marie's contributions were essential to the "new chemistry of Lavoisier." Marie maintained the laboratory, helped with the experiments, recorded most of the observations and results, and drew the sketches that appeared in Lavoisier's notebooks and publications. Many other chemists, such as John Dalton (1766–1844),

Humphry Davy (1778–1829), and Joseph Gay-Lussac (1778–1850) all made major contributions to the field during this period.

Today, chemists are experimenting with the creation of new types of molecules that have remarkable promise in a broad array of fields such as medicine, electronics, and even the creation of new physical structures. One example of this is the creation of diamond lattice structures that theorists like Arthur C. Clarke have proposed could be used to build space elevators. Through a chemical process, a diamond filament could be created that could be extended up ("grown") from the equator of the Earth all the way into space. This incredibly strong yet thin structure could then serve as the backbone for an electrically driven cable car system to carry materials and people cheaply and safely into low Earth orbit. Such experiments represent the fusion of chemistry with other fields of science and engineering in ways that will potentially have a profound impact on our economic, social, and geographic systems.

Other discoveries on the horizon in the field of chemistry will almost certainly contribute to extending human life and providing cures for a range of diseases, from diabetes to cystic fibrosis to cancer. For example, in the past 30 or 40 years, the average life expectancy of an American increased by 15% or 20%. This is due to the introduction of new drugs and chemically based treatments, as well as the ability to perform complex surgeries and procedures such as organ transplants, which are made possible by blocking autoimmune rejection systems with drugs and other chemically related procedures.

Measurement in Chemistry

Chemistry, like all the sciences, requires careful measurement. Only a certain amount of a chemical substance will be sufficient to act as a catalyst to begin a chemical reaction. Temperature, when combined with pressure and other forces, determines the rate and strength of most chemical reactions. Understanding the variables that affect chemical reactions largely depends on measurement.

Estimating Volume

The use of consistent volumetric measures was not only important for the early development of science but was essential to commerce. If, for example, liquid goods, such as wine or oil, were to be sold, it was necessary to establish standard measures of volume to determine a consistent and uniform price for a commodity. In ancient Greece, the basic volumetric measure was the *kheonike*. A *kotule* was a liquid measure. Measures such as these were important because they provided a standard by which objects could be measured. Thus the establishment of a standard amount of a kotule (whatever amount a kotule actually was) made it possible to have fixed prices as well as uniform means of taxation.

Experiment 58: Estimating Volume

To get as accurate an estimate as possible, sometimes you have to break the process down into several steps. In this activity, you will answer the question "How much water do students drink from the water fountains in my school in one day?"

Materials You Will Need for This Activity

• The water fountains in your school

What You Will Do

Image 8.3. Child Drinking From Water Fountain

SOURCE: Photo by Jean-Marie Buxton.

1. Estimate how much water the typical student drinks from a water fountain each time he or she gets a drink. Think about how you could refine the accuracy of this estimate. How could you take a measurement to help you?
2. Estimate how many times the typical student drinks from a water fountain in a typical school day (think about how you could refine the accuracy of this estimate).
3. Estimate how many students are in your school (think about how you could refine the accuracy of this estimate).
4. Using all the information you have gathered so far, how can you create an estimate of the total amount of water drunk from all water fountains in your school in one day? (Think about how you could refine the accuracy of this estimate.)

What you will learn: You can estimate a large and complex total amount by breaking the estimate down into more manageable parts and then summing the estimates of its parts.

Core concept demonstrated: Improving the accuracy of estimations

Thinking like a scientist: What if you required a more accurate measure of water fountain use than you could get from estimating? What are some things you could do to further increase the accuracy? How do city planners and developers make the plans for infrastructure (electricity, water, sewage, etc.) when new parts of a city are built?

Correlation With National Science Standards: A.2; G.3

In modern chemistry, there is the need to be able to replicate an experimental process, whether it involves baking a cake in your kitchen or conducting an experiment in a highly sophisticated laboratory. In either case, precise volumetric measures make a scientific approach possible.

Volume is a measure of how much space an object (or some amount of matter) takes up. The volume of a regularly shaped solid object can be found mathematically by multiplying the object's length, times width, times height. For a liquid, however, volume is generally found using a calibrated (or graduated) container. This could be a measuring cup, a beaker, a flask, or a graduated cylinder. In some chemical experiments, volume must be measured with a high degree of accuracy. In other experiments, estimating the volume will be sufficient. The following investigation will let you practice estimating volume. (See Experiment 58.)

Measuring Temperature Using a Thermometer

A thermometer is a device that measures the temperature of things. *Thermo* refers to heat and *meter* to measure. Thus a thermometer measures the heat of an object. The Italian scientist Galileo Galilei (1564–1642) invented one of the earliest thermometers. It involved glass balls partially filled with liquid that were suspended in a tall cylinder of water (see Image 8.4). The balls would rise or fall in the water depending on its temperature. This occurred because as the temperature of the water in the column increased the water expanded slightly, becoming less dense in the process. Balls that would remain floating at a higher density began to sink as the density of the water in the column lessened. (See Experiment 59.)

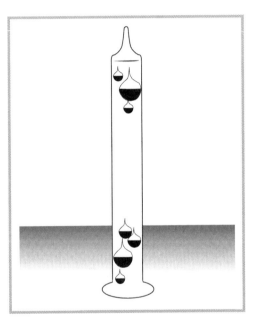

Image 8.4. A Galilean Thermometer

Counting Particles: Understanding Parts per Thousand

In chemistry, the properties of a compound can depend upon very small variations in the amount of a given substance. The effects of chemical substances can also change depending on their concentrations. For example, hydrogen peroxide at low concentrations (diluted in water) is an effective antiseptic. At high concentrations, however, the same substance is a very powerful base that can cause severe chemical burns. Thus, understanding and controlling the concentration of a chemical is an important concept in chemistry. You can see the effect of changing concentrations in the following experiment on serial dilution using color. (See Experiment 60.)

 **Experiment 59:** **Making a Thermometer**

In the following activity, you will build a working thermometer.

Materials You Will Need for This Activity

- Clear bottle
- Rubber stopper to fit bottle, with hole in center
- Rigid plastic tubing to fit hole in stopper, 24″ long
- Water
- Food coloring
- Candle wax (paraffin)
- Scotch tape
- Cardboard strip, 10″ × 2″
- Regular lab thermometer

What You Will Do

1. Carefully place the tubing through the hole in the stopper.
2. Color $\frac{1}{2}$ cup of room temperature water with food coloring. Pour this into the glass bottle so that it is $\frac{1}{4}$ full.
3. Place the stopper in the flask so that it makes a tight fit. The tube end should be in the liquid, almost touching the bottom. Pour a little colored water into the top of the tube through the open end until its level is about halfway up the part of the tube above the stopper.
4. Use wax to seal the tube to the stopper and the stopper to the bottle so that there is an airtight seal.
5. Cut slits in the top and bottom of the cardboard to slide it on the tube above the stopper.
6. Mark the water level on the cardboard and its temperature as room temperature (you can measure what this temperature is with the regular thermometer).
7. Place both the regular thermometer and your thermometer in a warm water bath. The water in the tube should rise up. Mark this new temperature on the cardboard.
8. Repeat a third time in an ice water bath and mark the new temperature.
9. You can make a scale and fill in the temperature points between the three points you have measured. You now have your very own working thermometer.

*Safety Note—The teacher or another adult should insert the tubing through the hole in the stopper using a lubricant.

(Continued)

(Continued)

What you will learn: Thermometers work because changing temperatures cause the liquid in the thermometer to expand or contract and thus rise or fall in the thin tube.

Core concept demonstrated: Response of a liquid to changing temperature

Thinking like a scientist: Why did Galileo and the other early scientists need to invent their own tools such as the Galilean thermometer? Do scientists today still invent their own tools? Why do most thermometers have tall thin tubes as part of their design?

Correlation With National Science Standards: A.1; B.4; E.4

Atoms, Elements, and Molecules

Most of the universe is composed of matter and energy. To a scientist, energy is the ability to do work and matter is any substance that has mass and occupies space. All matter is composed of elements. Elements are physical substances that are composed of a single type of atom. For example, pure silver contains only one type of atom, silver atoms. An atom is the smallest particle that an element can be divided into while still retaining its chemical properties. Atoms can be further broken down into subatomic particles. Since the early 1900s, a number of subatomic particles have been discovered, but the three most common are the proton and neutron (which together make up the nucleus of the atom) and the electron (which is a very small particle located outside of the nucleus).

Molecules are collections of atoms of more than one element, where those elements exist in a definite, fixed ratio. Thus, table salt (sodium chloride, NaCl) is always composed of equal numbers of sodium atoms and chlorine atoms. Water (hydrogen dioxide, H_2O) is always composed of twice as many hydrogen atoms as oxygen atoms. The atoms in a molecule are joined together by bonds. The three most common types of bonds are ionic bonds (where atoms gain or lose electrons to other atoms), covalent bonds (where atoms share electrons), and hydrogen bonds (where a weak electrical attraction holds atoms together). Atoms and molecules are difficult to visualize because they are so extremely small. Objects at the atomic level are so small that our everyday understanding of things does not suffice. As with topics like interplanetary distances or geologic time, scales that are very large and very small are quite difficult to comprehend. The use of models can help us understand these scales.

Experiment **60:** Serial Dilution of Colored Liquid

In the following activity, you will make a serial dilution to show how the concentration of a chemical compound can change

Materials You Will Need for This Activity

- Four 250-milliliter beakers
- Water
- Salt
- Blue or green food coloring
- Stirring rod
- Balance

Image 8.5. Serial Dilution

SOURCE: Photo by Jean-Marie Buxton.

To watch a video clip related to this concept, go to the Student Resource CD bound into the back of your textbook.

What You Will Do

1. Mark each of the beakers 1 through 4.
2. Using a graduated cylinder, measure 100 ml of water into beaker #1.
3. Add 3 grams of salt and 2 drops of food coloring.
4. Now measure 50 ml of solution #1 from beaker #1 using your graduated cylinder and pour it into beaker #2. Add 50 ml of water to beaker #2. Stir.
5. Next measure 50 ml of solution #2 with your graduated cylinder, and pour it into beaker #3. Add 50 ml of water to beaker #3. Stir.
6. Measure 50 ml of solution #3 with your graduated cylinder. Pour it into beaker #4. Add 50 ml of water to beaker #4. Stir.
7. Measure 50 ml of solution #4 with your graduated cylinder and put aside (this is so that all four beakers have the same amount of liquid).
8. Observe and describe the contents of the four beakers. How are they similar? How are they different?

What you will learn: Each beaker had the concentration of both salt and coloring halved compared to the previous beaker by adding an equal amount of plain water to the salt water. The nature of the substance (colored salty water) did not change, but with each dilution, its concentration decreases.

Core concept demonstrated: Concentration of a chemical substance

Thinking like a scientist: If the initial concentration of salt in beaker #1 is 3%, what is the salt concentration in beaker #2? Beaker #3? Beaker #4? How could you find out the concentration of salt in beaker #1 if you were not told what it is?

Correlation With National Science Standards: A.1; B.4

Building Simple Molecules

The English chemist John Dalton (1766–1844) proposed that the properties of all matter depend upon their atomic composition. In chemical reactions, groups of atoms (or molecules) that were joined together in one way separate and rejoin in new ways, forming molecules with new properties. These atoms and molecules are much too small to observe with the naked eye. Even with the most powerful electron microscopes, things at the atomic scale often remain fuzzy and indistinct. Scientists build a variety of models to help them visualize molecules and their interactions. (See Experiment 61.)

Physical Properties of Molecules

Evaporation is the process by which a liquid is transformed into a gas. Evaporation can only occur when a liquid is present and when the relative humidity in the air is less than 100%. Evaporation also requires energy, generally in the form of heat. This explains why a puddle of water will evaporate quickly on a hot, dry day and much more slowly when the weather is cold or wet. Additionally, different liquids will evaporate at different rates even under the same conditions. (See Experiment 62.)

Elements You Eat

When you think of chemistry, it is possible that the first image that comes to your mind is that of the periodic table of the elements. The periodic table organizes the physical elements into groups, or "periods," based on similar behaviors or characteristics—most notably, how one element interacts with other elements to form molecules. The Russian chemist Dmitri Ivanovich Mendeleev (1834–1907) is generally credited as the father of the periodic table, although much had already been discovered about elements by others before him. Mendeleev published his table in 1869 (see Image 8.6). In the roughly 150 years since Mendeleev's work, many new elements have been added to the periodic table. While some of the chemical elements that have been identified are quite rare, we interact with others on a daily basis. In fact, you must eat many elements every day to remain healthy. (See Experiment 63.)

Matter

The States of Matter and the Organization of Matter: Physical and Chemical Changes

As we mentioned earlier, matter is any substance that has mass and occupies space. Sometimes forces such as heat and pressure change can result in changes in the state of matter of molecules, from solid to liquid to gas. This change in state is a physical change because the basic elements and

(Text continues on page 273)

THE PERIODICITY OF THE ELEMENTS

The Elements	Their Properties in the Free State t [1]	a [2]	d [3]	$\frac{A}{d}$ [4]	Composition of the Hydrogen and Organo-metallic Compounds RH_m or $R(CH_3)_m$ [5]	Symbols R [6]	A [6]	Composition of the Saline Oxides R_2O_n [7]	Properties of the Saline Oxides d [8]	$\frac{(2A+n'16)}{d'}$ [9]	V [10]	Small Periods or Series [11]
Hydrogen	<−200°	—	<0·05	20	m = 1	H	1	1 = n	0·917	19·6	<−20	1
Lithium	180°	—	0·59	12		Li	7	1†	2·0	15	− 9	2
Beryllium	(900°)	—	1·64	5·5		Be	9	— 2	3·06	16·3	+ 2·6	
Boron	(1300°)	—	2·5	4·4	3 — —	B	11	— — 3	1·8	39	10	
Carbon	>(2500°)	—	<2·0	> 6	4 — — —	C	12	— — — 4	>1·0	<88	<19	
Nitrogen	−203°	—	<0·7	> 20	3 — —	N	14	1 — 3* — 5*	1·64	66	< 5	
Oxygen	<−200°	—	<1·0	> 16	2 —	O	16					
Fluorine	—	—	—	—	1	F	19	—				
Sodium	96°	071	0·98	23		Na	23	1†	2·6	24	−22	3
Magnesium	500°	027	1·74	14	2 —	Mg	24	— 2†	3·6	22	− 3	
Aluminium	600°	023	2·6	11	3 — —	Al	27	— — 3	4·0	26	+ 1·3	
Silicon	(1200°)	008	2·3	12	4 — — —	Si	28	— — 3 4	2·65	45	5·2	
Phosphorus	44°	128	2·2	14	3 — —	P	31	1 — 3* 4* 5*	2·39	59	6·2	
Sulphur	114°	067	2·07	15	2 —	S	32	— 2 — 4* 5* 6*	1·96	82	8·7	
Chlorine	−75°	—	1·3	27	1	Cl	35½	1 — 3 — 5* — 7*				
Potassium	58°	084	0·87	45		K	39	1†	2·7	35	−55	4
Calcium	(800°)	—	1·6	25		Ca	40	— 2†	3·15	36	− 7	
Scandium	—	—	(2·5)	(18)		Sc	44	— — 3†	3·86	35	(0)	
Titanium	(2500°)	—	(5·1)	(9·4)		Ti	48	— — — 4	4·2	38	(+5)	
Vanadium	(2000°)	—	5·5	9·2		V	51	— 2 3 4 5	3·49	52	6·7	
Chromium	(2000°)	—	5·5	8·0		Cr	52	— 2 3 — — 6*	2·74	73	9·5	
Manganese	(1500°)	—	7·5	7·3		Mn	55	— 2† 3 4 — 6* 7*				
Iron	1400°	012	7·8	7·2		Fe	56	— 2† 3 — — 6*				
Cobalt	(1400°)	013	8·6	6·8		Co	58½	— 2† 3 —				
Nickel	1350°	017	8·7	6·8		Ni	59	— 2† 3				
Copper	1054°	029	8·8	7·2		Cu	63	1† 2†	Cu_2O 5·9	24	9·8	5
Zinc	1433°	—	7·1	9·2		Zn	65	— 2†	5·7	25	4·8	
Gallium	30°	—	5·96	12	3 — —	Ga	70	— — 3	Ga_2O_3 (5·1)	(36)	(4·0)	
Germanium	900°	—	5·47	13	4 — — —	Ge	72	— 2 — 4	4·7	44	4·5	
Arsenic	500°	006	5·7	13	3 — —	As	75	— — 3 — 5*	4·1	56	6·0	
Selenium	217°	—	4·8	16	2 —	Se	79	— — 4 — 6*				
Bromine	−7°	—	3·1	26	1	Br	80	1 — — 5* — 7*				
Rubidium	39°	—	1·5	57		Rb	85	1†				6
Strontium	(600°)	—	2·5	35		Sr	87	— 2†	4·3	48	−11	
Yttrium	—	—	(3·4)	(26)		Y	89	— — 3†	5·05	45	(−2)	
Zirconium	(1500°)	—	4·1	22		Zr	90	— — — 4	5·7	43	−0·2	
Niobium	—	—	7·1	13		Nb	94	— — — 3 5*	4·7	57	+6·2	
Molybdenum	—	—	8·6	12		Mo	96	— 2 3 — 4 — 6*	4·4	65	6·8	
							(1)					
Ruthenium	(2000°)	010	12·2	8·4		Ru	103	— 2 3 4 — 6 — 8				
Rhodium	(1900°)	008	12·1	8·6		Rh	104	— 2 3 4 — 6				
Palladium	1500°	012	11·4	8·3		Pd	106	1† 2 — 4				
Silver	950°	019	10·5	10		Ag	108	1†	Ag_2O 7·5	31	11	7
Cadmium	320°	031	8·6	13	2 —	Cd	112	— 2†	8·15	31	2·5	
Indium	176°	046	7·4	14	3 —	In	113	— 2 3	In_2O_3 7·18	38	2·7	
Tin	230°	023	7·2	16	4 — — —	Sn	118	— 2 — 4	6·95	43	2·8	
Antimony	432°	012	6·7	18	3 — —	Sb	120	— — 3 4 5	6·5	49	2·6	8
Tellurium	455°	017	6·4	20	2 —	Te	125	— — 4 — 6*	5·1	68	4·7	
Iodine	114°	—	4·9	26	1	I	127	1 — 3 — 5* — 7*				
Cæsium	27°	—	1·88	71		Cs	133	1†				
Barium	—	—	3·75	36		Ba	137	— 2†	5·1	60	6·0	
Lanthanum	(600°)	—	6·1	23		La	138	— — 3†	6·5	50	+1·3	
Cerium	(700°)	—	6·6	21		Ce	140	— — 3 4	6·74	50	2·0	
Didymium	(800°)	—	6·5	22		Di	142	— — 3 — 5				
							(14)					
Ytterbium	—	—	(6·9)	(25)		Yb	173	— — 3	9·18	43	(−2)	10
							(1)					
Tantalum	—	—	10·4	18		Ta	182	— — — — 5	7·5	59	4·6	
Tungsten	(1500°)	—	9·6			W	184	— — — 4 — 6	6·9	67	8	
							(1)					
Osmium	(2500°)	007	22·5	8·5		Os	191	— — 3 4 — 6 — 8				
Iridium	2000°	007	22·4	8·6		Ir	193	— — 3 4 — 6				
Platinum	1775°	005	21·5	9·2		Pt	196	— 2 — 4				
Gold	1045°	014	19·3	10		Au	198	1 — 3	Au_2O (12·5)	(33)	(13)	11
Mercury	−39°	—	13·6	15	2 —	Hg	200	1† 2†	11·1	39	4·5	
Thallium	294°	031	11·8	17	3 —	Tl	204	1† — 3	Tl_2O_3 (9·7)	(47)	(4·3)	
Lead	326°	029	11·3	18	4 — — —	Pb	206	— 2† — 4	8·9	53	4·2	
Bismuth	268°	014	9·8	21	3 — —	Bi	208	— — 3 — 5				
							(5)					
Thorium	—	—	11·1	21		Th	232	— — — 4	9·86	54	2·0	12
							(1)					
Uranium	(800°)	—	18·7	13		U	240	— — — 4 — 6	(7·2)	(80)	(9)	

SOURCE: From the first English edition of Dmitri Mendeleev's *Principles of Chemistry*, 1891, translated from the Russian fifth edition (Wikimedia Commons http://commons.wikimedia.org/wiki/Image:Mendeleev_Table_5th_II.jpg.).

Image 8.6. The First English Translation of Mendeleev's Periodic Table

Experiment 61: **Marshmallow Molecule Models**

In the following activity, you will make a model of one of the most important molecules, a water molecule, using marshmallows.

Materials You Will Need for This Activity

- Large marshmallows to represent oxygen atoms
- Small marshmallows (colored if possible) to represent hydrogen atoms
- Toothpicks to represent the bond between atoms.

What You Will Do

1. Take two small marshmallows (the hydrogen atoms) and one large marshmallow (the oxygen atom).
2. Stick them together with toothpicks so that the two small marshmallows stick out of either side of the large marshmallow at angles.
3. Using more marshmallows, build several more water molecules like the first and connect them in a chain as shown in Image 8.7.
4. Use the Internet, books, and other resources to find pictures of other molecules and then build marshmallow models of these molecules as well.

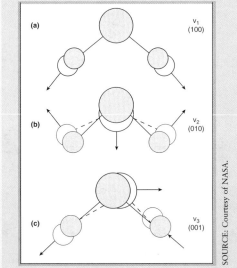

Image 8.7. A Diagram of the Molecular Form of Water Molecules

SOURCE: Courtesy of NASA.

What you will learn: Atoms come in different sizes and combine in a variety of ways, from simple to complex, in order to form molecules. Water is one of the simplest molecules.

Core concept demonstrated: Bonding of atoms into molecules

Thinking like a scientist: Look at your molecule. Why is the chemical formula for water H_2O? How many atoms are there in a molecule of table salt (NaCl)? In a molecule of sulfuric acid (H_2SO_4)?

Correlation With National Science Standards: B.1; G.4

Experiment **62:** Evaporating Molecules

To watch a video clip related to this concept, go to the Student Resource CD bound into the back of your textbook.

In the following activity, you will observe how water and alcohol molecules behave differently under the same conditions.

Materials You Will Need for This Activity

- Cup of water
- Bottle of isopropyl alcohol
- Ruler
- Paper towel

- 2 small plastic cups (8 or 10 oz)
- 2 large plastic cups (16 or 20 oz)
- Pencil
- Tape

What You Will Do

1. Place the two large cups upside down on a table.
2. Lay the pencil across the cups as a bridge and tape it in place.
3. Balance the ruler across the pencil like a see-saw.
4. Cut two identical strips from a paper towel and label one "W" for water and the other "A" for alcohol.
5. Dip the "W" strip of towel in a cup of water until completely wet. Do the same with the "A" strip of towel and the cup of alcohol.
6. Place one strip of towel on each end of the ruler (like two children on a see-saw) and position the ruler so it is balanced again.
7. Keep an eye on your experiment over the next 30 minutes and observe what happens.

What you will learn: Molecules of alcohol evaporate more quickly at room temperature than molecules of water. Thus, the towel soaked with alcohol will lose mass faster than the towel soaked with water.

Core concept demonstrated: Different molecules react differently to their environment.

Thinking like a scientist: Even though you cannot observe molecules of a substance directly, how can you study their behaviors indirectly? Aside from studying evaporation, what are some other ways you could indirectly study the behavior of molecules?

Correlation With National Science Standards: A.2; B.4

Experiment 63: Elements You Eat

In the following activity, you will look at nutritional labels to see which elements are common in the food you eat.

Materials You Will Need for This Activity

- A variety of nutritional labels from a range of foods such as cereals, soups, canned fruits and vegetables, dairy, canned meats, "junk food," etc.

What You Will Do

1. Make a data table with three columns to record the type of food, chemical elements present, and amount of element present (or percentage of recommended daily allowance).
2. Examine at least 10 nutritional labels from different kinds of foods and record the information in your data table.
3. Look at the results of your completed table. What patterns or observations can you make?

What you will learn: A number of chemical elements, such as iron, calcium, magnesium and potassium (to name a few), are necessary parts of a healthy diet and found in many common foods.

Core concept demonstrated: Chemical elements are an essential part of your daily life.

Thinking like a scientist: Why are some chemical elements important for your health? Find an appropriate book or Web site on nutrition and explore the role each of the elements on your data table plays in keeping your body healthy. Which types of foods that you examined contained the most elements you need to be healthy? Which contain the least?

Correlation With National Science Standards: B.1; F.1

Image 8.8. Hot Air Balloon

In September, 1804, chemist Joseph Gay-Lussac ascended in a hot air balloon to study the atmosphere.

SOURCE: Photograph courtesy of the Smithsonian Institution (http://www.centennialofflight.gov/essay/ Lighter_than_air/early_scientific_balloons/LTA7G1.htm).

molecules are not altered; they are just rearranged. In contrast, in a chemical change a new substance is formed. For example, when a piece of paper is burned, molecules of ash and carbon dioxide are created—molecules that were not there before the paper was burned.

Hot Air Rises

All of the substance that makes up the universe exists primarily in three different states of matter: solids, liquids, and gases. Gases are the most elusive of the three states of matter. Gases have relatively low densities and expand and contract with changes in pressure and temperature. A gas has no shape or size of its own and can expand without limit. The air we breathe, for example, is a gas that consists of nitrogen, oxygen, hydrogen, and other trace elements. When air is heated up it expands and rises (see Image 8.8). The particles that make up a gas move faster when they are heated. Perhaps you have seen hot air rise on the surface of a road when you drive down it on a hot day. Things off in the distance appear wavy because the rising hot air in the atmosphere distorts the light and what you are seeing. (See Experiment 64.)

Densities of Liquids

Have you ever looked at the salad dressings in a supermarket? Many are made of oil and vinegar. If they have been sitting on the shelf and no one has picked them up, the oil and vinegar will have separated into two distinct layers. When you shake the bottle, the two separate chemical compounds (oil and vinegar) merge together to create a substance with properties different from the properties of the original layers. You can demonstrate this by tasting the separate oil and vinegar layers of the dressing—neither one is particularly appealing. But when you combine them and taste the resulting mixture, you will see that it has a very different flavor than either the separate oil or the vinegar. There is a synthesis of the two flavors that gives you something totally new. (See Experiment 65.)

Experiment **64:** Hot Air Rises

You can demonstrate hot air rising by making a simple hot air detector with a piece of paper and a string.

Materials You Will Need for This Experiment

- A piece of paper
- Scissors
- Needle and thread
- Burning electric light

What You Will Do

1. Draw a large spiral on a piece of paper.
2. Cut along the line of the spiral so that the paper uncoils and hangs down like a snake or spiral ramp.
3. Knot the end of a piece of thread and string it through a small hole poked in the top of the spiral so that the spiral can hang down from the thread.
4. Suspend the spiral from the thread above a burning electric light bulb. Be careful not to burn yourself. The hot air currents generated by the light bulb should set the spiral slowly spinning.

What you will learn: The heat from the burning light bulb will cause the particles that make up the air to move faster and rise, causing the paper spiral to move.

Core concept demonstrated: Heating a gas will cause it to expand and rise.

Thinking like a scientist: What are the implications of hot air rising, as you have discovered in this experiment? Think about a hot air balloon. How does the way it works relate to this experiment? How does rising hot air affect weather?

Correlation With National Science Standards: A.2; B.3; B.5

Experiment 65: Densities of Liquids

To watch a video clip related to this concept, go to the Student Resource CD bound into the back of your textbook.

In the following activity, you will explore the property of *density* as it applies to various liquids.

Materials You Will Need for This Activity

- 4 small plastic 8-ounce cups
- A tall, clear 16-ounce plastic cup
- Corn syrup
- Vegetable oil
- Water
- Isopropyl alcohol
- Food coloring (any color)
- Balance
- Plastic spoon

What You Will Do

Image 8.9. Illustration of an Early Version of the Classic Density of Liquids Experiment

SOURCE: Good (1893).

1. Use a permanent marker to label the four small plastic cups *vegetable oil, corn syrup, alcohol,* and *water*. Draw a horizontal line on each cup 5 cm from the bottom to serve as the fill line.
2. Fill each cup to the fill line with the liquid that matches the label of the cup (vegetable oil, corn syrup, alcohol, and water).
3. Add three drops of food coloring to the water and stir.
4. Find the mass of each cup on the balance and record the result.
5. Into the 16-ounce plastic cup, slowly pour the heaviest liquid first, then the second heaviest, then the third heaviest, and finally the lightest.
6. Observe and describe what happens to the three liquids in the cup.
7. Stir the liquids with the plastic spoon and observe again. What do they look like?
8. Set each cup aside and observe it periodically over the next 30 minutes. What do you observe?

What you will learn: Liquids of different densities will tend to layer, with the densest liquid on the bottom and the least dense on the top. These layers can be disturbed by agitating the liquid, but when given time to settle, the layers will separate.

Core concept demonstrated: Density of liquids

Thinking like a scientist: If the vegetable oil was poured in the cup first, then the corn syrup, and then the water and alcohol, would the oil stay at the bottom of the cup? Why or why not?

Correlation With National Science Standards: A.1; B.1

Making Salt Crystals

The atoms in most molecules form repeating three-dimensional patterns. The atom patterns in minerals often result in crystalline structures. These crystalline structures can have a wide range of forms, ranging from simple forms such as cubes to highly complex, multifaceted crystals. Crystals form when a liquid containing the necessary elements either cools and solidifies (as in the case of magma) or evaporates, leaving the solid component behind, as you will observe in the following activity. (See Experiment 66.)

Bonding

As noted earlier, bonding is the chemical process by which elements join together to form molecules. The periodic table shows that there are only 118 chemical elements. There are many more than 118 chemical substances in nature, however. This is because the 118 elements react with one another to create new substances called chemical compounds. A compound forms when multiple atoms of two or more elements bond together. Chemical bonding determines the basic characteristics of materials. Why, for example, does soap make water "wetter," and what does this mean? Why does a varnish adhere to the surface of a piece of wood while a bead of water rolls down and off the same material? The answers to these as well as many other chemical questions have to do with chemical bonding.

SOURCE: Photograph by Markus Gayda (Wikimedia Commons, http://commons.wikimedia.org/wiki/ Image:Wasserläufer_bei_der_Paarung._crop.jpg).

Image 8.10. A Water Strider Skating Across the Surface of a Pond Due to Surface Tension

Surface Tension. Have you ever seen an insect like a water strider zip across a pond or slow-moving stream as though it were ice skating? Have you wondered why it didn't fall in the water? The reason is surface tension (see Image 8.10). Surface tension is a property found in all liquids: the surface contracts and resembles a thin invisible elastic skin. (See Experiment 67.)

Separating Mixtures

Chemical elements and molecules combine to form compounds, mixtures, and **solutions**. The fundamental distinction is that once the molecules have combined and reacted to form a compound, they cannot be separated into their constituent parts by physical means. A mixture, on the other hand, can be reversed and the original materials can be separated. A solution is simply a liquid mixture or compound composed of one substance dissolved into another. (See Experiment 68.)

 **Experiment 66: Making Salt Crystals**

To watch a video clip related to this concept, go to the Student Resource CD bound into the back of your textbook.

In this activity, you will create salt crystals from a solution of salty water.

Materials You Will Need for This Activity

- Glass jar
- Pencil
- Thread or string
- Salt

What You Will Do

1. Fill a jar half full with hot (but not boiling) water.
2. Gradually stir the salt into the water until no more salt will dissolve.
3. Tie a thread or string to the middle of pencil and hang the string down into the jar of salty water (but don't let the thread touch the bottom of the jar).
4. Set the jar aside to let the water evaporate.
5. Observe the jar each day and record your observations.

What you will learn: As the water evaporates from the jar, salt crystals will form on the thread. These crystals will be of various sizes but will all have the same crystalline structure.

Core concept demonstrated: The separation of a mixture into its components

Thinking like a scientist: Think about salty ocean water. What happens to the salt when the seawater evaporates? How come rainwater isn't salty? Can the process of forming crystals from cooling or evaporation be reversed? Why or why not?

Correlation With National Science Standards: A.1; B.4; F.3

Compounds, mixtures, and solutions can be clearly seen in cooking. Think about the creation of a dish like minestrone soup. When a chef makes a pot of soup, he or she combines a variety of ingredients to create something that is delicious and nutritious. A chef might start with water and then add tomato, carrots and beans, and small bits of macaroni. Salt and the herb basil are added, and when cooked, the result is a tasty dish. If you first line up all your ingredients on the kitchen counter, you can see these as your starting substances. If you simply dump them all in a pot of water, you have created a mixture, because you could, with little trouble, separate all the ingredients again—no chemical reactions have taken place to alter the ingredients. Once you cook the soup, however, the heat causes chemical reactions to take place that fundamentally change the substances (as evidenced by their changed taste), making it impossible to return them to their original state. Thus, the cooked soup is a chemical compound. The soup broth is also an example of a solution because some of the ingredients dissolved into the water.

To watch a video clip related to this concept, go to the Student Resource CD bound into the back of your textbook.

Experiment 67: Floating a Needle on Water

In the following activity, you will see surface tension at work.

Materials You Will Need for This Activity

- A wide-brimmed glass full of water
- A needle
- A fork

What You Will Do

1. Place the needle across the tines of the fork.
2. Drop the needle gently onto the surface of the water.
3. If you do not break the surface with the point of the needle, it should "float" despite being denser than the water.

SOURCE: Illustration by Poyet from Good (1893).

Image 8.11. Floating Needle

What you will learn: The needle will remain on top of the water because of the water's surface tension.

Core concept demonstrated: Surface tension affects the properties of liquids.

Thinking like a scientist: Why does this experiment only work with a light object like and needle and not with a heavier object like a nail? How does an insect like a water strider use surface tension to help it survive?

Correlation With National Science Standards: A.1; B.1

 **Experiment 68:** **Separating Mixtures**

In the following activity, you will investigate how to separate mixtures by physical means.

Materials You Will Need for This Activity

- Magnets
- Filter paper
- Funnels
- Beakers
- Sieve
- Small jars or beakers
- Sand
- Salt
- Rice
- Iron filings
- Marbles
- Crushed herb (e.g., oregano, basil)
- Water

Image 8.12. A Bowl of Cereal: Is It a Mixture?

SOURCE: Photo by Jean-Marie Buxton.

What You Will Do

1. You will need to make the four sample mixtures (see below) in advance. Place the samples in the small jars.
2. Sample 1: Combine equal amounts of sand and salt.
3. Sample 2: Combine equal amounts of rice and iron filings.
4. Sample 3: Combine equal amounts of water and marbles and then freeze this sample to make a solid.
5. Sample 4: Combine equal amounts of a crushed herb (e.g., oregano or basil) and water.
6. For each of the four samples, think about how you could separate the mixture into its two components. Possible strategies you could use are separation by dissolving, by magnetism, by evaporation, by melting, or by filtration.
7. Try your ideas, and see how each works.

What you will learn: Using basic physical procedures, a mixture can be separated into its original components.

Core concept demonstrated: Difference between compounds and mixtures

Thinking like a scientist: What other compounds and mixtures do you experience in your dally life? How can you tell which are compounds and which are mixtures? Think, for example, about cement. What is it made of? Is it a compound or a mixture? How can you tell? What about Jell-O? Is it a compound or a mixture? How can you tell? How are cement and Jell-O similar and different?

Correlation With National Science Standards: A.1; B.4

Making Water "Wetter" With Soap

All of us have been told to wash our hands with soap to get them really clean. But why do soap and water wash away dirt better than just water alone? Soap has a long history. There are recipes for soap on Sumerian clay tablets dating from 2500 B.C. These soaps were mixtures of various oils or fats plus ashes. The ash contained sodium hydroxide (lye); sodium hydroxide and oils are the main ingredients in soap to this day (see Image 8.13).

Soap works to remove dirt by reducing the surface tension of water. Water normally has a high surface tension, meaning that it likes to cling to itself, which is why it tends to bead or form drops. Soap molecules react with water molecules so that one end of the water molecule is no longer attracted to other water molecules. This hydrophobic (water-hating) end will then bond with a dirt molecule and the other end of the water molecule will still bond with other water molecules, thus washing away the water molecule with the dirt attached. Thus, it has sometimes been said that soap makes water "wetter." Still, not all soaps clean equally well, as you will see in Experiment 69.

Temperature

Temperature is one of the most important variables in chemistry. Temperature affects the properties of materials, the rates of chemical reactions, and the states of matter. For example, when sweetened milk is stirred at a low enough temperature, it becomes delicious ice cream. The temperature of ocean water is largely responsible for the ocean currents as well as the amount of oxygen that the water can absorb, factors that play a major role in the lives of ocean creatures and humans. Likewise, heating and cooling of the Earth's atmosphere influences the weather patterns we experience. The strain and load bearing capacity of metals is similarly affected by temperature, as could be seen in the collapse of the World Trade Center buildings on September 11, 2001.

Evaporation: Effects on Temperature

Have you ever stood in front of a fan on a really hot day to cool off, or felt better when a breeze blew on you? Do you know why these things make you feel cooler? You feel cooler because of the evaporation of sweat from your body. The evaporation of sweat is the primary way that heat is dispelled from the body and body temperature is kept under control. When the sweat evaporates from the surface of your skin, it absorbs energy from the skin's surface. This loss of energy cools the skin. The faster the liquid evaporates, the cooler the surface gets. Still, not all liquids evaporate at the same rate. Could a liquid other than water cause more cooling due to evaporation? (See Experiment 70.)

Experiment **69:** Comparing Soaps

In the following activity, you will test the relative cleaning effectiveness of several different soaps.

Materials You Will Need for This Activity

- 6 small square pieces of cloth from the same piece of material
- 5 numbered samples of soap and detergent (brands unknown)—solid, powder, and liquid
- 6 small containers half full of water in which to wash the cloth
- 6 plastic spoons
- 1 bottle of ketchup
- 1 watch or clock with a second hand
- 1 permanent marker

Image 8.13. Adding Lye to Grease in Soap Making

SOURCE: Photograph by Russell Lee, 1939. Courtesy of the Library of Congress Prints and Photographs Division, Washington, DC.

What You Will Do

1. Using the bottle of ketchup, stain all six squares of cloth in the same way.
2. Label each cloth with one of the soap sample numbers.
3. Label the last cloth "C" for control.
4. Place an equal amount of soap on five of the cloths (leave the control cloth untreated).
5. Rub the soaps into the stains and then wash each cloth in a separate container of water.
6. Stir the cloths in the water for five minutes using the plastic spoons.
7. After five minutes, rinse each cloth in tap water and lay them out for observation.
8. Rank order the six cloths from cleanest to dirtiest.

What you will learn: Soaps help to remove stains by allowing water molecules to bond more easily with dirt molecules. Different soaps perform in different ways.

Core concept demonstrated: Chemical bonding

Thinking like a scientist: Which type of soap—solid, powder, or liquid—seemed to be most effective in removing the stain? Did the control sample get any cleaner after washing it in plain water? Why might this be the case?

Correlation With National Science Standards: A.1; B.4; E.5; F.1; G.1

Experiment **70:** Evaporation of Alcohol and Water

In the following activity, you will compare the cooling capabilities of evaporating water and alcohol.

Materials You Will Need for This Activity

- 2 thermometers
- 2 pieces of cloth
- 2 rubber bands
- 2 small beakers
- Water
- Rubbing alcohol

What You Will Do

1. Look at the thermometers and record the initial room temperature.
2. Use the rubber bands to secure one piece of cloth to the bottom third of each of the two thermometers.
3. Dip the cloth attached to one thermometer in the beaker of water to wet the cloth.
4. Dip the cloth attached to the other thermometer in the beaker of rubbing alcohol.
5. GENTLY and CAREFULLY, wave the two thermometers back and forth to increase the natural rate of evaporation.
6. Take a temperature reading from each of the two thermometers each minute for five minutes, continuing to gently wave the thermometers in the same way between readings.

What you will learn: Alcohol evaporates from surfaces faster than water, creating more and faster cooling.

Core concept demonstrated: Temperature change due to evaporation

Thinking like a scientist: How much more effective was the alcohol at lowering the temperature than the water? If other liquids are better at cooling, why do we sweat water rather than something else, like alcohol?

Correlation With National Science Standards: A.1; B.1; B.3

Hot and Cold Water Interactions

Have you ever gone swimming in a lake or in the ocean and noticed that the water near the surface is warm, but the water gets colder as you go deeper? This happens because hot water rises and cold water sinks. This fact is very important in the creation of ocean currents and climate patterns. For example, coastal areas tend to have less extreme seasonal temperature changes because of the moderating effects of the oceans. You can see how different temperatures of water interact by conducting the following experiment. (See Experiment 71.)

Making Ice Cream

I scream, you scream, we all scream for ice cream! Nearly everyone likes ice cream, but do you know how ice cream is made? It actually involves a chemical process.

SOURCE: Courtesy of the Library of Congress Prints and Photographs Division, Washington, DC.

Image 8.14. Making Ice Cream at the W.C. Wicks Residence on Route 1, East Stroudsburg, Pennsylvania, 1946

The history of ice cream seems to date back to the fourth century B.C. when the Roman emperor Nero (A.D. 37–68) ordered ice to be brought from the mountains and mixed with fruit toppings. Other stories tell that King Tang (A.D. 618–697) of China had his chef create ice and milk desserts. This method was likely brought from China to Europe, where it became particularly popular with the French royal court. George Washington is said to have impressed his guests at his presidential inauguration by serving "iced cream," but it was not until the first ice cream parlor opened in New York City in 1776 that the frozen treat became available to the masses (see Image 8.14). (See Experiment 72.)

🐚 Pressure

Along with temperature and volume, pressure is a key variable necessary for understanding chemical behaviors. Pressure is defined as the force per unit area. In the case of gases, this force comes from the gas molecules hitting each other and the sides of the container holding the gas, if the gas is in an enclosed area. We measure air pressure using a barometer. Traditional barometers compare the force of the air pressing down from above with the force being applied by a column of liquid in a closed tube. The higher the column of liquid rises, the more force the air is exerting and the higher the barometric pressure.

To watch a video clip related to this concept, go to the Student Resource CD bound into the back of your textbook.

Experiment 71: Hot and Cold Water Mixtures

In the following activity, you will observe the interactions of hot and cold water.

Materials You Will Need for This Activity

- 2 small clear plastic vials
- 2 rubber bands
- 2 popsicle sticks
- 2 medium (500 ml) beakers
- Red and blue food coloring
- Hot and cold water

SOURCE: Photo by Jean-Marie Buxton

Image 8.15. Hot and Cold Water Interactions

What You Will Do

1. Use the rubber bands to attach one popsicle stick to each plastic vial, to make a handle for lowering the vials into the beakers.
2. Use the food coloring to dye a small amount (about 50 ml) of the hot water red and a small amount of the cold water blue.
3. Pour un-dyed hot water into one of the 500 ml beakers, filling it about half way.
4. Pour un-dyed cold water into the other 500 ml beaker, filling it about half way.
5. Fill one plastic vial with the blue cold water and gently submerge the vial into the beaker of hot water. What do you observe?
6. Fill the other plastic vial with the red hot water and gently submerge the vial into the beaker of cold water. What do you observe?

What you will learn: The blue cold water will remain in the vial because it is denser that the hot water surrounding it. Any blue water that escapes the vial will sink to the bottom of the beaker. Only when the cold water heats up will it start to mix with the surrounding water. The red hot water will leave the vial and float to the surface because it is less dense than the surrounding water.

Core concept demonstrated: Hotter water is less dense than colder water.

Thinking like a scientist: If cold water sinks below warm water, why does ice float?

Correlation With National Science Standards: A.1; B.3; B.4; B.6

Experiment **72:**   Making Ice Cream

In the following activity, you will learn how salt affects the freezing point of water as you make ice cream.

Materials You Will Need for This Activity

- $\frac{1}{2}$ cup milk
- $\frac{1}{8}$ teaspoon vanilla
- 1 tablespoon sugar
- 4 cups crushed ice
- 4 tablespoons coarse salt
- 2 quart-size zip-lock bags
- 1 gallon-size zip-lock freezer bag
- 1 thermometer

What You Will Do

1. Mix the milk, vanilla, and sugar together in one of the quart-size bags.
2. Seal tightly, allowing as little air to remain in the bag as possible (too much air left inside the bag may force the bag to open during shaking).
3. Place this bag inside the other quart-size bag, again leaving as little air as possible inside the bag, and seal it completely. (By double bagging, the risk of salt and ice leaking into the ice cream is minimized.)
4. Put the two bags inside the gallon-size bag, then add the ice and salt to the gallon bag. Again, let all the air escape and seal the bag.
5. You may elect to have one control group add only ice but no salt in the above step.
6. Take an initial temperature reading of the ice inside the gallon bag.
7. Shake and massage the bag for five minutes, making sure that the ice surrounds the cream mixture.
8. Take a second temperature reading of the ice mixture.
9. Continue shaking for an additional three to five minutes. Check the consistency of the ice cream and continue shaking for several more minutes, if necessary.
10. Take a final temperature reading, remove the ice cream, and enjoy.

What you will learn: Adding salt to the ice changes the chemical composition of the ice in a way that lowers the freezing point (it also raises the boiling point). This lower freezing point means that the temperature of the salty ice will drop lower than the temperature of ice alone and will allow the ice cream to solidify. If you used the control bag of just ice with no salt, you can see the difference in its temperature. **Core concept demonstrated:** Depression of freezing point

Thinking like a scientist: What do you predict would happen if you repeated this experiment using half as much salt while leaving all other amounts the same? Why? If you used twice as much ice, leaving all other amounts the same? Why? Where else can you apply this understanding of temperature change in real life?

Correlation With National Science Standards: A.1; B.4; B.6; F.10; G.2

We are generally unaware of the dynamics of pressure in our daily lives; however, there are certain times that we feel these effects. Your ears pop when you take off or land in an airplane or when you dive into a deep pool. You find it hard to breathe when you are at the top of a mountain. A scuba diver gets the bends when she comes up too quickly. All of these examples are results of pressure affecting our bodies.

Burning Candles: A Temperature/Pressure Relationship

Robert Boyle (1627–1691) is best known for his work concerning the pressure of gases, an issue that is of critical importance to the study of chemistry. In 1662, he published what became known as Boyle's law, which states that at constant temperature, the volume of a gas is inversely proportional to its pressure. Boyle knew that temperature also affected the pressure of gases, but did not add the effect of temperature into his theories. It was many years later that the French scientist Jacques Charles (1746–1823) proved that the volume of a gas depended on its temperature. You will explore both Boyle's and Charles's work concerning gases and their behavior in Experiment 73. (See Experiment 73.)

Creating a Vacuum

Among the most important experiments in the seventeenth century was one performed by Otto von Guericke (1602–1686) involving the creation of a vacuum. This experiment came to be known as the "Magdeburg Sphere" experiment, after the town in Germany in which it took place and where Guericke was also the mayor. In his experiment, he put two large identical metal hemispheres together, extracted the air from them with a pump, and then tried to pull them apart using two teams of horses (see Image 8.16). Because of the vacuum created inside the spheres, it was impossible to pull the spheres apart. (See Experiment 74.)

SOURCE: Ferrari's *Philosophia Peripatetica*, 1745.

Image 8.16. Illustration of Otto von Guericke's "Magdeburg Sphere" Experiment

 **Experiment 73:** **Burning Candles**

To watch a video clip related to this concept, go to the Student Resource CD bound into the back of your textbook.

In the following activity, you will observe a temperature/pressure relationship.

Materials You Will Need for This Activity

- Petri dish
- Birthday candle
- Small piece of clay
- Matches
- Water
- Erlenmeyer flask

What You Will Do

1. Stick the candle upright in the center of the Petri dish using the piece of clay.
2. Fill the Petri dish $\frac{2}{3}$ full of water.
3. Write a hypothesis of what you think will happen when the candle is lit and then covered by the Erlenmeyer flask.
4. Light the candle, wait several seconds, and then quickly cover it with the inverted flask. Observe what happens.
5. Repeat the procedure, making any additional observations you can.
6. Do several more trials to see whether you can control how high the water rises in the flask.
7. Explain what you have observed.

Image 8.17. Burning Candles

What you will learn: The hot air that is initially trapped in the flask expands, and some of this air escapes through the water under the flask. After the candle is extinguished and the remaining air in the flask begins to cool, it will contract, leaving a partial vacuum. The water will then push up into the flask until the pressure inside and outside the flask is equalized.

Core concept demonstrated: Temperature, pressure, and volume interactions of a gas

Thinking like a scientist: You probably did not observe the bubbles during the first or second trials. Why not? What does this say about the importance of multiple trials and careful observations when conducting scientific investigations?

Correlation With National Science Standards: A.1; B.3; B.5; B.6; G.4

Creating a Simple Vacuum

You can recreate the effect of Guericke's experiment in a somewhat different way by making your own vacuum with two glasses and a lit candle.

Materials You Will Need for This Experiment

- Two identical wide-brimmed glasses
- A short candle
- A heavy piece of paper with a small hole in its center ($\frac{1}{4}$ inch)
- A small bowl of water
- Matches or lighter

What You Will Do

1. Very lightly dampen the paper.
2. Place the candle in the bottom of one the glasses.
3. Light it.
4. Next, quickly put the piece of paper over the top of the glass with the candle burning in it.
5. Then invert the second glass and place it exactly over the first, so that the rims are aligned with the paper in between.
6. Wait for a few minutes and then carefully try to pull the two glasses apart.

What you will learn: As in the previous burning candle experiment (Experiment 73), the hot air that is initially trapped in the glass expands, and some of this air escapes past the piece of paper. After the candle is extinguished and the remaining air in the glass begins to cool, it will contract, leaving a partial vacuum. This vacuum will keep the two glasses locked together.

Core concept demonstrated: A vacuum can create a powerful seal.

Thinking like a scientist: In burning buildings, what happens to the air? Why would a fireman who has to deal with a back draft be interested in this experiment? Why would it affect how he or she might fight a fire?

Correlation With National Science Standards: A.1; B.4; B.5; B.6; G.4

SOURCE: Photo by Henrik Reinholdson (Wikipedia, http://en.wikipedia.org/wiki/Image: Diving_bell.jpg).

Image 8.18. Early Diving Bell

How Air Pressure Changes With Depth

Legend has it that Alexander the Great (356–323 B.C.) went to the bottom of the Mediterranean Sea near Turkey in a diving bell (see Image 8.18). The diving bell was open at its bottom. It didn't fill up with water because the air pressure contained inside the bell could only be compressed to a certain point. As a result, water could not make its way into the empty space inside the diving bell. (See Experiment 75.)

Fuels

The use of fuels plays a central role in our modern industrial and post-industrial world. Burning fossil fuels remains an efficient way of making energy. Crude oil, natural gas, and coal are the primary examples of fossil fuels. These fuels are important resources, not only for producing energy, but also as sources of the various organic chemicals used in the manufacture of products such as paints, detergents, plastics, cosmetics, and even some medicines. The burning of fossil fuels also has negative environmental consequences, however. Emissions from burning fossil fuels seem to enhance the greenhouse effect, as well as contribute to smog and other forms of air pollution. Additionally, the transportation of fuels, especially oil, creates the risk of accidents and spills that are environmentally devastating.

There continues to be a growing interest in so-called "alternative fuels" that would reduce the world's dependence on the burning of fossil fuels. These alternative fuel sources include nuclear power, solar power, tidal power, geothermal power, and a variety of fuel cell (battery) technologies. It is possible to imagine that in the future a combination of some or all of these fuel sources will create a more sustainable energy production system to provide the world's population with the energy we all need for a more comfortable and efficient lifestyle.

Measuring the Energy in Batteries

The amount of electricity that a battery generates depends on the chemical reaction going on inside it. The first battery was invented by the Italian scientist

Experiment 75:   Cartesian Diver

You can see how air pressure works in a diving bell by constructing a Cartesian diver.

Materials You Will Need for This Activity

- A plastic eye dropper or pipette
- A metal nut
- A 1-liter plastic bottle with cap (filled to the top with water)
- A tall cup of water
- Scissors

Image 8.19. An Early Version of the Cartesian Diver

SOURCE: Illustration by Erle (1884).

What You Will Do

1. Use the scissors to cut the tube off the plastic eyedropper, leaving only about $\frac{1}{4}$ inch of the tube above the cut.
2. Screw the metal nut onto the remaining piece of tube on the end of the dropper. This will be your "diver."
3. Place the diver into the cup of water—does it sink or float? Why?
4. Keeping the diver in the water, squeeze some of the air out. What happens? Why?
5. Adjust the water level in the diver until it just barely floats in the cup.
6. Transfer the diver from the cup to the one-liter plastic bottle and put the cap on the bottle.
7. Squeeze the bottle in the middle and hold the squeeze. Record what happens to the diver.
8. Release the squeeze on the bottle. Record what happens to the diver.
9. Repeat squeezing and releasing the bottle several times. Carefully observe the diver as you do this.
10. Draw a labeled diagram of the squeezed and unsqueezed state.

What you will learn: Squeezing the bottle increases the water pressure inside and compresses the air in the diver. This increases the density of the diver and causes it to sink. Releasing the bottle decreases the water pressure inside and allows the air to expand. This decreases the density of the diver and causes it to rise.

Core concept demonstrated: Effect of pressure on a gas

Thinking like a scientist: How might a submarine use a similar principle to dive and surface in the ocean? Scuba divers sometimes get a painful condition call the "bends," or decompression sickness, when they come up to the surface too quickly after a dive. How might this condition be related to the Cartesian diver?

Correlation With National Science Standards: A.1; B.5; E.4; G.2

Alessandro Volta (1745–1827). He created his battery by stacking alternating layers of zinc, blotting paper soaked in salt water, and silver. Batteries of this kind became known as a *voltaic pile* (see Image 8.20). If one attached a wire to the top and bottom of the pile, the battery could generate electricity. In the following activity, you will construct your own voltaic pile. (See Experiment 76.)

Harnessing Solar Energy

The sun generates enormous amounts of energy. This energy makes life on Earth possible. Solar energy is collected in many different ways. Plants, for example, absorb the sun's energy and use it to produce food through photosynthesis. In a certain sense, a plant is a very sophisticated solar engine that is translating solar energy into power that allows it to grow. Humans have likewise been harnessing solar energy for a long time. You may think that solar-powered devices are a relatively new invention, but in fact, they date back nearly 150 years (see Image 8.21). In the 1860s and 1870s, there was a growing movement to harness solar energy out of concern that one day "all the coal will have been used up." History is repeating itself today, as a concern about the limited quantities of petroleum has again led to increased interest in renewable energy sources such as solar energy. (See Experiment 77.)

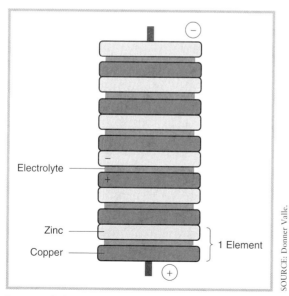

Electrolyte

Zinc

Copper

1 Element

SOURCE: Donner Valle.

Image 8.20. Voltaic Pile

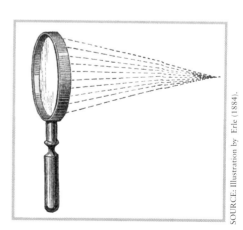

SOURCE: Illustration by Erle (1884).

Image 8.21. Focusing Light With a Magnifying Glass

 **Experiment 76:**   **Building a Voltaic Pile**

In the following activity, you will make your own Voltaic pile.

Materials You Will Need for This Activity

- Pile of coins (pennies, nickels, dimes)
- Paper towels
- Salt
- Water
- Volt meter
- Modern "D" battery

What You Will Do

1. Make a saturated salt solution (Dissolve as much salt as the water will hold. Warm water will allow more salt to be dissolved.)
2. Cut several paper towels into small squares and soak the paper towel pieces in the salt solution.
3. Create your pile by alternately stacking pennies and nickels with a piece of wet paper towel between each coin (note that there must be a different type of coin on the top and bottom of the pile).
4. Use the voltmeter to measure the voltage and current that your pile produces by placing the meter's contact points on the top and bottom of the stack of coins.
5. Try a different number of layers and see what effect it has on voltage.
6. Try alternating pennies and dimes and see what happens.
7. Now use the voltmeter on the modern "D" cell battery. How does your voltaic pile compare to the modern dry cell battery in terms of the amount of electricity it generates?

What you will learn: The battery is a type of fuel that generates electricity through a chemical reaction that leads to a flow of electrons. The stronger the chemical reaction, the greater the current the battery can produce.

Core concept demonstrated: Electricity generated by a battery

Thinking like a scientist: What would the world be like if we did not have batteries? Think about portable radios, iPods, computers, cell phones, flashlights, and similar types of devices. How would we power these devices if we did not have batteries? How would their use change as a result?

Correlation With National Science Standards: A.2; B.3; B.4; B.6; F.10; G.4

Experiment 77: Making a Solar Water Heater

In the following activity, you will design and build a solar water heater.

Materials You Will Need for This Activity

- 2 identical jars, milk cartons, or yogurt containers
- Metallic car windshield reflector or cardboard covered with aluminum foil
- Water
- Thermometer
- Plastic wrap

What You Will Do

1. Pour 100 ml of water into each of the two jars or containers, and cover each jar with plastic wrap to limit the loss of heat.
2. Take an initial temperature reading of the water in each jar.
3. Place both jars in direct sunlight.
4. Position the windshield reflector or foil-covered cardboard to reflect as much light as possible onto one of the jars of water.
5. Take additional temperature readings of each jar every five minutes for one hour.

What you will learn: The jar surrounded by the solar reflector has much more sunlight focused upon it and is therefore able to absorb and store a greater amount of solar energy.

Core concept demonstrated: Concentration and storage of solar energy

Thinking like a scientist: Why do most satellites rely on solar energy? If your house was powered by solar energy, how could you have power at night when the sun was not shining on your house?

Correlation With National Science Standards: A.1; B.3; B.4; B.6; E.5

Energy in Fossil Fuels

You have probably seen wood burning in a fireplace. The energy stored within the piece of wood is consumed and quickly released by the catalytic force of the fire. This process releases both light and heat. Other organic materials have energy stored in them as well. Coal, for example, is a type of rock created by the compression of organic materials (mostly ancient plants). Within the coal is a great deal of compressed and concentrated energy that can be released when the coal is burned. But how about a peanut? Does it have energy stored in it as well (see Image 8.22)? (See Experiment 78.)

SOURCE: Courtesy of Library of Congress Prints and Photographs Division, Washington, DC.

Image 8.22. Peanut Vendor

Joseph Severio, 11-year-old peanut vendor, had been pushing his cart two years when this photo was taken in Wilmington, Delaware.

Experiment 78: Peanut Power

In the following activity, you will measure the amount of energy stored in a peanut.

Materials You Will Need for This Activity

- A small bag of unsalted, shelled peanuts
- A cork
- A needle
- A large metal juice can
- A small metal soup can with paper label removed

- A can opener
- A hammer
- A large nail
- A metal skewer
- A cup of water
- A thermometer
- Matches or a lighter

What You Will Do

1. Push the eye of the needle into the smaller end of the cork and the pointed end of the needle into a peanut, so the peanut is standing upright.
2. Use the can opener to remove the two ends of the large juice can. (Watch out for sharp edges!)
3. Using the hammer and nail, punch holes around the bottom of the large can (these are air holes, which will make the can act like a chimney).
4. Remove the top of the soup can and, using the hammer and nail, punch two holes near the top of the can exactly opposite each other so that the skewer can slide through.
5. Pour $\frac{1}{2}$ cup of room temperature water into the small can. Put the thermometer into the water and record the temperature.
6. Carefully light the peanut with a match or lighter.
7. As soon as the peanut has caught fire, place the large can over the nut. Balance the skewer holding the small can on the top of the large can so that the small can is suspended above the burning peanut.
8. Allow the nut to burn until it goes out.
9. Stir the water with the thermometer. Measure and record the temperature a second time.

* Safety note—The teacher or other adult should prepare or carefully supervise the preparation of the can, for safety reasons.

What you will learn: The temperature of the water will rise because of the energy released from the peanut as it burns.

Core concept demonstrated: Chemical potential energy

Thinking like a scientist: Where did the energy in the peanut come from? How was it stored in the nut? Are peanuts a viable source of fuel? Why or why not? Are peanuts a renewable or nonrenewable source of energy?

Correlation With National Science Standards: A.1; B.3; B.4; B.6; F.3

Student Study Site

The Companion Web site for *Teaching Science in Elementary and Middle School* http://www.sagepub.com/buxtonstudy

Visit the Web-based student study site to enhance your understanding of the chapter content and to discover additional resources that will take your learning one step further. You can enhance your understanding of the chapters by using the study materials, which include chapter objectives, flashcards, activities, practice tests, and more. You'll also find special features, such as Resources for Experiments, the Links to Standards from U.S. States and associated activities, Learning From Journal Articles, Theory Into Practice resources, Reflections on Science exercises, a Science Standards-Based Lesson Plan Project, and PRAXIS resources.

Reflections on Science

1. The study of chemistry covers a range of topics, including organic chemistry, inorganic chemistry and physical chemistry. What do these various topics have in common that make them all chemistry?

2. We interact with a wide variety of chemicals in our day-to-day lives. Make a list of as many kinds of chemicals as you can that you use on daily basis. See if you can categorize these chemicals into groups.

3. Temperature, pressure, and volume are all interrelated in understanding the chemical properties of matter, and especially gases. Reflect on the experiments you have done in this chapter and summarize what you now know about the relationship between temperature, pressure, and volume.

Internet Connections: Chemistry

The following Web sites provide additional resources that may prove useful in teaching about chemistry:

American Chemical Society: Web site for elementary and middle school chemistry
http://www.chemistry.org/portal/a/c/s/1/acsdis play.html?DOC=kids%5ccc_kidspage_index.html

American Chemical Society: Web site of links to other resources for elementary and middle school chemistry

http://www.chemistry.org/portal/a/c/s/1/acsdis play.html?DOC=education\wande\index .html

Oregon Museum of Science and Industry: Chemistry activities and experiments
http://www.omsi.edu/visit/chemistry/

Miami Museum of Science: Exploration of pH
http://www.miamisci.org/ph/index.html

Polymer Science Learning Center: Activities for kids
http://www.pslc.ws/paul.html

Umea University (Sweden): Links to a wide variety of chemistry education resources
http://www.anachem.umu.se/eks/pointers.htm

References

Erle, T. (1884). *Science in the nursery*. London: Griffith and Farran.

Good, A. (1893). *La science amusante* (Vols. 1–3). Paris: Le Librarie Larousse.

Holmyard, E. J. (1990). *Alchemy*. New York: Dover.

Standen, A. (1958). *Science is a sacred cow*. Boston: Dutton.

Understanding and Teaching Physics

9

Consider the following quotes about physics:

G ive me a lever long enough and a fulcrum on which to place it, and I shall move the world.

—**Archimedes**

T hose who are not shocked when they first come across quantum mechanics cannot possibly have understood it.

—**Niels Bohr**

I am become death, the destroyer of worlds.

—**J. Robert Oppenheimer (1904–1967), U.S. physicist, quoting from the *Bhagavad Gita* at the first atomic test in New Mexico, 1945.**

W hat I am going to tell you about is what we teach our physics students in the third or fourth year of graduate school. . . . It is my task to convince you not to turn away because you don't understand it. You see, my physics students don't understand it. . . . That is because I don't understand it. Nobody does.

—**Richard P. Feynman (1990, p. 9)**

❧ The Place of Physics in Science Education

What do you think of when you see or hear the word "physics"? Do you think about mad scientists in laboratories creating weird experiments? Do you think about objects in motion? The dynamics of water pouring from a glass? The rotation of a wheel on an automobile or wagon? The striking of a hammer against a nail? The opening of a door on a hinge? A drop of water splashing in a mud puddle? Do you think of forces that make it possible for us to heat our homes, bring light into dark places, and—through inventions like the atomic bomb—destroy the Earth? Do you think about computers and their logic circuits and the Internet and access to massive amounts of knowledge and the exchange of information? The opening quotes of this chapter highlight the mystique and the power that are generally attributed to physics. Yet physics can be as mundane and as simple as it can be esoteric and arcane. Physics is as much a part of our everyday world as is biology, only many people fail to recognize this fact.

Physics is considered by many to be the most foundational of the sciences. As physicists are fond of pointing out, at the most fundamental level, all science is physics. This is because physics governs the fundamental particles and interactions that define the workings of the natural world. The challenging (and often counterintuitive) nature of this fact means that traditionally, physics is placed last in the organization of the science curriculum. Consider that in the typical high school, physics is an elective course offered only to juniors and seniors. While the study of physics can be highly abstract and mathematical, we believe that physics is the scientific discipline that most readily lends itself to simple and manageable inquiry-based experiments at the elementary and middle school level. Rolling balls down ramps, constructing simple electric circuits, changing the pitch of a musical instrument, and many other examples we will explore in this chapter provide opportunities for children to engage in a wide range of inquiry-based science activities.

Physics may very well be the most ancient of all human sciences. When cavemen first looked up at the starry firmament in the sky, they began to relate to the fundamental aspects of physics as a science. As Cro-Magnon humans began to develop tools, they employed the basic laws of physics (the discovery, for example, of the lever as a simple tool).

Physics is essential to humans as tool makers (*homo faber*). It was with tools that human beings overcame their weakness compared to other animals. A club (a simple lever) suddenly made it possible for hunters to battle stronger and fiercer animals. Many of the great engineering accomplishments of antiquity were, likewise, tied to basic physics. The construction of the pyramids involved a knowledge of physical principles embedded in basic tools such as the lever, pulley, and rollers. The great cathedrals of Medieval Europe were also constructed on the basis of knowledge of physics applied to engineering and architecture (see Image 9.1).

SOURCE: Photo by Ivan Vighetto.

Image 9.1. An Example of Renaissance Architecture

The modern field of physics essentially emerged in the late Renaissance with the discoveries of scientists such as Leonardo Da Vinci (1452–1519) and Galileo Galilei (1564–1642). Its development continued into the early modern period and, some people would argue, helped create modern culture through the work of scientists such as Isaac Newton (1643–1727), Nicolas Copernicus (1473–1543), and Johannes Kepler (1571–1630). Physics, in the form of astronomy, opened up an awareness of the vast reaches of our solar system and, in turn, the universe (see Image 9.2). It also brought into focus the microscopic world that determines biological systems: amoebas, parasites, and single-cell structures.

Much of the progress since the Enlightenment has been a direct result of discoveries in the field of physics. An example of this is the steam engine, originally invented by Isaac Watts (1674–1748) to pump water from the depths of coal mines in Wales (see Image 9.3). By the nineteenth century, the steam engine was being used in other industries, most importantly railroads, which redefined the understanding of time and distance in Western culture. In the United States, the invention of the railroad made possible the opening up and settlement of the interior of the continent, and vast lands and territories now became available for settlers (see Image 9.4).

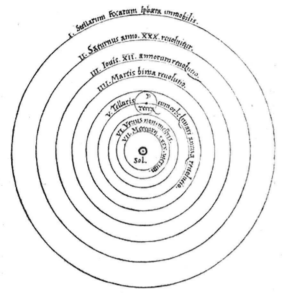

Image 9.2. The Solar System as Conceived by Copernicus

SOURCE: Copernicus (1543).

Discoveries and inventions based on an understanding of physics expanded by the beginning of the twentieth century. It is hard to believe, but only a little more than 100 years ago, men could not fly. The discovery of powered flight set in motion a series of historic events that have been pivotal in our culture's subsequent history. Think for a moment what the twentieth century would have been like without powered flight. How would people have moved around, communicated, conducted business, or conducted war without this remarkable invention?

Closer to our own era, the power of physics has taught us about the fragility of the world and our potential to destroy it. In 1945, we exploded our first atomic bomb, and in doing so, made it possible to eliminate human life on the Earth (see Image 9.5).

The basic principles of physics, discovered over the last couple of thousand years, surround us in our day-to-day lives, yet we take most of these principles for granted. If we look at a wheelbarrow or bicycle, for example, we can see simple machines like the wheel and axle and lever working together to create a mechanical advantage that makes people's work easier (see Image 9.6). More recent inventions, such as the internal combustion engine, have used basic principles of physics to revolutionize the way we live.

The study of physics has increasingly moved from a macro to a micro world, one in which things are evident that were invisible to previous

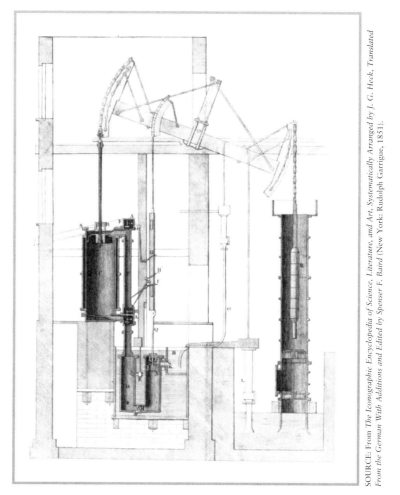

SOURCE: From *The Iconographic Encyclopedia of Science, Literature, and Art. Systematically Arranged by J. G. Heck, Translated From the German With Additions and Edited by Spenser F. Baird* (New York: Rudolph Garrigue, 1851).

Image 9.3. Isaac Watts' Engine, Used to Pump Water out of Coal Mines

generations. Consequently, the science of physics presents new possibilities that have the potential to profoundly redefine our lives. One of the most exciting developments in recent years has been the invention of electronic computing, which has become faster, more efficient, and cheaper every year. The processing power of the personal computer is literally tens of times greater than it was only a decade ago. Hand-held devices now have the power that university "supercomputers" had just 20 years ago.

Other new developments are also coming to the fore. Nanotechnology, for example, represents a whole new field of physics in which we can

SOURCE: Courtesy of the National Archives.

Image 9.4. Joining the Tracks for the First Transcontinental Railroad, Promontory, Utah Territory, 1869.

The transcontinental railroad connected the east and west coasts of the United States, making possible the economic and social unification of the country.

literally "grow" microscopic machines (see Image 9.7). As a result, it will be possible to create computers of virtually unlimited power that make only minimal use of energy, or create machines so small that they can perform operations and manipulations at the cellular level.

In the rest of this chapter, we introduce 25 core experiments in physics, which we think provide a foundation for teachers working in the classroom.

Measurement in Physics

Measurement is essential to the science of physics. Physics would not be possible without a range of measurement tools, whether to establish standards for weight, the duration of a period of time, or the size of an object.

Image 9.5. The Bombing of Nagasaki

A dense column of smoke rose more than 60,000 feet into the air over the Japanese port of Nagasaki after an atomic bomb, the second ever used in warfare, was dropped on the industrial center August 8, 1945, from a U.S. B-29 Superfortress.

SOURCE: Courtesy of the National Archives.

SOURCE: Courtesy of the National Archives.

Image 9.6. A Bicycle from 1886: A Combination of Simple Machines

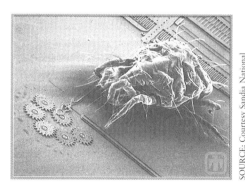

SOURCE: Courtesy Sandia National Laboratories, SUMMiT™ Technologies, http://www.mems.sandia.gov

Image 9.7. A Mite Examines a Gear Chain Created Using Nanotechnology

Standards for Measuring Length

One of the most important developments of modern science has been the establishment of standards for measuring length. This is something that we largely take for granted today, but it is, in fact, a relatively recent invention.

In ancient Egypt, the basic unit of length was a cubit, which is the distance from one's elbow to the fully extended tip of one's middle finger (see Image 9.8). The problem, of course, with this type of unit is that it is different depending on the length of an individual's arm.

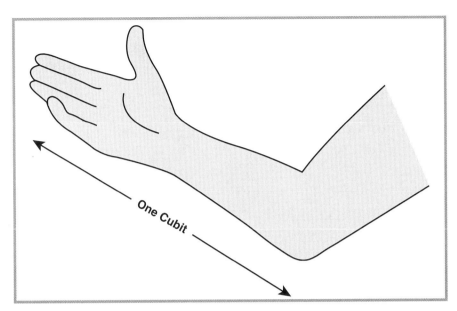

Image 9.8. One Cubit

The need quickly developed for a standard and dependable unit of measurement.

Among the most common and natural units of measurement is the foot. Early cultures logically used the length of a human foot to mark off a space. In England, the length of a foot was derived from King Henry I (1068–1135), whose foot measured 12 inches in length. Henry's foot may have included his shoe, since the average length of a human foot is just over nine inches. Whatever the case, a standard was set that we now follow today in England (at least in part) and in the United States.

Other countries, such as France and Germany, use the metric system, which is based on the unit of a meter, which is 1/10,000,000 of the distance from the Earth's pole to the equator along the Meridian through Paris. Considerable confusion exists when one has to measure across different units (feet versus meters); hence, the tendency in science is to base most measurements on the metric system, which is formulated on a base-10 decimal system that is easier to manipulate than the base-12 system used for a foot.

Scientists draw a distinction between accuracy and precision in measurement. *Accuracy* refers to how close the measured result is to reality. For example, if you weigh 150 pounds and a scale measures your weight as 160 pounds, the scale is not very accurate. There are many factors that

Experiment **79**: Using Standard and Nonstandard Units of Length

In the following activity, you will discover why standard units of measurement are important to scientists.

Materials You Will Need for This Activity

- Your feet
- A standard 12-inch ruler or a tape measure

What You Will Do

Image 9.9. One Foot

1. Have each person in the group measure the length of the room using his or her foot as the standard unit of measurement. Measure the distance accurately, putting one foot in front of the other.
2. Record your results in a column on the blackboard.
3. Circle the highest and lowest measurements.
4. Average all of the measurements together.
5. Repeat the same measurement using a standard 12-inch ruler.
6. Put the results on the blackboard and compare them with the highest and lowest measurements, as well as with the average measurement.

What you will learn: Measures using nonstandard units can be highly variable and unreliable. Such measures make accurate scientific investigation almost impossible. Using standard measuring tools makes accurate measurement possible for scientific inquiry.

Core concept demonstrated: The importance of accurate measurement through the use of standardized units.

Thinking like a scientist: What are the implications for science of sloppy or inaccurate measurements? Think about how careful measurement is a foundation of scientific thought. Imagine that you lived in a time before the use of standard units for measurement. How might you convince people of the need for standard units? What might their objections be to this new idea? Where would the units of measurement come from?

Correlation With National Science Standards: A.1; A.2; G.1

affect accuracy, including the reliability of the instrument, the conditions under which the measurement is done, and human error. *Precision* refers to the repeatability of a measurement. That is, if you measure your height three times and you get the same result each time, the measurement is precise. If you get substantially variable measurements, those measurements are imprecise. Precision can also be influenced by variables such as the reliability of the instrument, the conditions under which the measurement is done, and human error. (See Experiment 79.)

Using a Balance to Measure Mass

The accurate and precise measurement of mass and weight is essential to the work of scientists. For practical purposes, the terms mass and weight are basically interchangeable here on Earth, but they are not synonymous. Weight is a measure of how much force you exert as a result of gravity pulling down on you. Thus, your weight will change as the force of gravity changes. In space, for example, you are "weightless." In contrast, mass is a measure of how much matter there is in an object. No matter where you are, your body contains the same amount of matter, and thus, your mass will not change, even if you are floating in outer space.

Image 9.10. Car Crash

In all the science disciplines, mass and weight are important variables. In physics, for example, the force of a moving object is dependent upon its mass and its acceleration (Force = Mass × Acceleration). Thus, a small car has less force than a large car as a result of its having less mass. As a consequence, the small car will suffer greater damage if there is a collision between the two (see Image 9.10).

In chemistry, mass determines the amount that will be produced by a chemical reaction. Thus, if you are creating salt by combining sodium and chlorine, the amount of salt created will depend on the amount of each element (sodium or chlorine) used to create the compound. (See Experiment 80.)

Using a Stopwatch to Measure Time

The accurate measurement of time is a requirement of many scientific experiments. In the sixteenth century, for example, the Italian scientist Galileo Galilei tried to calculate the rate of acceleration due to gravity. His experiment to determine this involved setting up an inclined plane or ramp and rolling

Experiment 80: Determining Relative and Absolute Mass Using a Pan Balance

In the following activity, you will use a pan balance to measure both the relative mass and absolute mass of objects.

Materials You Will Need for This Activity

- A pan balance
- 5 assorted small objects of various masses
- A set of calibrated gram masses

What You Will Do

1. Using the pan balance, weigh each object and put them in order from lightest to heaviest.
2. Record your results.
3. Now, use the calibrated masses to determine the exact mass of each object in grams.
4. Order the objects again from lightest to heaviest, based on their weight in grams.

Image 9.11. Balance

What you will learn: A pan balance can be used to compare the masses of objects (relative masses) or can be used to find the absolute mass of an object by using a set of calibrated weights.

Core concept demonstrated: The accurate determination of mass

Thinking like a scientist: When would determining the relative masses of two objects be sufficient—that is, simply knowing which of two objects is heavier? When is knowing the absolute mass of an object necessary?

Correlation With National Science Standards: A.1; A.2; B.1

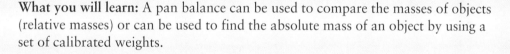

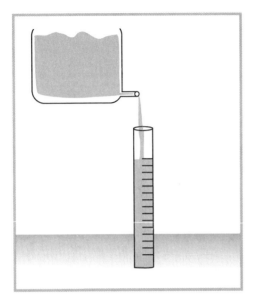

Image 9.12. Water Clock

balls down it. In doing so, he kept the incline of the plane constant and measured the acceleration of the rolling ball using a water clock (see Image 9.12).

Galileo, and other scientists, were limited by the accuracy of the clocks and timepieces available to them. Today, stopwatches that are accurate to one-hundredth of a second can be purchased for a few dollars and make experiments based on the precise measurement of time relatively easy to do. (See Experiment 81.)

Force: Gravity, Velocity, Acceleration, Newton's Laws

Force is one of the fundamental concepts in physics. We intuitively know what a force is from our daily interactions with the world around us. We can't see forces, but we do see their effect on objects all the time. We see a ball fly through the air and then hit the ground. We see the Moon orbit the Earth. We see an airplane fly across the sky. All of these actions are the result of forces. To a physicist, a force is simply a push or a pull that acts upon some object. Gravity is one example of a force, lift is another example, and friction is a third.

The great physicist Isaac Newton, who has been mentioned throughout this book, is probably best known for his three laws concerning the behavior of moving objects. Together, these laws do much to explain the role that forces play in the motion of objects. Proposed by Newton in 1687, the first law of motion states that if the forces on an object are in balance, the object's speed and direction of motion won't change. This is often referred to as the Law of Inertia. Newton's second law concerns forces and acceleration, stating that the net force of a moving object can be found by multiplying the object's mass times its acceleration. This is often referred to as the Law of Dynamics. His third law states that every action has an equal and opposite reaction. This is often referred to as the Action-Reaction Law.

While later studies of force and motion, including Albert Einstein's famous theories of relativity, have shown Newton's laws of motion to be inaccurate at the molecular level and at speeds approaching the speed of light, when it comes to describing the motion of everyday objects in our experience, Newton's laws continue to be suitable, over 400 years after he developed them.

Experiment 81: Using a Stopwatch to Measure Time

In the following activity, you will practice taking accurate measurements of time using a stopwatch.

Materials You Will Need for This Activity

- A stopwatch
- A pad of paper
- A pencil or pen

What You Will Do

1. Have a classmate sign his or her name on the pad as quickly as he or she can, 10 times.
2. Using a stopwatch, measure how much time this took.
3. Have your classmate repeat this procedure a second time.
4. Compare the measured time of the first and second trials.
5. Now change places: you sign your name and your classmate measures you. Repeat a second time.
6. Compare the results from the four trials.

What you will learn: Measurement of time can be highly variable. Accuracy in measuring time can be heavily influenced by human error in starting and stopping the stopwatch. Precision in measuring time often varies because repeated tasks frequently take different amounts of time to complete.

Core concept demonstrated: The accurate measurement of time

Thinking like a scientist: Could Galileo have conducted his experiments without first inventing the water clock? Why or why not? Why do the timers used in the Olympic Games frequently measure to an accuracy of one-thousandth of a second?

Correlation With National Science Standards: A.1; A.2; G.1

Inertia

You have experienced **inertia** when you brake quickly in a car, but your body continues to move forward. Perhaps you have seen a magician or entertainer on television pull a tablecloth out from under a table full of plates and silverware without disturbing anything. This is possible because of inertia. (See Experiment 82.)

Experiment 82: **Flipping a Card Off Your Finger While Leaving a Quarter in Place**

In the following activity, you will demonstrate the concept of inertia without the risk of breaking any cups and dishes.

Materials You Will Need for This Activity

- A 3″ × 5″ card or a playing card
- A quarter

What You Will Do

1. Place the quarter on top of the card and then balance both the card and the quarter on top of your hand.
2. With your other hand, hold your index finger against your thumb and flick it hard and with an even stroke against the edge of the card.
3. With a little bit of practice, you should able to flick the card off your hand while the quarter stays in place.

What you will learn: The inertia of the quarter will keep it from moving off your hand. The force from your snapping finger is only transferred to the card.

Core concept demonstrated: Objects at rest are subject to the force of inertia.

Thinking like a scientist: What would happen if there was a sticky substance between the card and the quarter? Why is the concept of inertia important in terms of designing safety features on airplanes and in automobiles?

Correlation With National Science Standards: B.2; B.5; G.4

Inertia is the tendency of an object to continue to move in the direction it is already going, or in the case of an object at rest, the tendency to remain at rest.

Centrifugal Force

Have you ever ridden a merry-go-round or a "scrambler ride" at an amusement park? If you were moving fast enough, you almost certainly felt yourself pushed away from the center of the ride (see Image 9.13). The same thing happens when you make a fast turn in a car. This effect is caused by centrifugal force. Centrifugal force is the tendency of a physical body turning around a central point to move away from that point. (See Experiment 83.)

Air Flow: Creating Lift

Have you ever wondered why an airplane can fly? It flies because of an aerodynamic principle that was discovered in the seventeenth century by the

Image 9.13. Loop the Loop, Coney Island, NY

SOURCE: Courtesy of the Library of Congress Prints and Photographs Division, Washington, DC.

Experiment **83:** Swinging a Bucket of Water in a Circle Without Getting Wet

You can demonstrate centrifugal force by conducting the following experiment.

Materials You Will Need for This Activity

- A plastic bucket with a handle or a large plastic cup
- Water

What You Will Do

1. Fill the plastic bucket or cup two-thirds full of water.
2. Pick up the bucket or cup and smoothly swing it up around your head, as shown in Image 9.14.
3. If you make a smooth continuous movement, the water should remain in the bucket.

SOURCE: Illustration by Poyet from Good (1893).

Image 9.14. Spinning Cup Experiment

What you will learn: The centrifugal force of the water being pushed against the bottom of the bucket will keep it from falling out when it is swung.

Core concept demonstrated: Physical objects can be influenced in their movement by centrifugal force.

Thinking like a scientist: What would happen if you slowed down the rotation of the bucket or cup? Is there a point where the water will spill out on you? Why is centrifugal force an important element in an amusement park ride like a roller coaster? Can you think of other amusement park rides in which centrifugal force is important?

Correlation With National Science Standards: A.2; B.2; B.5

Swiss mathematician Jakob Bernoulli (1654–1705). Bernoulli was famous for his work in probability and various aspects of physics. Bernoulli's principle about air pressure states that air moving at a high speed has lower pressure than air that is still or moving more slowly. An airplane wing is flat on the bottom and curved on its top and leading edge, so air moving across the top of the wing is forced to move more quickly, thus lowering its air pressure relative to the air moving below the wing (see Image 9.15). This creates lift, which makes it possible for the plane to fly. (See Experiment 84.)

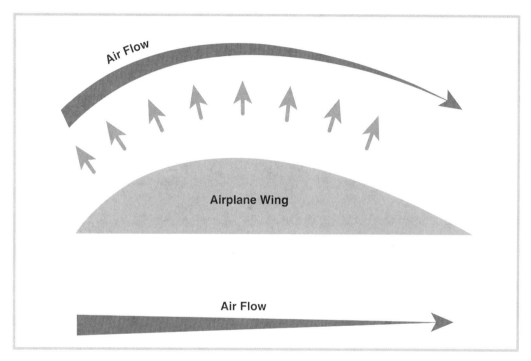

Image 9.15. Airflow Over a Wing

Forms of Energy

Energy can take many different forms, including light, heat, sound, motion, and pressure. All of these forms of energy, however, can be placed into two categories, **potential energy** and **kinetic energy**. Potential energy is the energy that is stored in an object, whereas kinetic energy is energy in motion. Potential energy can be in the form of chemical energy, such as gas that can be burned; nuclear energy, such as hydrogen atoms that can be

Experiment 84: Demonstrating "Lift" With a Ping-Pong Ball and Straw

In the following activity, you will demonstrate Bernoulli's Principle.

Materials You Will Need for This Activity

- A flexible straw
- A ping-pong ball
- Scissors

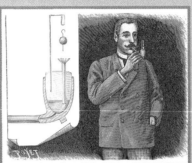

Image 9.16. Version of the Airflow Experiment

SOURCE: Illustration by Poyet from Good (1893).

What You Will Do

1. Take the short end of the straw before the bend and cut four slits and fold them back.
2. Place the long end of the straw in your mouth, and balance the ping-pong ball on the other end of the straw.
3. Gently blow on the straw.
4. The ping-pong ball will rise on the air current and stay there, captured by the air current flowing around the ball as a result of the two different air pressures.

What you will learn: The ball cannot escape the air stream because Bernoulli's principle is at work. The still air around the fast flowing air that surrounds the ball exerts greater pressure, holding it in place. These same forces make it possible for an airplane wing to lift.

Core concept demonstrated: Differences in air pressure can affect the aerodynamic properties of surfaces.

Thinking like a scientist: What would the world be like if the properties of "lift" did not exist (Think of planes, boats, and birds)? What happens to lift as you go higher in the atmosphere or even into space? Do spaceships need wings?

Correlation With National Science Standards: A.1; B.2; B.5

fused; stored mechanical energy, like a spring that is wound or a rubber band that is stretched; or gravitational energy, like a rock poised to fall off a cliff. Kinetic energy can also be found in many forms, such as electrical energy, as current runs through a wire; thermal energy, such as water boiling on the stove; sound energy, such as the music you hear when you turn on the radio; or electromagnetic energy, such as the light you see or the microwaves that can cook your food.

Trading Potential and Kinetic Energy With Superballs

Energy can be transferred between potential and kinetic states, as is shown by tossing a ball in the air and letting it bounce off the ground. This effect can be magnified through the use of highly elastic rubber balls called superballs. (See Experiment 85.)

Modeling Nuclear Decay and Half-Life

Almost all of us have seen watch faces that glow in the dark. On many watches, this is made possible because the numbers are painted with a radioactive paint. As one atomic element decays into another on the paint, particles are released into the air that cause the watch face to glow. This is a visible demonstration of nuclear decay. The process of nuclear decay is highly regular and can be used to measure time. In fact, the first atomic clock was built in 1955 by the National Physical Laboratory in England and the United States Naval Observatory (see Image 9.17). This clock used radioactive cesium as standard for measure. Cesium decay makes it possible to break a second into 30 billion parts. As a result, tremendous accuracy is possible. (See Experiment 86.)

SOURCE: Courtesy of the United States Naval Observatory.

Image 9.17. The U.S. Navy Master Atomic Clock Sits Behind a Historic Navy Clock

Static Electricity

Have you ever dragged your feet across a carpet and touched a doorknob or counter and received a shock? What you experienced was static electricity. Static electricity is caused when excess electrons are gathered together in large enough numbers that they discharge when in contact with an object that has significantly fewer electrons. The uneven charges tend to even out, or equalize, whenever possible. (See Experiment 87.)

Experiment 85:   Bouncing Superballs

In the following activity, you will see how potential energy is transformed into kinetic energy.

Materials You Will Need for This Activity

- One large and one small superball
- A meter stick

What You Will Do

1. Place the meter stick against a flat wall and measure a height of one meter.
2. Estimate how high each ball will bounce when dropped from the one meter mark.
3. Next, drop each ball from the one meter mark and measure the height of each bounce. What do you find?
4. Next, drop both balls together with the small ball immediately on top of the larger ball. What happens?

What you will learn: When a single ball is dropped, it will not bounce back as high as the point from which it was released. When stacked balls are dropped, a portion of the kinetic energy of the bottom ball is transferred to the top ball, causing it to bounce higher than the point from which it was released.

Core concept demonstrated: The transfer of potential to kinetic energy

Thinking like a scientist: Why is the transfer of potential energy to kinetic energy an important principle in physics? How is it related to old-fashioned pinball machines and bumper cars in amusement parks? How does it explain why dominos stacked in a row fall? What might be some of the consequences of this principle for different aspects of life? Think, for example, about how automobiles in car crashes are affected by the transfer of potential to kinetic energy.

Correlation With National Science Standards: A.1; A.2; B.2; B.5

Experiment 86: Modeling Nuclear Half-Life

In the following activity, you will model nuclear half-life with a simple physical model. A nuclear half-life is the time it takes for one-half the amount of a radioactive element to decay or transform itself into another, more stable element.

Materials You Will Need for This Activity

- A bag of M&M candies (60 M&Ms)

What You Will Do

1. Place the 60 M&Ms in a pile in front of you. Each M&M represents one atom of your nuclear material.
2. Assume that the half-life of your modeled radioactive material is one minute. This means that in one minute, half your atoms will decay and be transformed into a more stable element.
3. In another minute, half of what is left will then decay. This pattern will continue, each minute leading to less and less of the radioactive material.
4. Create a table showing how many M&Ms are left after one minute, two minutes, three minutes, five minutes, and ten minutes.

What you will learn: Most of a radioactive substance decays in its first few half-lives, but the decay will continue indefinitely. Note that in this model, the M&Ms are being removed to represent the decay, but in reality matter is not being destroyed, it is just being transformed from the radioactive state to a more stable element or isotope.

Core concept demonstrated: Nuclear decay

Thinking like a scientist: How long does it take for a decaying substance to finally totally disappear? Why is this the case?

Correlation With National Science Standards: B.1; B.4; G.1

Experiment **87**: Creating an Electroscope to Detect Static Electricity

In the following activity, you will make a very simple but effective device to detect electrical charges in the atmosphere. It is called an electroscope.

Materials You Will Need for This Activity

- A piece of aluminum foil
- A 3″ × 5″ index card
- A glass jar
- A paper clip
- A piece of silk or wool
- Classroom objects made of different materials (e.g., wood, glass, plastic, rubber, metal)

What You Will Do

1. Cut two strips of aluminum foil about l cm wide by 4 cm long.
2. Open up a paper clip so that there is a hook on one end and it is straightened out on the other end.
3. Push the straight side of the paper clip through the middle of an index card, and tape it so that the hook is hanging down from the card.
4. Place the two foil strips on top of each other and then push the hook end of the paper clip through them so that the foil leaves hang down from the hook.
5. Lay the card over the jar so that the foil strips hang inside.
6. Rub the various classroom objects with the piece of silk or wool to try to build up a static electric charge.
7. Bring each charged object close to the hook and observe what happens.

What you will learn: Rubbing the objects with the silk or wool deposits excess electrons onto them. When the charged object is brought near the paper clip, some of the electrons in the foil leaves are pulled up into the paper clip, giving the two foil leaves a positive charge and causing them to repel each other. The amount that the foil leaves spread apart is proportional to the charge of the object.

Core concept demonstrated: Static electricity builds a charge that can be detected.

Thinking like a scientist: What would happen if you used other materials besides wool or silk to rub the glass? Is there a connection between the small amount of static electricity being generated here and the reason for lightning strikes?

Correlation With National Science Standards: A.1; A.2; B.4; B.5; B.6; G.4

Simple Machines

Simple machines are basic tools that make work easier to do. They are called "simple" because they generally have few or no moving parts. Simple machines still require energy to do work. In fact, doing work using a simple machine does not require less energy than doing the same work without the simple machine. What the simple machine generally does is to spread out the energy required over a greater time or distance. This means that a smaller force can be exerted at any given point in time. The most common types of simple machines are the lever, the inclined plane, the screw, the pulley, the wedge, and the wheel and axle.

Many more complex mechanic devices are also based on one or a combination of simple machines. A bicycle, for example, uses levers, pulleys, screws, and wheels and axles. Many other common tools are also simple machines. A crow bar is a simple lever. A winch is a type of pulley. A graded highway is a type of ramp. In the following activities, you will explore the working of several simple machines.

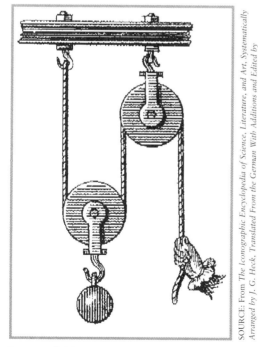

Image 9.18. Drawing of a Two-Pulley System

SOURCE: From *The Iconographic Encyclopedia of Science, Literature, and Art, Systematically Arranged by J. G. Heck, Translated From the German With Additions and Edited by Spenser F. Baird* (New York: Rudolph Garrigue, 1851).

Pulleys

According to the Roman historian Plutarch, the ancient Greek scientist and inventor Archimedes (287–212 B.C.) moved an entire warship full of men by himself using a pulley system. A pulley is a grooved wheel with a rope or cable wrapped in the groove. Pulleys reduce the amount of force needed to move heavy objects. They do this by increasing the distance over which the force necessary to move an object is applied. In the end, the same amount of work is done, but in a much easier way. Multiple wheels on a pulley multiply this effect (see Image 9.18). (See Experiment 88.)

Ramps

Among the most important constructions in the ancient world were the Egyptian pyramids. Thousands of years after they were built, we continue to marvel at the means by which they were constructed. Ramps were essential in the building of the pyramids. Like pulleys, ramps make it possible to do things that require great amounts of force by distributing work over a greater distance and time. (See Experiment 89.)

Experiment 88: Experimenting With Pulleys

In the following activity, you will experiment with pulleys to learn how they make the work of an object easier.

Materials You Will Need for This Activity

- A piece of rope
- A single pulley
- A double pulley
- A spring scale
- A heavy object to lift

What You Will Do

1. First, attach one end of the rope to your heavy object and the other end to a spring scale. Lift the object with the weight hanging down from the spring scale. Record how much force is shown on the scale.
2. Next, thread the rope over the wheel of the single pulley. Lift and record the force that is shown on the spring scale.
3. Set up a double pulley system as shown in Image 9.18.
4. Using the double pulley system, lift the object and record the force that is shown on the spring scale.
5. Compare the results for each of your measurements.

What you will learn: Pulleys reduce the force required to lift an object by increasing the length over which that reduced force must be applied.

Core concept demonstrated: The mechanics of a pulley and pulley systems

Thinking like a scientist: When you see pictures or movies of people on sailboats, they are often pulling on ropes to raise and lower the sails. Why do they use pulleys with these ropes? Pulleys were common tools in industrial and commercial settings in the nineteenth century. Why do you think they are less common today?

Correlation With National Science Standards: A.1; B.5; B.6; F.4; F.10

Experiment **89:** Experimenting With Ramps

In the following activity, you will pull a heavy object up ramps with different inclines. You will determine how much force it takes to drag the same object up each slope.

Materials You Will Need for This Activity

- A flat smooth wooden board
- A piece of rope
- A heavy object that can be easily attached to the rope
- A spring scale

What You Will Do

1. First, attach one end of the rope to your heavy object and the other end to a spring scale.
2. Set the ramp at an incline with one end raised two inches above the horizontal surface.
3. Pull the object up the incline using the spring scale and record how much force was required. Repeat this process with the ramp set at four inches, then six inches, and finally eight inches.

What you will learn: The steeper the ramp, the more force it takes to move the same object.

Core concept demonstrated: Ramps as simple machines

Thinking like a scientist: How are ramps used to create roads and streets in hilly areas? Why is the grade of a road often an important issue? If you were in a wheelchair, why would the grade of a ramp be an import issue for you?

Correlation With National Science Standards: A.1; B.5; B.6; E.4; F.10

Levers

Archimedes is most famous for having said that given a long enough lever and a place to stand, he could move the Earth (see Image 9.19). A lever is a rigid bar or plank with a pivot point or fulcrum that can be used to move another object. It works in much the same way as a pulley or ramp by distributing over a greater distance the force needed to move an object. (See Experiment 90.)

SOURCE: Engraving from *Mechanics Magazine*, London, 1824.

Image 9.19. Archimedes With a Lever

Sound

Hearing is one of the senses that we use to interpret and make meaning of our surroundings. It is arguably the second most important sense to modern humans, after sight. The basis for understanding sound is the physics of **waves**. Sound is actually a wave that is created by a vibrating object and then passed through a medium from one location to another. A wave can be thought of as a disturbance that carries energy through a medium. The medium that waves move through is usually air, but it can also be a liquid such as water or a solid such as the wood of your front door. In physics lessons on sound, waves are often demonstrated by using a tuning fork. As the two tines of the tuning fork vibrate back and forth, they send waves out through the surrounding air molecules, allowing us to hear the ringing sound of the fork. The sounds we hear can be altered as a result of **resonance**

Experiment 90: Experimenting With Levers

In the following activity, you will learn how levers provide a mechanical advantage.

Materials You Will Need for This Activity

- Wooden sticks with lengths of 6 inches, 1 foot, and 2 feet
- A small triangular wooden block
- A heavy object to move

What You Will Do

1. Place the triangular block on a flat surface.
2. Place the heavy object next to the block.
3. Position the six-inch wooden stick as a lever under the heavy object using the piece of triangular wood as a fulcrum.
4. Try to lift the object off the table using the lever.
5. Next, repeat the procedure using the one-foot stick as your lever.
6. Repeat again using the two-foot stick.
7. Describe the effort required to move the object each time.

What you will learn: Levers of different lengths reduce the force necessary to move an object by increasing the distance over which that lessened force is applied. The longer the lever, the easier it is to move the weight.

Core concept demonstrated: The lever as a simple machine

Thinking like a scientist: How does your arm work as a lever? Is it easier for someone with a longer arm to lift up a heavy object than someone whose arm is shorter? Why?

Correlation With National Science Standards: A.1; B.5; B.6; E.4; F.10

(an echo) or the dynamics of different harmonic forms such as a vibrating string of a violin.

Sound Conduction

Sounds are waves within the **frequency** range of human hearing. Sound waves must be conducted through a medium. Media can include the air; water; or a solid such as metal, wood, or even cloth. Despite the fact that we are used to hearing sound conducted through a gas (air), sound waves actually travel more efficiently through liquids and solids because the molecules the waves pass through are more compact. (See Experiment 91.)

Harmonics

In 1761, the American scientist and inventor Benjamin Franklin (1706–1790) created a new musical instrument called the glass armonica (see Image 9.20). Franklin's armonica consisted of a series of overlapping bowl-shaped glasses.

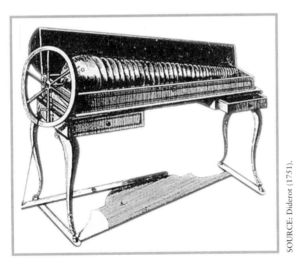

When the edges of the different bowls were rubbed, they made different sounds. It was actually possible to play very complex pieces of music using this instrument. In fact, the great Austrian composer Wolfgang Amadeus Mozart (1756–1791) wrote a quintet for the glass armonica, flute, oboe, viola, and violoncello. (See Experiment 92.)

Resonance

Sound waves can actually cause a stationary object to vibrate and move. This occurs because of resonance. Resonance can be defined as a prolonging of sound by reflection or the vibration of other objects. (See Experiment 93.)

SOURCE: Diderot (1751).

Image 9.20. Drawing of a Glass Armonica

Light and Color

There is longstanding debate in physics about whether light is a wave or a stream of particles. Whatever the case, light exhibits many behaviors characteristic of a wave, such as the ways light reflects and refracts, how it undergoes interference, and how it exhibits the Doppler effect.

Optics is the study of the physics of light and color. Optics determines what we see or do not see in the world. Light refracting through the atmosphere turns the sky blue. Lenses bring images into sharper focus both near and far. Colors blend together to create different forms for us to see and experience.

Experiment 91: Demonstrating the Conduction of Sound

In the following activity, you will hear how sound is conducted through different media.

Materials You Will Need for This Activity

- A large spoon
- A piece of heavy string about 20 inches in length

What You Will Do

1. Wrap the middle portion of the string around the spoon, leaving both ends of the string to hang down.
2. Hold the two ends of the string between your thumb and index fingers of each of your hands, with the spoon hanging down in the middle.
3. With the strings taut, place an end in each of your ears. Gently strike the spoon against the edge of a table or other hard surface.
4. Describe what you hear.

What will you learn: The sound of the spoon striking the table will be conducted through the spoon and into the two pieces of string. You will hear the sound through the strings.

Core concept demonstrated: Sound waves propagate through a solid medium as well as through air.

Thinking like a scientist: What happens if you are in a vacuum and try to hear something? Can you hear an explosion in outer space? If you were trapped outside a spaceship and needed to get in, how could you transmit a sound to someone on the inside? Sound travels through air at a speed of approximately 700 MPH. Do you think it travels at the same speed through other media? How could you experiment to find out?

Correlation With National Science Standards: A.1; B.4; B.6; F.10

Experiment 92: Experimenting With Harmonic Sound

In the following activity, you can explore harmonic sound of the type created by a glass armonica.

Materials You Will Need for This Activity

- A wine glass or goblet (one with a thin rim will work best)
- Several plastic cups (hard plastic, not disposable)
- A spoon
- A pitcher full of water

What You Will Do

1. The teacher will pour a small amount of water into the wine glass, wet her index finger, and run it along the edge of the glass.
2. Listen carefully and you should be able to hear a ringing sound coming from the glass.
3. Add more water and listen to how the ringing sound changes as the height of the column of air in the glass changes.
4. Pour different amounts of water into each of the plastic cups.
5. Tap the side of each cup with the spoon and listen carefully to the resulting sound.
6. You can create an instrument like Ben Franklin did by arranging the cups with water at different heights.

* Safety Note—The teacher should do the wine glass portion of the activity as a demonstration because thin-rimmed wine glasses can easily break.

What you will learn: The sound created by your finger running across the surface of the glass or the spoon hitting the glass will change according to the length of the column of air it travels through.

Core concept demonstrated: Sound is altered when its waves pass through different-sized columns of air.

Thinking like a scientist: Have you ever thought about why the pipes on a pipe organ are of different sizes? How does the size of the pipes affect the air that is forced through them? How does this create a complex musical instrument?

Correlation With National Science Standards: A.1; B.1; B.6; E.4; G.4

Experiment **93:** Experimenting With Resonance

You can see how resonance works by completing the following activity.

Materials You Will Need for This Activity

- Two wine glasses or goblets, each $\frac{1}{4}$ full of water
- A thin piece of wire that can stretch across the mouth of one of the glasses and be bent down on either side

What You Will Do

1. Place the piece of bent wire across the top of one of the glasses.
2. Place the two glasses next to each other.
3. Rub your finger lightly across the rim of the glass without the wire, as was done in Experiment 92 to produce the sound.
4. Experiment with doing this until you generate a ringing sound from the wire laying across the other glass.

* Safety Note—As with the wine goblet in Experiment 92, it is recommended that the teacher does this experiment because it involves a fragile glass goblet. Alternatively, the same concept can be demonstrated by cutting out both ends of an oatmeal canister and covering them with wax paper. Rice grains can be put on the top and the "drum" tapped on the bottom. The rice grains will "dance" on the top, showing that the sound waves can cause other objects to vibrate.

What you will learn: You should be able to observe the wire begin to vibrate or "dance." This is because you have achieved the resonant frequency of the water in the cup. A resonant frequency is a natural frequency of vibration that is determined by the vibrating object. It is easy to get an object to vibrate at its resonant frequency.

Core concept demonstrated: Sound waves can cause other objects to vibrate or resonate.

Thinking like a scientist: Think about the following phrase: The speaker's ideas resonated with me. What does this mean? How is it related to the experiment you just conducted? Why would the concept of resonance potentially be important to someone designing a building or bridge? Think about a tall skyscraper in the wind. Have you ever used a tuning fork in music? Why would it have something in common with a flagpole being blown in a strong wind?

Correlation With National Science Standards: A.2; B.5; B.6

Persistence of Vision

All of us have watched movies, but have you thought much about why they work? Motion pictures are possible because of the phenomenon of the persistence of vision. When an image is projected onto the retina of your eye, it remains there unchanged for approximately one-tenth of a second. Motion pictures take advantage of this phenomenon by flashing slightly changing or "moving" images in front of your eyes. As these flash by you, the images merge into a continuous set of "motion pictures."

The first modern motion picture device was a simple toy called a *thaumatrope* (meaning "wonder-turner" in Greek.). It was discovered by a nineteenth-century scientist by the name of John Ayrton Paris (1785–1856). Paris was interested in studying the physiology of the eye and was the first person to do systematic research on the retina. He invented the thaumatrope in order to demonstrate that the retina took "snapshots" of images and transferred them to the brain. (See Experiment 94.)

Color Blending

Colors are created by blending or combining the three primary colors (red, yellow, and blue) with each other or with the three secondary colors (violet, orange, and green). These six colors make up what is known as the color wheel. The Scottish physicist James Clerk Maxwell (1831–1879) created a very simple device for blending colors using a top. (See Experiment 95.)

Bending Light

Nearly all of us have seen a rainbow in the sky, or in a soap bubble caught in the sunlight. Have you ever wondered where these colors come from? The British physicist Sir Isaac Newton (1642–1727) was the first person to describe the optical properties of a soap bubble and prism. The light we see from the sun, as well as from light bulbs and other artificial sources, appears to be white. In fact, it is the combination of all of the colors of the electromagnetic spectrum. Newton observed that light going through a transparent soap bubble, or material such as glass, could be broken up into component colors or wavelengths. This is a result of the physical properties of the glass in a prism or other medium that spreads or bends the light waves in slightly different directions. This process is called *refraction*. Refraction allows us to see the various wavelengths of light as distinct colors. (See Experiment 96.)

🐜 Electricity and Magnetism

Magnetism is one of the most extraordinary forces found in physics. The interaction of magnetism and electricity makes possible the creation of electric motors and other types of electrical devices. The magnetic field generated by our planet enables us to navigate across the planet's surface using

(Text continues on page 334)

Experiment 94: Making a Thaumatrope

To watch a video clip related to this concept, go to the Student Resource CD bound into the back of your textbook.

You can easily make your own thaumatrope to explore the persistence of vision.

Materials You Will Need for This Activity

- 2 short pieces of string 6 inches each in length
- Scissors
- A felt tip pen
- A 3-inch square of cardboard

What You Will Do

1. Cut a circle out of the piece of cardboard.
2. Punch two holes on opposite edges of the piece of cardboard.
3. Tie a piece of string to each hole.
4. Draw a picture of a bird one side of your cardboard circle and a picture of a bird cage on the other side.
5. The two images should be upside down relative to each other and each face north and south, with the string being on the east and west points of the circle.
6. Place the strings between the thumb and index finger of both of your hands.
7. Rapidly spin the paper disk, and you will see the two images merge together.

SOURCE: Photography courtesy of the Library of Congress.

Image 9.21. Animal Locomotion by Eadweard Muybridge

In 1872, the railroad baron Leland Stanford hired the photographer Eadweard Muybridge to determine whether racing horses had all four of their legs off the ground at the same time when they ran. Muybridge set up a trip system on a race course with multiple cameras, each set to expose its shutter as the horse and its rider went by. Muybridge determined that around the middle of each stride the horse did, indeed, have all four feet off the ground.

What you will learn: The retina in your eye holds onto the images it records for approximately one-tenth of a second. Because your brain cannot process information received from the retina that goes by it too fast, it perceives that what are actually separate images are merged together.

Core concept demonstrated: Phenomenon of the persistence of vision

Thinking like a scientist: How is much of what we see in the world an illusion? Do scientific devices make it possible for us to see things in new ways? Think, for example, about stop-motion photography. What does it reveal to us about the world that we would not otherwise know or perceive?

Correlation With National Science Standards: A.1; B.1; B.2; E.4; G.4

Experiment 95:   **Color Blending**

In the following activity, you will make a color-blending top similar to Maxwell's.

Materials You Will Need for This Activity

- 4 or 5 pieces of colored construction paper or thin cardboard
- A 2- or 3-inch stub of sharpened pencil
- Scissors

What You Will Do

1. Cut out two three-inch circles of cardboard, each of a different color.
2. Punch a hole through the center of each circle so that the pencil can fit snugly through the hole, thus making your top.
3. Next, cut a slit from the edge to center of each colored disk.
4. Slide the two colored circles together and fit the pencil through both holes.
5. You should be able to rotate the two colored disks so that they will have different amounts of color showing on the surface of your top.
6. Experiment with different proportions of each as you spin the top. Different shades of color should appear.

What you will learn: By adjusting the relative proportions of colors to one another, colors can be changed and modified.

Core concept demonstrated: New colors are created by the combination of primary and secondary colors.

Thinking like a scientist: Why is color-blending important to a painter? How many colors is it possible to create from the three primary colors, the three secondary colors, or all six together? What happens if you vary the amount of colored material between each color? How many different shades of colors are potentially available?

Correlation With National Science Standards: A.2; B.2; B.3; E.4; G.4

Experiment **96:** Bending Light

In the following activity, you will use a soap bubble to observe how light bends.

Materials You Will Need for This Activity

- Soap bubble solution or liquid detergent
- A soap bubble pipe or blower
- A tall cup or glass
- A small bowl
- A lamp, candle, or powerful flashlight
- A piece of solid white paper or cardboard

Image 9.22. Bending Light Through a Soap Bubble

SOURCE: Illustration by Poyet from Good (1893).

What You Will Do

1. Blow a large bubble and set it on the rim of a glass.
2. Place a light source behind the bubble and project its image onto a sheet of white paper. You may need to darken the room to see more clearly.
3. Sketch and record what you observe on the sheet of white paper.

What you will learn: A spectrum of colors will appear on the piece of paper that is projected through the bubble from the light source. Note that the colors seen through the soap bubble are not the same as the colors viewed through a prism. Colors seen on soap bubbles are due to *interference*, whereas colors seen when light passes through a prism are due to *dispersion*.

Core concept demonstrated: White light consists of many different colors.

Thinking like a scientist: Why do rainbows appear in the sky? What are the colors found in the spectrum? What order do they appear in a spectrum? How does the order they appear in affect the properties of light and color? Think about light bulbs (fluorescent, tungsten, black light, etc.). Why do they project different types of light?

Correlation With National Science Standards: A.1; B.1; B.3; G.2

compasses. Magnets are essential in state-of-the-art medical imaging technology that diagnoses illnesses without invasive surgery.

Magnetic Fields

The English scientist Michael Faraday (1791–1867) was the first person to discover that magnets produce magnetic fields that have distinct patterns and shapes. These fields are produced by the movement of electrical charges that can shape and influence nearby objects. While magnets come in many different shapes and forms, no matter how different they are, they each have a positive and a negative pole and produce similar magnetic fields that run between their poles.

Magnetic fields are invisible under normal circumstances. Faraday, however, found that their shape or pattern could be observed by manipulating iron filings with a magnet placed under a piece of glass or paper. (See Experiment 97.)

Electrical Circuits

The idea that electricity represents the flow of electrons was first discovered by Hans Christian Oersted (1777–1851). While demonstrating the heat-generating properties of a voltaic pile (an early type of electrical battery; see Chapter 8, Image 8.20), he noticed that the needle on a compass placed near it would align itself with the electrical charge from a wire connected to the battery. As a result, he concluded that electrical currents created magnetic fields.

Soon other scientists, such as Andre Ampère and Michael Faraday, began to experiment with electricity and magnetism, leading to a number of important discoveries, including the invention of electromagnets and the electric motor. An electrical circuit is a closed path through which electrical current travels. Circuits are important because they provide us a means by which to control the flow of electricity. (See Experiment 98.)

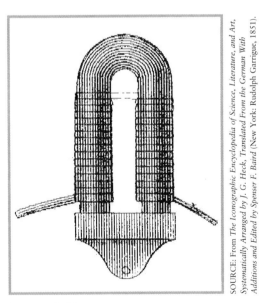

SOURCE: From *The Iconographic Encyclopedia of Science, Literature, and Art, Systematically Arranged by J. G. Heck, Translated From the German With Additions and Edited by Spenser F. Baird* (New York: Rudolph Garrigue, 1851).

Image 9.23. An Early Electromagnet

Electromagnets

Within a week of hearing about Oersted's discovery, Andre Ampère (1775–1836) demonstrated that electrical currents were like magnetic fields, in that they could oppose or attract each other according to the orientation of their poles (see Image 9.23). Soon other scientists, such as Michael Faraday, began to experiment with electricity, leading to a number of important discoveries, including the invention of the electric motor. (See Experiment 99.)

Experiment 97: Observing Magnetic Fields

In the following activity, you will study the shape of a magnetic field.

Materials You Will Need for This Activity

- A piece of glass or clear plastic
- Iron filings
- A bar magnet

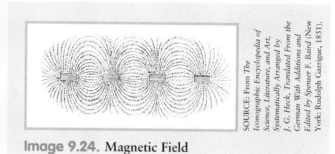

Image 9.24. Magnetic Field

SOURCE: From *The Iconographic Encyclopedia of Science, Literature, and Art, Systematically Arranged by* J. G. Heck, Translated From the German With Additions and Edited by Spenser F. Baird (New York: Rudolph Garrigue, 1851).

What You Will Do

1. Sprinkle a small amount of iron filings on top of the glass or plastic.
2. Slowly pass the bar magnet back and forth under the glass.
3. Observe the behavior of the iron filings.

* Safety Note—Iron filings can be quite dangerous if they get on your fingers and you then rub your eyes. Thus, safety goggles should always be worn when using iron filings, or this activity should be done as a teacher demonstration on the overhead projector.

What you will learn: All magnets exert a magnetic field that has predictable lines of magnetic force. These field lines are invisible but can be made visible through the use of iron filings.

Core concept demonstrated: All magnets have a magnetic field.

Thinking like a scientist: What happens when two magnets are brought close together? Does this have something to do with their magnetic fields? What do you think the field lines, as seen with iron filings, would look like as the two magnets are moved closer together or farther apart?

Correlation With National Science Standards: A.1; B.1; B.3; G.1; G.4

Experiment 98: Making a Simple Circuit

In the following activity, you will explore the construction of simple circuits.

Materials You Will Need for This Activity

- Insulated wire with stripped ends (2 per student)
- D-cell batteries, 1 per student
- Flashlight bulbs, 1 per student (have a few extra bulbs on hand in case one is dropped)

What You Will Do

1. With one piece of wire, a D battery, and a flashlight bulb, try to light the bulb.
2. Record *all* of the configurations that you try, even those that don't work. It might take a while to find ways that work. The idea is to explore possible configurations until you find some that do work.
3. Now, take a second piece of wire and try to light the bulb using both wires.
4. Again, record all configurations you try.

What you will learn: Electrical circuits only allow for the flow of electricity when the circuit is closed, such that the electricity can flow from one pole of the battery to the other pole.

Core concept demonstrated: Electrical flow through a circuit

Thinking like a scientist: How is the electrical circuit that powers an appliance in your house similar to the circuit you constructed to light the bulb? How is it different? What happens when you turn a light switch on or off?

Correlation With National Science Standards: A.1; B.2; B.3; B.6; E.4; G.2; G.4

 **Experiment 99: Making an Electromagnet**

To watch a video clip related to this concept, go to the Student Resource CD bound into the back of your textbook.

In the following activity, you will construct an electromagnet, a device which, like the electric motor, takes advantage of the relationship between electricity and magnetism.

Materials You Will Need for This Activity

- 1.5-volt battery
- 1 meter of insulated wire with the ends stripped
- A nail
- About a dozen small paper clips

What You Will Do

1. Wrap the wire tightly around the nail. Start about 15 cm from one end of the nail. Make small concentric loops and continue until you have reached about 15 cm from the other end of the nail.
2. Connect one end of the wire to the positive terminal of the battery.
3. Connect the other end of the wire to the negative terminal of the battery.
4. The nail will now act as an electromagnet as long as there is current running through the wire.
5. To test that the nail is now magnetized, you can try to pick up individual paper clips with the nail.
6. Unwrap about half the wire from around the nail and pick up paper clips with your electromagnet again. What do you observe?

What you will learn: The loops of wire circling the nail pass electrical current around the nail, thus producing a magnetic field. The more loops of wire, the more current circling the nail, and the stronger the magnetic field that is produced.

Core concept demonstrated: An electric field can be used to harness the power of a magnet.

Thinking like a scientist: How is an electromagnet different from a permanent magnet? What advantages might an electromagnet have over a permanent magnet? For what can an electromagnet be used?

Correlation With National Science Standards: A.1; B.3; B.4; B.6; E.4; G.2; G.4

Experiment 100: Designing Your Own Experiment

By this point, you have conducted a number of experiments that demonstrated core science principles. Now it is your turn to design and carry out your own experiment. You can base your experiment on one of the investigations you have already done. Most science is done this way; the scientist considers his or her past experiments and this leads to related questions that require further experimentation. Sometimes, however, a scientist will begin to experiment in a whole new area of research. You can choose either approach. Use the format below to consider what you will need, what you will do, and what you might learn from your experiment. Good luck!

Materials You Will Need for This Experiment

-
-
-
-

What You Will Do

1.
2.
3.
4.
5.

What you will learn: What did you learn by completing your experiment? Did you learn or come to better understand a science concept? Did you learn or become more comfortable with a science process or technique? Did you learn something else about the design of science experiments?

Core concept demonstrated: What core concept do you believe was demonstrated by your experiment?

Thinking like a scientist: How successful was your experiment? How do you know? Why was this the case? What new questions are raised by completing your experiment?

Correlation With National Science Standards: Look at the standards listed in the Appendix and decide which standards your experiment meets.

Student Study Site

The Companion Web site for *Teaching Science in Elementary and Middle School* http://www.sagepub.com/buxtonstudy

Visit the Web-based student study site to enhance your understanding of the chapter content and to discover additional resources that will take your learning one step further. You can enhance your understanding of the chapters by using the study materials, which include chapter objectives, flashcards, activities, practice tests, and more. You'll also find special features, such as Resources for Experiments, the Links to Standards from U.S. States and associated activities, Learning From Journal Articles, Theory Into Practice resources, Reflections on Science exercises, a Science Standards-Based Lesson Plan Project, and PRAXIS resources.

Reflections on Science

1. Physics is composed of many subtopics, such as force and motion, electricity and magnetism, sound and light, and nuclear physics. What do these topics have in common that makes them all fit under the general umbrella of physics?

2. Physicists sometime make the claim that all the other sciences (chemistry, biology, etc.) are, at the most fundamental level, actually physics. What do you think is the physicists' rationale for making this claim?

3. The most famous physicists, such as Galileo, Newton, Einstein, and Hawking, are all prototypically eccentric white males. What strategies can you think of for teaching physics in ways that will be engaging and inviting for all learners?

4. Complete Experiment 100 on page 338.

Internet Connections: Physics

The following links provide additional resources for teaching the physical sciences:

Frank Potter's Science Gems
http://www.sciencegems.com/

NASA Quest Teacher Resources
http://quest.arc.nasa.gov/index.html

Amusement Park Physics
http://www.learner.org/exhibits/parkphysics/

Bad Physics (Common Misconceptions)
http://www.geoffers2000.freeserve.co.uk/main. htm

Science Education Resource Page: Physics and Chemistry
http://serp.la.asu.edu/ChemPhy_dir/ChmPhy Idx.html

EDC Center for Science Education
http://cse.edc.org/

References

Copernicus, N. (1543). *De revolutionibus orbium coelestium, libri VI.* Nuremberg: Ioh. Petreius.

Diderot, D. (Ed.). (1751). *Encyclopédie, ou dictionnaire raisonné des sciences, des arts et des métiers.* Paris: Le Breton.

Feynman, R. P. (1990). *QED: The strange theory of light and matter.* London: Penguin Books.

Good, A. (1893). *La science amusante* (Vols. 1–3). Paris: Le Librarie Larousse.

Part III
Making the Transition From Preservice Teacher to Inservice Teacher

By this point, you have had ample opportunity to consider both the content and the process of teaching science at the elementary and middle school level. You should feel confident that you know how to begin your journey toward being an effective teacher of science. Hopefully, you even feel excited by the prospect of teaching science to children. Still, as you are surely aware, graduating from a teacher-training program is just the beginning, rather than the end, of your journey. Once you are a teacher in your own classroom, you will still have many opportunities to seek further professional development as a teacher of science. Our concluding chapter in *Teaching Science in Elementary and Middle School: A Cognitive and Cultural Approach* discusses how to make the most of these professional development experiences and continue your growth as a science teacher.

By looking at teacher certification and recertification requirements across several states, you will get a sense of similarities and differences in state requirements for teacher qualification. By considering innovative new approaches to professional development, such as Japanese lesson study, video study groups, and action research, you will be brought up to date on the wide range of professional development opportunities that are available to teachers in today's schools. We also make the case for going beyond your school and school system to consider what can be gained from joining professional organizations and attending professional conferences, returning to university for graduate studies, and eventually pursuing National Board Certification to truly become a master teacher. Finally, we discuss how you can take your science teaching to the next level by pursuing grant funding to support your use of inquiry-based science learning. This chapter is meant to help you look beyond becoming a new teacher of science and toward becoming a leader in the efforts to create meaningful, inquiry-based science learning experiences for all children.

Teacher Professional Development

Growing as a Teacher of Science

Consider the following quotes about teacher professional development:

New teachers are among the more vulnerable professionals in schools: they need to be nurtured and supported in the profession. Despite all of their youthful and idealistic enthusiasm, most new teachers are both frightened and overwhelmed by the demands of teaching. They expect (and should receive) well-planned and implemented professional development that helps them learn about their work as they make those first, tentative steps in the profession. They need the opportunity to try new things, and they need to be challenged about preconceived and stereotypical notions that circulate about teaching particular groups of students.

—**Ladson-Billings (2001, p. 24)**

It is only by introducing the young to great literature, drama, and music and to the excitement of great science that we open to them the possibilities that lie within the human spirit—enable them to see visions and dream dreams.

—**Eric Anderson**

History of Teacher Professional Development

All teachers, including teachers of science, have had the same primary responsibility since schools were first established in this country: to foster the development of educated citizens. However, the meaning of educated citizens, and thus the corresponding role of the teacher, as well as the nature of teacher preparation and professional development to support this responsibility, have changed a great deal over time.

It is worth remembering that in the nineteenth century, many teachers were themselves poorly educated and many had little more than an elementary education. There was also little emphasis on teachers taking further action to advance their own learning. Much less was known about educational psychology or theories of learning, and consequently, the prevailing wisdom was that any teacher education should focus on subject matter knowledge, with little attention paid to the relationship between teaching and learning.

By the beginning of the twentieth century, there was a movement for the professionalization of teaching. By the mid-1950s, science education as a field was largely established in the programs of most schools and colleges of education. It was during this time that the foundations of contemporary science education were developed. As discussed in Chapter 2, the launch of the Russian satellite Sputnik in 1957 led to a major reform in science education. The demand for enhanced academic content for students meant that teacher professional development needed to shift its focus to using the new wave of enriched science curriculum materials that were being produced with the assistance of scientists. This era saw the rise of "teacher workshops" in which teachers would work with a curriculum expert to consider how to best use the new materials. It is worth noting, however, that for the curriculum developers, the emphasis was on creating "teacher-proof" materials that would simply ask the teacher to follow directions rather than make decisions about how to best implement the curriculum.

The 1960s and 1970s saw the creation of the Elementary and Secondary Education Act, the Americans With Disabilities Act, and the rise of programs such as Head Start, in which the federal government began to play a larger role in the education system. These programs and the resulting funding began to attract more young people to the teaching profession, particularly in high-poverty urban areas. While increased funding was going into these large-scale federal programs, there was not a corresponding increase in funding for teacher professional development because the attempts to improve education were focused more on the policy level.

In the 1980s, the publication of the report *A Nation at Risk* (1983) and, later, the National Governors' Association *Goals 2000* report (1989), led to a new wave of educational reform, one that focused again on teachers and their qualifications. Making the claim that most teachers were underprepared to teach the material expected of them, the new focus of education reform became school leadership, teacher quality, and accountability. One of the results of this new policy push was that many states began to pay more attention to preservice teacher education and teacher certification. A new wave of teacher tests was implemented that focused on basic skills, to ensure minimum competency levels. By the 1990s, most teacher licenses were tied to some level of performance on a standardized test or series of tests, in addition to the coursework taken in a teacher preparation program. On the inservice professional development side, many states developed enhanced requirements for renewing teacher certification, which were generally tied to accumulating a certain number of professional development credits every few years. Approaches such as the Madeline Hunter model, which presented a list of components of effective lessons in a very prescriptive way, led to a model of professional development that valued conformity of implementation and teacher evaluations based on the degree of this conformity. At the same time, attempts to address the issue of school leadership led to models of "site-based management" and "school-level improvement teams" that gave teachers a new degree of influence on school-level decision making.

The Current State of Teacher Professional Development

The trends that began in the aftermath of the publication of *A Nation at Risk* and the *Goals 2000 Report* have generally strengthened and continued into the first decade of the twenty-first century, leading to the passage of the No Child Left Behind Act (NCLB) in 2001. NCLB was the most significant federal attempt to influence public education since the Elementary and Secondary Education Act in the 1960s. The accountability mandates instituted by states, largely in response to NCLB, have come to focus primarily on student achievement as measured by test scores. In nearly all states with student accountability testing, these tests have been aligned with a new wave of state standards and benchmarks for content-area knowledge. Thus, professional development in its current form tends to focus on these content standards and benchmarks on the one hand, and on preparing students for high-stakes tests on the other.

There is an awareness today that the teacher-proof curriculum attempted in the reforms of the 1960s is neither feasible nor desirable; instead, successful student learning outcomes will only result from good teaching, and good teaching can best be developed and enhanced though good professional development. But what do we know about the features of good professional development? NCLB, for example, requires states to provide "high-quality" professional development to all teachers but provides no specific guidance as to what constitutes high-quality professional development. We do know that much of the professional development that does take place is not highly effective. We know that "one shot" professional development, where an expert on a given topic provides a single workshop, has little lasting impact on teachers' classroom practice.

The National Science Education Standards (NSES) discussed in Chapter 2 sought to provide some guidance by outlining teacher professional development standards as one of the six strands of standards presented. These standards point to the knowledge, skills, and dispositions that teachers should continually work to develop throughout their teaching careers and that high-quality professional development opportunities should be committed to fostering. There are four professional development standards presented in the NSES.

Professional development standard A states that professional development for teachers of science should focus on learning core science content through inquiry-based teaching methods. For example, professional development experiences should allow teachers to engage in scientific investigations in ways that build on their current understandings, extend those understandings further, and allow them to reflect on both the processes and outcomes of the science that was learned.

Professional development standard B states that professional development for teachers of science should emphasize understanding how knowledge about science, knowledge about learning, and knowledge about teaching can be brought together in ways that enhance student learning of science. This is educational philosopher Lee Shulman's concept of "pedagogical content knowledge": knowledge about how best to teach specific content topics that develops from teaching those concepts. The experienced teacher learns to reflect on such things as analogies that are more or less successful, common misconceptions that students have about the topic, and so on. To support this standard, professional development experiences for teachers of science should build on opportunities to connect and integrate aspects of science and science education through inquiry-based activities and reflections.

Professional development standard C states that professional development for teachers of science needs to support the development of and appreciation for lifelong learning. To this end, professional development activities should provide regular opportunities for individual and collegial examination and reflection on classroom and institutional practice, as well as opportunities for teachers to receive feedback about their teaching and to understand, analyze, and apply that feedback to improve their practice.

Professional development standard D highlights the need for professional development programs for teachers of science to be coherent and integrated. As such, professional development activities need to provide long-term experiences that build upon and support learning over time; support individual teacher needs and interests as well as the needs of the school; foster collaboration among teachers as well as between teachers and administrators, parents, community leaders, and others; and recognize the unique history, culture, and organization of each specific school environment.

When taken together, these professional development standards provide guidance for professional development experiences that build on current understandings of teaching and learning in ways that are empowering for teachers. School districts, universities, and other entities that provide inservice teacher professional development have been modifying their professional development activities to build on these new models.

Theory Into Practice 10.1

Recertification Requirements Across States

Because educational policymaking is within the purview of state government rather than federal government in the United States, each state has the right and responsibility to develop its own teacher certification and teacher recertification guidelines.

In this activity, you will compare and contrast the recertification guidelines for your state with another state of your choice.

Below arc Web sites where you can find recertification guidelines for several states. A search of the Internet should enable you to locate such guidelines for other states.

Virginia: http://www.pen.k12.va.us/VDOE/Compliance/TeacherED/remanual.pdf

Texas: http://www.sbec.state.tx.us/SBECOnline/certinfo/renewcertonline.asp

Illinois: http://www.isbe.state.il.us/certification/html/experienced_teacher.htm

Maryland: http://www.wcboe.k12.md.us/content/d_hr_recert.cfm#jan 1999

Consider the following questions as you compare recertification requirements:

1. What seems to be the goal of the recertification requirements?

2. What does each state seem to want experienced teachers to continue to learn about?

3. How do the goals of the recertification programs seem to align with the kinds of professional development that are discussed in the remainder of this chapter?

🦗 Action Research: From Research "On" to Research "With"

Traditional educational research is largely done by university researchers and is most commonly disseminated in scholarly journals that are not targeted at practicing K–12 teachers. For this reason, traditional research generally has only limited usefulness for classroom teachers. This research is often done "on" or "about" teachers. An alternative model of educational research, known as teacher research or action research, can be conceptualized as research "with" teachers. In teacher research, teachers extend the reflection they should already be doing as part of their ongoing professional development to include systematic attempts to answer some of the questions raised by these reflections. The teacher will undertake research in her or his classroom or school to address a specific question in order to improve a specific aspect of teaching or to evaluate and implement a specific educational plan.

Because teachers have generally not received training in research methodology as part of their teacher preparation, the kinds of research that teachers are prepared to undertake are somewhat different from the research conducted by trained university researchers. Teachers will also need support from someone with more research experience to guide them in the process. However, because the research questions that teacher researchers are likely to ask are localized and contextualized in their classroom or school and are not necessarily meant to be generalized, the model of teacher as researcher can be successful as a vehicle for professional development. Issues to consider in designing or participating in an action research project include the following:

- Select a research question that is concrete, relevant to your teaching, and on a topic that will hold your interest—you will spend a lot of time thinking about it!
- Remember that your main role as a teacher is to teach your students—don't take on a research project that will interfere with your teaching responsibilities.
- The method of data collection should not be too demanding on the teacher's time, yet the method must also be rigorous and reliable enough to allow teachers to draw conclusions they can trust and develop classroom strategies based on those conclusions.
- Ethical treatment of all participants in research is of critical importance. University researchers are required to get training in ethical treatment of participants, training that teachers doing action research will not receive. Still, the fundamental principle is simple: The participants in your research must be protected to the best of your ability from any negative consequences that could result from their participation. In classroom research, common ethical issues include keeping student information confidential; ensuring that students who wish not to participate do not face any negative consequences for this decision; and, because your students are minors, ensuring that you have parental consent for student participation.

Teachers will need support to successfully conduct action research. This support generally will come from teaching colleagues who are also interested in conducting action research and from a research coordinator (usually a college or university faculty member trained in educational research) who provides guidance to the group as a whole and one-on-one support as needed. Teacher researchers must formulate a question they are interested in answering and then determine the kind of information that they will need to gather in order to answer the question satisfactorily and reliably. The answer that the teacher researcher comes to in the end should primarily be of use to the teacher herself, in terms of pointing to the success of a new practice, the need to change an existing practice, and so on. These findings may potentially be of interest and use to other teachers as well, however, so creating venues for teacher researchers to share their action research is another task that the research coordinator ought to consider.

Teacher action research can, in the right circumstances and with the right support, be a powerful professional development tool that empowers the teacher to think in new ways about her classroom practice and how it can be improved. There is much conversation today about the need for data-driven decision making. Teacher action research provides one method for engaging in this practice while at the same time fostering the development of new skills and individual change and growth in the teacher.

Japanese Lesson Study

Lesson study, also commonly referred to as Japanese lesson study, is a relatively new (at least in the U.S.) professional development technique that highlights the detailed analysis of individual teaching lessons. In Japan, teachers are expected to improve their teaching over time through "lesson study," in which multiple teachers, most often in pairs, plan, observe, analyze, and refine classroom lessons together. These lessons are referred to as "research lessons" and are carefully selected to allow the participating teachers to focus on particular teaching aspects of interest. Lesson study became better known in the U.S. as a result of the Third International Mathematics and Science Study video project (TIMSS Video). Conducted in 1995 and again in 1999, the TIMSS Video compared the teaching styles and techniques of eighth-grade math teachers in various countries. In-depth comparisons of teaching practices in Japan, Germany, and the United States pointed to distinct cultural patterns of teaching. Japanese teachers generally pointed to lesson study as one of the key components of their highly successful elementary mathematics and science instruction. Since the TIMSS Video, lesson study has rapidly gained in popularity as a professional development model in many sites across the United States. The key features of successful lesson study projects include the following:

- They help teachers think about long-term goals of education, such as fostering critical thinking skills or shaping lifelong learners, rather than just short-term goals of having students meet certain benchmarks or standards.
- There is careful selection of "research lessons" that focus on topics and approaches that will address specific, short-term subject matter goals and also clearly connect with the long-term goals for students.
- They clarify the goals of teaching a particular unit or lesson and how it connects with the reasons for teaching the discipline at all. For example, what is important to know about light, why is this important, and how does knowing certain things about light help us clarify why it is important to know something about physics?
- There is detailed study of how students respond to the research lessons. What did they learn? Were they engaged and focused on the lesson? How did students respond and relate to each other? Other teachers in the group observe the lesson, and then the group meets to discuss to what degree the lesson met its learning objectives. One of the goals is for teachers to learn to be accurate observers of what is happening in the classroom in order to determine whether the lesson is contributing to student learning.

Accurate observation is a skill that is especially relevant for teachers of science. Thus, the lesson study approach to teacher professional development provides teachers with opportunities to research, create, try, and evaluate lesson plans to determine whether they are helping students learn. It allows groups of teachers to research, develop, and practice lessons and techniques that have direct impact on their students while also examining their personal beliefs about teaching. As with action research, lesson study fosters a professional development context in which teachers work collaboratively on topics that they wish to study in a way that can support development of content knowledge, pedagogical knowledge, and pedagogical content knowledge. It also fosters the development of social capital in the school as teachers develop closer professional relationships with other teachers, sharing resources, ideas, and support. Perhaps most important, because lesson study builds professional relationships while directly targeting teaching areas in which the teachers themselves want to improve, lesson study groups often become ongoing school-based professional development projects that can last for years. In Japan, participation in lesson study is an ongoing expectation that is simply seen as one part of the teacher's job. Some school districts in the U.S. are beginning to explore the use of lesson study in this way, as professional development that promotes the lifelong learning of the teacher while leading to enhanced student achievement.

Theory Into Practice 10.2

The TIMMS Video Project

The following Web site has video clips from various classrooms that participated in the TIMMS Video Study:

http://nces.ed.gov/pubs2003/timssvideo/

Watch the video clips and then answer the following questions:

1. What similarities do you see in terms of what teachers of math and science do in the different countries?

2. What clear and obvious differences do you see in terms of what teachers of math and science do in the different countries?

3. Pick a video clip that seemed very different to you and watch it a second time. Do you see any similarities the second time that you missed when watching it the first time?

4. Do you think all teachers should be asked to watch videos of how teachers in other countries teach? Why or why not?

Video Study Groups

One outgrowth of the Japanese lesson study movement is a professional development technique sometimes referred to as video study groups. While videotaping lessons is not part of the traditional Japanese lesson study technique, it was primarily because of the videos taken in Japanese teachers' classrooms as part of the TIMSS Video Study that the lesson study model began to be known and disseminated in U.S. schools. Video study groups share many features with Japanese lesson study. Groups of teachers agree to meet regularly in ongoing professional development aimed at exploring and reflecting on actual classroom practice in a systematic and supportive way. As with lesson study, teachers begin by selecting a topic they wish to improve upon or better understand in their classroom. They then carefully craft a lesson plan, often with input from other members of the group, that will highlight the topic in question. The topic could be anything from a particular content objective, to a new classroom management technique, to a new instructional or formative assessment technique. The teacher then teaches this target lesson in her or his class and has the lesson videotaped by a colleague.

The teacher group meets later, watches the video together, and reflects on key issues. Having a video that can be watched repeatedly makes for an excellent self-reflective tool because it allows teachers to revisit their practice from a new perspective while sharing this practice with trusted colleagues. As with all of the innovative professional development approaches that are discussed here, learning to use video study groups effectively takes practice and training. It is helpful, at least at the beginning of a project, to have an expert, such as a trained university researcher who has had successful experiences working as part of a video study group, as a participant. This individual can share her or his experiences with how and why video study groups benefit participating teachers and can deliver procedural training and share tips and potential pitfalls.

It is natural that, initially, feedback on video lessons will focus on what has been referred to as "show and tell" discussions of what is happening in the classroom during the lesson. With practice, teachers can move beyond show and tell and begin to explore deeper issues that the teacher who is sharing the video cares about. Again, this is much like the philosophy behind the Japanese lesson study approach.

For this shift toward deeper issues to take place, trust must be developed among the participants. Allowing others to see and critique him or her puts the teacher in a vulnerable position, making trust and a sense of collective purpose critical issues that must be developed among this group. This need for trust holds true for the other nontraditional professional development strategies discussed in this chapter as well. In traditional short-term workshop-based professional development, trust is not an important issue because there is no real requirement for teacher buy-in or participation. The presenter typically shares an approach that he or she is advocating, and each individual teacher then makes a decision whether or not he or she will actually try to implement it. There may or may not be follow-up later to discuss what teachers did in the classroom. The kinds of professional development advocated in this chapter, whether teacher action research, Japanese lesson study, or video study groups, are all meant to be ongoing, team based, and devoted to issues that participating teachers identify as important to them. These approaches have the potential to be very powerful for the same reason that they can make teachers feel vulnerable—they take the art of teaching, which is largely seen as an individual endeavor, and make it communal.

Parental Involvement and Parental Engagement

There is a long history of research dating back to the 1960s that clearly demonstrates how engaging parents in their children's learning contributes significantly to the students' academic success. Just as trust is important in professional development, when working with parents it is important to develop a trusting relationship. Most parents will generally assume that you, as their child's teacher, have good intentions and want their child to succeed in school. Still, many parents are hesitant to become more involved in their child's learning. There can be many reasons for this: They may feel they do not have enough time to become more involved, they may lack self-confidence in their own level of education, there may be mistrust based on negative experiences they had in school, or they may be concerned about their legal standing or immigration status. Each of these parental concerns can be mitigated to some degree by taking gradual steps to build trust in the relationship. As that trust increases, many parents will start to become more engaged in their children's learning.

There are many ways to promote parental involvement in science education. The following are some strategies that can be used to begin this process. Note that if your class has a significant number of parents whose first language is not English, you may consider having these communications and resources translated into the relevant language(s).

1. Keep parents informed about what is going on in your classroom. Send home a weekly newsletter; create a class Web site; and/or e-mail parents updates about class projects, ongoing assignments, homework, and the like.

2. If you create a class Web site, also use it to suggest resources that could be used by parents to help students with their work and interesting places in the community that have either formal or informal opportunities for families to engage in science learning together.

3. Identify and send home a list of appropriate videos/DVDs that emphasize science concepts that will be of interest to children. Check your local library and video rental store to see what is available. Parents can then borrow/rent these and watch them with their children. Additionally, you can create a classroom library of videos that students can borrow and watch at home with their family or friends.

4. Create a book list organized by science topic and reading level that you can send home to parents (and post on the class Web site). Parents can take their children to the library to check out books from this list and read them together.

5. Hold a family science night at school. Students prepare hands-on inquiry-based science activities and then family members come to school in the evening and the students guide them through the activities, sharing what they have learned about the science concepts involved.

6. There are currently many educational toys and games that support the development of science concepts. Some of these can be rather expensive, but not all are. Around the holidays, provide parents with a list of toys and games that reinforce scientific thinking and suggest places in your community where they might be able to purchase these games.

For all of the above suggestions, make it clear to parents that these are not assignments or expectations, but simply suggestions and opportunities for parents to support their children's learning. Emphasize that while some cost money, others are free, and while all require some time commitment, most can be done in a flexible way in short chunks of time as available.

You will observe that nearly all of the above suggestions have embedded in them the notion of parents learning science along with their children. Unless parents work in a scientific field, it is unlikely that they will have a particularly strong science background. Having parents learn with their children will help them become more comfortable with science themselves and can, in turn, lead to a greater willingness to become further involved in their children's learning.

Over time, if a teacher is committed to fostering parental involvement, at least some parents will make the shift from only being involved at the request of the teacher to more actively engaging with the teacher and school. These parents may begin helping in the classroom and giving the teacher feedback about aspects of their child's science learning. This is generally a very good thing, indicating that there is a level of trust that allows for open and honest communication. It is important to remember, however, that you are the teacher and you must ultimately make the decisions about what goes on in the classroom. It is possible for parents to become overly involved, and at that point, if you have developed a level of trust you will be able to talk with the parent in a candid and open way about an appropriate level of involvement.

Theory Into Practice 10.3

Parent Interview

In the following activity, you will interview a parent of an elementary or middle school student about his or her conceptions of science and science instruction.

1. First, can you please tell me your name?

2. How many children do you have?

3. How old are they?

4. What do you think of when you hear the word "science"?

5. What do scientists do?

6. What kinds of people become scientists?

7. Do you have any relatives, friends, or acquaintances that use science? In what ways?

8. Do you ever engage in activities that you think of as being related to science? Tell me about this.

9. Do you engage in any science-related activities with your children? Tell me about this.

10. What kinds of science homework do your children bring home from school?

11. Do you think your child(ren) find science class difficult or easy? Interesting or boring? Why do you think so?

12. What do you think about your children's prospects for a career in science? Why do you think so?

🐌 Professional Organizations: NSTA

There are a number of professional organizations dedicated to supporting the work of teachers in science. The largest professional organization specifically dedicated to supporting the work of science teachers is the National Science Teachers Association (NSTA). NSTA has over 55,000 members nationwide, and the organization engages in a wide range of activities to forward the teaching of science in the United States. NSTA is especially interested in professional development of practicing teachers and how professional development can be used to promote increased interest and support for the teaching of science. The following are some of the NSTA resources that may prove useful to you as a teacher of science. The NSTA strongly encourages interested teachers to become members of the organization (see their Web site for membership information), but many of the resources discussed below are available to non-members.

1. *Professional Journals and Publications*. NSTA publishes journals targeted to each level of science teaching. The journal *Science and Children*

is targeted to the elementary teacher and the journal *Science Scope* is aimed specifically at the middle science teacher (there is also *The Science Teacher,* targeting high school, and *College Science Teaching,* to support the teaching of undergraduates). Both *Science and Children* and *Science Scope* provide a mix of suggestions for activities, teachers' experiences with attempting new instructional and assessment strategies, reviews of new materials and books relevant to science teaching, and announcements about upcoming events of interest to teachers of science. NSTA members receive the journal of their choice by mail and online; however, most elementary and middle school libraries subscribe to the appropriate level journal, so teachers should have access to issues of that journal at school.

2. *Conferences.* Each year, the NSTA holds a national conference and a series of regional conferences. The conferences are well organized and well attended, especially the national conference, and they provide teachers with a wide range of opportunities and experiences to enhance their science teaching. These include hundreds of practical workshops covering the full range of science disciplines and grade levels. Teachers can hear from other teachers who are engaged in innovative practices in curriculum, instruction, assessment, and professional development, as well as from university researchers and teacher educators, school and district administrators, policy makers and others who are interested in improving science education. There are also displays from the major book and materials publishers where teachers can make purchases or simply get ideas. Attending an NSTA conference also provides opportunities to build and strengthen professional networks that extend beyond one's local school or district.

3. *Awards and Recognition Programs.* NSTA is involved in a number of programs that support and recognize both teachers and students for exceptional ideas or achievements in science education. These awards include cash awards, school supplies and materials, and trips to the NSTA national convention. Programs administered by NSTA include the Toyota TAPESTRY Grants for Teachers, the Craftsman NSTA Young Inventors Awards Program, the Toshiba NSTA ExploraVision Awards, the Shell Science Teaching Award, and the Robert Carleton Award. Information about each of these awards, including who is eligible to apply and how to apply, can be found on the NSTA Web site (see below).

4. *NSTA Web Site.* The NSTA Web site is a thorough and comprehensive site with information on all the topics that have been discussed in this section—membership, journals, conferences, awards—as well as many other topics. Some features of the site are restricted to "members only," but most of the site is publicly accessible. The address of the NSTA Web site is http://www.nsta.org/.

Advanced Study

At some point in your teaching career, you may decide you want to advance your education and do graduate work at a local university or college. Most colleges and universities provide various opportunities for advanced study, including programs in science education. If you live in or near a large metropolitan area, you are likely to have a number of schools and programs to choose from. If you live in a less populous area, your choices may be limited. In either case, choosing a program that meets your needs and expectations is an important part of the process. Visit college and university Web sites to find out what programs and faculty are available, areas of specialization, requirements of the program, cost, admissions requirements, and other issues that will be important to you. In addition to getting information from the Web site, you will probably want to schedule a visit to the campus to speak with a program representative. If possible, you may also want to speak with a student currently in the program. A fellow student can sometimes provide the best information about whether the program will meet your needs. It is worth noting that nearly all school districts in the country give a salary increase to teachers with a master's or other advanced degree in education. Getting more education pays in more ways than one.

In addition to university graduate programs, there are many other opportunities available to teachers interested in ongoing education. Nearly all school districts provide professional development opportunities for their teachers through courses, workshops, summer institutes, and so on. Participation in these activities generally earns the teacher "continuing education credits" that can be used to obtain recertification, but unlike university credits, these district credits do not count toward any type of advanced degree.

Additionally, other resources in your community such as museums, parks, and community colleges often offer teacher workshops and other programs that can enhance your skills and abilities as a teacher of science. You can learn about such opportunities by going to the organization's Web site or by calling and inquiring about educational programs. The Web site for your school district and/or your state department of education are also good places to check for opportunities for advanced study.

National Board Certification

The most rigorous and prestigious certification currently available to a teacher is known as National Board Certification (NBC). The National Board of Professional Teaching Standards (NBPTS) is an independent, nonprofit organization founded with the goal of creating a symbol of professional teaching excellence that would be recognized by teachers, administrators, and the community at large. The focus of the NBC program is to support teachers in meeting high professional standards and demonstrating the accomplished application of those standards in their teaching through a series of performance-based assessments.

Teacher participation in NBC is completely voluntary; as of yet, no school district has made NBC a requirement to hold any teaching position. Because it is voluntary, the standards are very rigorous. To become National Board certified, teachers go through an intensive assessment process that can take several years to complete. The teacher's work is judged by a board of his or her peers and must demonstrate each of a series of accomplished practices. NBC complements, but does not replace, the regular state licensing procedures that all teachers must go through. State licensing systems generally set the minimum standards for teachers to maintain their positions. In contrast, NBC establishes advanced standards for experienced teachers.

NBC requires the teacher to produce a teaching portfolio that includes student work samples, videos of lessons, and a thorough analysis of the candidate's teaching and students' learning. Written components address the candidate's content knowledge, pedagogical knowledge, and pedagogical content knowledge. To be eligible to apply, the teacher must have three years of classroom teaching experience. To find out more about NBC and to locate teachers in your area who are already National Board certified, see the NBPTS Web site at http://www.nbpts.org/.

Theory Into Practice 10.4

Interviewing an NBCT in Your School District

Begin by identifying teachers in your area who are National Board certified. One way to do this is to check the NBPTS Web site (http://www.nbpts.org/). Alternatively, you could contact local schools directly and inquire about the presence of NBC teachers.

Contact one or more of these teachers and ask whether they would be willing to discuss the NBC process with you. Because part of being National Board certified is being a teacher leader, they should be willing to make time to speak with you. Use the following questions as a guide for this conversation.

1. How long have you been teaching?

2. At what point did you become interested in pursuing National Board Certification?

3. What people or events influenced your decision to pursue National Board Certification? In what ways?

4. Can you describe the process of becoming National Board certified?

5. What was the most challenging thing about the process?

6. What was the most enjoyable thing about the process?

7. What advice would you give to a colleague who is considering beginning the process?

Applying for Grants

One of the largest challenges facing many teachers of science is the need for material resources. While the activities and experiments presented in this book were intentionally selected to highlight the ability to teach conceptually rich inquiry-based science with ordinary household objects, it is still true that even simple materials cost money. Schools (especially elementary schools) that do not have a tradition of teaching hands-on, inquiry-based science are unlikely to have abundant material resources to support this kind of teaching. As a new teacher, you have not had the opportunity to build your own collection of supplies. Your school administration may have some funding to support the purchase of science supplies, but this is likely to be quite limited. In short, many new teachers of science feel that they are faced with the choice of not teaching hands-on science or buying the materials needed to do so on their own.

Another option you should consider is to apply for a small grant. While writing a funding proposal can be somewhat time consuming, it does have several payoffs. First, if you are successful, you will be able to purchase the resources you need to be a more effective teacher of science. Second, whether or not you are funded, the process of writing the proposal is a valuable professional development experience in its own right, requiring you to think clearly about what you want to do and why and then communicate those ideas to other people. Even if you are not funded the first time, you are likely to get feedback on your proposal that will increase your chances of getting funded the next time around. Below are listed a number of Web sites that provide information on opportunities for grant funding. Before you commit the time needed to write a grant proposal, be sure to carefully read over the material about the grant, both to make sure that you are eligible to apply and to be sure that the grant meets your needs.

Grants for K–12
http://www.technologygrantnews.com/grant-index-by-type/k-12-grants.html

This index provides a guide to grants for school programs, curriculum development, and staff professional development for teachers, as well as grants for specific topic areas such as science. This is a large site that is used by teachers, school administrators, and districts.

Ciba Specialty Chemicals Exemplary Middle Level and High School Science Teaching Awards
    http://www.nsta.org/cibateacher
    A competitive award made to one middle school and one high school teacher each year for exemplary science teaching. The recipient receives $1,000, a one-year membership in NSTA, and up to $500 to attend NSTA's National Convention.

Delta Education/CPO Science Awards for Excellence in Inquiry-Based Science Teaching
    http://www.nsta.org/deltacpo
    This award is open to any K–12 teacher and recognizes three teachers each year who use inquiry-based science to enhance teaching and learning in their classroom. The award is $1,500 toward expenses to attend the NSTA National Convention, plus a $1,500 prize.

Estes/Space Foundation/NSTA "Space Educator Award"
    http://www.nsta.org/estes
    This award is for Grade 4–12 teachers with at least three years of teaching experience who demonstrate excellence in teaching space science. The award is $1,000 and up to $500 to attend the NSTA Convention, plus travel and tuition expenses to attend the Space Discovery Graduate Course in Colorado Springs, Colorado.

Shell Science Teaching Award
    http://www.nsta.org/shell
    This award recognizes one outstanding K–12 science teacher who has had a positive impact on his or her students, school, and community through exemplary science teaching. The award includes $10,000 and an all-expense-paid trip to NSTA's National Convention; two finalists will also receive all-expense-paid trips to the convention.

Toyota TAPESTRY Grants for Teachers
    www.nsta.org/programs/tapestry/program.htm
    The Toyota TAPESTRY program awards numerous grants to K–12 teachers each year to support innovative projects that enhance science education at the school level. Small teams of teachers generally apply together for this grant. The awards include 50 grants of up to $10,000 each plus 20 "mini-grants" of $2,500 each. Specific topics for funding are sometimes required for a given year, so read the funding description carefully if you are considering applying.

Vernier Technology Awards
    http://www.nsta.org/vernier
    The Vernier Technology Awards recognize innovative use of data collection technology using a computer, graphing calculator, or other hand-held in the science classroom. One of the awards is at the K–5 level and two awards are at the middle school level. Each award is $1,000 toward expenses to attend the NSTA National Convention, $1,000 in cash for the teacher, and $1,000 in Vernier Products.

    A search on the Internet will uncover many other grant opportunities, both for science and for teaching in general, for which you might be eligible. As with all of the professional development topics discussed in this chapter, it is valuable to conceptualize, develop, and reflect on ideas for grants with some of your peers and colleagues. If there is one clear lesson that we have learned about teacher professional development in recent years, it is that the activity, whether it be action research, lesson study, applying for a grant, or anything else, must be guided primarily by teacher needs and interests and then supported as much as possible by collaborative support structures. When this becomes the focus, professional development has the potential to lead to substantive and lasting improvements in teacher practice and in student learning.

Theory Into Practice 10.5

If I Had $500 . . .

Imagine that you have just been offered $500 to enhance your teaching of science with the condition that you provide a clear justification and rationale for how you will spend the money.
    What would you do?
    What would you buy?
    Make a list of how you would spend the money and why you would spend it in this way. How would this enhance the science learning of your students?
    Now look at the grants listed above. Do any of these grants seem likely to fund your idea?
    If one seems to be a good match, consider applying as soon as you have your own classroom.

Student Study Site

The Companion Web site for *Teaching Science in Elementary and Middle School* http://www.sagepub.com/buxtonstudy

Visit the Web-based student study site to enhance your understanding of the chapter content and to discover additional resources that will take your learning one step further. You can enhance your understanding of the chapters by using the study materials, which include chapter objectives, flashcards, activities, practice tests, and more. You'll also find special features, such as Resources for Experiments, the Links to Standards from U.S. States and associated activities, Learning From Journal Articles, Theory Into Practice resources, Reflections on Science exercises, a Science Standards-Based Lesson Plan Project, and PRAXIS resources.

Reflections on Science

1. Why do you think teacher professional development has changed over the past decade? What kinds of professional development do you believe teachers need to be successful in teaching hands-on, inquiry-based science?

2. What sorts of school policies and practices might support effective teacher professional development?

What sorts of school policies and practices might hinder effective teacher professional development? Why?

3. Inexperienced young teachers are sometimes intimidated by parents who may question their practices or decision making. What can you do as a new teacher to foster a successful relationship with your students' parents? What are some things you should avoid doing?

References

Ladson-Billings, G. (2001). *Crossing over to Canaan: The journey of new teachers in diverse classrooms.* San Francisco: Jossey-Bass.

National Commission on Excellence in Education. (1983). *A nation at risk:* *The imperative for educational reform.* Washington, DC: U.S. Department of Education.

National Governors' Association. (1989). *Goals 2000: National education goals of the Governors' Education Summit.* Washington, DC: U.S. Department of Education.

Appendix

*The National Science Education
Standards for Science Content*

As mentioned in Chapter 2 of this text, one of the cornerstones of the standards is the idea of systemic reform, the notion that for science education reform to be successful, no one piece of the reform can be changed without consideration of how the other aspects of the education system must also respond. Thus, for example, changes in science curriculum must be accompanied by changes in instruction, assessment, professional development, and administrative support.

That said, since the dissemination of the national standards much of the focus has been on the content standards and the question of what science should be taught in our schools if we are to develop a truly science-literate society. When states have set their own science standards and benchmarks, they have tended to focus on science content standards to a larger degree than on the other aspects of systemic reform.

Below we list the science content standards as presented in the National Science Education Standards (NSES). It is to these standards that the 100 core experiments presented in Part II of this text are aligned. When you are developing your own lessons in the classroom, you will most likely be asked to record in your lesson plans which of your state's content standards your lessons are addressing. We undertook a similar exercise with our experiments, but using the NSES as opposed to the state standards for any given state. Still, as you are likely to see by investigating the standards for your state, most states developed their science content standards to be closely aligned with the NSES content standards.

Content Standard A: Science as Inquiry

All students should develop

> A.1. Abilities necessary to do scientific inquiry
> A.2. Understandings about scientific inquiry

Content Standard B: Physical Science

All students should develop an understanding of

B.1. Properties and changes of properties in matter
B.2. Motions and forces
B.3. Transfer of energy

Content Standard C: Life Science

All students should develop understanding of

C.1. Structure and function in living systems
C.2. Reproduction and heredity
C.3. Regulation and behavior
C.4. Populations and ecosystems
C.5. Diversity and adaptations of organisms

Content Standard D: Earth and Space Science

All students should develop an understanding of

D.1. Structure of the Earth system
D.2. Earth's history
D.3. Earth in the solar system

Content Standard E: Science and Technology

All students should develop

E.1. Abilities of technological design
E.2. Understandings about science and technology

Content Standard F: Science in Personal and Social Perspectives

All students should develop understanding of

F.1. Personal health
F.2. Populations, resources, and environments
F.3. Natural hazards
F.4. Risks and benefits
F.5. Science and technology in society

Content Standard G: History and Nature of Science

All students should develop understanding of

G.1. Science as a human endeavor
G.2. Nature of science
G.3. History of science

Glossary

Like all fields of study, science has a specialized vocabulary that helps scientists communicate with each other clearly and efficiently. To the student of science, however, this specialized vocabulary can be a bit overwhelming and confusing. Additionally, science sometimes takes terms with an everyday meaning and uses them in a particular and sometimes unrelated way (e.g., mass, theory). The following glossary is meant to help you make better sense of this scientific vocabulary.

Accuracy	How close a measured result is to reality.
Advance organizer	Any tool or strategy that helps to connect new ideas to prior knowledge to aid the learner in conceptualizing how the new idea fits into a broader framework.
Anemometer	A tool used to measure wind speed.
Aquifer	A rock formation that is porous and permeable enough to store water.
Assessment	Systematic analysis of student work to help the teacher understand to what degree students have or have not gained mastery of the instructional goals and objectives.
Astronomy	The study of the stars and the other cosmological features.
Atmosphere	Earth's relatively thin covering of gases.
Atom	The smallest particle that an element can be divided into while still retaining its chemical properties.
Biology	The study of life in all its myriad forms.
Biome	A large area containing similar flora, fauna, and microorganisms.
Biosphere	All of Earth's living organisms.
Cells	The basic unit of life and the building blocks for all organisms, whether plants or animals.
Census	A count of all of a given type of organism in a given location.

Chemistry	The study of matter and its interaction with energy.
Classifying	The grouping or ordering of objects or events into categories.
Climate	The long-term atmospheric and hydrologic patterns that help us to understand the weather.
Communication	The sharing of scientific findings and questions so that other members of the scientific community can both challenge and build upon one's findings and hypotheses.
Communism	The idea that science is a communal activity, in that scientists share their work with their community for the common good.
Compound	A chemical substance made of chemically bonded elements in a fixed ratio that cannot be separated by physical means.
Concept map	A diagram consisting of bubbles (called "nodes") that contain descriptions of relevant concepts and arrows (called links or "propositions") that connect nodes with labels describing the nature of the linkage between the concepts.
Constructivism	A theory of learning based on the idea that learners construct knowledge and meaning for themselves by interacting with the world in which they live. Thus, each individual's understanding of an idea will be somewhat different because of differing prior knowledge and experience.
Control of variables	A variable is any factor that could change, intentionally or unintentionally, during the course of scientific inquiry. Only one variable at a time should be changed. The rest should be held constant, or controlled.
Cosmology	The search for origins and attempts to answer questions such as how the Universe began.
Creativity	Exploring a question, problem, or phenomenon in a variety of ways, often involving "thinking outside the box."
Density	The ratio of the mass of an object divided by the volume it occupies.
Diagnostic assessment	Assessment done at the beginning of a new instructional unit or theme to provide the teacher with information about what her students already know about the topic to be studied.

Disinterestedness	The idea that scientists should have no emotional or financial attachments to their work.
DNA	An amino acid used by biological systems to store and transfer information about the organism using a genetic code.
Earth and space science	The range of science disciplines that study the physical properties of the Earth, its various systems, and the place of the Earth within the larger cosmos.
Ecosystem	The dynamic interactions between plants, animals, microorganisms, and their environment. Within an ecosystem, each organism has its own niche, or role, to play.
Element	A physical substance that is composed of a single type of atom.
Energy	The ability to do work.
Energy system	The energy that powers all Earth's systems.
English Language Learners	Students who speak a language other than English as their home language and are learning English as an additional language (also referred to as ELL, ESOL, or LEP students).
Eucaryotes	Organisms whose cells contain a nucleus, including protozoa, algae, plants, fungi, and animals.
Evolution	A change in the gene pool of a population over time.
Exceptionality	Any physical or mental condition that places a student outside the norm as related to school activity. This can include students with a physical impairment (such as vision or hearing loss), learning disabilities, emotional disabilities, or gifted or talented students.
Force	A push or a pull that acts upon some object.
Formative assessment	Assessment that is ongoing throughout the course of a unit of study to monitor student progress.
Frequency	The number of times that a repeated event occurs in a certain period of time.
Fuel	A substance that can be used to produce energy.

Gas	A state of matter that has no shape or size of its own and can expand without limit.
Gene	A hereditary unit that can be passed on from generation to generation of an organism.
Germination	The process by which a seed sprouts and begins to grow into a plant.
Greenhouse effect	The effect of carbon dioxide on temperature as a result of trapped gases in a planet's atmosphere.
Hydrosphere	Earth's circulating water systems.
Inertia	The tendency of an object to continue to move in the direction it is already going, or in the case of an object at rest, the tendency to remain at rest.
Inferring	Drawing a conclusion about something based on previously gathered information.
Informed skepticism	Proponents of new scientific theories must provide evidence to support their theories, and the rest of the scientific community has a responsibility to be open to new ideas but to rigorously question their accuracy and validity.
Kinetic energy	Energy in motion.
Lithosphere	Earth's surface and interior.
Magnetism	An attractive or repulsive force caused by the interaction of charged particles.
Mass	A measure of how much matter there is in an object; no matter where the object is, it still contains the same amount of matter and thus, has the same mass.
Matter	Any substance that has mass and occupies space.
Measurements	Using tools to quantify variables such as length, mass, volume, temperature, time, and so on.
Meteorologist	A scientist who studies weather and climate.
Mineral	A naturally occurring solid with a definite chemical composition and crystal structure.
Mixture	A combination of substances that can be separated into its parts.
Molecule	A collection of atoms of more than one element, where those elements exist in a definite, fixed ratio.

Monera	Organisms whose cells lack a nucleus, such as bacteria and blue-green algae.
Observations	Using all appropriate senses and tools to gather information and describe a process, object, or event.
Optics	The study of the physics of light and color.
Organized skepticism	The idea that scientists should wait until "all the facts are in" before a judgment is made about a particular theory.
Orrery	A three-dimensional model that demonstrates the rotation of the planets around the sun and relative to each other.
Paradigm shift	The idea that science does not build upon itself in a linear fashion, but rather that it builds gradually for a time through routine science practice and then takes sudden and revolutionary leaps in unexpected directions.
Photosynthesis	The process in green plants by which chloroplasts in plant cells produce the sugars that serve as food for the plant.
Physics	The study of the fundamental materials of the universe, the forces these materials exert on one another, and the results of these forces.
Plate tectonics	The geologic forces that cause convection currents beneath the Earth's surface, leading to the motion of the Earth's plates and resulting in continental drift.
Portfolio	A compilation of one's professional work that can include lesson plans, personal reflections, observations, and even poetry or art. It serves both as a tool for professional development and as an interview tool when searching for a teaching position.
Potential energy	The energy that is stored in an object.
Precision	The repeatability of a measurement.
Predicting	Stating an outcome for some future event based on past experience, observation, or other evidence.
Pressure	A measure of force per unit of area.
Project-based science	Integrated science units, usually several weeks long, that provide students with an overarching problem or context for inquiry.

Replicability	If the same procedures are conducted under the same conditions, then the same results should be achieved.
Resonance	A prolonging of sound by reflection or the vibration of other objects.
Rock	Naturally occurring solids composed of one or more minerals.
Scientific inquiry	A process of trying to explain observations made of the natural world around us.
Scientific literacy	Possessing a sufficient amount of science knowledge to use appropriate scientific processes and principles when making decisions related to science and technology.
Scientific theory	A theory is not a guess or a hunch. In science, a theory is a self-consistent model that describes the behavior of objects or phenomena. Thus, gravity is a theory, despite the fact that we are highly confident that if we drop an apple on Earth it will fall toward the center of the planet until something gets in its way.
Situated cognition	A theory that explains learning through its situation in social relationships, social organization, and learning within a community.
Soil	A complex mix of organic and inorganic materials that is essential for life on Earth. It typically includes small particles of rock, plant material in various states of decomposition, animal material both living and dead, and a variety of minerals.
Solution	A combination of substances that has the same concentration of all its parts throughout and can be separated by some physical process into its constituent substances.
Sputnik 1	The world's first artificial satellite, launched by the Soviet Union on October 4, 1957.
Summative assessment	Assessment aimed at gaining a more comprehensive picture of the degree to which each student has gained mastery of the key concepts addressed in a given unit or theme.
Sundial	The oldest known device for measuring time and probably the most ancient of all scientific instruments. Any object that uses the length and position of shadows to tell time.

Systematicity	Following a previously determined, systematic plan in order to optimize the ability to control variables and other aspects of a well-controlled inquiry process.
Temperature	The heating or cooling of a substance that results from the movements of the molecules in the substance.
Universalism	The idea that scientific results should be analyzed objectively and be verifiable or repeatable, without regard for the scientist's personal or social attributes.
Vacuum	The absence of all matter.
Volume	A measure of how much space a substance takes up.
Wave	A disturbance that propagates through space, often transferring energy.
Weather	The variety of atmospheric events that we observe daily.
Weight	A measure of how much force an object exerts as a result of gravity pulling down on it; thus, weight will change as the force of gravity changes.
Work	A change in the energy of an object caused by a force.

Index

AAAS. *See* American Association for the Advancement of Science

Absolute mass, 309 (Experiment 80)

Academic competitions, 114

Academy of Natural Sciences, The, 65 (Web site)

Accuracy, 306, 308, 365

Acid rain, 219–220 (Experiment 36)

Action-Reaction Law, 310

Action research, 124–125, 128, 347–349

Additive changes to science curriculum, 106

Adenine, 236 (Experiment 46)

Advanced study, 357

Advance organizers, 73, 365

Aesthetic benefits to science education reform, 53, 54 (image)

African American scientists, 90, 92, 93 (table), 117 (Web site)

Ahlgren, A., 99–100

AIDS, 25, 61

Air, hot, 273, 274 (Experiment 64)

Air flow, 313, 315, 316 (Experiment 84)

Airplanes, 9 (image), 302

Air pollution, 191, 194 (Experiment 24)

Air pressure, 73

Alaska, climate of, 184

Alchemy, 13, 261

Alcohol, evaporation of, 271 (Experiment 62), 282 (Experiment 70)

Alexander, Archibald, 93 (table)

Alexander the Great, 289

Alvarez, Luis Walter, 94 (table)

American Association for the Advancement of Science (AAAS), 35 (Web site), 99, 146

American Association of University Women, 117 (Web site)

American Chemical Society, 296 (Web site)

Americans with Disabilities Act, 95, 344

Ampère, Andre, 334

Amusement park physics, 313, 339 (Web site)

Anatomy, human, 41 (image), 252–253 (Experiment 56), 253, 255

Anderson, Eric, 343

Anemometers, 187–188 (Experiment 20), 365

Animals, 221–224
  cells of, 221, 223–224 (Experiment 38)
  census, 224, 225 (Experiment 39)
  experimental, 63 (Theory Into Practice 2.5)
  eye placement on, 242, 243 (image)
  in Linnaean classification system, 214 (Experiment 33)
  locomotion of, 331 (image)
  skeleton reconstruction of, 221, 222 (Experiment 37)

Antarctic Ocean, 195

Antibiotics, development of, 61

Apollo 11, 204

Appendicitis, 7

Aquifers, 175, 177, 180
    (Experiment 16), 365
Archimedes, 299, 321, 324
Architecture, 301 (image)
Arctic Ocean, 195
Arkansas Science Teachers Association,
    35 (Web site)
Arm, human, 252–253 (Experiment 56),
    253, 255
Armonicas, glass, 326
Art Forms in Nature (Haeckel), 54 (image)
Artifacts, in portfolio, 140
Asian tsunami, 170
Aspirin, 249
Assessment, 126–127
    authentic, 138
    cumulative, 126, 127
    definition of, 365
    diagnostic, 126, 366
    formative, 126–127, 367
    ongoing, 126–127
    post-assessment, 126, 127
    pre-assessment, 126
    summative, 126, 127, 370
Assignments, leveling, 115
Astronomy, 202 (Web site)
    definition of, 365
    earth and space science, 161, 163–167
    experiments, 163–164 (Experiment 7),
        165–166 (Experiment 8), 168
        (Experiment 9)
    physics, 301, 302 (image)
    scientific inquiry in, 17–18
Atlantic Ocean, 195
Atmosphere, 189, 191–194
    definition of, 151, 365
    experiments, 192 (Experiment 22),
        193 (Experiment 23), 194
        (Experiment 24)
Atmospheric cycle, 182, 183–184
    (Experiment 18)
Atomic bombs, 9, 10 (image),
    302, 305 (image)

Atomic clocks, 317
Atoms, 266, 268, 270 (Experiment 61), 365
Atwater, M. M., 89, 105
Australia, rabbit introduction into, 246
Ausubel, David, 73
Authentic assessment, 138
Automobiles, invention of, 20
Awards and recognition programs, 356

Bacon, Francis, 6, 7 (image)
Bacteria, 61, 226, 229–230 (Experiment 42)
Banking model of education, 58–59
Banks, J., 105
Banneker, Benjamin, 93 (table)
Barba, R. H., 96
Barton, A. C., 57
Basch, Linda, 87
Bateson, Gregory, xxi, 20–21, 27, 150
Batteries, 289, 291, 292 (Experiment 76)
Baudelaire, Charles, 72
Bears, eye placement on, 242, 243 (image)
Beaufort wind scale, 188 (Experiment 20)
Bell, Alexander Graham, 97 (table)
Benacerraf, Baruj, 94 (table)
Benchmarks for Science Literacy, 99
Benzene ring, 17
Bernoulli, Jakob, 315, 316 (Experiment 84)
Bernoulli's Principle, 315, 316 (Experiment 84)
Berra, Yogi, 121
Bhagavad Gita, 299
Biceps, 252–253 (Experiment 56)
Bicycles, 302, 305 (image), 321
Big Bang theory, 155, 157
Billiards, 23–24
Bill Nye the Science Guy, 44
Binocular vision, 242, 243 (image),
    244 (Experiment 50)
Biological Sciences Curriculum Study, 51, 78
    Biology, xxv, 203–257, 256–257
    (Web sites)
    animals, 221–224, 222 (Experiment 37),
        223–224 (Experiment 38),
        225 (Experiment 39)

biomes and ecosystems, 243, 246–249,
    247 (Experiment 52), 248–249
    (Experiment 53), 250
    (Experiment 54)
classification, 209, 210 (image), 211,
    212 (Experiment 31), 213
    (Experiment 32), 214 (Experiment 33)
definition of, 365
ethics in, 204
evolution, 237, 239, 241–242
    (Experiment 49), 241–243, 244
    (Experiment 50), 245 (Experiment 51)
genetic code, 232, 234, 236–237,
    236 (Experiment 46), 238–239
    (Experiment 47), 240 (Experiment 48)
human body and human health, 249,
    251–255, 251 (Experiment 55), 252–253
    (Experiment 56), 254–255 (Experiment 57)
measurement in, 205–208, 206
    (Experiment 28), 207 (Experiment 29),
    208 (Experiment 30)
organism building blocks, 226, 230–232,
    231 (Experiment 43), 233–234
    (Experiment 44), 235 (Experiment 45)
other living organisms, 224, 226, 227
    (Experiment 40), 228 (Experiment 41),
    229–230 (Experiment 42)
plants, 211, 215–220, 216 (Experiment 34),
    217–218 (Experiment 35),
    219–220 (Experiment 36)
quotations about, 203
in science education, 204
Biomes and ecosystems, 243, 246–249, 365
    experiments, 247 (Experiment 52), 248–249
    (Experiment 53), 250 (Experiment 54)
Biosphere, 151, 365
Biosphere 2 project, 257 (Web site)
Birds:
    beak models, 239, 241–242 (Experiment 49)
    census of, 224, 225 (Experiment 39)
    instruction units on, 75–76
Black scientists, 90, 92, 93 (table), 117 (Web site)
Bloom's Taxonomy, 114–115

Bohr, Niels, 299
Bombs, atomic, 9, 10 (image), 302, 305 (image)
Bonding, 266, 276, 278 (Experiment 67), 280,
    281 (Experiment 69)
Book lists, 353
Books in library, estimating, 153
    (Experiment 1)
Booms (equipment), 196
Boston Museum of Science, 65 (Web site)
Bouchet, Edward Alexander, 93 (table)
Boyle, Robert, 286
Boyle's Law, 286
Brachiosaurus dinosaurs, 242
Brackish water, 197 (Experiment 25)
Bradley, Omar, 9
Brandt, Hennig, 13
Bread, 226, 228 (Experiment 41)
Breathing, measuring peak flow rate
    of, 205, 206 (Experiment 28)
Brewster, David, 42–43, 45 (image)
Brickhouse, N., 89
British system of measurement, 137
Bruner, Jerome, 59, 78
Bybee, R., 56 (Theory Into Practice 2.3)

Calcite, 176–177 (Experiment 14)
California Academy of Sciences,
    The, 65 (Web site)
*California Content Standards
    for Science,* 57
Callinicus, 260
Canada Science and Technology
    Museum, 66 (Web site)
Candles, burning of, 232, 287 (Experiment 73)
Cannon, Annie Jump, 18, 33
Canopy layer, of rainforest, 185, 188
Carbon dioxide, effect on temperature
    changes, 248–249 (Experiment 53)
Carbon monoxide, discovery of, 261
Carnegie Science Center, 65 (Web site)
Cartesian divers, 73, 290 (Experiment 75)
Carver, George Washington, 93 (table)
Cell membrane, 215

Cell packing, 226, 230, 231 (Experiment 43)

Cell phones, 8, 9 (image)

Cells, 215, 256 (Web site)
  animal, 221, 223–224 (Experiment 38)
  definition of, 365
  as natural forms, 232, 235 (Experiment 45)
  plant, 215, 217, 217–218 (Experiment 35)

Cell wall, 215

Census, 221, 224, 225 (Experiment 39), 365

Center for Educational Resources, 202 (Web site)

Center for Learning Technologies in Urban
    Schools, The (LETUS), 85 (Web site)

Centers for Disease Control, 147 (Web site)

Centrifugal force, 313, 314 (Experiment 83)

Cesium, 317

Chambered nautilus seashells, 21

Charles, Jacques, 286

Charts:
  KWL, 76
  soil classification, 179 (image)

Checklist, safety, 146–147

Chemical History of a Candle,
    The (Faraday), 43–44

Chemical potential energy, 295
    (Experiment 78)

Chemical weapons and poisons, 261

Chemistry, xxv, 259–297, 296 (Web sites)
  atoms, elements, and molecules,
      266–268, 269 (image), 270
      (Experiment 61), 271 (Experiment 62),
      272 (Experiment 63)
  definition of, 366
  fuels, 289, 291–295, 292 (Experiment 76), 293
      (Experiment 77), 295 (Experiment 78)
  inorganic, 260
  matter, 268, 273–280, 274 (Experiment 64),
      275 (Experiment 65), 277 (Experiment
      66), 278 (Experiment 67), 279
      (Experiment 68), 281 (Experiment 69)
  measurement in, 262–266, 263 (Experiment
      58), 265–266 (Experiment 59),
      267 (Experiment 60)
  organic, 260

  physical, 260
  pressure, 283, 286–289, 287 (Experiment 73),
      288 (Experiment 74), 290 (Experiment 75)
  quotations about, 259
  in science education, 260–262
  temperature, 280, 282–283, 282
      (Experiment 70), 284 (Experiment 71),
      285 (Experiment 72)

Chernobyl nuclear power plant accident,
    61, 62 (image)

Chinchar, Alan, 42 (image)

Chloroplast, 217

Cholera, 27–28

Chromatography, 237, 238–239
    (Experiment 47)

Chromosomes, 237

Ciba Specialty Chemicals Exemplary
    Middle Level and High School Science
    Teaching Awards, 360

Circuits, electrical, 334, 336 (Experiment 98)

Clarke, Arthur C., 6, 262

Classification, 209, 210 (image), 211
  definition of, 366
  developing systems of, 213 (Experiment 32)
  Linnaean system of, 136, 209,
      211, 214 (Experiment 33)
  science process skills, 136
  soil, 179 (image)
  using senses, 209, 212 (Experiment 31)

Classroom observation, 124–125, 142 (Web site)

Class Web sites, 353

Climate, 182, 184, 211, 366
  See also Weather and climate

Clocks:
  atomic, 317
  water, 308, 310

Clouds, 182, 183–184 (Experiment 18), 189,
    192 (Experiment 22)

Coal, 289, 294

Cognition, situated, 80–81, 370

Cognitive demand, 114–115

Cold fusion, 28–29

Cole, M., 80

Cole, Rebecca, 93 (table)

Collaborative group work, 124–125

College Science Teaching, 356

Collins, Harry, 28, 29

Color:

   blending of, 330, 332 (Experiment 95)

   of clouds, 189, 192 (Experiment 22)

   scattering of, 189, 191, 192

      (Experiment 22), 193 (Experiment 23)

   See also Light

Colorado teacher proficiency themes, 138

Columbus, Christopher, 33

Columbus Egg Problem, 33

Comenius, Jan Amos, 41, 43 (image)

Communication, 8, 9 (image), 24–25, 137, 366

Communism, 32, 366

Community, in sociocultural

   theory, 80–82

Compasses, 152, 154 (Experiment 2)

Competitions, science, 114

Compounds, 260, 276–278, 366

Computing, electronic, 303

Conant, F. R., 96

Concentration of chemical substances, 264,

   267 (Experiment 60)

Concept maps, 73–74, 74–75

   (Theory Into Practice 3.1), 366

Conceptual literacy, 57

   (Theory Into Practice 2.3)

Concrete physical models, 47, 48 (image)

Conferences, 356

Connecticut Yankee in King Arthur's Court, A

   (Twain), 6, 38, 39 (image)

Consequences, unintended, 246, 250

   (Experiment 54)

Constructivism, 69, 70, 85 (Web site), 366

Continuing education credits, 357

Control of variables, 24, 366

Convection currents, 167, 169

   (Experiment 10), 170

Cooking, 277–278

   See also Food

Copernicus, Nicolas, 149, 301, 302 (image)

Cosmology, 155, 157, 159–160

   (Experiment 5), 366

Cosmos, 155, 157–161, 158

   (Experiment 4), 159–160

   (Experiment 5), 162 (Experiment 6)

Council for Exceptional Children,

   118 (Web site)

Covalent bonds, 266

Craftsman NSTA Young Inventors

   Awards Program, 356

Creativity, 25–26, 366

Crick, Francis, 234, 237

Cross-age tutoring, 108

Crystalline rocks, 177

Crystals, 173, 174 (Experiment 13),

   276, 277 (Experiment 66)

Cubits, 305–306

Cumulative assessment, 126, 127

Curie, Marie, 91 (table)

Currents, convection, 167, 169

   (Experiment 10), 170

Curriculum:

   multicultural education and, 106–107

   teacher-proof, 344, 345

Cytoplasm, 215

Cytosine, 236 (Experiment 46)

Dalton, John, 261–262, 268

D'Amato, J. D., 97

Davy, Humphry, 261–262

DeBoer, G. E., 51

Delta Education/CPO Science Awards

   for Excellence in Inquiry-Based

   Science Teaching, 360

Demeter, 161, 165

Density, 137, 273, 275 (Experiment 65), 366

Departments of education, state,

   145–146

Developmental psychologists, 59

Dewey, John, 45–47

Diagnostic assessment, 126, 366

Diamond lattice structures, 262

Dietz, Robert, 170

Direction, determining using compass, 152, 154 (Experiment 2)

Disabilities. *See* Exceptionalities

Diseases, 7–8, 254–255 (Experiment 57), 255, 261, 262

Disinterestedness, 32, 367

Dispersion, 333 (Experiment 96)

Dissection, owl pellet, 221, 222 (Experiment 37)

Diversity in science/science education, 87–119

  classroom strategies for, 102–115

  education reforms and, 99–102

  English language learners, 96–98, 110–112, 112 (Theory Into Practice 4.5), 118

  exceptionalities, students with, 95–96, 97(table), 108–110, 110 (Theory Into Practice 4.4), 118

  gender, 89–90, 91 (table), 102–104, 104 (Theory Into Practice 4.3), 117

  history of, 88–98

  mapping, 102 (Theory Into Practice 4.2)

  quotations about, 87

  race/ethnicity, 90, 92, 93–94 (table), 95, 104–107, 117

  socioeconomic status, 95, 107–108

Diving bells, 289, 290 (Experiment 75)

DNA, 33, 232, 234, 236–237

  definition of, 367

  experiment, 236 (Experiment 46)

Dough, action of yeast in, 226, 228 (Experiment 41)

Douglas, William O., 87

Dreams, role in scientific discoveries, 17

Drew, Charles Richard, 93 (table)

Duschl, R., 89

DVDs/videos, 353

Dynamics, Law of, 310

Dyson, Freeman, 14

Earth:

  composition, layers, movements, and impacts in surface features, 167, 169–173, 169 (Experiment 10), 171 (Experiment 11), 172–173 (Experiment 12)

cycles of, 175, 177, 180–182, 180 (Experiment 16), 181–182 (Experiment 17), 183–184 (Experiment 18)

photograph taken from moon, 204 (image)

tilt of, 165–166 (Experiment 8)

Earth and space science, xxv, 149–202, 202 (Web sites)

  astronomy, 161, 163–164 (Experiment 7), 163–167, 165–166 (Experiment 8), 168 (Experiment 9)

  atmosphere, 189, 191–194, 192 (Experiment 22), 193 (Experiment 23), 194 (Experiment 24)

  content standards, 364

  cosmos, 155–154, 157–161, 158 (Experiment 4), 159–160 (Experiment 5), 162 (Experiment 6)

  definition of, 367

  Earth cycles, 175, 177, 180–182, 180 (Experiment 16), 181–182 (Experiment 17), 183–184 (Experiment 18)

  Earth's composition, layers, movements, and impacts in surface features, 167, 169–173, 169 (Experiment 10), 171 (Experiment 11), 172–173 (Experiment 12)

  measuring and estimating in, 152–155, 153 (Experiment 1), 154 (Experiment 2), 156–157 (Experiment 3)

  quotations about, 149–150

  rocks and minerals, 173–175, 174 (Experiment 13), 176–177 (Experiment 14), 178–179 (Experiment 15)

  in science education, 150–152

  water and oceans, 195–200, 197 (Experiment 25), 198–199 (Experiment 26), 199–200 (Experiment 27)

  weather and climate, 182, 184–189, 186 (Experiment 19), 187–188 (Experiment 20), 190–191 (Experiment 21)

Earthquakes, 170, 172–173 (Experiment 12)

Earth Sciences Curriculum Project, 51

*Easy Introduction to the Knowledge
    of Nature and Reading the Holy Scriptures,
    An* (Trimmer), 41–42
Ecological niches, 242, 245 (Experiment 51)
Economic benefits to science
    education reform, 52, 53 (image)
Ecosystems, 246, 367
    See also Biomes and ecosystems
EcoTarium, 66 (Web site)
EDC Center for Science Education,
    339 (Web site)
Edison, Thomas Alva, 24, 97 (table)
Editors, 242, 243 (image)
Education, banking model of, 58–59
Educational toys and games, 353
Education reforms:
    benefits to, 52–54, 55 (image), 56
    diversity and, 99–102
    history of, 344–355
    personal effect of, 52 (Theory Into
        Practice 2.2)
    science education and, 49–51, 52 (Theory
        into Practice 2.2), 57–58, 143–144
    Sputnik and, 49–51, 344
    standards-based, 51, 52
        (Theory Into Practice 2.2), 79
Egg frying experiment, 162 (Experiment 6)
Egypt:
    anatomical records, early, 253
    pyramids, 321
Einstein, Albert, 97 (table), 121, 310
Eisenhart, M., 57
EKGs, 205
Electrical circuits, 334, 336 (Experiment 98)
Electricity, 330, 334–337
    generated by batteries, 289, 291, 292
        (Experiment 76)
    static, 317, 320 (Experiment 87)
    See also Magnetism
Electric motors, 25, 70–71, 72 (image)
Electromagnets, 25, 70, 334, 337 (Experiment 99)
Electronic computing, 303
Electronic portfolios, 140 (Theory Into
    Practice 5.5), 142 (Web site)

Electrons, 266
Electroscopes, 320 (Experiment 87)
Elementary and Secondary Education
    Act, 344
Elements, 266
    definition of, 367
    in food, 268, 272 (Experiment 63)
    periodic table of, 268, 269 (image)
Elephants, 242
Emergent layer, of rainforest, 188
Emerson, Ralph Waldo, 149
*Encyclopédie, ou Dictionnaire Raisonné des
    Sciences, des Arts, et des Métiers*
    (Encyclopedia, or a Systematic
    Dictionary of the Sciences, Arts,
    and Crafts), 39, 40 (image)
Endoplasmic reticulum, 215
Energy:
    coal as source of, 289, 294
    definition of, 367
    forms of, 315, 317–320, 318
        (Experiment 85), 319
        (Experiment 86), 320 (Experiment 87)
    kinetic, 315, 317, 318
        (Experiment 85), 368
    potential, 295 (Experiment 78), 315,
        317, 318 (Experiment 85), 369
    solar, 157, 161, 162 (Experiment 6),
        291, 293 (Experiment 77)
Energy system, 151, 367
Engines, steam, 8 (image), 301, 303 (image)
English language learners, xxiv, 96–98,
    110–112, 112 (Theory Into Practice 4.5),
    118 (Web site)
    definition of, 367
    translation of materials for parents, 353
English moths, 237, 239
Environmental benefits to science education
    reform, 53, 55 (image)
Environmental Protection Agency,
    147 (Web site)
Erosion, 171 (Experiment 11)
Estes/Space Foundation/NSTA
    "Space Educator Award," 360

Estimation:
    in Earth and space science, 152, 153
        (Experiment 1)
    large numbers of objects, 152, 153
        (Experiment 1)
    size of very small objects, 205,
        207 (Experiment 29)
    volume, 262–264, 263 (Experiment 58)
    See also Measurement
Ethics:
    in biology, 204
    experimental animals, treatment of,
        63 (Theory Into Practice 2.5)
    research participants, treatment of, 348
    in science, 61, 62 (image), 63
Ethnicity/race, 90, 92, 93–94 (table),
    95, 104–107, 117 (Web site)
Eucaryotes, 224, 367
Evaporation, 268, 271 (Experiment 62), 280,
    282 (Experiment 70)
Evolution, 237, 239, 241–243
    definition of, 367
    experiments, 241–242 (Experiment 49), 244
        (Experiment 50), 245 (Experiment 51)
    intelligent design versus, 13
Exceptionalities:
    definition of, 367
    scientists with, 97(table)
    students with, 95–96, 108–110, 110 (Theory
        Into Practice 4.4), 118 (Web site)
Expanding universe, 155, 157,
    159–160 (Experiment 5)
Experience gap, narrowing, 108
Experiments:
    designing, 77, 338 (Experiment 100)
    limitations on, 17–18
    modifying for students with disabilities,
        110 (Theory Into Practice 4.4)
Explorit Science Center, 65 (Web site)
Exponential functions, 288
    (Experiment 30)
Extension activities, 114
Exxon Valdez oil spill, 196
Eye placement on animals, 242, 243 (image)

Family science nights, 353
Faraday, Michael, 17, 25, 43–44, 70–71, 334
Ferm, Ransom K., 150
Fernbank Museum of Natural
    History, 65 (Web site)
Feynman, Richard P., 17, 299
Fibonacci, Leonardo, 21
Fibonaccian sequence, 21, 23, 288
    (Experiment 30)
Field experiences, 128–129
Finkel, E., 57
Finlay, Carlos, 94 (table)
5Es model, 78
Fizz test (mineral identification),
    176–177 (Experiment 14)
Fleischmann, Martin, 28
Flies, 122–123
Flight, powered, 9 (image), 302
Floating needle on water, 278 (Experiment 67)
Florida:
    science education materials, 146
    teacher proficiency themes, 138
Florida Museum of Natural History,
    The, 65 (Web site)
Flu epidemic, 255
Food:
    bacteria in, 226, 229–230 (Experiment 42)
    chemical experiments involving, 260
    choices of, 249, 251 (Experiment 55)
    compounds, mixtures, and solutions
        in, 277–278
    elements in, 268, 272 (Experiment 63)
    nutritional labels on, 272 (Experiment 63)
Food webs, 246, 247 (Experiment 52)
Foot, as standard of measurement,
    306, 307 (Experiment 79)
Force, 308, 310, 312–315
    centrifugal, 313, 314 (Experiment 83)
    definition of, 137, 367
    experiments, 312 (Experiment 82),
        314 (Experiment 83), 316
        (Experiment 84)
Ford, Henry, 97 (table)
Forest floor, 185

Formative assessment, 126–127, 367
Fort Worth Museum of Science and History, 65 (Web site)
Fossil fuels, 161, 289, 294
Fradd, S., 57
Franklin, Benjamin, 25, 326
Franklin, Rosalind, 33, 234, 237
Franklin Institute, 202 (Web site)
"Freedom" (space station), 42 (image)
Freezing point, 285 (Experiment 72)
Freire, Paulo, 59
Frequency, 326, 367
Freshwater salinity, 197 (Experiment 25)
Froebel, Friedrich, 45
Fuels, 289, 291–295
    alternative, 289
    definition of, 367
    experiments, 292 (Experiment 76), 293 (Experiment 77), 295 (Experiment 78)
    fossil, 161, 289, 294
Functional literacy, 56 (Theory Into Practice 2.3)
Fungi, 226, 228 (Experiment 41)

Galaxies, spiral, 21, 22 (image)
Galena, 176–177 (Experiment 14)
Galilean telescopes, 205
Galilean thermometers, 264
Galileo, 6, 7 (image)
    physics, 301
    thermometers, 264
    water clock use, 308, 310
Games, educational, 353
Gardner, H., 114
Gases, 273, 274 (Experiment 64), 368
Gay-Lussac, Joseph, 261–262
Gender:
    in collaborative group work, 124–125
    diversity in science/science education, 89–90, 91 (table), 102–104, 104 (Theory Into Practice 4.3), 117 (Web site)
    See also Women scientists
General Electric Corporation, 40–41

Generation, spontaneous, 122–123
Genes, 237, 368
Genetic code, 232, 234, 236–237
    experiments, 236 (Experiment 46), 238–239 (Experiment 47), 240 (Experiment 48)
Genetic defects, 237, 240 (Experiment 48)
Gente, Arnold, 170
Genus, 209
Geological Society of America, 202 (Web site)
Geologic time, 155, 156–157 (Experiment 3)
Georgia Institute of Technology, 77–78
Germination, 215, 216 (Experiment 34), 368
Germ theory, 53–54, 55 (image)
Gifted and talented students, 112–115, 115 (Theory Into Practice 4.6)
Giraffes, 242
Girls, strategies for working with, 102–104, 104 (Theory Into Practice 4.3)
    See also Gender
Glass armonicas, 326
Global positioning system (GPS), 8
Glucometers, 205
Goal changes to science curriculum, 106–107
Goals 2000 (National Governors' Association), 344
Golden Mean, 21
Golden Section (Phi), 21, 22 (image)
Good, Arthur, 43, 44, 45 (image)
Good, R., 88
Goodall, Jane, 91 (table)
Goodyear, Charles, 16
Gowan, D., 73
GPS. See Global positioning system
Grants, 359–361, 361 (Theory Into Practice 10.5)
"Greek fire," 260
Greenhouse effect, 189, 246, 248–249 (Experiment 53), 368
Grosser, Arthur, 259
Groundwater, pollution effect on, 180 (Experiment 16)
Guanine, 236 (Experiment 46)
Guericke, Otto von, 286

Gunpowder, 260–261
Gwynne, Peter, 87

Habitats, 245 (Experiment 51)
Hades, 161, 165
Haeckel, Ernst, 54 (image), 210
    (image), 232
Hair, estimating width of, 207 (Experiment 29)
Hands-on model of science education, 45–47
Hardness test (mineral identification),
    176–177 (Experiment 14)
Harmonics, 326, 328 (Experiment 92)
Hawaii, climate of, 184
Hawking, Stephen, 97 (table)
Hay, as source of animal feed, 14–15
Hay Theory of History, 14–15
Head Start, 344
Hearing impairments, 109
Hearing loss, 237, 240 (Experiment 48)
Heart rates, measuring, 205
Henry I (king), 306
Herbert, Don, 44
Hess, Harry, 170
Hewitt, N. M., 90
Hidden shapes activity, 19 (Theory Into
    Practice 1.2), 20 (image)
Hildegard of Bingen, Saint, 91 (table)
Hippocrates, 253
Hispanic scientists, 92, 94 (table), 117 (Web site)
History:
    Hay Theory of, 14–15
    "Whig" interpretation of, 39
History and nature of science content standards, 364
Hodgkin, Dorothy Crowfoot, 91 (table)
Holmes, Arthur, 167, 170
Holmyard, E. J., 261
Hook, Robert, 205
Howard University, 90, 92 (image)
Howes, E., 90
Hubble, Edwin, 155, 157
Human body and health, 249, 251–255, 251
    (Experiment 55), 252–253 (Experiment 56),
    254–255 (Experiment 57)

Hurricanes, 151, 151 (image), 185
Hutton, James, 150
Huxley, Thomas Henry, 5
Hydrogen bonds, 266
Hydrosphere, 151, 368
Hypatia, 91 (table)
Hypothesis box activity, 29–31
    (Theory Into Practice 1.3)

Ice cream, 280, 283, 285 (Experiment 72)
Icons used in text, xxiv
IDEA. *See* Individuals With
    Disabilities Education Act
Igneous rocks, 177
Illinois recertification guidelines, 347 (Web site)
Illiteracy, 56 (Theory Into Practice 2.3)
Illnesses, 7–8, 254–255
    (Experiment 57), 255, 261, 262
Imperial (British) system of measurement, 137
Inclusive education, 95–96
Independent science projects, 114
Indiana University, 35 (Web site)
Indian Ocean, 195
Individuals With Disabilities
    Education Act (IDEA), 95
Inertia, 310, 312–313, 312
    (Experiment 82), 368
Infectious disease, spreading of,
    254–255 (Experiment 57), 255
Inferring, 136, 368
Influenza epidemic, 255
Information processing model
    of learning, 75–76
Informed skepticism, 26–27, 368
Ingenhousz, Jan, 232
Ingersoll, Robert G., 121
Inorganic chemistry, 260
*Inquiry and the National Science
    Education Standards,* 99
Inquiry-based teaching methods, 346
Institute and Museum of the
    History of Science, 65 (Web site)
Intelligences, multiple, 114

Intelligent design, 13
Interbreeding, 209
Interference, 333 (Experiment 96)
Interviews:
    parent, 354–355 (Theory Into Practice 10.3)
    teacher, 134–135 (Theory Into Practice 5.4)
Inventions, importance of, 48
        (Theory Into Practice 2.1)
    See also specific inventions
Ionic bonds, 266
Isabella, Queen, 33

Jackson, Jesse, 87
Japanese lesson study, 349–351,
        351 (Theory into Practice 10.2)
John Paul III (pope), 5
Journals, professional, 355–356
Joyce, Jeremiah, 42
Jung, Carl, 5

Kaleidoscopes, 42–43, 45 (image)
Katrina, Hurricane, 151 (image), 185
Keilhau, B. M., 149
Kekulé, Till, 17
Kepler, Johannes, 301
Kheonike, 262
Kinetic energy, 315, 317, 318
        (Experiment 85), 368
Knowledge, challenges in
        demonstrating or gaining, 109–110
Kobe, Japan earthquake, 170
Kotule, 262
Kuhn, Thomas, 27, 32
KWL charts, 76

Ladson-Billings, G., 343
Lava, 177
Lave, Jean, 80–81, 82
Lavoisier, Antoine, 25, 261
Lavoisier, Marie, 261
Lawless, D., 69
Law of Dynamics, 310
Law of Inertia, 310

Learning:
    design-based, 77–78, 79 (Theory Into
        Practice 3.2), 85 (Web site), 369
    information processing model of, 75–76
    lifelong, 346, 350
    styles of, 114
    theories of, 83 (Theory Into
        Practice 3.3)
    through rediscovery, 70–74
    See also Teacher professional development
Learning by Design project, 77–78,
        85 (Web site)
Learning centers, 115
Learning disabilities, 109
Learning impairments, 109
Least restrictive environment, 95–96
Lee, O., 57
Leeuwenhoek, Anton van, 205
Legitimate peripheral participation, 80–81
Lemke, J. L., 59
Length, standards for measuring, 305–308,
        307 (Experiment 79)
Leonardo da Vinci, 301
Leopold, Aldo, 203
Leschak, Peter M., 121
Lesson study, 349–351, 351
        (Theory into Practice 10.2)
LETUS. *See* Center for Learning
        Technologies in Urban Schools, The
Leveling assignments, 115
Levers, 299, 324, 325 (Experiment 90)
Life expectancy, 7–8
Lifelong learning, 346, 350
    See also Teacher professional development
Life science content standards, 364
    See also Biology
Light:
    red-shifted, 155, 157
    refraction of, 330, 333 (Experiment 96)
    See also Color
Light bulbs, invention of, 24
Linguistically diverse students.
    See English language learners

Linnaean classification system, 136,
209, 211, 214 (Experiment 33)
Linnaeus, Carl, 136, 209
Liquids:
densities of, 273, 275 (Experiment 65)
serial dilution of, 267 (Experiment 60)
Literacy, scientific, 56–57, 56–57
(Theory Into Practice 2.3), 370
Lithosphere, 151, 368
Loving, C., 88
Lundstrom, John, 13
Luster test (mineral identification), 176–177
(Experiment 14)
Lyell, Charles, 150
Lysosome, 215

Machines, simple, 321–324, 322
(Experiment 88), 323 (Experiment 89),
325 (Experiment 90)
Madeline Hunter model, 345
"Magdeburg Sphere" experiment, 286
Maggots, generation of, 122–123
Magic versus science, 6, 13
Magma, 177
Magnetism, 330, 334, 335 (Experiment 97),
337 (Experiment 99), 368
See also Electricity
Magnetism test (mineral identification),
176–177 (Experiment 14)
Magnetite, 176–177 (Experiment 14)
Manchester Museum, 65 (Web site)
Marcus Aurelius (emperor), 121
Marion, S., 57
Marker experiment, 238–239 (Experiment 47)
Marshmallow molecule models,
270 (Experiment 61)
Martin, J. R., 73
Maryland recertification guidelines, 347
(Web site)
Mason, C. L., 96
Mass, 137, 308, 309 (Experiment 80), 368
Master's degree, 357
Matches, safety, 13

Matter, 268, 273–280
definition of, 368
experiments, 274 (Experiment 64), 275
(Experiment 65), 277 (Experiment 66),
278 (Experiment 67), 279 (Experiment 68),
281 (Experiment 69)
physical and chemical changes in, 268, 273
Maxwell, James Clerk, 330
Mayer, Maria Goeppert, 91 (table)
McBay, S. M., 105
McClintock, Barbara, 89
Measurement:
in biology, 205–208, 206 (Experiment 28),
207 (Experiment 29), 208 (Experiment 30)
in chemistry, 262–266, 263 (Experiment 58),
265–266 (Experiment 59), 267
(Experiment 60)
definition of, 368
in Earth and space science, 152, 154
(Experiment 2), 155, 156–157
(Experiment 3)
of heart rates, 205
imperial (British) system of, 137
of mass using balance, 308, 309
(Experiment 80)
metric system of, 137, 306
of peak flow rate of breathing, 205,
206 (Experiment 28)
in physics, 304–310, 307 (Experiment 79),
309 (Experiment 80), 311 (Experiment 81)
of population change, 288, 288
(Experiment 30)
as science process skill, 137
standards for measuring length, 305–308, 307
(Experiment 79)
of time, 308, 310, 311 (Experiment 81)
of wind, 185, 187–188 (Experiment 20)
See also Estimation
Medical research, 253
Mendeleev, Dmitri Ivanovich, 268, 269 (image)
Mentoring, 114
Merton, Robert, 31–32
Metamorphic rocks, 177

Metaphors, 60 (Theory Into Practice 2.4)

Meteorologists, 184, 368

Methods changes to science curriculum, 106

Metric system, 137, 306

Miami Museum of Science, 65 (Web site), 296 (Web site)

Microscopes, 77 (image), 205, 226, 227 (Experiment 40)

Mind and Nature (Bateson), xxi, 20–21

Mineral Information Institute, 202 (Web site)

Minerals, 202 (Web site)

definition of, 175, 368

identification strategies, 175, 176–177 (Experiment 14)

See also Rocks and minerals

Minestrone soup, 277–278

Minimal surfaces, 232, 235 (Experiment 45)

Mixtures, 276–278

definition of, 368

of gases, 189

hot and cold water interactions, 280, 283, 284 (Experiment 71)

separating, 279 (Experiment 68)

Mobility impairments, 109, 110

Modeling for Understanding in Science Education (MUSE), 85 (Web site)

Models:

animal cell, 223–224 (Experiment 38)

aquifers, 180 (Experiment 16)

banking, 58–59

bird beak, 239, 241–242 (Experiment 49)

concrete physical, 47, 48 (image)

convection currents, 169 (Experiment 10)

DNA double helix, 236 (Experiment 46)

earthquake-resistant structures, 172–173 (Experiment 12)

expanding universe, 159–160 (Experiment 5)

5Es, 78

greenhouse effect, 248–249 (Experiment 53)

hands-on, 45–47

human arm, 252–253 (Experiment 56), 253, 255

information processing, 75–76

Madeline Hunter, 345

marshmallow molecule, 270 (Experiment 61)

phases of the moon, 163–164 (Experiment 7)

plant cell, 217–218 (Experiment 35)

seasons, changing, 165–166 (Experiment 8)

smog, 194 (Experiment 24)

solar system, 158 (Experiment 4)

Molecules, 266

building, 268, 270 (Experiment 61)

definition of, 368

physical properties of, 268, 271 (Experiment 62)

Molina, Mario, 94 (table)

Molten rock, 177

Monera, 224, 369

Monturiol, Narciso, 94 (table)

Moon phases, 161, 163–164 (Experiment 7)

Moths, English, 237, 239

Motion pictures, 25–26, 330

Motors, electric, 25, 70–71, 72 (image)

Mountain building and erosion, 171 (Experiment 11)

Mozart, Wolfgang Amadeus, 326

Mr. Wizard, 44

Mulkay, Michael, 32

Multicultural education, 104–107

Multi-dimensional literacy, 57 (Theory Into Practice 2.3)

Multiple intelligences, 114

Multiple representations, 111

MUSE. *See* Modeling for Understanding in Science Education

Museums, 65–66 (Web sites), 132–133 (Theory Into Practice 5.3)

Muybridge, Eadweard, 331 (image)

Mythology, and changes in seasons, 161, 165

Nagasaki, bombing of, 305 (image)

Nanotechnology, 303–304, 305 (image)

NASA Quest Teacher Resources, 339 (Web site)

National Association of Bilingual Education,
    118 (Web site)
National Board Certification (NBC), 357–359,
    358–359 (Theory Into Practice 10.4)
National Board of Professional Teaching
    Standards (NBPTS), 357–358
National Council of Teachers of Mathematics
    (NCTM), 51
National Defense Education Act, 50
National Governors' Association, 344
National Research Council (NRC), 99, 146,
    *see also National Science Education
    Standards*
National Science Education Standards:
    components of, 101, 143–144, 145
    development of, 99
    diverse learners and, 100–102
    educational reform and, 51
    professional development
        standards, 346
    science content standards, 363–364
    science education goals, 56
        (Theory Into Practice 2.3), 57
National Science Teachers Association
    (NSTA), 356 (Web site)
    national science standards, 146
    nature of science, 35 (Web site)
    as professional organization, 355–356
    safety, 147 (Web site)
    science education reforms, 99
Nation at Risk, A, 52, 344
Natural History Museum of Los
    Angeles County, 66 (Web site)
Natural selection, 237, 239
Nautilus seashells, chambered, 21
NBC. *See* National Board Certification
NBPTS. *See* National Board of Professional
    Teaching Standards
NCLB. *See* No Child Left Behind Act
NCTM. *See* National Council
    of Teachers of Mathematics
Needham, James G., 203
Needles, floating on water, 278 (Experiment 67)

Nero (emperor), 283
Nespor, Jan, 81–82
Neutrons, 266
Newbery, John, 41
New Madrid, Missouri earthquakes, 170
New Mexico Museum of Natural History
    and Science, The, 66 (Web site)
Newton, Isaac:
    moving objects, 310
    nature of science, 5, 6
    physics, 301
    portraits of, xxii, xxii (image), 7 (image)
    refraction, 330
    as scientist with disabilities, 97 (table)
Newtonian reflecting telescopes, 205
*Newtonian System of Philosophy,
    The,* 41, 44 (image)
New York City, social and geographic
    structures in, 250 (Experiment 54)
1984 (Orwell), 8
Nitrous oxide, discovery of, 261
No Child Left Behind Act (NCLB), 58, 345
Nominal literacy, 56 (Theory Into Practice 2.3)
Norms, scientific inquiry, 31–32
North Carolina Museum of Life
    and Science, 66 (Web site)
Notebaert Nature Museum, The, 65 (Web site)
Novak, Joseph, 73
NRC. *See* National Research Council
*NSES. See National Science Education
    Standards*
NSTA. *See* National Science Teachers
    Association
Nuclear bombs, 9, 10 (image), 302,
    305 (image)
Nuclear decay and half-life, 317,
    319 (Experiment 86)
Nuclear fusion, 161
Nuclear power, 61, 62 (image)
Nucleus, 215
Numerical literacy (numeracy), 56
Nutrition, 249, 251 (Experiment 55)
Nutritional labels, 272 (Experiment 63)

Oakes, J., 90
Observation, xxv, 121–135
    classroom, 124–125, 142 (Web site)
    definition of, 369
    forms for, 129, 130–131 (Theory
        Into Practice 5.2), 132–133
        (Theory Into Practice 5.3),
        134–135 (Theory Into Practice 5.4)
    quotations about, 121
    science lesson, 130–131 (Theory
        Into Practice 5.2)
    scientific, 122–123, 142 (Web site)
    traffic pattern experiment, 123–124
        (Theory Into Practice 5.1)
    See also Science process skills
Oceans:
    floor of, 196, 198–199 (Experiment 26)
    oil spill clean-up, 196, 199–200 (Experiment 27)
    salinity of, 195–196, 197 (Experiment 25)
    temperature of water, 280, 283
    See also Water
Ochoa, Ellen, 94 (table)
Ochoa, Severo, 94 (table)
Odyssey of the Mind, 114
Oersted, Hans Christian, 334
Oil spill clean-up, 196, 199–200
    (Experiment 27)
Ongoing assessment, 126–127
"On the Mode of Communication of Cholera"
    (Snow), 27
Oppenheimer, J. Robert, 299
Optical telescopes, 205
Optics, 326, 369
Orbus Sensualium Pictus (Comenius),
    41, 43 (image)
Oregon Museum of Science and Industry, 66
    (Web site), 296 (Web site)
Organelles, 215
Organic chemistry, 260
Organism building blocks, 226,
    230–232, 231 (Experiment 43), 233–234
    (Experiment 44), 235 (Experiment 45)
Organizations, professional, 355–356

Organized skepticism, 32, 369
Orienteering, 152, 154 (Experiment 2)
Orrery, 47, 48 (image), 369
Orwell, George, 8
Owl pellet dissection, 221, 222
    (Experiment 37)
Oxford English Dictionary, 6
Oxygen, 189, 211, 261
Ozone layer, 189

Pacific Ocean, 195
Pagels, Heinz, 38
Pakistan earthquake, 170
Pangaea, 167
Paracelsus, 261
Paradigms and paradigm shifts, 32–33, 369
Parents:
    interviewing, 354–355 (Theory Into
        Practice 10.3)
    involving and engaging, 108, 352–355,
        354–355 (Theory Into Practice 10.3)
Paris, John Ayrton, 25, 42, 43, 330
Pasteur, Louis, 16
"Pattern that connects," xxi, 20–21
Peak flow rate, measuring, 205, 206
    (Experiment 28)
Pedagogical content knowledge, 346
Pedagogical features of text, xxii–xxiv
"Pedigree of Man" (Haeckel), 210 (image)
Peer teaching, 128
Peer tutoring, reciprocal, 108
Periodic table of elements, 268, 269 (image)
Peripheral participation, legitimate, 80–81
Persephone, 161, 165
Persistence of vision, 330, 331
    (Experiment 94)
Phantascopes, 25–26
Phi (Golden Section), 21, 22 (image)
Phillips, P., 90
Philosophy in Sport (Paris), 42
"Philosophy of Toys, A" (Baudelaire), 72
Phones, cell, 8, 9 (image)
Phosphorus, discovery of, 13

Photosynthesis, 211, 232, 233–234
    (Experiment 44), 291, 369
Physical chemistry, 260
Physical science content standards, 364
    See also Chemistry; Physics
Physical Science Study Committee, 51
Physics, xxv, 299–340, 339 (Web sites)
    amusement park, 313, 339 (Web site)
    definition of, 369
    electricity and magnetism, 330, 334–337,
        335 (Experiment 97), 336
        (Experiment 98), 337 (Experiment 99)
    energy forms, 315, 317–320, 318
        (Experiment 85), 319 (Experiment 86),
        320 (Experiment 87)
    force, 310, 312–315, 312
        (Experiment 82), 314
        (Experiment 83), 316 (Experiment 84)
    light and color, 326, 330, 331
        (Experiment 94), 332 (Experiment 95),
        333 (Experiment 96)
    machines, simple, 321–324, 322
        (Experiment 88), 323 (Experiment 89),
        325 (Experiment 90)
    measurement in, 304–310, 307
        (Experiment 79), 309 (Experiment 80),
        311 (Experiment 81)
    quotations about, 299
    in science education, 300–304, 305 (image)
    sound, 324, 326, 327 (Experiment 91), 328
        (Experiment 92), 329 (Experiment 93)
Piaget, Jean, 24, 47, 69, 70, 71
Pinch, Trevor, 28, 29
Planets, 158 (Experiment 4)
    See also Cosmos
Plank, Max, 26–27
Plants, 215–220
    cells of, 215, 217, 217–218 (Experiment 35)
    climate and, 211
    germination of, 215, 216 (Experiment 34)
    growth of, 219, 219–220 (Experiment 36)
Plate tectonics, 167, 170, 171
    (Experiment 11), 369

Plutarch, 321
Polio, 7
Pollution:
    air, 191, 194 (Experiment 24)
    water, 180 (Experiment 16)
Polymerase chain reaction, 237
Polymer Science Learning Center,
    296 (Web site)
Pond water, 226, 227 (Experiment 40)
Pons, Stanley, 28
Poor students, 95, 107–108
Population change, measuring,
    288, 288 (Experiment 30)
Portfolios, xxv, 137–140, 142 (Web site)
    content and structure of, 138–139
    definition of, 369
    electronic, 140 (Theory Into Practice 5.5)
    professional development themes
        in, 139–140
    professional statement and portfolio
        introduction in, 139
Positional terms and phrases, 111
Post-assessment, 126, 127
Postman, Neil, 5, 37
Potato chip packing experiment, 231
    (Experiment 43)
Potential energy, 295 (Experiment 78), 315, 317,
    318 (Experiment 85), 369
Poverty, 95, 107–108
Practical benefits to science education reform,
    53–54, 55 (image)
Practicum teaching experiences, 128–129
Pre-assessment, 126
Precision, 308, 369
Predicting, 136–137, 369
Pressure, 283, 286–289
    definition of, 369
    experiments, 287 (Experiment 73), 288
        (Experiment 74), 290 (Experiment 75)
Prey, eye placement on, 242, 243 (image)
Priestly, Joseph, 232, 261
*Principles and Standards for School
    Mathematics*, 51

Procedural literacy, 57 (Theory Into
    Practice 2.3)
Professional development standards, 346
    See also Teacher professional development
Professional journals and publications,
    355–356
Professional organizations, 355–356
Professional statement, in portfolio, 139
Progress, science as, 39–41, 42 (image), 61
Project-based science, 77–78, 79 (Theory
    Into Practice 3.2), 85 (Web site), 369
Protons, 266
Psychologists, social and developmental, 59
Publications, professional, 355–356
Public Law 94-142 (Individuals with
    Disabilities Education Act), 95
Pulleys, 321, 322 (Experiment 88)
Pyramids, Egyptian, 321
Pyrite, 175, 176–177 (Experiment 14)

Quackwatch, 35 (Web site)
Quartz, 176–177 (Experiment 14)
Quimby, Edith Hinckley, 91 (table)

Rabbits, introduction into Australia, 246
Race/ethnicity, 90, 92, 93–94 (table), 95,
    104–107, 117 (Web site)
Radiation waste, 61, 62 (image)
Radiolarians, 232
Railroads, invention of, 301, 304 (image)
Rainfall, tracking, 184 185, 186
    (Experiment 19)
Rainforests, 185, 190–191 (Experiment 21)
Ramps, 321, 323 (Experiment 89)
Reader's guide, in portfolio, 139
Reagan, Ronald, 40–41
Recertification requirements, 347
    (Theory Into Practice 10.1)
Reciprocal peer tutoring, 108
Recognition programs, 356
Redi, Francesco, 122–123
Rediscovery, learning through, 70–74
Red-shifted light, 155, 157

Rees, Martin, 149
Reflecting on field experiences, 128–129
Reflections, in portfolio, 140
Reforms. *See* Education reforms
Refraction, 330, 333 (Experiment 96)
Relative mass, 309 (Experiment 80)
Religion and science, 41–42
Replicability, 23, 28, 370
Representations, multiple, 111
Research lessons, 349, 350
    See also Lesson study
Resonance, 324, 326, 329
    (Experiment 93), 370
Ribosomes, 215
Rickover, Hyman, 50
Robert Carleton Award, 356
Rock cycle, 177, 181–182 (Experiment 17)
Rocks and minerals, 173–175,
    174 (Experiment 13), 176–177 (Experiment
    14), 178–179 (Experiment 15), 370
Rogoff, B., 80
Rosebery, A. S., 96
Rosser, S. V., 89, 90
Rossiter, M., 89
Roth, W.-M., 69
Rubber, vulcanized, 16
Rudolph, J. L., 50
Rutherford, F. J., 99–100

Sabin, Florence Rena, 91 (table)
Sabin, Louis, 61
Safety, 146–147, 147 (Web site)
Salad dressings, 273
Salinity, of water, 195–196, 197 (Experiment 25)
    See also Salt
Salk, Jonas, 7
Salt:
    freezing point of ice and, 285 (Experiment 72)
    table, 266
    See also Salinity, of water
Salt crystals, 276, 277 (Experiment 66)
San Francisco earthquake, 170
Scaffolding, 107–108

Scales:
  geologic time, 155, 156–157 (Experiment 3)
  solar system, 155, 158 (Experiment 4)
  as tool, 81 (image)
School-level improvement teams, 345
School of Mathematics Study Group, 51
Science:
  concepts versus science process skills, 136
  content standards, 363–364
  definition of, 6
  development of disciplines, 6
  ethics in, 61, 62 (image), 63
  importance of, 7–10, 13–15
  learning language of, 59–60
  magic versus, 6, 13
  metaphors in, 60 (Theory Into Practice 2.4)
  nature of science cards activity, 11–12
      (Theory Into Practice 1.1)
  paradigms and paradigm shifts in, 32–33
  in personal and social perspectives, 364
  as progress, 39–41, 42 (image), 61
  project-based, 77–78, 79 (Theory Into
      Practice 3.2), 85 (Web site), 369
  religion and, 41–42
Science Amusante, La (Good), 44, 45 (image)
Science and Children, 355–356
Science and technology content
      standards, 364
Science as inquiry content standards, 363
Science competitions, 114
Science content, importance of, 143–145
Science Controversies On-line: Partnerships in
      Education (SCOPE), 85 (Web site)
Science education:
  biology in, 204
  chemistry in, 260–262
  creating context for, 2
  Earth and space science in, 150–152
  educational reforms and, 49–51, 52 (Theory
      into Practice 2.2), 57–58, 143–144
  goals of, 58–60
  hands-on model of, 45–47
  historical role of, 39, 41–47, 48 (image)
  physics in, 300–304, 305 (image)

  reforms in, 52–54, 55 (image), 56, 143–144
  Sputnik and, 49–51
  state standards, 145–146
Science fairs, 114
Science for All Americans
      (Rutherford & Ahlgren), 99–100
Science Museum of Virginia,
      66 (Web site)
Science museums, 65–66 (Web sites),
      132–133 (Theory Into Practice 5.3)
Science Olympiad, 114
Science process skills, 136–137
  See also Observation
Science Scope, 356
Science Teacher, The, 356
Science-technology-society movement, 51
Science World, 66 (Web site)
Scientific Dialogues (Joyce), 42
Scientific inquiry, xx
  in astronomy, 17–18
  combining qualities to address
      scientific questions, 27–29
  definition of, 370
  norms of, 31–32
  process of, 16–18
  qualities of, 23–27
Scientific literacy, 56–57, 56–57
      (Theory Into Practice 2.3), 370
Scientific observation, 122–123
  Web site, 142 (Web site)
Scientific theory, 370
Scientists:
  African American, 90, 92, 93
      (table), 117 (Web site)
  with disabilities, 97 (table)
  Hispanic, 92, 94 (table), 117 (Web site)
  stereotypical, 88, 98 (Theory
      Into Practice 4.1)
  women, 33, 91 (table)
SciTech Hands-On Museum,
      66 (Web site)
SCOPE. *See* Science Controversies
      On-line: Partnerships in Education (SCOPE)
Seashells, chambered nautilus, 21

Seasons:
   changes in, 161, 165, 165–166
      (Experiment 8)
   orrery for teaching about, 47, 48 (image)
Second-language activity, sheltered,
      112 (Theory Into Practice 4.5)
Section 504 of the Rehabilitation Act, 95
Sedimentary rocks, 177
Seed germination, 215, 216 (Experiment 34), 368
Semiotics, social, 59–60
Severio, Joseph, 294 (image)
Seymour, E., 90
Shadows, 167, 168 (Experiment 9)
Shapes, hidden, 19 (Theory Into
      Practice 1.2), 20 (image)
Sheep, eye placement on, 243 (image)
Shell Science Teaching Award, 356, 360
Sheltered second-language activity, 112
      (Theory Into Practice 4.5)
Shulman, Lee, 346
Simple machines, 321–324, 322
      (Experiment 88), 323 (Experiment 89),
      325 (Experiment 90)
Simulations:
   earthquake, 172–173 (Experiment 12)
   hearing loss, 240 (Experiment 48)
   oil spill clean-up, 199–200 (Experiment 27)
   sonar, 198–199 (Experiment 26)
   spread of infectious disease, 254–255
      (Experiment 57)
Site-based management, 345
Situated cognition, 80–81, 370
Size, estimating, 205, 207 (Experiment 29)
Skeleton reconstruction, animal,
      221, 222 (Experiment 37)
Skepticism, informed, 26–27, 368
Skepticism, organized, 32, 369
Skimmers, 196
Sky, color of, 191, 193 (Experiment 23)
Skyhooks, 72–73
Smithsonian National Museum of Natural
      History, The, 66 (Web site)
Smog, 191, 194 (Experiment 24)
Snow, John, 27–28

Soap, 280, 281 (Experiment 69)
Social psychologists, 59
Social semiotics, 59–60
Sociocultural theory, 80–82
Socioeconomic status, 95, 107–108
Soda water, discovery of, 261
Soil, 175, 178–179 (Experiment 15),
      211, 370
Solar energy, 157, 161, 162 (Experiment 6),
      291, 293 (Experiment 77)
Solar system, 155, 158 (Experiment 4),
      302 (image)
   See also Cosmos
Solutions, 276–278, 370
Sonar simulation, 198–199 (Experiment 26)
Sorbents, 196
Sound:
   conduction of, 326, 327 (Experiment 91)
   harmonic, 326, 328 (Experiment 92)
Sound waves, 324, 326, 329 (Experiment 93)
Southern Ocean, 195
Soviet Union, 49–50
Space elevators, 262
Space science. See Earth and space science
Species, 209
Speech impairments, 109
Spinning cup experiment, 314 (Experiment 83)
Spiral galaxies, 21, 22 (image)
Spontaneous generation, 122–123
Sputnik, 49–51, 344, 370
St. Louis Science Center, 66 (Web site)
Standards:
   professional development, 346
   science education, 51, 52 (Theory
      Into Practice 2.2), 79, 143–146
   state, 145–146
   See also National Science
      Education Standards
Standen, A., 259
Stanley, W., 89
State departments of education, 145–146
State recertification requirements,
      347 (Theory Into Practice 10.1)
State science education standards, 145–146

State teacher proficiency themes, 138, 139–140
Static electricity, 317, 320 (Experiment 87)
Steam engines, 8 (image), 301, 303 (image)
Stereoscopic vision, 242, 243 (image), 244 (Experiment 50)
Stereotypical scientists, 88, 98 (Theory Into Practice 4.1)
Stevenson, Adlai E., 203
Stingley, Norman, 26
Stirrups, invention of, 15
Stopwatches, 310, 311 (Experiment 81)
Streak test (mineral identification), 176–177 (Experiment 14)
Structure of Scientific Revolutions, The (Kuhn), 32
Students:
    with exceptionalities, 95–96, 108–110, 110 (Theory Into Practice 4.4), 118 (Web site)
    gifted and talented, 112–115, 115 (Theory Into Practice 4.6)
    poor, 95, 107–108
Student work, in portfolio, 140
Study groups, video, 351–352, 351 (Theory into Practice 10.2)
Substitution to science curriculum, 106
Sugar blood level, measuring, 205
Summative assessment, 126, 127, 370
Sundials, 167, 168 (Experiment 9), 370
Superballs, 26, 317, 318 (Experiment 85)
Supplemental materials to text, xxv–xxvi
Surfaces, minimal, 232, 235 (Experiment 45)
Surface tension, 276, 278 (Experiment 67), 280, 281 (Experiment 69)
Susruta Samhita, 253
Sweat, evaporation of, 280
Swedish Museum of Natural History, The, 66 (Web site)
Systematicity, 24, 371
Szasz, Thomas, 38
Szent-Györgyi, Albert, 37

Table salt, 266
Tang (king), 283

Teacher action research, 124–125, 128, 347–349
Teacher interview form, 134–135 (Theory Into Practice 5.4)
Teacher professional development, 343–362
    action research, 347–349
    advanced study, 357
    current state of, 345–346
    grant applications, 359–361, 361 (Theory Into Practice 10.5)
    history of, 343–345
    Japanese lesson study, 349–351, 351 (Theory into Practice 10.2)
    National Board Certification (NBC), 357–359, 358–359 (Theory Into Practice 10.4)
    parental involvement and engagement, 352–355, 354–355 (Theory Into Practice 10.3)
    professional organizations, 355–356
    recertification requirements, 347 (Theory Into Practice 10.1)
    video study groups, 351–352, 351 (Theory into Practice 10.2)
Teachers of English to Speakers of Other Languages (TESOL), 118 (Web site)
Teacher workshops, 344
Teaching, peer, 128
Teaching context, in portfolio, 139
Telescopes, 205
Television science education programs, 44
Temperature:
    chemistry, 280, 282–283, 284 (Experiment 71), 285 (Experiment 72)
    definition of, 371
    effect of carbon dioxide on, 248–249 (Experiment 53)
    effect on weather, 280
    effects on evaporation, 280, 282 (Experiment 70)
    measuring, 264, 265–266 (Experiment 59)
    ocean water, 280, 283
Teresi, D., 106

Terms and phrases, positional, 111
Terrarium, rainforest, 190–191 (Experiment 21)
TESOL. *See* Teachers of English to Speakers of Other Languages
Texas recertification guidelines, 347 (Web site)
Text:
    distinguishing features of, xx–xxii
    icons used in, xxiv
    organization of, xxiv–xxv
    pedagogical features of, xxii–xxiv
    supplemental materials, xxv–xxvi
Textbooks, learning theories in, 83 (Theory Into Practice 3.3)
Textual literacy, 56
Thalidomide, 249
Tharp, Roland G., 97
Thaumatropes, 25, 330, 331 (Experiment 94)
Thermal inversion, 191
Thermometers, 264, 265–266 (Experiment 59)
"Thinking out of the box" puzzle, 33
Third International Mathematics and Science Study (TIMSS), 99, 349, 351, 351 (Theory Into Practice 10.2)
Thompson, Darcy Wentworth, 230
Thoreau, Henry David, 69
Thymine, 236 (Experiment 46)
Time:
    geologic, 156–157 (Experiment 3)
    measuring, 308, 310, 311 (Experiment 81)
TIMSS. *See* Third International Mathematics and Science Study
"Tom Telescope" books, 41, 44 (image)
Tonso, K., 89, 90
Tools, 111–112, 300
Toshiba NSTA ExploraVision Awards, 356
To Understand is to Invent (Piaget), 70
Toyota TAPESTRY Grants for Teachers, 356, 361
Toys, 72–73, 353
Traffic pattern observation experiment, 123–124 (Theory Into Practice 5.1)

Trains, steam-powered, 8 (image)
Transpiration, 232, 233–234 (Experiment 44)
Transportation, 8, 9 (image)
Traweek, S., 90
Treatise on the Kaleidoscope (Brewster), 42–43, 45 (image)
Triceps, 252–253 (Experiment 56)
Trimmer, Sarah, 41–42
Tsunamis, 170
Tuberculosis, 7
Tuning forks, 324
Turner, Charles Henry, 93 (table)
Tutoring, 108
Twain, Mark, 6, 38, 39 (image)

Umea University, 296 (Web site)
Understory layer, of rainforest, 185
Unintended consequences, 246, 250 (Experiment 54)
United States Geological Survey, 202 (Web site)
Universalism, 31–32, 371
Universe, expanding, 155, 157, 159–160 (Experiment 5)
University of Arizona Biology Project, The, 256 (Web site)
University of California, Berkeley, 35 (Web site)
University of Chicago laboratory school, 45–47
University of Georgia Museum of Natural History, 66 (Web site)
University of Illinois Committee on School Mathematics, 51
University of Maryland Mathematics Project, 51
University of Utah, 28
U.S. Navy Master Atomic Clock, 317

Vacuum, 286, 288 (Experiment 74), 371
Variables, control of, 24, 366
Vegetable oil experiment, 232, 235 (Experiment 45)
Vernier Technology Awards, 360
Vertical enrichment activities, 114
Videos/DVDs, 353

Video study groups, 351–352, 351
  (Theory into Practice 10.2)
Virginia recertification guidelines, 347 (Web site)
Vision:
  persistence of, 330, 331 (Experiment 94)
  stereoscopic, 242, 243 (image),
    244 (Experiment 50)
Visual impairments, 109
Volta, Alessandro, 25, 289, 291
Voltaic pile, 291, 292 (Experiment 76)
Volume, 137, 262–264, 263 (Experiment 58), 371
Von Baeyer, H., 17
Vulcanization, 16
Vygotsky, Lev, 24, 47, 59, 73

Warren, B., 96
Washington, George, 283
Water, 195–200
  brackish, 197 (Experiment 25)
  chemical composition of, 266, 270
    (Experiment 61)
  evaporation of, 271 (Experiment 62), 282
    (Experiment 70)
  floating needle on, 278 (Experiment 67)
  hot and cold water interactions, 280, 283,
    284 (Experiment 71)
  making "wetter" with soap, 280, 281
    (Experiment 69)
  pollution of, 180 (Experiment 16)
  pond, 226, 227 (Experiment 40)
  salinity of, 195–196, 197 (Experiment 25)
  See also Oceans
Water clocks, 308, 310
Water cycle, 175, 177, 180 (Experiment 16)
Water fountain experiment, 263 (Experiment 58)
Water heaters, solar, 293 (Experiment 77)

Watson, James, 234, 237
Watts, Isaac, 301, 303 (image)
Waves, 324, 326, 371
Weapons, 260–261
Weather and climate, 151, 182,
    184–189, 280, 371
  experiments, 186 (Experiment 19),
    187–188 (Experiment 20), 190–191
    (Experiment 21)
Web-Based Inquiry Science Environment
    (WISE), 85 (Web site)
Wegener, Alfred, 167, 170
Weight, 308, 371
Wenger, Etienne, 80–81, 82
"Whig" interpretation of history, 39
White, L. T., 15
Wilkins, Maurice, 234, 237
Williams, Daniel Hale, 93 (table)
Wilson, Edward O., 203
Wind, measuring, 185, 187–188 (Experiment 20)
Wind turbines, 72 (image)
WISE. See Web-Based Inquiry Science
    Environment
Women scientists, 33, 91 (table)
  See also Gender
Work, 70, 371
Workshops, teacher, 344
Wright, Steven, 259
Wright brothers, 9 (image)

Yeast, 226, 228 (Experiment 41)
Yogurt, 226, 229–230 (Experiment 42)
Young, Roger Arliner, 93 (table)

Zeus, 161, 165
Zoetropes, 26

About the Authors

Cory A. Buxton is Assistant Professor of Education at the University of Miami. His research uses anthropological and sociolinguistic lenses to explore the interactions of culture, language, and tool use in urban science classrooms. He also studies the ways in which students, teachers, and schools both conform to and resist the current political pressures of high-stakes assessment and how such assessments differentially influence "at-risk" and "high-performing" schools. Buxton began his career as a geologist and became interested in teaching science while serving as a U.S. Peace Corps volunteer in Guatemala. He then taught in urban New Orleans and rural Colorado before receiving his Ph.D. from the University of Colorado at Boulder. Since then, Buxton has taught graduate and undergraduate courses in science methods, the nature of science, feminist critiques of science, theories of learning, instructional technology, and ethnographic research methods. The current collaboration with Provenzo has resulted in the creation of a text that draws upon many of these diverse interests.

Eugene F. Provenzo, Jr. is Professor of Education at the University of Miami. The author of a wide range of books on education and culture, he has a particular interest in technology and the history of science, as well as constructivist models of learning. His book *Video Kids: Making Sense of Nintendo* (Harvard University Press, 1991) was the first scholarly book to look in detail at issues of race, gender, and violence in video games. A national media figure, he has appeared on *Good Morning America*, the *Today Show, ABC World News Tonight*, the *CBS Evening News*, and has been profiled in *People* magazine. He is currently editing a three-volume encyclopedia on the social and cultural foundations of education for SAGE Publications and is also the editor for SAGE of *Critical Issues in Education: An Anthology of Readings* (2006). He is an avid sculptor and collage artist, a toy designer and inventor, and divides his time between teaching and researching in Miami and restoring a circa-1850 house in Staunton, Virginia with his wife Asterie Baker Provenzo and his red tabby Maine Coon cat Fred.